PRAISE FOR M.F.K. FISHER

"M.F.K. Fisher . . . brings onstage a peach or a brace of quail and shows us history, cities, fantasies, memories, emotions."
—PATRICIA STORACE, *The New York Review of Books*

"Food is what she wrote about, although to leave it at that is reductionist in the extreme. What she really wrote about was the passion, the importance of living boldly instead of cautiously; oh, what scorn she had for timid eaters, timid lovers, people who took timid stands, or none at all, on matters of principle." —*San Francisco Examiner*

"I do not know of anyone in the United States who writes better prose."
—W. H. AUDEN, author of *The Age of Anxiety*

"M.F.K. Fisher is our greatest food writer because she puts food in the mount, the mind, and the imagination all at the same time. Beyond the gastronomical bravura, she is a passionate woman; food is her metaphor."
—SHANA ALEXANDER, *New York Times* bestselling author of *Nutcracker*

"Poet of the appetites." —JOHN UPDIKE, author of *Rabbit, Run*

"She writes about fleeting tastes and feasts vividly, excitingly, sensuously, exquisitely. There is almost a wicked thrill in following her uninhibited track through the glories of the good life."
—JAMES BEARD, author of *The James Beard Cookbook*

"She writes about food as others do about love, but rather better."
—CLIFTON FADIMAN, author of *Lifetime Reading Plan*

"If I were still teaching high school English, I'd use [Fisher's] books to show how to write simply, how to enjoy food and drink, but, most of all, how to enjoy life. Her books and letters are one feast after another."
—FRANK McCOURT, Pulitzer Prize–winning author of *Angela's Ashes*

"This enlightening cornucopia of writings toasts the pleasures of food, drink and celebration in literature . . . This is a refreshing, nourishing and fulfilling sampler from a connoisseur of a genre she has created." —*Publishers Weekly*

"This is unique . . . a collection of excerpts from world literature, concerned with eating and drinking . . . There's gastronomy in fantasy and nonsense, in history of pioneering, in regional writing, in studies of manners. And always—in her inimitable way—there is M.F.K. Fisher." —*Kirkus Reviews*

Here Let Us Feast

Here Let Us Feast

A Book of Banquets

M.F.K. FISHER
With a New Introduction by Betty Fussell

COUNTERPOINT
Berkeley, California

For Norah Kennedy Barr

Library of Congress Cataloging-in-Publication Data
Names: Fisher, M. F. K. (Mary Frances Kennedy), 1908–1992, author.
Title: Here let us feast : a book of banquets / M.F.K. Fisher ;
    with a new introduction by Betty Fussell.
Description: Berkeley, California : Counterpoint, [2018] | Includes index.
Identifiers: LCCN 2018008260 | ISBN 9781640090835
Subjects: LCSH: Literature—Collections. | Dinners and dining in literature. |
    Gastronomy—History.
Classification: LCC PN6071.G3 F5 2018 | DDC 808.8/03564—dc23
LC record available at https://lccn.loc.gov/2018008260

Jacket designed by Nicole Caputo
Book designed by Jordan Koluch

COUNTERPOINT
2560 Ninth Street, Suite 318
Berkeley, CA 94710
www.counterpointpress.com

Printed in the United States of America

TABLE OF CONTENTS

INTRODUCTION

Reader, you're in for a treat. Taste one page, and I bet—as with a potato chip—you can't eat just one. We're here for a feast created by an adventurer like no other, our unique poet-philosopher of the stove, Mary Frances Kennedy Fisher.

It was she who taught us that words are to be devoured the same way we devour buttered popcorn or a mug of beer; that while the need to devour something belongs to all animals, the need to have it mean something is entirely human. Pop that seed over a fire or ferment it into a drink. And celebrate human ingenuity in transforming the necessities of survival into the arts of cooking and eating, reading and writing. That's what feasts mean.

Her method was metaphor, her aim discovery, her manner seductive. If she was close to having been born a California gal with a bold knife and fork in her mouth, she was also born with a typewriter on her tongue. And it did no harm that she looked like a Hollywood glamour gal rather than an aproned Fannie Farmer.

To sense how daring this author was in both subject and method, look at the momentous global events happening when she published this, her sixth book, in 1946. World War II in both Japan and Germany had ended. Hitler, Mussolini, and Hirohito were dead. The Holocaust had been unmasked in Dachau. Hiroshima had been annihilated by the first atomic bomb.

And look what was happening in her personal life in this same period. She'd buried two suicides—her younger brother and her second husband—and birthed two daughters, one illegitimate, the other by a third husband. She'd published both fiction and nonfiction books, written gags for Hope and Crosby at Paramount Studios, begun a couple of novels, and splattered the pages of the nation's top glossies like *Vogue, The Atlantic Monthly*, and *Gourmet*.

Why in this time of global and personal tragedy did she choose the impossibly low subject of food? Particularly when American food books meant recipe books by either home economists teaching diet and health or by commercial companies pushing a brand. The big sellers were *Trader Vic's Book of Food and Drink, Betty Crocker Cookbook*, and *Magic Chef Cooking*.

In contrast, she presented the countless feasts of other men at other times woven together by a voice of elegance, wit, irony, and laugh-aloud buffoonery, the kind of writing she attributed to gastronome Brillat-Savarin, who "clears fustiness from the tongue of the mind like dry champagne."

To be savored, not gulped or gobbled like the fast food of instant twitters and tweets. We have to slow down to enjoy her banquet of selections laid out like a buffet table with a timeline that begins in Genesis and ends with Ernest Hemingway.

And with an arrangement of cultural dishes that places the bloodied altars of ancient Aztecs next to the "Poison Tree" of William Blake; the toilets and vomitoria of Petronius's ancient Rome next to the royal feasts described by Samuel Pepys and Madame de Sévigné; Dickens's *Christmas Carol* pottage next to Connelly's *Green Pastures* fish fry.

Through her voice, we sample "fried new-born mice in China, white rhino hump in South Africa, termites in Africa, bees picked on wing and fried in butter in Asia." Throughout her journey, she makes us eat words, sniff sentences, roll them around on our tongues, savor the shocking combination of flavors.

By the end of the banquet, it is we who have been transformed in our daily lives by her accounts of "the manners and meanings of broken bread, poured wine, and the communion of two or three of us gathered together."

It's the ultimate alembic transforming water into wine, bread into flesh, gut into soul. I hope by the end, you'll feel like I do. Not overstuffed, but lucky to have been invited.

BETTY FUSSELL
Santa Barbara
2017

THE FEAST OF KNOWLEDGE

Now the serpent was more subtil than any beast of the field which the Lord God had made. And he said unto the woman, Yea, hath God said, Ye shall not eat of every tree of the garden?

And the woman said unto the serpent, We may eat of the fruit of the trees of the garden:

But of the fruit of the tree which is in the midst of the garden, God hath said, Ye shall not eat of it, neither shall ye touch it, lest ye die.

And the serpent said unto the woman, Ye shall not surely die:

For God doth know that in the day ye eat thereof, then your eyes shall be opened, and ye shall be as gods, knowing good and evil.

And when the woman saw that the tree was good for food, and that it was pleasant to the eyes, and a tree to be desired to make one wise, she took of the fruit thereof, and did eat, and gave also unto her husband with her; and he did eat.

Genesis III: 1–6

THE BOOK AND THE FLEA

That's a valiant flea that dare eat his
breakfast on the lip of a lion.

—SHAKESPEARE,
King Henry V

This book is about feasting. It is a collection of excerpts—sentences, and paragraphs, and even pages—concerned with man's fundamental need to celebrate the highpoints of his life by eating and drinking. It is true that such a subject is not always connected, perforce, with the fine art of gastronomy, but still it is honest and intrinsically necessary in any human scheme, any plan for the future, any racial memory.

Men have always feasted, in huts and palaces and temples, in an instinctive gesture of gratitude to their gods for the good things that have come to them, and it is symbolical of their basic trust and artlessness that bread and wine, the good things themselves, are what they offer back. It is their way of admitting, subconsciously or not, that hunger is more than a problem of belly and guts, and that the satisfying of it can and must and does nourish the spirit as well as the body.

Food for the soul is a part of all religion, as ancient savages know when they roast a tiger's heart for their god, as Christians know when they partake of Body and Blood at the mystical feast of Holy Communion.

That is why there can be an equal significance in a sumptuous banquet for five thousand heroes, with the king sitting on his iron throne and minstrels singing above the sound of gnawed bones and clinking cups, or in a piece of dry bread eaten alone by a man lifting his eyes unto the hills.

That is why, to my mind, there can be nothing irreverent or illogical about putting together in one collection of feasts such apparently disparate things as St. Luke's story of the Last Supper and Lewis Carroll's tea-party for Alice in Wonderland, the fish fry for the Lord God in His green pastures and Trimalchio's gluttonous orgy in decadent Rome.

There is, of course, one obvious danger to any such arbitrary choosing, and I am aware of it but not afraid: I know that anyone who reads this book may wonder why in the name of intelligence and taste and even common sense I have chosen as I have. Why have I left out Falstaff, and Sancho Panza, and Chaucer's gourmande nun? How have I dared print Maginn's *Story Without a Tail* and ignore Thomas Love Peacock's erudite and slyly ribald drinking songs? The answer is only that this is part of what I have read and remembered as good, in some thirty-odd years. In as many more the whole thing could be different, the choice a wider one . . . if not narrower!

I have always found gastronomy a fulfilling subject, and have read much about it without surfeit. I know just what anyone knows who has read the books I have read, with anything like my own keen if unscholarly interest: that is, I have a sketchy but personally entertaining fund of common knowledge, some of it faulty, much of it garbled by time and my own interpretations of it, all of it alive for me . . . not sleeping in my brain.

There are several authoritative and even interesting books, full of dates and such, which are much safer than this one could possibly be for a reader who wants to know the chemical formula for manna, when and how Solomon feasted the Queen of Sheba, what Elizabeth of England spent in one year on her breakfast ale. And there are lists telling just what are the gastronomical classics . . . lists which almost certainly will never include *The Peterkin Papers*, or *Jorrocks's Jaunts and Jollities*, but will lend much more weight than this book's index to anyone's need to be a well-read gastronome.

I have read the lists, and the books, and I still have the temerity, not bland or smug but quite conscious of its implications, to make this present collection public.

I am a valiant flea indeed, thus to dare perch upon the lip of such a lion as the literature of feasting! My breakfast has been good. I shall hop back, again and again, to feed my little body and my growing soul upon such inexhaustible nourishment.

HERE LET US FEAST, AND TO THE FEAST BE JOIN'D
DISCOURSE, THE SWEETER BANQUET OF THE MIND.

Pope's Homer

Here
Let Us
Feast

IN THE BEGINNING

The Bible

Genesis 1: 1-3

In the beginning God created the heaven and the earth.

And the earth was without form, and void; and darkness was upon the face of the deep. And the Spirit of God moved upon the face of the waters.

And God said, Let there be light.

There has never been a mightier telling of our genesis than this from the King James version of the Bible, nor, quite probably, will there ever be one. It is with us always, incomprehensible in our youth, equally mysterious as we age, a subtle incantation to remind us of our awful beginning.

There is one other telling of it that may last a long time too. It is in *The Green Pastures*, a play that broke like sunlight between the first and second great wars of the twentieth century. It is told in human terms, about a fish fry held in Heaven but as real with its smells and tastes and table-sounds as any like feast day on Earth. It is a fine reassurance of the dignity of men and angels inside their varicolored skins, of Heaven and the Lord God and how the Earth began.

Since any thinking body knows that angels, like ordinary men, must eat and drink, it opens this way:

From *The Green Pastures* by Marc Connelly, 1890–1980

In the darkness many voices are heard singing "Rise, Shine, Give God the Glory." They sing it gayly and rapidly. The lights go up as the second verse ends. The chorus is being sung diminuendo by a mixed company of angels. That is, they are angels in that they wear brightly colored robes and have wings protruding from their backs. Otherwise they look and act like a company of happy Negroes at a fish fry. The scene itself is a pre-Creation Heaven with compromises. In the distance is an unbroken stretch of blue sky. Companionable varicolored clouds billow down to the floor of the stage and roll overhead to the branches of a live oak tree which is up left. The tree is leafy and dripping with Spanish moss, and with the clouds makes a frame for the scene. In the cool shade of the tree are the usual appurtenances of a fish fry: a large kettle of hot fat set on two small parallel logs, with a fire going underneath, and a large rustic table formed by driving four stakes into the ground and placing planks on top of the small connecting boards. On the table are piles of biscuits and corn bread and the cooked fish in dish pans. There are one or two fairly large cedar or crock "churns" containing boiled custard, which looks like milk. There is a gourd dipper beside the churns and several glasses and cups of various sizes and shapes from where the custard is drunk.

The principal singers are marching two by two in a small area at the R. of the stage. Two MAMMY ANGELS are attending to the frying beside the kettle. Behind the table a MAN ANGEL is skinning fish and passing them to the cooks. Another is ladling out the custard. A MAMMY ANGEL is putting fish on bread for a brood of cherubs, and during the first scene they seat themselves on a grassy bank upstage. Another MAMMY ANGEL is clapping her hands disapprovingly and beckoning a laughing BOY CHERUB down from a cloud a little out of her reach. Another MAMMY ANGEL is solicitously slapping the back of a GIRL CHERUB who has a large fish sandwich in her hand and a bone in her throat. There is much movement about the table, and during the first few minutes several individuals go up to the table to help themselves to the food and drink. Many of the women angels wear hats and a few of the men are smoking cigars. A large boxful is on the table. There is much laughter and chatter . . .

And gossip. And tomfoolery. It all sounds fine and real, and when the Lord God enters, and a reverent hush falls over the angels, He is fine and real too. "He is the tallest and biggest of them all," which is as it should be. "He wears a white shirt with a white bow tie, a long Prince Albert coat of black alpaca, black trousers, and congress gaiters...."

It is quite natural, by now in the telling of the story, that when God rears back and passes a few miracles to improve the flavor of the custard, rain should result, and then the creation of the earth itself. All the angels lean over the railing to see, looking down admiringly at it, and Gabriel says:

GABRIEL

[*Gazing down.*] Yes, suh. Dat'd make mighty nice farming country. Jest look at dat south forty over dere. You ain't going to let dat go to waste, is you, Lawd? Dat would be a pity an' a shame.

GOD

[*Not turning.*] It's a good earth. [GOD *turns, room is made for Him beside* GABRIEL *on the embankment.*] Yes. I ought to have somebody to enjoy it. [*He turns, facing the audience. The others, save for the* CHOIR, *who are lined up in two rows of six on an angle up right, continue to look over the embankment.*] Gabriel! [GOD *steps down from the embankment two paces.*]

GABRIEL

[*Joining him.*] Yes, Lawd.

GOD

Gabriel, I'm goin' down dere.

GABRIEL

Yes, Lawd.

GOD

I want you to be my working boss yere while I'm gone.

GABRIEL

Yes, Lawd.

GOD

You know dat matter of dem two stars?

GABRIEL

Yes, Lawd.

GOD

Git dat fixed up! You know dat sparrow dat fell a little while ago? 'Ten to dat, too.

GABRIEL

Yes, Lawd.

GOD

I guess dat's about all. I'll be back Saddy. [*To the* CHOIR.] Quiet, angels. [*The* CHOIR *stops singing. Those on the embankment circle down stage.* GOD *goes to embankment. Turns and faces the company.*] I'm gonter pass one more miracle. You all gonter help me an' not make a soun' caize it's one of de most impo'tant miracles of all. [*Nobody moves.* GOD *turns, facing the sky, and raises His arms above His head.*] Let there be man!

And that was a version of the beginning, since everything must have one, of man and his hungers.

The angels who watched it take shape, below their iron balcony rail, were well-fed happy angels, full of fried fish and biscuits and "custard," and probably God Himself was the only one who knew, there at the picnic, that the men He created down on earth would not always feast as well.

Things that have meant security and happiness may have been sung in terms of food and drink since The Beginning. David did that in his Psalms. Jesus made miracles with bread and wine and fishes to give strength to the oppressed spirits in Roman Palestine. This was their promise of milk and honey in a better land. . . .

Israel sang a little song: "Spring up, O well; Sing ye unto it"; and the well did spring up to slake his people's thirst. When we know that wandering tribes still sing thus, there is the whole story of our trust in God to ponder, kept living for us by men who since the first have thought much on it. A table has been set before us, and we can sing with David:

Psalm 23
The Lord is my shepherd; I shall not want.

He maketh me to lie down in green pastures: he leadeth me beside the still waters.

He restoreth my soul: he leadeth me in the paths of righteousness for his name's sake.

Yea, though I walk through the valley of the shadow of death, I will fear no evil: for thou art with me; thy rod and thy staff they comfort me.

Thou preparest a table before me in the presence of mine enemies: thou anointest my head with oil; my cup runneth over.

Surely goodness and mercy shall follow me all the days of my life: and I will dwell in the house of the Lord for ever.

By the time a story five thousand years old, or three thousand, comes to our ears, it has lost its trappings. It is as simple as any story can possibly be, because it is like a piece of driftwood that once has been a tree, with all its boughs and twiglets—a silvery noble fragment now, with faint carvings on it from the long-dead sea worms, but no other outward sign of its illimitable travel.

The Bible is like that, perhaps more so than any other collection of the stories of man. Every old language, though, has its revered lot of them. One mouth after another has discarded ornamentation in the telling; one hurried or persecuted scribe after another has cut off this little descriptive phrase and that little prettiness. What is left for us to read is as straightforward as Genesis, as direct as a Chinese poem.

The problem, then, is whether we are ready to read it. The sins and omissions of everything we have learned about it, from our devout grandmothers to our glib professors, tend to push us away from it into the safe void of disinterest and boredom. Through all our young years we learn the emasculated legends of Joseph's coat and baby Moses floating in the bulrushes, and we shun the hints of pain and awfulness in the stories of Jesus Christ. Then we retreat angrily, from what we have been told by our elders, or have read dutifully in the family Bible; we laugh in resentment, and call ourselves agnostic with all the enthusiasm of adolescence. That makes it easy and delightful to ape our teachers, a little later, and to agree, with only a sneaked glance over our shoulder at Grandmother's patient ghost, that the Bible is indeed "literature," a fascinating collection of myths and fairy tales.

How good it is to be free of the intellectual restrictions of Sunday School! And how disturbing we find it, a little later, to discover a sincere wistfulness, a wish confessed half-mockingly that we could feel devout, credulous, stupid enough to read the Book as some older people seem to! We hate to confess such a lacuna in our chain of culture.

Many people, like me, content themselves with the surety that one day, soon or late, they will be able to read, and mark, and inwardly digest the great feast that awaits. They will hardly suspect, as I did not, that the awaited realization of a true wish may come through some such a thing as the printed word *gluttony*.

It happened to me when I decided to make a collection of feasts that I had read about. I knew that I must include the first one, about the Apple on the Tree. I could find it, in the Bible I unthinkingly include among my other reference books because of my early and my later educations: easy, because I went to a school where we were taught more about the tribes of Israel and their battles than we ever suspected about Napoleon, or Sherman's march through Georgia, or Bismarck. I found the passages I wanted, and then, in the New Testament, the ones about the miracles of the loaves and fishes, the water changed to wine, all of those. . . .

And it grew clear to me that the priests and the storytellers, the great singers and the teachers, everywhere and always showed their people real food, real wine, to prove to them the truths of spiritual nourishment. A great catch of fishes from an empty sea, or water springing from a dry stone: such things were told of over and over to sustain men whose hope of Heaven dwindled and grew faint as their stomachs cried out.

I read more, excited at last to have found for myself a thread to follow through the long books. Then I remembered about concordances, on a hot gray day in July, 1945, an important day for me, in the New York Public Library, with the dim roar of a rainstorm outside the enormous room and all about me the rustle and squint and faint sour smell of reading. I found two thick black books on the reference shelves, and sat looking at them for several minutes, timid and inept. Finally I decided to search for the word Gluttony. And that was the beginning of pleasure and joy and great strength for me, because suddenly I was able, after long waiting, to read the Bible and know why and how, without duty to my grandmother or my professor or anything in the world but my own awakened understanding.

It was dark in the wet streets when I went away that night, but I was not tired, and the next days I came back and feasted more, as after a long fast.

I read Maschil's 78th Psalm about the greedy children of Ephraim, how they mocked God, asking Him to prove Himself by setting up a table for them in the wilderness, and how He rained down the corn of heaven upon them, "flesh also upon them as dust, and feathered fowls like as the sands of the sea," and how with their mouths still bulging He smote them, those fat lustful pigs. He was a just God, Maschil sang, for He filled them full in their mockery and then roared out with mirth and rage and smote them....

I read about Esau and Jacob, that story so full of treachery and slyness, about the dull-witted hairy man who let his brother and his empty belly cheat him into selling his birthright for a bowl of hot cooked soup, a mess of pottage. There was more to the story, which I had forgotten or never known, and I followed enviously the deft telling of how Jacob and his doting foxy mother made a fool again of Esau, and betrayed him to his blind old father, again with savory meat, but this time cooked as Isaac loved it, "two good kids from the goats." That was evil in the pot, for fair!

I read of the happy gaffer Abraham, how when he learned that he was to become the father of all the Hebrew race, and he ninety-nine and his wife Sarah an old barren woman, begot ready a little feast for the three celestial strangers who brought him the good news. He asked them to share a morsel of bread with him. Then hospitably, as it tells in Genesis:

Genesis XVIII. 6–8

... Abraham hastened into the tent unto Sarah, and said, Make ready quickly three measures of fine meal, knead it, and make cakes upon the hearth.

And Abraham ran unto the herd, and fetcht a calf tender and good, and gave it unto a young man; and he hasted to dress it.

And he took butter, and milk, and the calf which he had dressed, and set it before them; and he stood by them under the tree, and they did eat.

This seems in every way a charming simple banquet, right for the Lord Himself, but it has often been questioned by gastronomers, with great respect of course, because of the peculiar sauce served with it. Perhaps the best justification to be found, if one be needed, is in the Reverend Mr. Richard Warner's *Antiquitates Culinariae*, which appeared in London in 1791. (The long s used then in printing may add a touch more spice to the discussion, if not to the sauce itself.)

> **From *Antiquitates Culinariae* by Richard Warner, circa 1791**
> . . . In the XVIIIth Chapter of Genefis, we have the picture of a patriarchal entertainment; which, though it does not boaft any of the *tricks of modern cookery*, nor rife perhaps to the *modern* idea of *good cheer*, yet prefents a very pleafing picture of comfortable living. . . . The only fngular circumftance in this beautiful picture of patriarchal fimplicity, is, the kind of fauce ferved up with the calf, *butter and milk.* This is elucidated, however, by the following anecdote taken from Ockley's Hiftory of the Saracens. *Abdomelick* the caliph, upon his entering into *Cufah,* made a fplendid entertainment. "When he was fat down, *Amrou* the fon of *Hareth,* an ancient *Mechzumian,* came in; he called him to him, and placing him by him upon his fopha, afked him what meat he liked beft of all that he had eaten. The old Mechzumian anfwered, an afs's neck well feafoned, and well roafted. You do nothing, fays Abdomelick; what fay you to a leg or a shoulder of a fucking lamb, well roafted, and *covered over with butter and milk.*"

It was exciting, in the big Library, to match such motley, to remember an old English book and fit it into the much older story I could now read with my fresh-opened eyes. I went on much longer than I should, but without impatience at the strictures of time because at last I knew that the Bible was for me. There it was, finally, and there was I, ready for it whenever I wanted it, without boredom or duty or youthful snobbery to hinder me.

I could read stories like the one of Esther, as intricate and bloody and finely constructed as any modern masterpiece of adventure, a book which begins with one of the rowdiest drunken parties I know of, and mounts to its ferocious denouement with a series of craftily arranged intimate suppers, full of fine food and tipsy self-betrayals.

I could hypnotise myself with the singsong of Leviticus, and see how all that Moses taught his wandering children about sanitation and prudence and common animal decency still helps to preserve them in ghettos and refugee camps.

Finally, with a different sense of exhilaration, a kind of humility at my impotence in the face of a mysticism beyond me, I could read the story of Jesus. At least I could understand the ever-present fact, stronger than ever in the books of the New Testament, that the way to teach a new faith and to promise Heaven is to tell it as Christ did, in terms of feasts, of full vineyards, of mighty catches of fish and brimming bottles. I read about how the Devil failed to tempt Jesus to turn a stone into bread, to prove Himself the Son of God, and how He did turn water into wine for a better purpose, at a wedding. And there was the miracle of the five loaves and the two fishes, which fed a multitude . . . God making something from nothing, much from little, Paradise from Hell.

It was all a part of man's hunger for what is true, and a sign to me of the significance of bread and wine and our intuitive reverence for it and its spiritual connotations. It was there, ready to be known, just as all that anyone can ever know about hunger and nourishment and the feasting of the soul is in the story of the Last Supper, waiting to be read and pondered on:

St. Luke XXII: 7–22

Then came the day of unleavened bread, when the passover must be killed.

And he sent Peter and John, saying, Go and prepare us the passover, that we may eat.

And they said unto him, Where wilt thou that we prepare?

And he said unto them, Behold, when ye are entered into the city, there shall a man meet you, bearing a pitcher of water; follow him into the house where he entereth in.

And ye shall say unto the goodman of the house, The Master saith unto thee, Where is the guestchamber, where I shall eat the passover with my disciples?

And he shall shew you a large upper room furnished: there make ready.

And they went, and found as he had said unto them: and they made ready the passover.

And when the hour was come, he sat down, and the twelve apostles with him.

And he said unto them, With desire I have desired to eat this passover with you before I suffer:

For I say unto you, I will not any more eat thereof, until it be fulfilled in the kingdom of God.

And he took the cup, and gave thanks, and said, Take this, and divide it among yourselves:

For I say unto you, I will not drink of the fruit of the vine, until the kingdom of God shall come.

And he took bread, and gave thanks, and brake it, and gave unto them, saying, This is my body which is given for you: this do in remembrance of me.

Likewise also the cup after supper, saying, This cup is the new testament in my blood, which is shed for you.

But, behold, the hand of him that betrayeth me is with me on the table.

And truly the Son of man goeth, as it was determined: but woe unto that man by whom he is betrayed!

II

GLORIOUS DESCENDANTS

China

Man is always in need of reassurance, and it is perhaps strange that one of the best ways to reassure him is to show him that he has ever been so, and that what he thought or ate or spoke five thousand years ago is the same now.

Arabs still relish the sticky manna that oozed from the tamarisk bark for the wandering Jews, although God has never seen fit to let it flow for them for many days in a miracle, horticulturally impossible, as He did for His Chosen People. American Indians still dance their old hypnotic steps to the Corn God, even if what they do crackles faintly with its cellophane packaging for the tourists who shyly watch them. And the Chinese still eat a bowl of fried rice or a fresh pink crab with the same intellectual gusto they showed a thousand years ago and much, much longer.

Yuan-Mei, who has been called the Brillat-Savarin of his country, and who wrote a scholarly cookbook in the eighteenth century, said, "Into no department of life should indifference be allowed to creep—into none less than the domain of cookery."

The Chinese have always known this, and as long ago as the time of the Emperor Sung Nung (2873–2689 B.C.), the great ruler himself tasted, and then had his clerks classify, a remarkable range of plants, so that his subjects could improve their health and add to their pleasures. By the first century A.D. the list had grown to include three hundred and sixty-five edible plants, as well as all the good animals from land and sea and air, with their medicinal and nutritive values carefully catalogued.

The appointment of Shuh I, however, as imperial dietitian to Chen Wang in 1115 B.C., is probably most indicative of the place fine cookery has always held in China. He was chief of the four royal medical officers, and his duty was to supervise the smallest details of cooking and serving food, with special care in observing the effects of various dishes on the spirits as well as the bodies of the diners!

"Through the centuries," adds Dr. Gwei-Djen Lu of Cambridge University, in writing about his country's gastronomy, "it is a fact that careful records were kept and improvements made accordingly. Who knows but that the amazing survival of Chinese culture is due to this!"

And that is why it is possible, I think, to read what a modern Chinese like Lin Yutang says about his national cuisine, and know in a reassuring way that it has been thus forever. In the same fashion what a young Chinese-American says about the feast given for his father in San Francisco is as truly Chinese as if it had happened in Canton; and when a woman of America, but with a Chinese mind, tells what food a peasant named Wang Lung eats with his wives O-Lan and Lotus, it can be now or a thousand years ago.

Lin, the young intellectual who discovered his own country after he came to this one; Pardee Lowe, whose father was mayor of Chinatown and who was named for a California governor; Pearl Buck, who came home to write of her spiritual homeland: the ways of telling their stories seem as diverse as their backgrounds, and yet they have one basic fellowship in an almost Biblical cleanness of style.

The vocabularies differ, just as one of the writers may have round eyes, another a Harvard turn of inflection, the third a scholarly aptitude for anathema. But Lin and Lowe and Pearl Buck are writing here, in their minds as well as on paper, a language so old that it has been stripped of any sharpness and gaucheries of style. It has been spoken for so long, and used so thoughtfully in the speaking, that it is as terse as St. Luke's parables, and as thin-drawn as the rage of Job.

All this makes Charles Lamb's redundant charm seem overblown, and his Saxon playfulness and wit a heavy thing indeed among the austere wordings of the real Chinese. And yet his ridiculous story of the first roast of pork is too jolly a one to pass by.

From A *Dissertation Upon Roast Pig* by Charles Lamb, 1775–1834

Mankind, says a Chinese manuscript, which my friend M. was obliging enough to read and explain to me, for the first seventy thousand ages ate their meat raw, clawing or biting it from the living animal, just as they do in Abyssinia to this day. This period is not obscurely hinted at by their great Confucius in the second chapter of his Mundane Mutations, where he designates a kind of golden age by the term Cho-fang, literally the Cook's Holiday. The manuscript goes on to say that the art of roasting, or rather broiling (which I take to be the elder brother), was accidentally discovered in the manner following: The swineherd Ho-ti, having gone out into the woods one morning, as his manner was, to collect mast for his hogs, left his cottage in the care of his eldest son Bo-bo, a great lubberly boy, who, being fond of playing with fire, as younkers of his age commonly are, let some sparks escape into a bundle of straw, which kindling quickly, spread the conflagration over every part of their poor mansion, till it was reduced to ashes. Together with the cottage (a sorry antediluvian makeshift of a building, you may think it), what was of much more importance, a fine litter of new-farrowed pigs, no less than nine in number, perished. China pigs have been esteemed a luxury all over the East, from the remotest periods that we read of. Bo-bo was in the utmost consternation, as you may think, not so much for the sake of the tenement, which his father and he could easily build up again with a few dry branches, and the labor of an hour or two, at any time, as for the loss of the pigs. While he was thinking what he should say to his father, and wringing his hands over the smoking remnants of one of those untimely sufferers, an odor assailed his nostrils unlike any scent which he had before experienced. What could it proceed from? Not from the burnt cottage—he had smelt that smell before; indeed, this was by no means the first accident of the kind which had occurred through the negligence of this unlucky young firebrand. Much less did it resemble that of any known herb, weed, or flower. A premonitory moistening at the same time overflowed his nether lip. He knew not what to think. He next stooped down to feel the pig, if there were any signs of life in it. He burnt his fingers, and to cool them he applied them in his booby fashion to his mouth. Some of the crumbs of the scorched skin had come away with his fingers, and for the first time in his life (in the world's life indeed, for before him no man had known it) he tasted—*crackling!* Again he felt and fumbled at the pig. It did not burn him so much now; still, he licked his fingers from a sort of habit. The truth at length broke into his slow understanding that it was the pig that smelt so, and the pig that tasted so delicious; and surrendering himself up to the new-born pleasure, he fell to tearing up whole handfuls of the scorched skin with the flesh next it, and was cramming it down his throat in his beastly fashion, when his sire entered amid the smoking rafters, armed with retributory cudgel, and finding how affairs stood, began to rain blows upon the young rogue's shoulders, as thick as hailstones, which Bo-bo heeded not any more than if they had been flies. The tickling pleasure which he experienced in his lower regions had rendered him quite callous to any inconveniences he might feel in those remote quarters. His father might lay on, but he could not beat him from his pig, till he had fairly made an end of it, when, becoming a little more sensible of his situation, something like the following dialogue ensued.

"You graceless whelp, what have you got there devouring? Is it not enough that you have burnt me down three houses with your dog's tricks, and be hanged to you, but you must be eating fire, and I know not what;— what have you got there, I say?"

"O father, the pig, the pig! do come and taste how nice the burnt pig eats."

The ears of Ho-ti tingled with horror. He cursed his son, and he cursed himself that ever he should beget a son that should eat burnt pig.

Bo-bo, whose scent was wonderfully sharpened since morning, soon raked out another pig, and, fairly rending it asunder, thrust the lesser half by main force into the fists of Ho-ti, still shouting out, "Eat, eat, eat the burnt pig, father, only taste; O Lord!"—with suchlike barbarous ejaculations, cramming all the while as if he would choke.

Ho-ti trembled in every joint while he grasped the abominable thing, wavering whether he should not put his son to death for an unnatural young monster, when the crackling scorching his fingers, as it had done his son's, and applying the same remedy to them, he in his turn tasted some of its flavor, which, make what sour mouths he would for a pretense, proved not altogether displeasing to him. In conclusion (for the manuscript here is a little tedious) both father and son fairly set down to the mess, and never left off till they had dispatched all that remained of the litter.

Bo-bo was strictly enjoined not to let the secret escape, for the neighbors would certainly have stoned them for a couple of abominable wretches, who could think of improving upon the good meat which God had sent them. Nevertheless, strange stories got about. It was observed that Ho-ti's cottage was burnt down now more frequently than ever. Nothing but fires from this time forward. Some would break out in broad day, others in the night time. As often as the sow farrowed, so sure was the house of Ho-ti to be in a blaze; and Ho-ti himself, which was the more remarkable, instead of chastising his son, seemed to grow more indulgent to him than ever. At length they were watched, the terrible mystery discovered, and father and son summoned to take their trial at Pekin, then an inconsiderable assize town. Evidence was given, the obnoxious food itself produced in court, and verdict about to be pronounced, when the foreman of the jury begged that some of the burnt pig of which the culprits stood accused might be handed into the box. He handled it, and they all handled it; and burning their fingers, as Bo-bo and his father had done before them, and nature prompting to each of them the same remedy, against the face of all the facts, and the clearest charge which judge had ever given—to the surprise of the whole court, townsfolk, strangers, reporters, and all present—without leaving the box, or any manner of consultation whatever, they brought in a simultaneous verdict of Not Guilty.

The judge, who was a shrewd fellow, winked at the manifest iniquity of the decision; and when the court was dismissed, went privily and bought up all the pigs that could be had for love or money. In a few days his Lordship's town-house was observed to be on fire. The thing took wing, and now there was nothing to be seen but fire in every direction. Fuel and pigs grew enormously dear all over the district. The insurance offices one and all shut up shop. People built slighter and slighter every day, until it was feared that the very science of architecture would in no long time be lost to the world. Thus this custom of firing houses continued till in process of time, says my manuscript, a sage arose, like our Locke, who made a discovery, that the flesh of swine, or indeed of any other animal, might be cooked (*burnt,* as they called it) without the necessity of consuming a whole house to dress it. Then first began the rude form of a gridiron. Roasting by the string or spit came in a century or two later; I forget in whose dynasty. By such slow degrees, concludes the manuscript, do the most useful, and seemingly the most obvious, arts make their way among mankind.

Without placing too implicit faith in the account above given, it must be agreed that if a worthy pretext for so dangerous an experiment as setting houses on fire (especially in these days) could be assigned in favor of any culinary object, that pretext and excuse might be found in ROAST PIG.

Of all the delicacies in the whole *mundus edibilis*, I will maintain it to be the most delicate—*princeps obsoniorum.*

I speak not of your grown porkers—things between pig and pork—those hobbydehoys: but a young and tender suckling, under a moon old, guiltless as yet of the sty, with no original speck of the *amor immunditiae,* the hereditary failing of the first parent, yet manifest—his voice as yet not broken, but something between a childish treble and a grumble—the mild forerunner, or *praeludium,* of a grunt.

He must be roasted. I am not ignorant that our ancestors ate them seethed, or boiled—but what a sacrifice of the exterior tegument!

There is no flavor comparable, I will contend, to that of the crisp, tawny, well-watched, not over-roasted *crackling,* as it is well called—the very teeth are invited to their share of the pleasure at this banquet in overcoming the coy, brittle resistance—with the adhesive oleaginous—O call it not fat! but an indefinable sweetness growing up to it—the tender blossoming of fat, fat cropped in the bud, taken in the shoot, in the first innocence—the cream and quintessence of the child-pig's yet pure food; the lean, not lean, but a kind of animal manna; or, rather, fat and lean (if it must be so) so blended and running into each other, that both together make but one ambrosian result, or common substance.

Behold him, while he is "doing"—it seemeth rather a refreshing warmth, than a scorching heat, that he is so passive to. How equably he twirleth round the string! Now he is just done. To see the extreme sensibility of that tender age! he hath wept out his pretty eyes—radiant jellies—shooting stars.

See him in the dish, his second cradle, how meek he lieth! Wouldst thou have had this innocent grow up to the grossness and indocility which too often accompany maturer swinehood? Ten to one he would have proved a glutton, a sloven, an obstinate, disagreeable animal—wallowing in all manner of filthy conversation. From these sins he is happily snatched away—

Ere sin could blight or sorrow fade,

Death came with timely care.

His memory is odoriferous—no clown curseth, while his stomach half rejecteth, the rank bacon; no coal-heaver bolteth him in reeking sausages; he hath a fair sepulchre in the grateful stomach of the judicious epicure—and for such a tomb might be content to die.

From *My Country and My People* by Lin Yutang, 1895–1976

The question has often been asked as to what we eat. The answer is that we eat all the edible things on this earth. We eat crabs by preference, and often eat barks by necessity. Economic necessity is the mother of our inventions in food. We are too overpopulated and famine is too common for us not to eat everything we can lay our bands on. And it stands to reason that in this positively exhaustive experiment on edibles we should have stumbled upon important discoveries, as most scientific or medical discoveries have been stumbled upon. For one thing, we have discovered the magic tonic and building qualities of ginseng, for which I am willing to give personal testimony as to its being the most enduring and most energy-giving tonic known to mankind, distinguished by the slowness and gentleness of its action. But apart from such accidental discoveries of medical or culinary importance, we are undoubtedly the only truly omnivorous animals on earth, and so long as our teeth last, we should continue to occupy that position. Some day a dentist will yet discover that we have the best teeth as a nation. Gifted with these teeth and driven by famine, there is no reason why we should not at some particular time of our national life suddenly discover that roasted beetles and fried bee's chrysalis are great delicacies. The only thing we have not discovered and will not eat is cheese. The Mongols could not persuade us to eat cheese, and the Europeans do not have a greater chance of doing so.

It is useless to use logical reasoning in the matter of our food, which is determined by prejudices. On both sides of the Atlantic Ocean two shellfish are common, the soft-shelled clam, *Mya arenaria*, and the edible mussel, *Mytilus edulis*. The species of these two mollusks are the same on both sides of the water. In Europe, mussels are eaten freely but not clams, while the reverse is the case on the American side, according to the authority of Dr. Charles W. Townsend (*Scientific Monthly*, July, 1928). Dr. Townsend also mentions the fact that flounders fetch high prices in England and in Boston but are considered "not fit to eat" by Newfoundland villagers. We eat mussels with the Europeans and eat clams with the Americans, but we don't eat oysters raw as the Americans do. It is useless, for instance, for anybody to convince me that snake's meat tastes like chicken. I have lived in China forty years without eating a snake, or seeing any of my relatives do so. Tales of eating snakes travel faster than tales of eating chicken, but actually we eat more chickens and better chickens than the white people, and snake-eating is as much a curiosity to the Chinese as it is to the foreigners.

All one can say is that we are very catholic in our tastes, and that any rational man can take anything off a Chinese table without any qualm of conscience. What famine dictates is not for us human mortals to choose. There is nothing that a man will not eat when hard pressed by hunger. And no one is entitled to condemn until he knows what famine means. Some of us have been forced in times of famine to eat babies—and even this must be humanly rare—but, thank God, we do not eat them raw as the English eat their beef!

If there is anything we are serious about, it is neither religion nor learning, but food. We openly acclaim eating as one of the few joys of this human life. This question of attitude is very important, for unless we are honest about it we will never be able to lift eating and cooking into an art. The difference of attitude regarding the problem of food is represented in Europe by the French and the English. The French eat enthusiastically, while the English eat apologetically. The Chinese national genius decidedly leans toward the French in the matter of feeding ourselves.

The danger of not taking food seriously and allowing it to degenerate into a slipshod business may be studied in the English national life. If they had known any taste for food their language would reveal it. The English language does not provide a word for *cuisine:* they call it just "cooking." They have no proper word for *chef:* they just call him a cook. They do not speak about their *menu,* but know only what are called "dishes." And they have no word for *gourmet:* they just call him "Greedy Gut" in their nursery rhymes. The truth is, the English do not admit that they have a stomach. No stomach is fit for conversation unless it happens to be "sick" or "aching."

The result is that while the Frenchman will talk about the *cuisine* of his *chef* with—what seems to the English mind—immodest gestures, the Englishman can hardly venture to talk about the "food" of his "cook" without impairing the beauty of his language. When hard pressed by his French host he might be willing to mutter between his teeth that "that pudding is awfully good" and there let the matter rest. Now if a pudding is good it is good for some definite reasons, and about these problems the Englishman does not bother himself. All the English are interested in is how to strengthen themselves against influenza, as with Bovril, and save the doctor's bills.

Now you cannot develop a national culinary art unless you are willing to discuss it and exchange your opinions on it. The first condition of learning how to eat is to talk about it. Only in a society wherein people of culture and refinement inquire after their cooks' health, instead of talking about the weather, can the art of *cuisine* be developed. No food is really enjoyed unless it is keenly anticipated, discussed, eaten, and then commented upon. Preachers should not be afraid to condemn a bad steak from their pulpits and scholars should write essays on the culinary art as the Chinese scholars do. Long before we have any special food, we think about it, rotate it in our minds, anticipate it as a secret pleasure to be shared with some of our closest friends, and write notes about it in our invitation letters, like the following: "My nephew just brought some special vinegar from Chinkiang and a real Nanking salted duck from Laoyuchai," or this, "This is the end of June, and if you don't come, you won't taste another shad till next May." Long before the autumn moon rises, a real scholar, like Li Liweng as he himself confesses, would plan and save money for the crabs, decide upon an historical place where he could have the crab dinner with his friends under the mid-autumn moon or in a wilderness of chrysanthemums, negotiate with some of his friends to bring wine from Governor Tuan Fang's cellar, and meditate upon it as the English meditate upon their champion sweepstakes number. Only in this spirit can the matter of feeding ourselves be elevated into the level of an art.

We are unashamed of our eating. We have "Su Tungp'o pork" and "Kiang bean-curd." In England, a Wordsworth steak or Galsworthy cutlet would be unimaginable. Wordsworth sang about "simple living and high thinking," but he failed to note that good food, especially fresh-cut bamboo shoots and mushrooms, counts among the real joys of a simple rural life.

The Chinese poets, with a more utilitarian philosophy, have frankly sung about the "minced perch and *shun*-vegetable soup" of their native home. This thought is regarded as so poetic that officials in their petition for resignment will say that they are "thinking of *shun*-vegetable" as a most elegant expression. Actually our love of fatherland is largely a matter of recollection of the keen sensual pleasures of our childhood. The loyalty to Uncle Sam is the loyalty to American doughnuts, and the loyalty to the *Vaterland* is the loyalty to *Pfannkuchen* and *Stollen,* but the Americans and the Germans will not admit it. Many Americans while abroad sigh for their ham and sweet potatoes at home, but they will not admit that this makes them think of home, nor will they put it in their poetry.*

The seriousness with which we regard eating can be shown in many ways. Anyone who opens the pages of the *Red Chamber Dream* or of any Chinese novel will be struck by the detailed and constant descriptions of the entire menu of what Taiyü had for breakfast or what Paoyü had at midnight. Cheng Panch'iao apotheosized rice congee in his letter to his brother:

> On cold days, when poor relatives or friends arrive, first hand them a bowl of fried rice in boiling water, with a small dish of ginger or pickles. It is the most effective means of warming up old people and the poor. In your days of leisure, swallow cakes made of broken rice, or cook "slipslop congee," and hold the bowl between your two hands and eat it with shrugged shoulders. On a cold frosty morning, this will make your whole body warm. Alas! Alas! I think I'll become a farmer for the remainder of my days!

The Chinese accept food as they accept sex, women, and life in general. No great English poet or writer would condescend to write a Cook Book, which they regard as belonging outside the realms of literature and worthy of the efforts of Aunt Susan only. But the great poet-dramatist Li Liweng did not consider it beneath his dignity to write about the cooking of mushrooms and all kinds of vegetarian and non-vegetarian foods. An-

---

* A striking fact is the frequency of words like "intestines" and "belly" in Chinese poetry. *E.g.,* "The bamboo shoots are fresh and my rice bowl is too small; the fish is delicious, and my wine-intestines widen."

other great poet and scholar, Yüan Mei, wrote a whole book on cooking, besides writing a most wonderful essay on his cook. He described his cook as Henry James described the English butler, as a man carrying himself with dignity and understanding in his profession. But H. G. Wells, who of all English minds is the one most likely to write about English food, evidently cannot write it, and no hope is to be expected from the less ency-clopedic minds. Anatole France was the type that might have left us some wonderful recipe for frying calf's liver or cooking mushrooms, possibly in his intimate letters, but I doubt very much whether he has left it as part of his literary heritage.

Two principles distinguish Chinese from European cooking. One is that we eat food for its *texture*, the elastic or crisp effect it has on our teeth, as well as for fragrance, flavor, and color. Li Liweng said that he was a slave to crabs, because they had the combination of fragrance, flavor, and color. The idea of texture is seldom understood, but a great part of the popularity of bamboo-shoots is due to the fine resistance the young shoots give to our teeth. The appreciation of bamboo-shoots is probably the most typical example of our taste. Being not oily, it has a certain fairy-like "fugitive" quality about it. But the most important principle is that it lends flavor to meat (especially pork) cooked with it, and, on the other hand, it receives the flavor of the pork itself. This is the second principle, that of mixing of flavors. The whole culinary art of China depends on the art of mixture. While the Chinese recognize that many things, like fresh fish, must be cooked in their own juice, in general they mix flavors a great deal more than Western cooks do. No one, for instance, knows how cabbage tastes until he has tasted it when properly cooked with chicken, and the chicken flavor has gone into the cabbage and the cabbage flavor has gone into the chicken. From this principle of mixture, any number of fine and delicate combinations can be developed. Celery, for instance, may be eaten raw and alone, but when Chinese see, in a foreign dinner, vegetables like spinach or carrots cooked separately and then served on the same plate with pork or roast goose, they smile at the barbarians.

The Chinese, whose sense of proportion is so wonderfully acute in painting and architecture, seem to have completely lost it in the matter of food, to which they give themselves wholeheartedly when they seat them-selves around a dinner table. Any big course, like the fat duck, coming after twelve or thirteen other courses, should be a sufficient meal in itself for any human being. This is due to a false standard of courtesy, and to the fact that as course after course is served during dinners, the people are supposed to be occupied in different wine-games or contests of poetry during the intervals, which naturally lengthens the time required and gives more time for the stomach to assimilate the food. Most probably the relatively lower efficiency of Chinese government officials is due directly to the fact that all of them are subjected to an inhuman routine of three or four dinners a night. One-fourth of their food goes to nourish them, and three-fourths to kill them. That accounts for the prevalence of rich men's ailments, like diseases of the liver and the kidney, which are periodically announced in the newspapers when these officials see fit to retire from the political arena for reasons of convenience.

Although the Chinese may learn from the West a great deal about a sense of proportion in arranging for feasts, they have, in this field as in medicine, many famous and wonderful recipes to teach the Westerners. In the cooking of ordinary things like vegetables and chickens, the Chinese have a rich store to hand to the West, when the West is ready and humble enough to learn it. This seems unlikely until China has built a few good gun-boats and can punch the West in the jaw, when it will be admitted that we are unquestionably better cooks as a nation. But until that time comes, there is no use talking about it. There are thousands of Englishmen in the Shanghai Settlement who have never stepped inside a Chinese restaurant, and the Chinese are bad evangelists. We never force salvation on anybody who does not come to ask for it. We have no gun-boats anyway, and even if we had, we would never care to go up the Thames or the Mississippi and shoot the English or the Americans into heaven against their will.

As to drinks, we are naturally moderate except as regarding tea. Owing to the comparative absence of distilled liquor, one very seldom sees drunkards in the streets. But tea-drinking is an art in itself. It amounts with some persons almost to a cult. There are special books about tea-drinking as there are special books about incense and wine and rocks for house decoration. More than any other human invention of this nature, the drinking of tea has colored our daily life as a nation, and gives rise to the institution of tea-houses which are approximate equivalents of Western cafés for the common people. People drink tea in their homes and in the tea-houses, alone and in company, at committee meetings and at the settling of disputes. They drink tea before breakfast and at midnight. With a teapot, a Chinese is happy wherever he is. It is a universal habit, and it has no deleterious effect whatsoever, except in very rare cases, as in my native district where according to tradition some people have drunk themselves bankrupt. This is only possible with extremely costly tea, but the average tea is cheap, and the average tea in China is good enough for a prince. The best tea is mild and gives a "back-flavor" which comes after a minute or two, when its chemical action has set in on the salivary gland. Such good tea puts everybody in good humor. I have no doubt that it prolongs Chinese lives by aiding their digestion and maintaining their equanimity of temper.

The selection of tea and spring water is an art in itself. I give here an example of a scholar in the beginning of the seventeenth century, Chang Tai, who wrote thus about his art of tasting tea and spring water, in which he was a great connoisseur with very few rivals in his times:

Chou Molung often spoke to me in enthusiastic terms about the tea of Min Wenshui. In September of a certain year, I came to his town, and when I arrived, I called on him at Peach Leaves Ferry. It was already afternoon, and Wenshui was not at home. He came back later and I found him to be an old man. We had just opened our conversation when he rose suddenly and said that he had left his stick somewhere and went out again. I was determined not to miss this chance of having a talk with him, so I waited. After a long while, Wenshui came back, when it was already night, and he stared at me, saying, "Are you still here? What do you want to see me for?" I said, "I have heard about your name so long, and am determined to have a drink with you today before I go!" Wenshui was pleased, and then he rose to prepare the tea himself. In a wonderfully short time, it was ready. Then he led me into a room where everything was neat and tidy, and I saw over ten kinds of Ching-ch'i pots and Hsüanyao and Ch'engyao teacups, which were all very rare and precious. Under the lamplight, I saw that the color of the tea was not distinguishable from that of the cups, but a wonderful fragrance assailed my nostrils, and I felt ever so happy. "What is this tea?" I asked. "Langwan," Wenshui replied. I tasted it again and said, "Now don't deceive me. The method of preparation is Langwan, but the tea leaves are not Langwan." "What is it then?" asked Wenshui smilingly. I tasted it again and said, "Why is it so much like Lochieh tea?" Wenshui was quite struck by my answer and said, "Marvelous! Marvelous!" "What water is it?" I asked. "Huich'üan," he said. "Don't try to make fun of me," I said again. "How can Huich'üan water be carried here over a long distance, and after the shaking on the way, still retain its keenness?" So Wenshui said, "I shan't try to deceive you any longer. When I take Huich'üan water, I dig a well, and wait at night until the new current comes, and then take it up. I put a lot of mountain rocks at the bottom of the jar, and during the voyage I permit only sailing with the wind, but no rowing. Hence the water still keeps its edge. This water is therefore better even than ordinary Huich'üan water, not to speak of water from other springs." Again he said, "Marvelous! Marvelous!" and before he had finished his sentence, he went out again. Soon he came back with another pot, and asked me to taste it. I said, "Its fragrance is strong, and its flavor is very mild. This must be spring tea, while the one we just had must be autumn tea." Then Wenshui burst into laughter and said, "I am a man of seventy, and yet have never met a tea connoisseur like you." After that, we remained fast friends.

That art is now almost gone, except among a few old art-lovers and connoisseurs. It used to be very difficult to get good tea on the Chinese national railways, even in the first-class carriages, where Lipton's tea, probably the most unpalatable to my taste, was served *with milk and sugar.* When Lord Lytton visited Shanghai he was entertained at the home of a prominent rich Chinese. He asked for a cup of Chinese tea, and he could not get it. He was served Lipton's, with milk and sugar.

But enough has been said to show that the Chinese, in their moments of sanity, know essentially how to live. The art of living is with them a second instinct and a religion. Whoever said that the Chinese civilization is a spiritual civilization is a liar.

From *Father and Glorious Descendant* by Pardee Lowe, 1904–?

The eve of Father's sixty-sixth birthday was at hand: As we gathered our respective families under the paternal roof, the Gregorian solar year and the fact that on the morrow Americans the nation over would celebrate

Mother's Day possessed no significance. As filial descendants of a father about to celebrate his Great Birthday we were living in *Ting Chow*, the fourteenth year of the Seventy-seventh Cycle.

As we suspected, sleep, except for the two baby grand-children, was out of the question. A natural family of eight had quadrupled and become the Greater Family, including all available relatives and clanspeople. Since there were not enough beds to accommodate our abnormally swollen household, young and old reconciled themselves to staying up all night. All except Father who, exhausted by the extensive preparations, for once did not need any coaxing to retire early.

The household waxed merry, as befitted the joyous character of the occasion. Stepmother started games to make the watch through the night pass quickly. The young and old women played Swallows; the young men, stud poker; and the old men gathered in the Great Hall and reminisced with pleasant sighs of the days when they were young and Chinatown was un-Americanized. When the lottery agent made his appearance, Stepmother invited each member of the Greater Family to mark a ticket at her expense. "For the sake of good fortune! Yours and Father's!" Life, she reminded us, was as much caprice as preordination. It was desirable to attain a state of delicate equilibrium, of course. But since uncertainties existed more frequently than certainties, an excess of good deeds and auspicious words, and an occasional lottery ticket, were required to weight the scales in the proper direction.

For those uninterested in games, Stepmother found tasks, such as stacking paper spirit offerings, revising banquet seating arrangements and invitational lists, cataloguing and displaying gifts, and preparing the meals to be eaten on the morrow. "There is so *much* to do!" exclaimed Stepmother. She sighed with weariness and sheer pleasure as she served the midnight repast: fried noodles boiled in chicken broth. Noodles, the ambrosial food, whose unusual length when eaten presaged endless longevity for the consumer. Anachronistically, the dessert that followed revealed how hopelessly intermingled Chinatown's customs had become. It consisted of American waffles with maple syrup, sugar doughnuts, and coffee. What special significance this had upon longevity, Stepmother never explained.

But when the clock struck three, while a mighty cosmopolitan American city lay fast asleep, our family put aside its games and prepared to felic-

itate Father according to immemorial Chinese custom. The zodiac pointed
to Gemini; it was the beginning of the twin-hour period sacred to the
Tiger. Stepmother, dressed in her formal robes, prepared an informal altar
on the roof. Only I, as the eldest son, accompanied her.

Pushing aside the roof door, I beheld the setting Stepmother had selected for her outdoor ritual. Its grandeur was breathtaking. The stars were
flickering and wavering before the steady onrush of the dawn. The Nob
Hill skyscraper apartment hotels molded themselves into a natural am-
phitheater of worship, beyond whose eastern rim rose the Coast Range
Mountains tipped with a sheen of pale rose. The still waters of the Bay
shimmered with silver, and above all there hung the suspension cables of
the world's longest bridge, like the quiescent strings of an orchestra of giant
harps awaiting, so it seemed, only Stepmother's command before breaking
forth into paeans of joy.

Preoccupation with the rites of worship made Stepmother totally
oblivious of these external glories. She was busy placing a tall stack of var-
iegated spirit money on the floor. Beside it she set out a number of small
dishes containing chopped pieces of boiled chicken, roast duck, barbecued
pork, snow-white sweetened biscuits, a small tumbler of rice whisky, a bowl
of boiled rice, and a pair of ceremonial chopsticks. Behind the offerings of
food, she arranged a bank of red altar candles which were flanked by a row
of incense sticks.

The altar arranged, Stepmother bowed humbly before it. Methodically
she lit the candles and incense which gave off a fragrant but choking fog of
smoke; set fire to the stack of ghost money; raised aloft each dish in ceremonial fashion, gravely proffering it to an imaginary person, and concluded
the ritual by pouring the rice whisky, as a libation, on the roof. During all
these movements, she mumbled her simple, informal prayers, while I stood
at one side, not actually participating, and yet worshiping with her in spirit.
My calm acceptance of Stepmother's rituals amazed me.

When I was young I remember that Stepmother's worship usually
stirred me to indignation. A "sound" Christian in the accepted sense of the
term then, I was aggressively intolerant of her strange religious ways. My
scoffing ceased, however, when an iconoclastic American college education
deprived me of the "rockbound faith" of the Puritan Fathers, and experience with comparative religions opened my eyes to the humility and sin-

cerity underlying Stepmother's worship. Barbaric it might have appeared in form and details to alien eyes. But not to mine that morning. Stepmother, her hands upraised to the emerald-blue of the morning skies, clasping a sheaf of fragrant incense, will forever symbolize for me the deeply religious heart whose prayers are grounded in universal humanity.

Meanwhile, the other prime mover of Father's Great Birthday, Maternal Aunt, had not remained idle. She transformed our mundane Occidental living room into a ceremonial hall by banking the four walls with baskets of giant roses, azaleas, daffodils, gladioli, and potted ferns. In the center of the room she had placed a large library table, covering it with an embroidered red-silk cover scintillating with glass beads. This was the family altar. More decorative than the one on the roof, it was similarly arranged with the customary incense, candles, and sacrificial offerings of food, beverages, and confections, which completely encircled a large photograph of Mother, bordered by vases of blood-red roses. Stepmother, undoubtedly influenced by an age of American pictorial realism, had substituted Mother's colored photograph for the traditional wooden ancestral tablet.

If we children had been raised in China, we would have known instinctively how to act at the Ceremony of Felicitation, which immediately followed. There certainly would have been no need for a master or mistress of ceremonies to teach us our prescribed duties. But, being by birth and training psychologically Americans, we were ignorant of Chinese customs. We pleaded with Maternal Aunt Jo to teach us the complicated rites. She agreed to serve as mistress of ceremonies.

Pair by pair, Maternal Aunt summoned us into the Great Ceremonial Hall. "Don't forget," she admonished, as the assembled Greater Family looked on, "to cast down your eyes and clasp your hands to suggest extreme humility."

We did not forget. We concentrated on each separate movement of the unaccustomed rites.

"The filial Elder Son and dutiful Elder Daughter-in-law," announced Maternal Aunt in Chinese.

My wife and I moved into the hall to within touching distance of the three chairs at the right of the family altar. In the chief seat of honor sat Father, resplendent in his full dress. To his right sat Stepmother, becomingly gowned in a modern-styled Chinese robe of lavender brocade. The chair on the left was conspicuously empty. I turned quickly to Maternal Aunt. She read the look of inquiry in my eyes.

"Reserved for Mother's spirit," she whispered. Maternal Aunt Jo seemed to know everything. "She, too, comes to receive the kowtows of felicitation." Maternal Aunt resumed her stern role as mistress of ceremonies.

"In honor of the exalted living parents," she commanded, "genuflect!"

We prepared to kneel. Maternal Aunt intoned the traditional salutations connected with "Worshiping the Birthday":

> *"Nien, Nien, Yow Kum Yut;*
> *Sur, Sur, Yow Kum Chie. . . ."*

Our hearts echoed the phrases as we knelt. "May every year see such a glorious day; may every spring witness such a happy morning."

The salutations, part song and part declamation, continued. Maternal Aunt chanted like an oratorio soloist inspired. She was felicitating Father just as Stepmother had worshiped Mother in the early dawn. In our behalf, she was wishing him health, wealth, and unlimited descendants.

"Three kowtows of respect for your August Parents!" Maternal Aunt whispered, remembering that we had a part to play.

We knelt and self-consciously bumped our foreheads three times on the carpeted floor in slow succession.

"Arise and serve your elders tea and sweetmeats!"

Concluding our kowtows, we rose from the floor, turned to the sideboard and picked up two cups of tea, already prepared. I presented my cup to Father in ceremonial fashion with both hands clasped around the tiny body of the cup. My wife presented a similar cup to Stepmother. In the same ritualistic manner we served them Chinese confections. "In order to sweeten the life of your parents," explained Maternal Aunt.

Father and Stepmother beamed with satisfaction. Our conduct was exceedingly "righteous" in their eyes, and they signified their pleasure by presenting us with two large red envelopes of ceremonial gift money, each filled with sixty-six pieces of silver, corresponding to the number of years in Father's life.

As we withdrew to one side of the ceremonial hall, Maternal Aunt, following the rules of precedence, summoned my younger twin brothers. It was their turn to symbolize ritualistically their filial devotion and loyalty. They entered awkwardly, nervous with suppressed excitement.

A violent tug of the arm aroused me from my musing. I was being addressed by Maternal Aunt in peremptory tones.

"Elder son, go fetch the grandson Tsu-I," she ordered.

Returning with Junior in my arms, my wife and I again prepared to kowtow. However, Junior was utterly unimpressed by the solemnity of the occasion; seeing his grandparents, he uttered one long loud shriek of joy. It shattered the spell woven out of the past. The ceremonious kowtows were ignored when Father rose from the seat of honor and clasped his grandson to his breast. The felicitation ceremonies were telescoped on a totally unexpected note of joy. Maternal Aunt was visibly annoyed. "That's not the way it's done!" she grumbled.

When the Period of the Tiger had given way to that of the Hare, the sun was already climbing into the heavens. The formal ceremony and the informal congratulations were fully completed. It was time for breakfast. Stepmother again served a meal characterized more by its symbolism than savoriness. Like everything we had eaten the night before, each ingredient in the breakfast of hot broth possessed the power to confer special virtues. The almonds were to fill us with filial piety, the eggs to confer fertility, and the honey to grant us a plenitude of familiar affection. Like the appetite, filial piety, we discovered, also grew stout on the food it fed upon.

The breakfast dishes were no sooner out of the way than the stairs resounded with the heavy footsteps of delivery men carrying loaded trays on their heads. "The 'Tea Ceremonial Gifts' have arrived!" shouted Stepmother. She rushed to the door to supervise their unloading.

"Tea Ceremonial Gifts" are customarily presented by the immediate members of the natural family, exclusive of the sons (who must bear the costs of the Longevity Feast and the robes of immortality), to their father on his Great Birthday. They come in huge lacquer red or yellow octagonal boxes, which are filled with various sweetmeats, pastries, and meats. According to Chinese etiquette, which stresses the rule: "As you receive, so shall you give," these presents are, in turn, apportioned equally to all those who have graciously proffered gifts. When they are delivered in person to each donor, they are then designated "The Acknowledgment of All Donors' Gifts."

"You must inspect each package for its proper contents," charged Stepmother to the assembled members engaged in wrapping the gifts. "We dare not violate the proprieties by favoring some and forgetting others."

The family spent the entire morning wrapping, checking, and addressing each gift package, which contained a small red envelope of ceremonial gift money, a pair of red chopsticks, and an apple-green rice bowl, and the following delicacies: "hour cakes," similar to little dumplings; peanuts; dried dragon-eye nuts, belonging to the Li-chee family; Chinese doughnuts flecked with sesame seeds and filled with black sweetened soybean centers; and a huge slab of barbecued pig, which arrived that morning mounted regally on a large wooden platter, its crackly red skin elaborately festooned with bright-red letters of longevity.

By noon, even Stepmother was satisfied with the progress that had been made. She looked about her and saw the room piled high with packages ready for delivery. She took a puff of her silver water pipe. Just one phrase of approbation passed her lips: *"Jun Ho Ah!"*

My brothers and sisters winked knowingly. Stepmother's "heart was contented."

When the zodiac pointed to Capricorn and it was the Period of the Cock, the members of the Greater Family gathered in the main banquet hall of the Blossoming Almond. As they bustled about in last-minute preparations, Stepmother reviewed my duties:

"In thirty years," she told me, "since you were a baby, the fundamentals of formal banqueting have not changed. An eldest son still serves as proxy for his parents. He still greets each guest outside the main door with a deep bow. He still remonstrates with them for spending so much money on gifts. He still passes them on to solicitous kinsmen and kinswomen. Do not forget, they too are part of our Family and are eager to help."

I was heartened by her reminder. My duty as Chief Host would be made immeasurably lighter by the fact that beside me stood my two brothers and back of them all our kinsfolk to attend their wishes. They would take the hat, remove the outer garment, and announce aloud the name of each new arrival. They would offer the guests tea, watermelon seeds, cigarettes and cigars in turn. Finally, before conducting them to their places, they would escort them to Father and Stepmother, who would rise from their seats of honor and cordially greet them.

At length, in strict conformance to Chinese custom, three hours after the arrival of the first guest and the hour designated on the invitation, Stepmother gave the signal for the feast to begin. It was already the Period of the Dog, and Aquarius was in the ascendancy, when she nudged Father into action. He raised aloft his goblet. Three hundred and fifty goblets followed in twinkling crescendo. The banquet was on.

The courses, owing to the belated start, were rapidly served. When they appeared, it was evident that Stepmother had outdone herself in her choice of dishes. There were bird's-nest soup; shredded shark fins with diced ham; turtles cooked with sweet and spicy herbs; broiled squabs; braised prawns floating in a miniature swamp of Holland peas and tomato-curry sauce; stewed eels with celery cubes and thin medallions of water chestnuts; boiled capons crammed with a stuffing composed of lotus seeds and bird's-nest; steamed Westlake duck smothered under a bower of parsley and as fragile as a toy balloon, but much, much more substantial; diced chicken with bamboo shoots and roasted walnuts.

Course followed course in seemingly endless procession. The guests signified their repletion by laying down their chopsticks upon the table; but kinsmen serving as hosts at each table refused to be convinced. Neither was Stepmother, for she signaled the waiters to bring in the crowning achievement of Chinese epicurean taste: boneless "duck-hung-in-the-oven," barbecued to the color of lacquer and the crispness of parchment, and with it "thousand-layer biscuits" soft as down, and a seasoning with the delightful taste of an equally charming euphuistic sound, "The Sauce of the Fairies of the Sea."

"Jun Ho Ah! Jun Ho Ah!" murmured the guests, eyes gleaming with pleasure.

When the last course was served, the ceremony of pledging the guests began. With a cup of reddish Chinese brandy, aptly entitled "The-skin-increases-five-times," in our hands, Father, my two brothers, and I approached each table. As the Chief Host, I bowed, thanked them for coming, urged them to enjoy themselves. We sipped twice from our cups.

The guests responded with shouts.

"Hail the Longevity Elder! *Kawn Pui! Kawn Pui!*" (Dry cup! Dry cup!)

Father bubbled with deep appreciative laughter. Although the doctors had forbidden him to drink, he simulated the draining of an empty goblet.

Upon our return, it was Stepmother's and my wife's turn to pledge the guests. Despite the fact that my wife was an American, there was less formality in their toasts. Stepmother was in fine fettle. As she made the rounds, she had a smile and quip for everybody. Her invitations to drink sparkled with wit. She was in her element and realized it. The guests showered her with praise. They knew that it was Stepmother's crusading spirit for the old way that had made the Longevity Feast possible. She had conceived and nourished it. Her trials and tribulations had been many, but now she was reaping the reward of all her arduous labors. Father's Longevity Feast was being staged beautifully, with a rare sense of the dramatic, and in full view of a Chinatown audience which was amazed and yet delighted at the glamorous spectacle of an American daughter-in-law, clad in Chinese robes, following filially in the footsteps of her mother-in-law and repeating gracious invitations to drink in smiling and faultless Cantonese.

While Stepmother had her moments of glory, Father came in for his share, too. A clansman high in the social hierarchy of the Community had been selected as Master of Ceremonies. He rose now to introduce the orators: five leaders of powerful Chinatown groups.

The chairman of the directing board of the Masculine Concord Consolidated Districts Benevolent Association praised Father for his lifelong service to his native district. The Chief Elder of the Four Brothers called Father one of "the cornerstones" of the organization. The official representative of the Chinese-American Society drew especial attention to Father's Americanism, his progressive outlook on life. A gray-haired Chinese minister of the gospel cited Father's philanthropic efforts on behalf of Chinatown's youth. And the President of Chinatown's Chamber of Commerce extolled Father's Nestorian service to the Community.

In most communities, living men are seldom granted the privilege of hearing their own eulogies; such honors are usually reserved for their death. This is not true of Chinese society. Longevity elders are always honored in this manner. The good points of the individual are traced, to the total embarrassment of the family, backward and forward, even unto the third and fourth generation.

This barrage of praise overwhelmed us. Father, on the other hand, seemed cool, imperturbable. His eyes were rigidly shut. Stepmother, who had been enjoying the speeches, was startled by Father's immovable silence. His closed eyes frightened her. Had Father suffered another stroke? To make sure that nothing was wrong, she pinched him. Father opened wide his eyes and smiled. "What's the matter?" they seemed to say. Then, noting Stepmother's worried expression, he added jocularly, "Nothing's wrong, is there?" But Stepmother and the rest of the family were stumped. We did not know whether Father had closed his eyes out of modesty, or in order to avail himself of a pleasant nap.

The time came for delivering the valedictory. The "Appreciative Reply to the Assembled Honored Guests" always fell to the lot of the eldest son. I was frightened. Although I had become inured to public speaking before American audiences, the thought of addressing my own people in classical Chinese, with stereotyped euphuistic phrases, an entirely strange medium for me, struck me with horror.

When the Master of Ceremonies turned to me, I became a tyro orator. The aplomb laboriously acquired by years of debates and addresses in English forsook me. The Chinese speech which I had committed to memory left me. I was speechless. As I rose with a heavy effort, it was another person, certainly not my usual self, that I saw reflected in the giant mirror hanging at the opposite end of the banquet hall. Instead of a flourishing delivery, this strangely familiar figure read haltingly from a piece of paper. The voice, like the paper, quavered and shivered. I record in full a free translation from that same valedictory:

"Highly respected relatives and friends: This evening, you, as honored guests, have by gathering in this hall shed brilliancy upon this occasion. Our family is indeed highly sensible of the unusual honor you have conferred upon us. We deeply appreciate your illustrious presence here. Your bounteous gifts have overwhelmed us. Your illimitable rich expressions of felicitation move us to humble transports of gratitude. Even though tonight's repast is of an excessively shabby quality, and we dare not designate it as a banquet, we nevertheless hope that each of you will share with us many cups of brandy. Furthermore, we pray that you drink many more before your departure. At this moment, on behalf of our family, I pledge each of you. I thank you again for your magnificently generous favors. I felicitate you from the depths of my soul. I respectfully salute you. My prayer is that your future shall be as your hearts desire—pleasant, prosperous, and unending!"

The banquet ended just two hours short of midnight in the Period of the Boar, sacred to the zodiacal sign of Pisces. As countless mothers bundled their sleepy children into overcoats for the homeward journey, there was a rush of kinsfolk to the door. Like a military guard of honor they formed into two ranks. Each guest passing between the lines was sped with ceremonious bows and handclasps. As was traditional, it was the eldest son again who spoke the last words of profuse appreciation.

Then there was a lull. Most of the remaining guests, I saw from my post at the door, were surrounding Father and Stepmother, extending to them the felicitations befitting their newly acquired stature as "The Longevity Elder" and "The Longevity Elder's Wife."

Two solid days and nights of ceremonies and feasting and preparations appeared not to have sapped the vitality of my parents at all. Father never looked more distinguished or alert than as he bowed gravely to his departing guests; while Stepmother was the very picture of vivacity. But a glance at my brothers and sisters revealed a totally different sight. Forty-two hours of meticulous observance of unfamiliar customs and strange rites, without any rest, coupled with their duties as hosts at the banquet, had done its deadly work.

My two married sisters groaned.

"This is just the beginning," they sighed.

I nodded my head wearily. Their meaning was clear. The Longevity Feast was only the beginning. A series of sumptuous celebrations were yet to be observed. Although we had purposely ignored Mother's Day, tomorrow would see us marking it with red letters. There would be another restaurant banquet for the Greater Family and a visit to Mother's grave. Within a week, Stepmother's own birthday would be commemorated, if not on such a grand scale as Father's, still with more than casual rejoicing. Following this would come the Chinese festival of the Fifth Day of the Fifth Moon with its emphasis upon rice tamales wrapped in triangular bamboo leaves, presents, and feasting; and then shortly after an American holiday, Memorial Day. Life at that moment seemed to stretch out into an endless chain of Western and Oriental holidays interspersed with family festivities.

But when we children saw how Father, erect and smiling in his splendid suit of Piccadilly cut, looked younger every second, and how rejuvenated he and Stepmother had become, we had no heart to protest our fate further.

"This feast was worth it!" exclaimed Younger Brother, his voice blurred with emotion.

"Yes," concurred my sisters. "The financial burdens are heavy and the efforts troublesome, but since they come only once a lifetime, we can and shall shoulder them gladly!"

"True," I added, "a decade must pass before we can again celebrate Father's Great Birthday." Experiencing a sudden feeling of softness, I asked myself what would those eventful ten years bring? Would it ever be the same?

I gazed once more on that scene of lively color and noise, Father's Longevity Feast. I wanted to fix it forever in my memory so that some day when Tsu-I grew to manhood, I could tell him the complete story of his Grandfather's Great Birthday. I would explain to him why the Longevity Party was such a success, and why even in the Western World, even in Chinatown, the old traditions prevailed. He would hear how Stepmother had seen her duty and performed it, in order to assure the family's future prosperity and to impress forever upon our hearts the primal lesson of Chinese family life, a lesson she and Father had both learned at their own parents' knees: "Among our people, children are begotten and nurtured for one purpose—to provide for and glorify their parents."

From *The Good Earth* by Pearl Buck, 1892–1973

. . . There were foods Wang Lung had never even heard of: lichee nuts and dried honey dates and curious cakes of rice flour and nuts and red sugar, and horned fish from the sea and many other things. These all cost money more than he liked to give out, and yet he was afraid to say, "You are eating my flesh," for fear Lotus would be offended and angry at him, and it would displease her, and so there was nothing he could do except to put his hand unwillingly to his girdle. And this was a thorn to him day after day, and because there was none to whom he could complain of it, the thorn pierced more deeply continually, and it cooled a little of the fire of love in him for Lotus.

And there was yet another small thorn that sprang from the first, and it was that his uncle's wife, who loved good food, went often into the inner court at meal times, and she grew free there, and Wang Lung was not pleased that out of his house Lotus chose this woman for friend. The three women ate well in the inner courts, and they talked unceasingly, whispering and laughing, and there was something that Lotus liked in the wife of his uncle and the three were happy together, and this Wang Lung did not like.

But still there was nothing to be done, for when he said gently and to coax her,

"Now, Lotus, my flower, do not waste your sweetness on an old fat hag like that one. I need it for my own heart, and she is a deceitful and untrustworthy creature, and I do not like it that she is near you from dawn to sunset."

Lotus was fretful and she answered peevishly, pouting her lips and hanging her head away from him,

"Now I have no one except you and I have no friends and I am used to a merry house and in yours there is no one except the first wife who hates me and these children of yours who are a plague to me, and I have no one."

Then she used her weapons against him and she would not let him into her room that night and she complained and said,

"You do not love me, for if you did you would wish me to be happy."

Then Wang Lung was humbled and anxious and he was submissive and he was sorry and he said,

"Let it be only as you wish and forever."

Then she forgave him royally and he was afraid to rebuke her in any way for what she wished to do, and after that when he came to her Lotus, if she were talking or drinking tea or eating some sweetmeat with his uncle's wife, would bid him wait and was careless with him, and he strode away, angry that she was unwilling for him to come in when this other woman sat there, and his love cooled a little, although he did not know it himself.

He was angry, moreover, that his uncle's wife ate of the rich foods that he had to buy for Lotus and that she grew fat and more oily than she had been, but he could say nothing, for his uncle's wife was clever and she was courteous to him and flattered him with good words, and rose when he came into the room.

And so his love for Lotus was not whole and perfect as it had been before, absorbing utterly his mind and his body.

III
HUNGRY FOR PHOENIX-EGGS
The Adventurers

There is in some few men of every land a special hunger, one which will make them forego the safe pleasures of their own beds and tables, one which initiates them into that most mysterious and ruthless sect, The Adventurers. It gnaws at them, a worm or a wolf in the vitals of their minds, so that they must turn away from the things they know about and go to the farthest places of the world. They must face pain and fever, and starvation itself, to feed that other, inner hunger ... and once having fed it, search for more food, like stuffed beggars under a banquet-table. And when they die, even if they live to do it in their old age and their beds, which is rare indeed, they still have their teeth set, their gullets yawning, for some new feast: a trip up one of the strange rivers of the Congo, a trek to the lost kingdom of Bui Yo Fan.

The little islands of Great Britain, for some reason, have given more initiates to the Adventurers than any other western country. The close small hills may seem too close and small for them, and send them searching for Everest's top snows. Or perhaps it is the cold boiled mutton and the countless puddings that push Englishmen beyond their known horizons, to subsist or not on locusts and baked phoenix-eggs!

Fortunately, the common pattern of an English gentleman includes a certain amount of good education, so that many of the wanderers have been able to write of the strange things they have fed upon . . . and of the three I have chosen for this book, two are British: Richard Burton and T. E. Lawrence. The third, Marco Polo, happened to be born in Venice in 1254, but his veins were filled with the same feverish hunger.

When he was seventeen, and started on the long road to the capital of Kublai Khan, Emperor of the Tartars, Marco Polo was already a good merchant and a member of the company of Venetian noblemen, as well as a gay and thoughtful courtier. His uncle and father, with whom he traveled for three and a half years before he reached the fabulous court, were returning to tell the Khan that a new Pope, in answer to his request for a company of one hundred missionaries to convert China to Christianity, had seen fit to send but two disinterested and ill-taught priests.

It is true that the Emperor's interest in the new religion was somewhat more political than holy, as inspired by his long talks with the two elder Polos about their own country and the effects there of Christianity, but, as Manuel Komroff says in the introduction to his edition of *The Travels of Marco Polo*, which I am using: ". . . regardless of the sinister motives of Kublai Khan, the Pope cannot be forgiven for having lost so welcome an opportunity; an opportunity for wisdom, if not for virtue. Had he sent a thousand men instead of a hundred, little impression would they have made in so vast a territory, but however little, that impression would have been important. A new religion might have resulted; for inasmuch as China has altered Buddhism, probably it would have distorted Christianity also."

The theory is an exciting one, and seems more than possible when we see the picture of China as it was then, rising from the pages of Marco Polo's long diary. It was a country far ahead of Europe, just then emerging from the Dark Ages, in almost every attribute of civilization, from the subtlety of its many arts and inventions to the natural courtesy of its people.

The charming Italian merchant soon became a favorite of Kublai Khan and special envoy to all parts of the Empire, and since he saw quickly that his ruler enjoyed his own detailed, amusing accounts of his missions, he kept from the beginning of his long stay there small books of comment. These were the skeleton of his final story, which he composed almost thirty years later in prison, a captive of the Genoese.

Marco's character was so flamboyantly typical of The Great Adventurer that almost nobody believed a word of what he wrote, much less what he told in the halls of Venice for the rest of his life, and for several hundred years his *Travels* were laughed at as a collection of gargantuan whoppers. The miracles that so casually studded his matter-of-fact merchant's recording of his adventures are commonplaces now, but in the thirteenth century it was incredible that the Chinese burned a black stone called coal, that there were coconuts as big as a man's head . . . or even that Christians and Jews could live side by side in freedom and tolerance as they did then in Asia. . . .

The return of the three Polos to Venice, after twenty-six years in the mythical lands of the Orient, is in tune with their whole fantastic story. At first their families refused to recognize the filthy strangers, who had almost forgotten their own tongue, but finally they were admitted to be alive and genuine and, as Mr. Komroff writes:

From the Introduction to *The Travels of Marco Polo*, 15th Century edited by Manuel Komroff, 1890–1974

A day or two later a grand feast was arranged to which all the old friends and relatives were asked. The three travellers were clothed in long robes of crimson satin, but these they removed before they sat down to the feast and they put on other robes of crimson damask, while the first were cut up and the cloth divided among the servants. Once during the course of the meal the travellers left the room and came back, this time in long robes of crimson velvet, and the damask garments were presented to some of the guests. When the dinner was finished the robes of velvet were removed and the travellers appeared dressed in the ordinary fashion of the day; and the velvet robes were likewise distributed to the guests in strict accordance with the Mongol custom.

This performance caused much wonder. But when the table had been cleared, and all the servants had been asked to retire from the hall, Marco Polo produced the coarse, shabby costumes which the three travellers had worn on their arrival. Then taking sharp knives they ripped the seams and pleats and let fall to the table quantities of rubies, carbuncles, sapphires, diamonds, emeralds, pearls, and other jewels of great value. Amazement bewildered and dumbfounded the guests; but if a shadow of doubt had remained in the minds of some regarding the identity of the travellers, it was now wholly dispersed. And all paid honour to the three gentlemen, agreeing that they could be no other than those of the merchant family.

Marco Polo's own chronicle is a completely unimaginative and humorless one, but is full of clear-headed observations which make a wonderful picture of the Eastern world as it was then. He wrote of the animals and plants he saw, and especially of what people ate, whether they were peasants or the Great Khan himself, and it is difficult to choose one detail that is more interesting than another. Those that follow could have been a hundred others:

From *The Travels of Marco Polo*, 15th Century
edited by Manuel Komroff, 1890–1974

[The Tartars] subsist entirely upon flesh and milk, eating the produce of their sport, and a certain small animal, not unlike a rabbit, which during the summer season is found in great abundance in the plains. But they likewise eat flesh of every description, horses, camels, and even dogs, provided they are fat. They drink mares' milk, which they prepare in such a manner that it has the qualities and flavour of white wine.

They make provision also of milk thickened and dried to the state of a paste, which is prepared in the following manner: They boil the milk, and skimming off the rich or creamy part as it rises to the top, put it into a separate vessel as butter; for so long as that remains in the milk, it will not become hard. The latter is then exposed to the sun until it dries. Upon going on service they carry with them about ten pounds for each man, and of this, half a pound is put, every morning, into a leathern bottle, with as much water as is thought necessary. By their motion in riding the contents are violently shaken, and a thin porridge is produced, upon which they make their dinner.

When his Majesty holds a grand and public court, those who attend it are seated in the following order: The table of the sovereign is placed on an elevation, and he takes his seat on the northern side, with his face turned towards the south; and next to him, on his left hand, sits the Empress. On his right hand are placed his sons, grandsons, and other persons connected with him by blood, upon seats somewhat lower, so that their heads are on a level with the Emperor's feet. The other princes and the nobility have their places at still lower tables; and the same rules are observed with respect to the females, the wives of the sons, grandsons, and other relatives of the Great Khan being seated on the left hand, at tables in like manner gradually lower; then follow the wives of the nobility and military officers: so that all are seated according to their respective ranks and dignities, in the places assigned to them, and to which they are entitled.

The tables are arranged in such a manner that the Great Khan, sitting on his elevated throne, can overlook the whole. It is not, however, to be understood that all who assemble on such occasions can be accommodated at tables. The greater part of the officers, and even of the nobles, on the contrary, eat, sitting upon carpets, in the halls; and on the outside stand a great multitude of persons who come from different countries, and bring with them many rare curiosities.

In the middle of the hall, where the Great Khan sits at table, there is a magnificent piece of furniture, made in the form of a square coffer, each side of which is three paces in length, exquisitely carved in figures of animals, and gilt. It is hollow within, for the purpose of receiving a capacious vase, of pure gold, calculated to hold many gallons. On each of its four sides stands a smaller vessel, containing about a hogshead, one of which is filled with mare's milk, another with that of the camel, and so of the others, according to the kinds of beverage in use. Within this buffet are also the cups or flagons belonging to his Majesty, for serving the liquors. Some of them are of beautiful gilt plate. Their size is such that, when filled with wine or other liquor, the quantity would be sufficient for eight or ten men.

Before every two persons who have seats at the tables, one of these flagons is placed, together with a kind of ladle, in the form of a cup with a handle, also of plate; to be used not only for taking the wine out of the flagon, but for lifting it to the head. This is observed as well with respect to the women as the men. The quantity and richness of the plate belonging to his Majesty is quite incredible.

Officers of rank are likewise appointed whose duty is to see that all strangers who happen to arrive at the time of the festival, and are unacquainted with the etiquette of the court, are suitably accommodated with places; and these stewards are continually visiting every part of the hall, inquiring of the guests if there is anything with which they are unprovided, or whether any of them wish for wine, milk, meat, or other articles, in which case it is immediately brought to them by the attendants.

At each door of the grand hall, or of whatever part the Great Khan happens to be in, stand two officers of a gigantic figure, one on each side, with staves in their hands, for the purpose of preventing persons from touching the threshold with their feet, and obliging them to step beyond it. If by chance any one is guilty of this offence, these janitors take from him his garment, which he must redeem for money; or, when they do not take the garment, they inflict on him such number of blows as they have authority for doing. But, as strangers may be unacquainted with the prohibition, officers are appointed to introduce and warn them. This precaution is used because touching the threshold is regarded as a bad omen. In departing from the hall, as some of the company may be affected by the liquor, it is impossible to guard against the accident, and the order is not then strictly enforced.

The numerous persons who attend at the sideboard of his Majesty, and who serve him with victuals and drink, are all obliged to cover their noses and mouths with handsome veils or cloths of worked silk, in order that his victuals or his wine may not be affected by their breath. When drink is called for by him, and the page in waiting has presented it, he retires three paces and kneels down, upon which the courtiers, and all who are present, in like manner make their prostration. At the same moment all the musical instruments, of which there is a numerous band, begin to play, and continue to do so until he has ceased drinking, when all the company recover their posture. This reverential salutation is made as often as his Majesty drinks. It is unnecessary to say anything of the victuals, because it may well be imagined that their abundance is excessive.

When the repast is finished, and the tables have been removed, persons of various descriptions enter the hall, and amongst these a troop of comedians and performers on different instruments. Also tumblers and jugglers, who exhibit their skill in the presence of the Great Khan, to the high amusement and gratification of all the spectators. When these sports are concluded, the people separate, and each returns to his own house.

One of those Englishmen who have most clearly gone out in the noonday sun was T. E. Lawrence, Lawrence of Arabia, probably the king of the peculiarly British race of Adventurers who have had to flee the cold-mutton limitations of their island for the hot, high-spiced intrigue of the Orient.

His book, *Seven Pillars of Wisdom: A Triumph,* is one of the most exciting prose poems in our language, for the oftentimes extraordinary phrases in it, magic ones: "this self-regardant picture," and then for the picture itself, of a short-boned man, abstemious as a monk making his retreat from the dangers of the world and the flesh, and yet still able to write of the "quick and delicate meals," the hot pools of yellow fat in others' feastings.

He wrote the story of the Arab Revolt, which was largely a machination to help the Arabs rebel against the Turks and thus aid England to defeat both Turkey and Germany at the same time. The detailed history of the astounding little *agent provocateur*'s subtleties for his country among the rebelling people is mysterious to an average human being in the same way that a perfect spider web is mysterious, but its unwavering humanity keeps it comprehensible, as in the following cool descriptions of how a ruler and his subjects nourished themselves:

From *The Seven Pillars of Wisdom* by T.E. Lawrence, 1888–1935

The routine of our life in camp was simple. Just before daybreak the army Imam used to climb to the head of the little hill above the sleeping army, and thence utter an astounding call to prayer. His voice was harsh and very powerful, and the hollow, like a sounding-board, threw echoes at the hills which returned them with indignant interest. We were effectually roused, whether we prayed or cursed. As soon as he ended, Feisal's Imam cried gently and musically from just outside the tent. In a minute, one of Feisal's five slaves (all freed men, but refusing discharge till it was their pleasure: since it was good and not unprofitable to be my lord's servant) came round to Sharraf and myself with sweetened coffee. Sugar for the first cup in the chill of dawn was considered fit.

An hour or so later, the flap of Feisal's sleeping tent would be thrown back: his invitation to callers from the household. There would be four or five present; and after the morning's news a tray of breakfast would be carried in. The staple of this was dates in Wadi Yenbo; sometimes Feisal's Circassian grandmother would send him a box of her famous spiced cakes from Mecca; and sometimes Hejris, the body slave, would give us odd biscuits and cereals of his own trying. After breakfast we would play with bitter coffee and sweet tea in alternation, while Feisal's correspondence was dealt with by dictation to his secretaries. One of these was Faiz el Ghusein the adventurous; another was the Imam, a sad-faced person made conspicuous in the army by the baggy umbrella hanging from his saddle-bow. Occasionally a man was given private audience at this hour, but seldom; as the sleeping tent was strictly for the Sherif's own use. It was an ordinary bell tent, furnished with cigarettes, a camp-bed, a fairly good Kurd rug, a poor Shirazi, and the delightful old Baluch prayer-carpet on which he prayed.

At about eight o'clock in the morning, Feisal would buckle on his ceremonial dagger and walk across to the reception tent, which was floored with two horrible kilims. Feisal would sit down at the end of the tent facing the open side, and we with our backs against the wall, in a semicircle out from him. The slaves brought up the rear, and clustered round the open wall of the tent to control the besetting suppliants who lay on the sand in the tent-mouth, or beyond, waiting their turn. If possible, business was got through by noon, when the Emir liked to rise.

We of the household, and any guests, then reassembled in the living tent; and Hejris and Salem carried in the luncheon tray, on which were as many dishes as circumstances permitted. Feisal was an inordinate smoker, but a very light eater, and he used to make-believe with his fingers or a spoon among the beans, lentils, spinach, rice, and sweet cakes till he judged that we had had enough, when at a wave of his hand the tray would disappear, as other slaves walked forward to pour water for our fingers at the tent door. Fat men, like Mohammed Ibn Shefia, made a comic grievance of the Emir's quick and delicate meals, and would have food of their own prepared for them when they came away. After lunch we would talk a little, while sucking up two cups of coffee, and savouring two glasses full of syrup-like green tea. Then till two in the afternoon the curtain of the living tent was down, signifying that Feisal was sleeping, or reading, or doing private business. Afterwards he would sit again in the reception tent till he had finished with all who wanted him. I never saw an Arab leave him dissatisfied or hurt—a tribute to his tact and to his memory; for he seemed never to halt for loss of a fact, nor to stumble over a relationship.

If there were time after second audience, he would walk with his friends, talking of horses or plants, looking at camels, or asking someone the names of the visible land features. The sunset prayer was at times public, though Feisal was not outwardly very pious. After it he saw people individually in the living tent, planning the night's reconnaissances and patrols—for most of the field-work was done after dark. Between six and seven there was brought in the evening meal, to which all present in headquarters were called by the slaves. It resembled the lunch, except that cubes of boiled mutton were sorted through the great tray of rice, *Medfa el Suhur*, the mainstay of appetite. We observed silence till all had eaten.

This meal ended our day, save for the stealthy offering by a barefooted slave of a tray of tea-glasses at protracted intervals.

. . . The chiefs of the Fitenna waited on us, and said that they were honoured to feast us twice a day, forenoon and sunset, so long as we remained with them; and they meant what they said. Howeitat hospitality was un-limited—no three-day niggardliness for them of the nominal desert law—and importunate, and left us no honourable escape from the entirety of the nomad's dream of well-being.

Each morning, between eight and ten, a little group of blood mares under an assortment of imperfect saddlery would come to our camping place, and on them Nasir, Nesib, Zeki, and I would mount, and with per-haps a dozen of our men on foot would move solemnly across the valley by the sandy paths between the bushes. Our horses were led by our servants, since it would be immodest to ride free or fast. So eventually we would reach the tent which was to be our feast-hall for that time; each family claiming us in turn, and bitterly offended if Zaal, the adjudicator, preferred one out of just order.

As we arrived, the dogs would rush out at us, and be driven off by onlookers—always a crowd had collected round the chosen tent—and we stepped in under the ropes to its guest half, made very large for the occa-sion and carefully dressed with its wall-curtain on the sunny side to give us the shade. The bashful host would murmur and vanish again out of sight. The tribal rugs, lurid red things from Beyrout, were ready for us, arranged down the partition curtain, along the back wall and across the dropped end, so that we sat down on three sides of an open dusty space. We might be fifty men in all.

The host would reappear, standing by the pole; our local fellow-guests, el Dheilan, Zaal, and other sheikhs, reluctantly let themselves be placed on the rugs between us, sharing our elbow-room on the pack-saddles, pad-ded with folded felt rugs, over which we leaned. The front of the tent was cleared, and the dogs were frequently chased away by excited children, who ran across the empty space pulling yet smaller children after them. Their clothes were less as their years were less, and their pot-bodies rounder. The smallest infants of all, out of their fly-black eyes, would stare at the company, gravely balanced on spread legs, stark-naked, sucking their thumbs and pushing out expectant bellies toward us.

Then would follow an awkward pause, which our friends would try to cover by showing us on its perch the household hawk (when possible a sea-bird taken young on the Red Sea coast) or their watch-cockerel, or their greyhound. Once a tame ibex was dragged in for our admiration: another time an oryx. When these interests were exhausted they would try and find a small talk to distract us from the household noises, and from noticing the urgent whispered cookery-directions wafted through the dividing curtain with a powerful smell of boiled fat and drifts of tasty meat-smoke.

After a silence the host or a deputy would come forward and whisper, "Black or white?"—an invitation for us to choose coffee or tea. Nasir would always answer "Black," and the slave would be beckoned forward with the beaked coffee-pot in one hand, and three or four clinking cups of white ware in the other. He would dash a few drops of coffee into the uppermost cup, and proffer it to Nasir; then pour the second for me, and the third for Nesib; and pause while we turned the cups about in our hands, and sucked them carefully, to get appreciatively from them the last richest drop.

As soon as they were empty his hand was stretched to clap them noisily one above the other, and toss them out with a lesser flourish for the next guest in order, and so on round the assembly till all had drunk. Then back to Nasir again. This second cup would be tastier than the first, partly because the pot was yielding deeper from the brew, partly because of the heel-taps of so many previous drinkers present in the cups; whilst the third and fourth rounds, if the serving of the meat delayed so long, would be of surprising flavour.

However, at last, two men came staggering through the thrilled crowd, carrying the rice and meat on a tinned copper tray or shallow bath, five feet across, set like a great brazier on a foot. In the tribe there was only this one food-bowl of the size, and an incised inscription ran round it in florid Arabic characters: "To the glory of God, and in trust of mercy at the last, the property of His poor suppliant, Auda abu Tayi." It was borrowed by the host who was to entertain us for the time; and, since my urgent brain and body made me wakeful, from my blankets in the first light I would see the dish going across country, and by marking down its goal would know where we were to feed that day.

The bowl was now brim-full, ringed round its edge by white rice in an embankment a foot wide and six inches deep, filled with legs and ribs of mutton till they toppled over. It needed two or three victims to make in the centre a dressed pyramid of meat such as honour prescribed. The centre-pieces were the boiled, upturned heads, propped on their severed stumps of neck, so that the ears, brown like old leaves, flapped out on the rice surface. The jaws gaped emptily upward, pulled open to show the hollow throat with the tongue, still pink, clinging to the lower teeth; and the long incisors whitely crowned the pile, very prominent above the nostrils' pricking hair and the lips which sneered away blackly from them.

This load was set down on the soil of the cleared space between us, where it steamed hotly, while a procession of minor helpers bore small cauldrons and copper vats in which the cooking had been done. From them, with much-bruised bowls of enamelled iron, they ladled out over the main dish all the inside and outside of the sheep; little bits of yellow intestine, the white tail-cushion of fat, brown muscles and meat and bristly skin, all swimming in the liquid butter and grease of the seething. The bystanders watched anxiously, muttering satisfactions when a very juicy scrap plopped out.

The fat was scalding. Every now and then a man would drop his baler with an exclamation, and plunge his burnt fingers, not reluctantly, in his mouth to cool them: but they persevered till at last their scooping rang loudly on the bottoms of the pots; and, with a gesture of triumph, they fished out the intact livers from their hiding place in the gravy and topped the yawning jaws with them.

Two raised each smaller cauldron and tilted it, letting the liquid splash down upon the meat till the rice-crater was full, and the loose grains at the edge swam in the abundance; and yet they poured, till, amid cries of astonishment from us, it was running over, and a little pool congealing in the dust. That was the final touch of splendour, and the host called us to come and eat.

We feigned a deafness, as manners demanded: at last we heard him, and looked surprised at one another, each urging his fellow to move first; till Nasir rose coyly, and after him we all came forward to sink on one knee round the tray, wedging in and cuddling up till the twenty-two for whom there was barely space were grouped around the food. We turned back our sleeves to the elbow, and, taking lead from Nasir with a low "In the name of God the merciful, the loving-kind," we dipped together.

The first dip, for me, at least, was always cautious, since the liquid fat was so hot that my unaccustomed fingers could seldom bear it; and so I would toy with an exposed and cooling lump of meat till others' excavations had drained my rice-segment. We would knead between the fingers (not soiling the palm), neat balls of rice and fat and liver and meat cemented by gentle pressure, and project them by leverage of the thumb from the crooked forefinger into the mouth. With the right trick and the right construction the little lump held together and came clean off the hand; but when surplus butter and odd fragments clung, cooling, to the fingers, they had to be licked carefully to make the next effort slip easier away.

As the meat pile wore down (nobody really cared about rice: flesh was the luxury) one of the chief Howeitat eating with us would draw his dagger, silver hilted, set with turquoise, a signed masterpiece of Mohammed Ibn Zari, of Jauf, and would cut crisscross from the larger bones long diamonds of meat easily torn up between the fingers; for it was necessarily boiled very tender, since all had to be disposed of with the right hand, which alone was honourable.

Our host stood by the circle, encouraging the appetite with pious ejaculations. At top speed we twisted, tore, cut, and stuffed: never speaking, since conversation would insult a meal's quality; though it was proper to smile thanks when an intimate guest passed a select fragment, or when Mohammed el Dheilan gravely handed over a huge barren bone with a blessing. On such occasions I would return the compliment with some hideous impossible lump of guts, a flippancy which rejoiced the Howeitat, but which the gracious, aristocratic Nasir saw with disapproval.

At length some of us were nearly filled, and began to play and pick; glancing sideways at the rest till they too grew slow, and at last ceased eating, elbow on knee, the hand hanging down from the wrist over the tray edge to drip, while the fat, butter, and scattered grains of rice cooled into a stiff white grease which gummed the fingers together. When all had stopped, Nasir meaningly cleared his throat, and we rose up together in haste with an explosive "God requite it you, O host," to group ourselves outside among the tent-ropes while the next twenty guests inherited our leaving.

Those of us who were nice would go to the end of the tent where the flap of the roof-cloth, beyond the last poles, drooped down as an end curtain; and on this clan handkerchief (whose coarse goat-hair mesh was pliant and glossy with much use) would scrape the thickest of the fat from the hands. Then we would make back to our seats, and re-take them sighingly; while the slaves, leaving aside their portion, the skulls of the sheep, would come round our rank with a wooden bowl of water, and a coffee-cup as dipper, to splash over our fingers, while we rubbed them with the tribal soap-cake.

Meantime the second and third sittings by the dish were having their turn, and then there would be one more cup of coffee, or a glass of syrup-like tea; and at last the horses would be brought and we would slip out to them, and mount, with a quiet blessing to the hosts as we passed by. When our backs were turned the children would run in disorder upon the ravaged dish, tear our gnawed bones from one another, and escape into the open with valuable fragments to be devoured in security behind some distant bush; while the watch-dogs of all the camp prowled round snapping, and the master of the tent fed the choicest offal to his greyhound.

Just as there is little difference between the Chinese cuisine of today and four thousand years ago (except perhaps in some such a minor matter as canned pineapple!), so the Arabs and the other tribes who for uncounted centuries have roamed the lands south and east of the Mediterranean celebrate their feast-days and fastings much as they always have. It does not matter whether photographers cover a meeting of princely oil magnates in Saudi Arabia for the next issue of *Life* magazine: the intricately simple manners of the diners will be the same as they were yesterday in 1986 B.C.

And in the village streets the same stinking dust still rises, and the same music still tinkles and clashes, as when Ma'aruf the Cobbler hated his wife in Cairo and a handsome young porter was seduced in Baghdad, perhaps eighteen hundred years ago, and were told about by Shahrazad in the thousand and one stories she unfolded to the Sultan to save her life.

Of course never were men so bold and potent as when she spoke of them, nor women so dazzling and generous; never did gold gleam so richly, nor wine flow in such deep rivers, nor feasts spread so many fabulous courses before such hungry superhuman beings. Flying carpets, and thrones cut from a single ruby, and six lovely virgins carved each from a diamond and standing on a golden pedestal: they all seem as real when Shahrazad speaks of them as does the man whose life was ruined because he broke wind on his marriage night, or the nagging Fatimah, "a whorish, worthless wretch" who wanted only bees' honey on her vermicelli cake. They are all part of the long dream, the completely impossible but comprehensible fairy tale, *The Arabian Nights' Entertainments*, where each of us who reads can lead his best secret life of adventure and love and satisfaction.

One of the reasons why this "book of a thousand nights and a night" can still transport us is that the Englishman whose version we read now was not only a great Orientalist but also one of that fabulous breed, a Great Adventurer. The same hunger that held Marco Polo in the court of Kublai Khan, and turned Lawrence into an Arab, drove Richard Burton all his life to explore and ask and struggle.

He went to Mecca, a pilgrim; he cut new paths in to the lakes of Central Africa, and risked his life in Somaliland, and wandered in South American jungles. Always he was working on his own "full, complete, uncastrated" translation of the *Thousand Nights and a Night*, and tingeing it with the exaggerated richness of his whole character.

It is hard to choose a banquet from all its feasts, just as it would be hard to pick one jewel from among the ropes and baskets and piles of precious stones lying loose in every corner of the book. So here is a little crumb from the hilarious story of Ma'aruf the Cobbler, to show at least the beginning of his revenge against Fatimah over the vermicelli cake; here is the beginning of the incredible adventure of the Porter and the Three Ladies of Baghdad, to show that no matter how they may have exhausted him later, they took care to nourish him first in all his senses; finally, here is the whole sad story of what happened when Abu Hasan, a sensitive if greedy man, ate too much at his wedding:

From *The Thousand Nights and a Night*, circa 13th Century
translated by Richard Burton, 1821–1890

There dwelt once upon a time in the God-guarded city of Cairo a cobbler who lived by patching old shoes. His name was Ma'aruf and he had a wife called Fatimah, whom the folk had nicknamed "The Dung"; for that she was a whorish, worthless wretch, scanty of shame and mickle of mischief. She ruled her spouse and used to abuse him and curse him a thousand times a day; and he feared her malice and dreaded her misdoings; for that he was a sensible man and careful of his repute, but poor-conditioned. When he earned much, he spent it on her, and when he gained little, she revenged herself on his body that night, leaving him no peace and making his night black as her book; for she was even as of one like her saith the poet:

> How manifold nights have I passed with my wife
> In the saddest plight with all misery rife:
> Would Heaven when first I went in to her
> With a cup of cold poison I'd ta'en her life.

Amongst other afflictions which befell him from her one day she said to him, "O Ma'aruf, I wish thee to bring me this night a vermicelli-cake dressed with bees' honey." He replied, "So Allah Almighty aid me to its price, I will bring it thee. By Allah, I have no dirhams to-day, but our Lord will make things easy." She rejoined, "I wot naught of these words; whether He aid thee or aid thee not, look thou come not to me save with the vermicelli and bees' honey; and if thou come without it I will make thy night black as thy fortune whenas thou marriedst me and fellest into my hand." Quoth he, "Allah is bountiful!" and going out with grief scattering itself from his body, prayed the dawn-prayer and opened his shop, saying, "I beseech thee, O Lord, to vouchsafe me the price of the Kunafah and ward off from me the mischief of yonder wicked woman this night!" After which he sat in the shop till noon, but no work came to him and his fear of his wife redoubled. Then he arose and, locking his shop, went out perplexed as to how he should do in the matter of the vermicelli-cake, seeing he had not even the wherewithal to buy bread. Presently he came up to the shop of the Kunafah-seller and stood before it distraught, whilst his eyes brimmed with tears. The pastry-cook glanced at him and said, "O Master Ma'aruf, why dost thou weep? Tell me what hath befallen thee." So he acquainted him with his case, saying, "My wife is a shrew, a virago who would have me bring her a Kunafah; but I have sat in my shop till past mid-day and have not gained even the price of bread; wherefore I am in fear of her." The cook laughed and said, "No harm shall come to thee. How many pounds wilt thou have?" "Five pounds," answered Ma'aruf. So the man weighed him out five pounds of vermicelli-cake and said to him, "I have clarified butter, but no bees' honey. Here is drip-honey, however, which is better than bees' honey; and what harm will there be, if it be with drip-honey?" Ma'aruf was ashamed to object, because the pastrycook was to have patience with him for the price, and said, "Give it me with drip-honey." So he fried a vermicelli-cake for him with butter and drenched it with drip-honey, till it was fit to present to Kings. Then he asked him, "Dost thou want bread and cheese?"; and Ma'aruf answered, "Yes." So he gave him four half dirhams worth of bread and one of cheese, and the vermicelli was ten nusfs. Then said he, "Know, O Ma'aruf, that thou owest me fifteen nusfs; so go to thy wife and make merry and take this nusf for the Hammam; and thou shalt have credit for a day or two or three till Allah provide thee with thy daily bread. And straiten not thy wife, for I will have patience with thee till such time as thou shalt have dirhams to spare." So Ma'aruf took the vermicelli-cake and bread and cheese and went away, with a heart at ease, blessing the pastry-cook and saying, "Extolled be Thy perfection, O my Lord! How bountiful art Thou!" When he came home, his wife enquired of him, "Hast thou brought the vermicelli-cake?"; and, replying "Yes," he set it before her. She looked at it and seeing it was dressed with cane-honey, said to him, "Did I not bid thee bring it with bees' honey? Wilt thou contrary my wish and have it dressed with cane-honey?" He excused himself to her, saying, "I bought it not save on credit"; but said she, "This talk is idle; I will not eat Kunafah save with bees' honey." And she was wroth with it and threw it in his face, saying, "Begone, thou pimp, and bring me other than this!" Then she dealt him a buffet on the cheek and knocked out one of his teeth. The blood ran down upon his breast and for stress of anger he smote her on the head a single blow and a slight; whereupon she clutched his beard and fell to shouting out and saying, "Help, O Moslems!" So the neighbours came in and freed his beard from her grip; then they reproved and reproached her, saying, "We are all content to eat Kunafah with cane-honey. Why, then, wilt thou oppress this poor man thus? Verily, this is disgraceful in thee!" And they went on to soothe her till they made peace between her and him. But, when the folk were gone, she sware that she would not eat of the vermicelli, and Ma'aruf, burning with hunger, said in himself, "She sweareth that she will not eat; so I will e'en eat." Then he ate, and when she saw him eating, she said, "Inshallah, may the eating of it be poison to destroy the far one's body." Quoth he, "It shall not be at thy bidding," and went on eating, laughing, and saying, "Thou swarest that thou wouldst not eat of this; but Allah is bountiful, and tomorrow night, and the Lord decree, I will bring thee Kunafah dressed with bees' honey, and thou shalt eat it alone." And he applied himself to appeasing her, whilst she called down curses upon him; and she ceased not to rail at him and revile him with gross abuse till the morning, when she bared her forearm to beat him. Quoth he, "Give me time and I will bring thee other vermicelli-cake." Then he went out to the mosque and prayed. . . .

Once upon a time there was a Porter in Baghdad, who was a bachelor and who would remain unmarried. It came to pass on a certain day, as he stood about the street leaning idly upon his crate, behold, there stood before him an honourable woman in a mantilla of Mosul silk, broidered with gold and bordered with brocade; her walking-shoes were also purfled with gold and her hair floated in long plaits. She raised her face-veil and, showing two black eyes fringed with jetty lashes, whose glances were soft and languishing and whose perfect beauty was ever blandishing, she accosted the Porter and said in the suavest tones and choicest language, "Take up thy crate and follow me." The Porter was so dazzled he could hardly believe that he heard her aright, but he shouldered his basket in hot haste saying in himself, "O day of good luck! O day of Allah's grace!" and walked after her till she stopped at the door of a house. There she rapped, and presently came out to her an old man, a Nazarene, to whom she gave a gold piece, receiving from him in return what she required of strained wine clear as olive oil; and she set it safely in the hamper, saying, "Lift and follow." Quoth the Porter, "This, by Allah, is indeed an auspicious day, a day propitious for the granting of all a man wisheth." He again hoisted up the crate and followed her; till she stopped at a fruiterer's shop and bought from him Shami apples and Osmani quinces and Omani peaches, and cucumbers of Nile growth, and Egyptian limes and Sultani oranges and citrons; besides Aleppine jasmine, scented myrtle berries, Damascene nenuphars, flower of privet and camomile, blood-red anemones, violets, and pomegranate-bloom, eglantine and narcissus, and set the whole in the Porter's crate, saying, "Up with it." So he lifted and followed her till she stopped at a butcher's booth and said, "Cut me off ten pounds of mutton." She paid him his price and he wrapped it in a banana-leaf, whereupon she laid it in the crate and said "Hoist, O Porter." He hoisted accordingly, and followed her as she walked on till she stopped at a grocer's, where she bought dry fruits and pistachio-kernels, Tihamah raisins, shelled almonds, and all wanted for dessert, and said to the Porter, "Lift and follow me." So he up with his hamper and after her till she stayed at the confectioner's, and she bought an earthen platter, and piled it with all kinds of sweetmeats in his shop, open-worked tarts and fritters scented with musk and "soap-cakes," and lemon-loaves and melon-preserves, and "Zaynab's combs," and "ladies' fingers," and "Kazi's tit-bits," and goodies of every description; and placed the platter in the Porter's crate. Thereupon quoth he (being a merry man), "Thou shouldest have told me, and I would have brought with me a pony or a she-camel to carry all this market-stuff." She smiled and gave him a little cuff on the nape saying, "Step out and exceed not in words, for (Allah willing!) thy wage will not be wanting." Then she stopped at a perfumer's and took from him ten sorts of waters, rose scented with musk, orange-flower, water-lily, willow-flower, violet, and five others; and she also bought two loaves of sugar, a bottle for per-fume-spraying, a lump of male incense, aloe-wood, ambergris, and musk, with candles of Alexandria wax; and she put the whole into the basket, saying, "Up with thy crate and after me." He did so and followed until she stood before the greengrocer's, of whom she bought pickled safflower and olives, in brine and in oil; with tarragon and cream-cheese and hard Syrian cheese; and she stowed them away in the crate saying to the Porter, "Take up thy basket and follow me." He did so and went after her till she came to a fair mansion fronted by a spacious court, a tall, fine place to which col-umns gave strength and grace: and the gate thereof had two leaves of ebony inlaid with plates of red gold. The lady stopped at the door and, turning her face-veil sideways, knocked softly with her knuckles whilst the Porter stood behind her, thinking of naught save her beauty and loveliness. Presently the door swung back and both leaves were opened, whereupon he looked to see who had opened it; and behold, it was a lady of tall figure, some five feet high; a model of beauty and loveliness, brilliance and symmetry and perfect grace. Her forehead was flower-white; her cheeks like the anemone ruddy bright; her eyes were those of the wild heifer or the gazelle, with eyebrows like the crescent-moon which ends Sha'aban and begins Ramazan; her mouth was the ring of Sulayman, her lips coral-red, and her teeth like a line of strung pearls or of camomile petals. Her throat recalled the antelope's, and her breasts, like two pomegranates of even size, stood at bay as it were; her body rose and fell in waves below her dress like the rolls of a piece of brocade, and her navel would hold an ounce of benzoin ointment. In fine she was like her of whom the poet said:

> On Sun and Moon of palace cast thy sight
> Enjoy her flower-like face, her fragrant light;
> Thine eyes shall never see in hair so black
> Beauty encase a brow so purely white:
> The ruddy rosy cheek proclaims her claim
> Though fail her name whose beauties we indite;
> As sways her gait I smile at hips so big
> And weep to see the waist they bear so slight.

When the Porter looked upon her his wits were waylaid, and his senses were stormed so that his crate went nigh to fall from his head, and he said to himself, "Never have I in my life seen a day more blessed than this day!" Then quoth the lady-portress to the lady-cateress, "Come in from the gate and relieve this poor man of his load." So the provisioner went in followed by the portress and the Porter and went on till they reached a spacious ground-floor hall, built with admirable skill and beautified with all manner colours and carvings; with upper balconies and groined arches and galleries and cupboards and recesses whose curtains hung before them. In the midst stood a great basin full of water surrounding a fine fountain, and at the upper end on the raised dais was a couch of juniper-wood set with gems and pearls, with a canopy like mosquito-curtains of red satin-silk looped up with pearls as big as filberts and bigger. Thereupon sat a lady bright of blee, with brow beaming brilliancy, the dream of philosophy, whose eyes were fraught with Babel's gramarye and her eyebrows were arched as for archery; her breath breathed ambergris and perfumery and her lips were sugar to taste and carnelian to see. Her stature was straight as the letter I and her face shamed the noon-sun's radiancy; and she was even as a galaxy, or a dome with golden marquetry, or a bride displayed in choicest finery, or a noble maid of Araby. The third lady rising from the couch stepped forward with graceful swaying gait till she reached the middle of the saloon, when she said to her sisters, "Why stand ye here? take it down from this poor man's head!" Then the cateress went and stood before him, and the portress behind him, while the third helped them, and they lifted the load from the Porter's head; and, emptying it of all that was therein, set everything in its place. Lastly they gave him two gold pieces, saying, "Wend thy ways, O Porter." But he went not, for he stood looking at the ladies and admiring what uncommon beauty was theirs, and their pleasant manners and kindly dispositions (never had he seen goodlier); and he gazed wistfully at that good store of wines and sweet-scented flowers and fruits and other matters.

They recount that in the City Kaukaban of Al-Yaman there was a man of the Fazli tribe who had left Badawi life and become a townsman for many years, and was a merchant of the most opulent merchants. His wife had deceased when both were young; and his friends were instant with him to marry again, ever quoting to him the words of the poet:

> Go, gossip! re-wed thee, for Prime draweth near:
> A wife is an almanac—good for the year.

So, being weary of contention, Abu Hasan entered into negotiations with the old women who procure matches, and married a maid like Canopus when he hangeth over the seas of Al-Hind. He made high festival therefor, bidding to the wedding-banquet kith and kin, Olema and Fakirs; friends and foes and all his acquaintances of that country-side. The whole house was thrown open to feasting: there were rices of five several colours, and sherbets of as many more; and kids stuffed with walnuts and almonds and pistachios and a camel-colt roasted whole. So they ate and drank and made mirth and merriment; and the bride was displayed in her seven dresses and one more, to the women, who could not take their eyes off her. At last, the bridegroom was summoned to the chamber where she sat enthroned; and he rose slowly and with dignity from his divan; but in so doing, for that he was over full of meat and drink, lo and behold! he let fly a fart, great and terrible. Thereupon each guest turned to his neighbour and talked aloud and made as though he had heard nothing, fearing for his life. But a consuming fire was lit in Abu Hasan's heart; so he pretended a call of nature; and, in lieu of seeking the bride-chamber, he went down to the house-court and saddled his mare and rode off, weeping bitterly, through the shadow of the night. In time he reached Lahej, where he found a ship ready to sail for India; so he shipped on board and made Calicut of Malabar. Here he met with many Arabs, especially Hazramis, who recommended him to the King; and this King (who was a Kafir) trusted him and advanced him to the captainship of his body-guard. He remained ten years in all solace and delight of life; at the end of which time he was seized with home-sickness; and the longing to behold his native land was that of a lover pining for his beloved; and he came near to die of yearning desire. But his appointed day had not dawned; so, after taking the first bath of health, he left the King without leave, and in due course landed at Makalla of Hazramut. Here he donned the rags of a religious; and, keeping his name and case secret, fared for Kaukaban a-foot; enduring a thousand hardships of hunger, thirst, and fatigue; and braving a thousand dangers from the lion, the snake, and the Ghul. But when he drew near his old home, he looked down upon it from the hills with brimming eyes, and said in himself, "Haply they might know thee, so I will wander about the outskirts, and hearken to the folk. Allah grant that my case be not remembered by them!" He listened carefully for seven nights and seven days, till it so chanced that, as he was sitting at the door of a hut, he heard the voice of a young girl saying, "O my mother, tell me the day when I was born; for such an one of my companions is about to take an omen for me." And the mother answered, "Thou wast born, O my daughter, on the very night when Abu Hasan farted." Now the listener no sooner heard these words than he rose up from the bench, and fled away saying to himself, "Verily thy fart hath become a date, which shall last for ever and ever; even as the poet said:

> As long as palms shall shift the flower;
> As long as palms shall sift the flour."

And he ceased not travelling and voyaging and returned to India; and there abode in self-exile till he died; and the mercy of Allah be upon him!

IV

THE PEACOCK'S PLUME

Egypt, Greece, Rome

The story of a nation's life, from its simple innocence at the beginning to its final corrupt, decadent end, can often most clearly be charted by its gastronomy. This is particularly true of Greece and Rome, but even their mother, Egypt, followed the inevitable pattern in a less splendid, less revolting way than theirs.

Records of the daily life of the Egyptians started in 2320 B.C., and although with the natural increase of the wealthy and leisured classes there came many signs of extravagance and ostentation, the whole long story is one of graciousness and comparative simplicity.

Even poor people lived well in that kindly climate, and the rich lands along the Nile grew every kind of fruit and grain and vegetable that man could hunger for. Melons and grapes and pomegranates flourished under the hot sun, and figs, probably the oldest cultivated fruits in the world, ripened and burst with honey. There were ovens from the beginning, as the wall-paintings show, and Egyptian bakers were in demand in every city around the Mediterranean for their delicious pastries and cakes.

Religious and social restrictions in diet were always numerous, as befits a fastidious people, but they increased to a fantastic point by the end of the pre-Christian era, so that the priests themselves led an almost impossibly ascetic life. It was of course their quasi-paternal wish to make their charges do likewise, and they denounced a hundred foods, including the highly popular garlic, as unclean. Apparently they had the usual modified success of such religious disciplinarians: in 450 B.C. Herodotus quoted a statement inscribed on the Great Pyramid that 16,000 talents had been paid out for onions, radishes, and the foul garlic for workingmen on that mighty pile of stones!

There is a certain historical monotony about the way kings have always eaten, and yet that very monotony, so splendidly banal, so fastuously routine, has always interested not only readers but writers. That is why it is much easier to know how Solomon banqueted, or an unnamed Egyptian ruler, or even Henry VIII of England, than it is to find a description of how pilgrims boiled their groats and bacon on the way to the Holy Land, or what besides wheat-cakes and melons the farmers ate along the Nile Delta while their masters feasted in the airy, flower-filled "big houses."

Certainly the Egyptian masters dined well, from what the writers and painters have told us. Probably no highly cultured civilization has surpassed the charm and gaiety of their banquets.

People came from long distances to attend them, rather as they were to do centuries later for the fiestas at the great haciendas of Early California. Men and women ate and drank and danced together, and played such games as draughts and checkers, in contrast to the strict segregation that had always existed in the countries farther east, and would later in Greece and Italy.

There were flowers everywhere, in garlands on the walls and chairs and tables and on all the heads, and elaborate evanescent decorations of glass and silk changed the rooms from one banquet to the next. Guests always separated upon their arrival, to be washed and perfumed in the retiring rooms by boy or girl slaves. Then they met to drink and listen to music for a time before the banquet began, usually a little after sundown. It was fashionable to drink a great deal of wine or beer, and women succeeded in making themselves as gloriously drunk as the men.

Their goblets were exquisite and much admired and discussed, and were made of everything from carved jewels and metals to the beautiful glassware that had existed in Egypt since about 2000 B.C. The tables were low and round, and everyone ate with fingers from the plates that were laid out or were held by slaves dressed in short girdles and necklaces of flowers and jewels. According to the wall-paintings of such affairs, the diners should really have had three elegantly beringed hands instead of two . . . one to hold the customary lotus or Nile-lily, another for the omnipresent goblet, and a third for eating the long courses of the feast!

The food itself, although it increased in richness as the culture of the nation developed, was always much simpler than that of corresponding periods in Athens or Rome. There were many kinds of baked fish and meat, and the usual excellent and highly prized breads, pastries, and cakes, and then artful mixtures of fresh and dried fruits. . . and floods of wine. And after the banqueters could eat and drink and dance no more, jugglers and tumblers entertained them, as they have entertained surfeited people since time began.

Such parties, of course, were possible only for people with money and leisure, but they have a pleasant sound about them, whereas the daily deadly piles of food needed to nourish a ruler, even in Egypt, seem foolish in the telling. One Pharaoh, an old report says, "fed 14,000 guests each day, and the quintals of meat, and of butter and sugar for the pastry-work alone, would seem incredible."

That sounds like Solomon! Each day his table needed thirty measures of fine flour, and threescore measures of meal; ten fatted oxen and twenty out of the pastures; one hundred sheep; and harts, roebucks, fallow deer, fatted fowl. . . . It is small wonder that he kept twelve stewards, eleven of them to travel constantly in search of new viands.

Such magnificence is apparently a part of being royal. It is only in this twentieth century that the spell has really been broken, and a king has been able to have two poached eggs on toast and a glass of milk for his lunch. The real danger of gastronomical decadence in a nation comes when the wealthy citizens begin to think that at table they too are kings. That happened in the last years of Greece's glory, and then again, even more sickeningly and dangerously, while Rome was riding for its fall. Both countries learned much from Egypt, but forgot what was good and simple in the teaching.

In the first days, the Greeks lived on cabbage, chestnuts, honey, and the like: food that was made for them by the gods. In some parts of their wild country it was thought to be effeminate and foolish to pay any attention to such a thing as sensuous pleasure in eating, and in Sparta a person who confessed that he liked to cook as well as to eat what he had prepared was exiled, in disgrace and contempt, for the rest of his life.

The Spartans themselves lived almost wholly on their famous black broth, which was supposed by many to be thickened hogs' blood, but was probably a soup of water, vinegar, salt, and boiled pork. It was known everywhere as the Spartans' elixir of bravery ... which makes Warner's comment in 1791 in *Antiquitates Culinariae* doubly amusing:

> What the ingredients of this sable composition were, we cannot exactly ascertain; but we may venture to say, it could not be a very *alluring* mess, since a citizen of Sybaris having tasted it, declared it was no longer a matter of astonishment with him, why the Spartans should be so fearless of death in battle, since any one in his senses, would much rather undergo the pains of dissolution, than to continue to exist on such execrable food.

Gradually even the Spartans lost their first asceticism, and a man who lived simply in Greece was looked upon as a curiosity. It was noted with a kind of awe, for instance, that Plato preferred common olives above all other food, although he would admit to an occasional hunger for good bread or pastry. More often than not a simple taste was scoffed at as pure stinginess by the luxury-fattened Greeks, and it was a slang expression to call a frugal or tight-wad person an Athenian, because the people of that city lived less extravagantly than their neighbors.

As interest in banqueting increased in the country, so did the kinds of spices and flavorings, until finally a meal was so distorted by weird tastes of asafetida and ambergris and such that the original meats and fishes were unrecognizable, and fashionably so.

The boundless hospitality of the early citizens never changed, though, and no matter how elaborate dinners became, they were always simple in the prime reason for their being: to welcome and nourish friends and strangers alike.

Women were excluded from Greek banquets, as they were later in Rome, being considered much less interesting than the food and wine, as well as deleterious to good conversation. Cup-bearers, however, could be girls; and at the end of any self-respecting dinner came the chosen hetaerae, women whose function it was to converse, sing, and be completely charming. As has always been the case, the men for whom they performed piped the tune for their behavior, so that at their best they were intelligent, witty, and beautiful companions, and at their most degraded they were a troupe of drunken whores.

As time passed and banqueting became more and more important to the soft, gluttonous Greeks, some of the greatest of their writers dwelt on it, in both pleasure and anger, so that it is easy for us now to know what happened so long ago upon those extravagantly inlaid dining-couches, upon those gold and purple cushions.

We can smell the heavy perfume that was sprayed into the air between the interminable courses, and taste it and the roses and the spices in each dish. We can drink the strong sweet wines of Corinth and of Samos and Chios and Tenedos, and listen to the piping voices of the boys and virgins as they sing and dance for us. And we can compliment our host upon his cook, who like most of them in Greece (and later in Rome) is probably a Sicilian who stands in the market-place surrounded by his pots and kettles, waiting to be hired for any such occasion.

If true to form he is a scamp and thief as well as an excellent chef, and fat and drunken to boot—but anything is forgivable when he can conjure up such delicacies as we have eaten: fried sole, "the fish of kings," and oysters and eels in a pie, and a suckling pig surrounded by roasted pullets, and then the almost obligatory peacock baked whole in his feathers, riding a sea of tiny stuffed ortolans. . . .

It is too easy, faced with such opulent dishes, to forget that the great Epicurus enjoins temperance above all other virtues!

Archestratus of Syracuse was the first great culinary authority of that era, about 330 B.C., and his lost poem "Gastronomy" was so important to all the writers on the subject after him that Atheneus called it "a treasure of light." A few fragments of this work remain, and the opening stanza of it shows clearly the stateliness of concept of that subject, which soon became blurred as lesser writers (and greater gluttons) took it over:

> I write these precepts for immortal Greece,
> That round a table delicately spread,
> Or three, or four, may sit in choice repast,
> Or five at most. Who otherwise shall dine,
> Are like a troop marauding for their prey.

Of the many Greeks who followed Archestratus, the most famous was Atheneus, the author of some ten cookery books and histories, of his own country and Rome, but best remembered for his astonishing *Deipnosophists* or *Banquet of the Learned*, probably written at the beginning of the third century A.D. This is, in twenty-five books, a seemingly endless and at times impossibly wandering account of an imaginary banquet, during which all the guests discuss their avocation, gastronomy. It is a superhuman hodgepodge of quotations, jokes, recipes, and strange facts about everything that could possibly be associated with eating and drinking, and it is one of the most tiresome and at the same time most delightful collections that anyone could possibly read.

It begins with a discussion of epicures: men like Pithyllus, who "not only had a covering to his tongue made of skin ... but he is the first who is said to have eaten his meat with fingerstalls on, in order to convey it to his mouth as warm as possible"; and Aristoxenus the philosopher, from whom hams cured in a certain way were called *aristoxeni* by the gourmets.

It was he who "out of his prodigious luxury used to syringe the lettuces which grew in his garden with mead in the evening, and then, when he picked them in the morning, he would say that he was eating green cheesecakes, which were sent up to him by the earth."

On and on Atheneus goes, through *Asparagus, Pickle, The Cactus* (which he thinks is really a form of artichoke, or perhaps vice versa), *Eels*, and *Turnips*: "Theophrastus says that there are two kinds of turnips, the male and the female ... but Diphilus ... says the turnip has attenuating properties, and is harsh and indigestible, and moreover is apt to cause flatulence. Diphilus goes on to say of the carrot, 'This vegetable is harsh but tolerably nutritious, and moderately good for the stomach; but it passes quickly through the bowels, and causes flatulence: it is indigestible, diuretic, and not without some influence in prompting men to amatory feelings. ...'"

On a page headed *The Gourd* there is this jolly lyric to Athens by Aristophanes:

> There you shall at mid-winter see
> Cucumbers, gourds, and grapes, and apples,
> And wreaths of fragrant violets
> Covered with dust, as if in summer.
> And the same man will sell you thrushes,
> And pears and honey-comb, and olives,

Beestings and tripe, and summer swallows,

And grasshoppers, and bullocks' paunches.

There you may see full baskets pack'd

With figs and myrtle, crown'd with snow;

There you may see fine pumpkins join'd

To the round rape and mighty turnip;

So that a stranger well may fear

To name the season of the year.

Atheneus occasionally remembers that he is supposed to be writing the conversation of a group of extremely erudite gastronomers at a feast, and inserts a minor detail about the banquet itself, as when, under *Pigs*, he says:

> ... when a pig was served up before us, the half of which was being carefully roasted, and the other half boiled gently, as if it had been steamed, and when all marveled at the cleverness of the cook, he, being very proud of his skill, said: "And, indeed, there is not one of you who can point out the place where he received the death wound; or where his belly was cut so as to be stuffed with all sorts of dainties. For it has thrushes in it, and other birds; and it has also in it parts of the abdomens of pigs, and slices of a sow's womb, and the yolk of eggs, and moreover the entrails of birds, with their ovaries, those also being full of delicate seasoning, and also pieces of meat shred into thin shavings and seasoned with pepper. . . ."

In discussing the delicious bird called the Porphyrion, Atheneus says that it is not only excellent for roasting, but "when it is kept in a house, watches those women who have husbands very closely: and has such instantaneous perception of anyone who commits adultery, that, when it perceives it, it gives notice to the master of the house, cutting its own existence short by hanging itself."

Atheneus writes rather scornfully that partridges are "much devoted to amatory enjoyment . . . so very eager to propagate their species that they fall into the hands of the hunters on that account, sitting on the tiles. They say, too, that when hen partridges are taken out to hunt, even when they see or smell a cock standing or flying down the wind, they become pregnant, and . . . immediately begin to lay eggs."

In spite of the unreal feeling that a succession of such tidbits gives, a kind of supragastronomical dizziness, the body of *The Deipnosophists* is fairly dull page-to-page reading, at least for anyone not completely fascinated by the history of obsolete Greek words for "hare," for instance. And even there, some such quotation as this one from the lost poem by Archestratus turns up:

> Many are the ways and many the recipes
> For dressing hares; but this is best of all,
> To place before a hungry set of guests,
> A slice of roasted meat fresh from the spit,
> Hot, seasoned only with plain simple salt,
> Not too much done. And do not you be vexed
> At seeing blood fresh trickling from the meat,
> But eat it eagerly. All other ways
> Are quite superfluous, such as when cooks pour
> A lot of sticky clammy sauce upon it,
> Parings of cheese, and lees, and dregs of oil,
> As if they were preparing cat's meat. . . .

Atheneus is perhaps most interesting on the subject of various forms of luxury. It is impossible not to be amused, in a horrid way, by the mention of an ancient king named Sagaus who used "out of luxury, to eat, till he arrived at old age, out of his nurse's mouth, that he might not have the trouble of chewing his own food"; of Demetrius, whose dinner at the beginning of his career "consisted of a kind of pickle, containing olives and cheese; but when he became rich he bought Moschion, the most skillful of all the cooks and confectioners of that age. And he had such vast quantities of food prepared for him every day, that, as he gave the cook what was left each time, Moschion in two years purchased three detached houses in the city."

And there was Anaxarchus, "who used to have a naked full-grown girl for his cup-bearer. And his baker used to knead the dough wearing gloves on his hands, and a cover on his mouth, to prevent any perspiration running off his hands, and also to prevent him from breathing on his cakes while he was kneading them.'"

Inevitably we move on this tide of luxury from Greece, where it was bad enough, to Rome, where never before in the world's history had it been equaled, even at the courts of Sardanapalus and Alexander.

Atheneus says, more than once, that it was Lucullus, the conqueror of Mithridates and of the king of Armenia, who brought back all their wealth to Rome and "was the first teacher of luxury. Now there is no one of those who are even tolerably well off who does not provide a most sumptuous table, and who has not cooks and a great many more attendants, and who does not spend more on his daily living than formerly men used to spend on their festivals and sacrifices."

Lucullus the Epicure it was of whom Juvenal wrote:

> Stretch'd on the unsocial couch, he rolls his eyes
> O'er many an orb of matchless form and size,
> Selects the fairest to receive his plate,
> And at one meal devours a whole estate.

Lucullus the General it was who built an aquarium for his special fish and then pierced a whole mountain between two of his farms to bring sea-water for it.

He it was who paid each of his carvers the fantastic sum of four thousand dollars a year, and had several dining rooms, where the meal "per head" cost from a few hundred dollars up to one thousand in the most beautiful chamber, dedicated to Apollo himself.

The stories of his famous lonely supper, when he chided the cooks for not surpassing themselves, since "Lucullus dined with Lucullus" that night, are as varied as the tellers, and for as many reasons, but it seems true that he was the king of the epicures, no swine at table, and only more insanely extravagant than his fellow citizens in that his income was larger than theirs.

It is a pity that other men, with almost as much wealth as the General's, did not possess his gift for balancing extravagance with good taste. Julius Caesar spent millions counted as high as twenty-five, although it seems incredible, in four months of supper-parties, and not one of them is remembered. Marc Antony gave his cook a whole town once, when Cleopatra praised the sauce . . . but how was that sauce made? And Heliogabalus, most profligate of all, depleted the treasury of the whole Roman Empire in four years, before he killed himself with gluttony: a possible revenge of the gods for his prize invention of sausages made of oysters, lobsters, and crabs, which he deemed more delicious than any of the exotic dishes he paid his courtiers to produce for him.

His end was less sad, gastronomically, than that of Septimus Severus. Septimus was dying of intolerably painful gout, the result of his piggishness, and when his physicians refused to end his dolor, he ordered the most fantastically rich meal he could imagine, and died deliberately of indigestion!

With such leaders before them, the Roman citizens, always good imitators, soon grew to behave as if they too were sated rulers. Their first simple living was easily forgotten, as it had been with the Greeks, and they eagerly exchanged elaborate banquets for the old national dish of porridge.

Ordinary merchants and doctors devoted themselves, like emperors, to learning to tell the locality of a wild boar's or a pike's death-place by a particular flavor, and kept aviaries in the country filled with thrushes. The little birds were fed on a diet of millet, wheat flour, and crushed sweet figs, whereas swans and white geese ate green figs for their livers!

Oyster-beds were cultivated carefully, with special feedings cast upon the waters as prescribed by the greatest gourmets, but it is doubtful if their diet was as fastuous as that of one emperor's conger eels, who are reported to have thrived on live slave-meat.

The interest in eating became a national obsession, and people spent every cent they could borrow or dig up on such things as four-pound mullets at a thousand dollars for three, a fact noted by Suetonius because it caused Tiberius to pass severe laws against such nonsense. The laws, of course, were soon ignored in the Romans' almost hysterical pursuit of new taste-adventures.

Every kind of sea-creature was hunted and cooked, except perhaps the dolphin, sacred as the pilot of Triton's car, and the mermaid! Rare turbots, and trout from the farthest icy lakes, were common fare at any good banquet, but the mullet remained favorite, perhaps because of its refinements of living and dying. Seneca once wrote of it, in telling of a banquet at which live fish were served in tall blown-glass vessels, so that each guest could enjoy the death-throes of his next course: "Look how it reddens! There's no vermilion like it; look at those lateral veins! See how the gray brightens upon its head— and now it is at its last gasp! It pales, and its inanimate body fades to a single hue. . . ."

(Seneca also wrote of his period's extravagance in less lightly ironical, angrier moods, as when he said: "I see the shell of the tortoise bought for immense sums and ornamented with the most elaborate care; I see tables and pieces of wood valued at the price of a senator's estate [Cicero's famous lemonwood table cost 200,000 sesterces, or about $7000!], which are all the more precious the more knots the tree has been twisted into by disease. I see murrhine cups, for luxury would be too cheap if men did not drink to one another out of hollow gems the wine to be afterward thrown up again.")

The ceremony of a banquet remained fairly static throughout the Republic and the Empire: it was the amounts of exotic food and the manners of the guests that changed. A well-ordered meal usually had nine guests, one of whom was elected dictator for the evening, to direct the singing, the conversation, and the formalities of drinking.

It was *de rigueur* to drink at least ten bumpers of wine: nine to the Muses, and one to Apollo. From there on the amount depended on how many mistresses must be saluted by each man challenged by the *dictator*. It is no wonder that various efforts were made to stay cool-headed, such as wearing wreaths of parsley and fresh roses, and even of small garden-lettuces!

The air was kept heavy with perfumes, which grew so fashionably expensive that one or two of the guests often contributed them, to help the host with his fantastic budget . . .

> . . . Nor fell
> His perfumes from a box of alabaster;
> That were too trite a fancy, and had savor'd
> O' the elder time—but ever and anon
> He slipped four doves, whose wings were saturate
> With scents, all different in kind—each bird
> Bearing its own appropriate sweets: these doves,
> Wheeling in circles round, let fall upon us
> A shower of sweet perfumery, drenching, bathing,
> Both clothes and furniture—and, lordlings all—
> I deprecate your envy, when I add,
> That on myself fell floods of violet odors.*

---

* Atheneus, *The Deipnosophists.*

The dictator barred all subjects in any way sad or unpleasant, since they might hinder digestion, and a kind of cocktail called the *promulsis* to strengthen the stomach was served first. It was made of boiled honey, wine, and a great many intricately measured spices. Then, to help the brave diners still more, raw lettuce was often presented between the first few courses, to cool and encourage the assaulted inwards.

Three guests lay on each of the three elaborately carved couches, with the lowest place on the middle couch reserved for the honored man. Each brought his own napkin. Ivory knives were furnished by the host, but because of the reclining position dictated by the couches, spoons and fingers were used most.

Greek wines were popular, but Campanian and Caecuban Falernian were most highly thought of, and were served hot in winter as a further aid to digestion.

The preoccupation of the gluttonous Romans with this sometimes painful subject is understandable for many obvious reasons, but perhaps a menu and one or two recipes will make it even clearer. Here, then, is "How to make thick sauce for a boiled chicken." It is from *De Re Culinaria*, which is a good picture of a master-cook at work, written probably by a man named Coelius who called himself Apicius in admiration for one of three brothers of that name. (These brothers were renowned gourmets, and correspondingly extravagant in their desires for strange dishes: Apicius III, who finally killed himself, once hired a large ship to look for a certain kind of shrimp, and after a month's severe voyage turned back in disgust when he found that ordinary fishermen ate the little sea-fleas.)

Put the following ingredients into a mortar: anise-seed, dried mint, and lazerroot [like asafetida]. Cover them with vinegar. Add dates. Pour in *liquamen* [juice from salted ferments of fish-guts], oil, and a small quantity of mustard seeds. Reduce all to a proper thickness, with sweet wine warmed; and then pour this same over your chicken, which should previously be boiled in anise-seed water.

And here, without pause for rumination on this ghastly thing, is a menu for a very ordinary and simple affair, not one to compete in any way with a truly Lucullan banquet:

GUSTUS (appetizer): sorrel, lettuce, oysters, eggs, sardines, radishes, mushrooms, pickles, served with Falernian wine mixed with Greek honey.

FIRST COURSE : conger eels, oysters, two kinds of mussels, thrushes on asparagus, fat fowls, ragout of all kinds of shellfish.

SECOND COURSE : shellfish, fig-peckers, haunches of venison, wild boar, pastry of small birds.

THIRD COURSE : sow's udder, boar's head, fricassee of fish, fricassee of sow's udders, various kinds of ducks, roast fowl, hares, sausages, roast pig, peacocks.

FOURTH COURSE : very elaborate set-pieces of pastry and Pirentine bread.

FIFTH COURSE : fruits and wines.

Seneca wrote bitterly of a Roman's life: *Edunt et vomant; vomant et edunt.* His meaning was clear, even to a person with little Greek and less Latin! The incredible procession of such food, all heavy with rich sauces and washed down on floods of sweetened wines, is nauseating even to think upon. It is no wonder that many diners took purgatives and emetics first, or even during a meal, to make room within themselves for more.

Special toilets and *vomitoria* built near the banquet-rooms were requisite in any thoughtful host's apartments, and it was considered a compliment to the cook to have to use them often. However, Romans must have been constructed much like other human beings except for their especially trained stomachs, and it is hard to know just what the natural or unnatural processes were in a man like Tiberius, who according to Suetonius spent two whole days and one night at a feast without leaving the table!

Little feathers on sticks were usually provided by the host in the *vomitorium*, much as a modern powder-room has its thoughtful supply of face-tissues and gargles, but it is interesting to know just what the emetics were made of, in case a guest preferred to arrive prepared to do his own heaving.

The nearest I can come to it, although I have looked hard for a recipe, is this one copied from an Elizabethan pamphlet. My druggist tells me that such things have changed little in two thousand years, so perhaps Mr. Marriott, "the great Eater of Grays-Inn," drank much the same potion in London in 1630 as was downed in Caesar's Rome:

... he would often follow the Fariars Rule for Drenches, which Receit best agreed with his body: for he would take Milk and Oyl with Aquavitae, Pepper, and Brimstone, all mingled together: a pottle at one time is nothing with him to scour his Maw.

It is too easy to grow sated with descriptions of such a way of life, which nonetheless hold a kind of sick fascination for us, and perhaps it is good to use them, if for no better reason, as a kind of emetic of the mental bowels, a scourer of the maw of our mind's gastronomy. That is why I have chosen, after one or two purple passages from Edgar Saltus' book on Rome, to print some of Trimalchio's notorious banquet, much as it bores me with its stuffy slang and strained rowdiness. I agree with the critics who condemn the "Oscar Wilde translation" as "reeking of stale perfume," but even so it seems better than most others procurable to modern readers.

After it comes a snippet from *Peregrine Pickle*, by Tobias Smollett: a slapstick account of an attempt to re-create, in eighteenth-century England, the supposed glories of a Roman banquet.

Then, to take the taste of all this indigestible mess from our mouths, I have put in a little section of *The Golden Ass*, because it is funny and fresh and delightful to eat with a man who turned into an ass after watching so many men who turned into swine instead. The translation of this book by Apuleius, the Greek turned Roman, was done in 1566 by an Englishman named Adlington whose Latin was sometimes shaky, but who had a fine fair sense of the book's flavor!

To table, then, and may there be no need of too drastic a purging afterward!

From *Imperial Purple* by Edgar Saltus, 1855–1921

In the hall, like that of Mecænas, one divided against itself, the upper half containing the couches and tables, the other reserved for the service and the entertainments that follow, the ceiling was met by columns, the walls hidden by panels of gems. On a frieze twelve pictures, surmounted by the signs of the zodiac, represented the dishes of the different months. Beneath the bronze beds and silver tables mosaics were set in imitation of food that had fallen and had not been swept away. And there, in white ungirdled tunics, the head and neck circled with coils of amaranth—the perfume of which in opening the pores neutralizes the fumes of wine—the guests lay, fanned by boys, whose curly hair they used for napkins. Under the supervision of butlers the courses were served on platters so large that they covered the tables; sows' breasts with Lybian truffles; dormice baked in poppies and honey; peacock-tongues flavored with cinnamon; oysters stewed in garum—a sauce made of the intestines of fish—sea-wolves from the Baltic; sturgeons from Rhodes; fig-peckers from Samos; African snails; pale beans in pink lard; and a yellow pig cooked after the Troan fashion, from which, when carved, hot sausages fell and live thrushes flew. Therewith was the mulsum, a cup made of white wine, nard, roses, absinthe, and honey; the delicate sweet wines of Greece; and crusty Falernian of the year six hundred and thirty-two. As the cups circulated, choirs entered, chanting sedately the last erotic song; a clown danced on the top of a ladder, which he maintained upright as he danced, telling meanwhile untellable stories to the frieze; and host and guests, unvociferously, as good breeding dictates, chatted through the pauses of the service; discussed the disadvantages of death, the value of Noevian iambics, the disgrace of Ovid, banished because of Livia's eyes.

Such was the Rome of Augustus.

. . . Caligula and Vitellius had been famous as hosts, but the feasts that Heliogabalus gave outranked them for sheer splendor. From panels in the ceiling such masses of flowers fell that guests were smothered. Those that survived had set before them glass game and sweets of crystal. The menu was embroidered on the table-cloth—not the mere list of dishes, but pictures drawn with the needle of the dishes themselves. And presently, after the little jest in glass had been enjoyed, you were served with Camels' heels; combs torn from living cocks; platters of nightingale-tongues; ostrich-brains, prepared with that garum sauce which the Sybarites invented, and of which the secret is lost; therewith were peas and grains of gold; beans and amber peppered with pearl dust; lentils and rubies; spiders in jelly; lion's dung, served in pastry. The guests that wine overcame were carried to bedrooms. When they awoke, there staring at them were tigers and leopards—tame, of course; but some of the guests were stupid enough not to know it, and died of fright.

From *The Satyricon* by Petronius Arbiter, circa 50 A.D.

Well! at last we take our places, Alexandrian slave-boys pouring snow-water over our hands, and others succeeding them to wash our feet and cleanse our toenails with extreme dexterity. Not even while engaged in this unpleasant office were they silent, but sang away over their work. I had a mind to try whether all the house servants were singers, and accordingly asked for a drink of wine. Instantly an attendant was at my side, pouring out the liquor to the accompaniment of the same sort of shrill recitative. Demand what you would, it was the same; you might have supposed yourself among a troupe of pantomime actors rather than at a respectable citizen's table.

Then the preliminary course was served in very elegant style. For all were now at table except Trimalchio, for whom the first place was reserved—by a reversal of ordinary usage. Among the other hors d'oeuvres stood a little ass of Corinthian bronze with a packsaddle holding olives, white olives on one side, black on the other. The animal was flanked right and left by silver dishes, on the rim of which Trimalchio's name was engraved and the weight. On arches built up in the form of miniature bridges were dormice seasoned with honey and poppy-seed. There were sausages too, smoking hot on a silver grill, and underneath (to imitate coals) Syrian plums and pomegranate seeds.

We were in the middle of these elegant trifles when Trimalchio himself was carried in to the sound of music, and was bolstered up among a host of tiny cushions, a sight that set one or two indiscreet guests laughing. And no wonder; his bald head poked up out of a scarlet mantle, his neck was closely muffled, and over all was laid a napkin with a broad purple stripe or laticlave, and long fringes hanging down either side. Moreover, he wore on the little finger of his left hand a massive ring of silver gilt, and on the last joint of the next finger a smaller ring, apparently of solid gold, but starred superficially with little ornaments of steel. Nay! to show this was not the whole of his magnificence, his left arm was bare and displayed a gold bracelet and an ivory circlet with a sparkling clasp to put it on. . . .

Meantime . . . a dish was brought in with a basket on it, in which lay a wooden hen, her wings outspread round her as if she were sitting. Instantly a couple of slaves came up, and to the sound of lively music began to search the straw, and pulling out a lot of peafowl's eggs one after the other, handed them round to the company.

Trimalchio turns his head at this, saying, "My friends, it was by my orders that hen was set on the peafowl's eggs yonder; but, by God! I am very
much afraid they are half-hatched. Still, we can but try whether they are
still eatable." For our part, we take our spoons, which weighed at least half
a pound each, and break the eggs, which were made of paste. I was on the
point of throwing mine away, for I thought I discerned a chick inside. But
when I overheard a veteran guest saying, "There should be something good
here!" I further investigated the shell, and found a very fine fat beccafico
[fig-pecker] swimming in yolk of egg flavoured with pepper.

Trimalchio had . . . been helped to all the dishes before us, [and] had
just announced in a loud voice that any of us who wanted a second supply
of honeyed wine had only to ask for it, when suddenly, at a signal from the
band, the hors d'oeuvres are whisked away by a troupe of slaves, all singing
too. But in the confusion a silver dish happened to fall and a slave picked it
up again from the floor. This Trimalchio noticed, and, boxing the fellow's
ears, rated him soundly and ordered him to throw it down again. Then
a groom came in and began to sweep up the silver along with the other
refuse. . . .

He was succeeded by two long-haired Ethiopians, carrying small
leather skins, like the fellows that water the sand in the amphitheatre, who
poured wine over our hands; for no one thought of offering water.

After being duly complimented on this refinement, our host cried out,
"Fair play's a jewel!" and accordingly ordered a separate table to be assigned
to each guest. "In this way," he said, "by preventing any crowding, the
stinking servants won't make us so hot."

Simultaneously there were brought in a number of wine-jars of glass
carefully stoppered with plaster, and having labels attached to their necks
reading FALERNIAN: OPIMIAN VINTAGE ONE HUNDRED YEARS OLD. . . .

Our applause was interrupted by the second course, which did not
by any means come up to our expectations. Still, the oddity of the thing
drew the eyes of all. An immense circular tray bore the twelve signs of the
zodiac displayed round the circumference, on each of which the Manciple
or Arranger had placed a dish of suitable and appropriate viands: on the
Ram, ram's-head-pease; on the Bull, a piece of beef; on the Twins, fried
testicles and kidneys; on the Crab, simply a Crown; on the Lion, African
figs; on the Virgin, a sow's haslet cut to shape and supporting a honeycomb.

Meanwhile an Egyptian slave was carrying bread round in a miniature oven of silver. . . .

Seeing us look rather blank at the idea of attacking such common fare, Trimalchio cried, "I pray you, gentlemen, begin; the best of your dinner is before you." No sooner had he spoken than four fellows ran prancing in, keeping time to the music, and whipped off the top part of the tray. This done, we behold underneath, on a second tray in fact, stuffed capons, a sow's paps, and as a centrepiece a hare fitted with wings to represent Pegasus. We noticed besides four figures of Marsyas, one at each corner of the tray, carrying little wine-skins which spouted out peppered fish-sauce over the fishes swimming in the Channel of the dish.

We all join in the applause started by the domestics and laughingly fall on the choice viands. . . . Finally, fresh servants entered and spread carpets before the couches, embroidered with pictures of fowling nets, prickers with their hunting spears, and sporting gear of all kinds. We were still at a loss what to expect when a tremendous shout was raised outside the doors, and lo and behold! a pack of Laconian dogs came careering round and round the very table. These were succeeded by another huge tray, on which lay a wild boar of the largest size, with a cap on its head, while from the tushes hung two little baskets of woven palm leaves, one full of Syrian dates, the other of Theban. Round it were little piglets of baked sweetmeat, as if at suck, to show it was a sow we had before us; and these were gifts to be taken home with them by the guests.

To carve the dish [appeared] a great bearded fellow, wearing leggings and a shaggy jerkin. Drawing his hunting knife, he made a furious lunge and gashed open the boar's flank, from which there flew out a number of fieldfares. Fowlers stood ready with their rods and immediately caught the birds as they fluttered about the table. Then Trimalchio directed each guest to be given his bird, and this done, added, "Look what elegant acorns this wild-wood pig's fed on." Instantly slaves ran to the baskets that were suspended from the animal's tushes and divided the two kinds of dates in equal proportions among the diners. . . .

At the end of this course Trimalchio left the table to relieve himself, and when he re-entered, and after wiping his brow and scenting his hands: "Pardon me, my friends," he said after a brief pause, "but for several days I have been costive. My physicians were non-plussed. However, pomegranate rind and an infusion of fir-wood in vinegar has done me good. And now I trust my belly will be better behaved. At times I have such a rumbling about my stomach, you'd think I had a bull bellowing inside me. So if any of you want to relieve yourselves, there's no necessity to be ashamed about it. None of us is born solid. I don't know any torment so bad as holding it in. It's the one thing Jove himself cannot stop.... I never hinder any man at my table from easing himself, and indeed the doctors forbid our baulking nature. Even if something more presses, everything's ready outside—water, close-stools, and the other little matters needful. Take my word for it, the vapours rise to the brain and may cause a fluxion of the whole constitution. I know many a man that's died of it, because he was too shy to speak out."

We thank our host for his generous indulgence, taking our wine in little sips the while to keep down our laughter. But little we thought we had still another hill to climb, as the saying is, and were only half way through the elaborations of the meal. For when the tables had been cleared with a flourish of music, three white hogs were brought in, hung with little bells and muzzled; one, so the nomenclator informed us, was a two-year-old, another three, and the third six. For my part, I thought they were learned pigs, come in to perform some of those marvellous tricks you see in circuses. But Trimalchio put an end to my surmises by saying, "Which of the three will you have dressed for supper right away? Farmyard cocks and pheasants and suchlike small deer are for country folks; my cooks are used to serving up calves boiled whole." So saying, he immediately ordered the cook to be summoned, and, without waiting for our choice, directed the six-year-old to be killed. Then speaking loud and clear, he asked the man, "What decuria do you belong to?"

"To the fortieth," he replied.

"Bought," he went on, "or born in my house?"

"Neither," returned the cook, "I was left you by Pansa's will."

"Then mind you serve the dish carefully dressed; else I shall order you to be degraded into the decuria of the outdoor slaves."

And the cook, thus cogently admonished, then withdrew with his charge into the kitchen.

But Trimalchio, relaxing his stern aspect, now turned to us and said: "If you don't like the wine, I'll have it changed; otherwise please prove its quality by your drinking. Thanks to the gods' goodness, I never buy it; but now I have everything that smacks good growing on a suburban estate of mine. I've not seen it yet, but they tell me it's down Terracina and Tarentum way. I am thinking at the moment of making Sicily one of my little properties; then, when I've a mind to visit Africa, I may sail along my own boundaries to get there." . . .

He was still in the middle of this nonsense, when a tray supporting an enormous hog was set on the table. One and all, we expressed our admiration at the expedition shown, and swore a more ordinary fowl could not have been cooked in the time—the more so as the hog appeared to be a much larger animal than the wild boar just before. Presently, Trimalchio, staring harder and harder, exclaimed, "What! What! Isn't he gutted? No! by heaven! He's not. Call the cook in."

The cook came and stood by the table, looking sadly crestfallen and saying he had clean forgotten. "What! forgotten?" cried Trimalchio; "To hear him, you would suppose he'd just omitted a pinch of pepper or a bit of cummin. Strip him!"

Instantly the cook was stripped, and standing between two tormentors, the picture of misery. But . . . Trimalchio, . . . a smile breaking over his face, "Well! well!" said he, "as you have such a bad memory, bowel him now, where we can all see."

Thereupon the cook resumed his tunic, seized his knife, and with a trembling hand slashed open the animal's belly. In a moment, the apertures widening under the weight behind, out tumbled a lot of sausages and blackpuddings.

At this all the servants applauded like one man, and chorussed, "Gaius for ever!" Moreover, the cook was gratified with a goblet of wine and a silver wreath, and received a drinking cup on a salver of Corinthian metal. . . .

Then, with the servants bustling in all directions, a boiled calf was borne in on a silver dish weighing two hundred pounds, and actually wearing a helmet. Then came Ajax, and rushing at it like a madman slashed it to bits with his naked sword, and making passes now up now down, collected the pieces on his point and so distributed the flesh among the astonished guests.

We had little time, however, to admire these elegant surprises; for all of a sudden the ceiling began to rattle and the whole room trembled. I sprang up in consternation, fearing some tumbler was going to fall through the roof. The other guests were no less astounded, and gazed aloft, wondering what new prodigy they were to expect now from the skies. Then lo and behold! the ceiling opened and a huge hoop, evidently stripped from an enormous cask, was let down, all round which hung suspended golden wreaths and caskets containing precious unguents. These we were invited to take home with us as mementos.

Then looking again at the table, I saw that a tray of cakes had been placed on it, with a figure of Priapus, the handiwork of the pastrycook, standing in the middle, represented in the conventional way as carrying in his capacious bosom grapes and all sort of fruits. Eagerly we reached out after these dainties, when instantly a new sell set us laughing afresh. For each cake and each fruit was full of saffron, which spurted out into our faces at the slightest touch, giving us an unpleasant drenching. . . .

After a short interval Trimalchio next ordered the dessert to be served; hereupon the servants removed all the tables and brought in fresh ones, and strewed the floor with saffron- and vermilion-coloured saw-dust and, a refinement I had not seen before, with [glass from a mirror] reduced to powder. The moment the tables were changed, Trimalchio remarked, "I could really be quite content with what we have; for you see your 'second tables' before you. However, if there is anything spicy for dessert, let's have it in.". . .

The Extra-Course now [came] in—thrushes of pastry, stuffed with raisins and walnuts, followed by quinces stuck over with thorns, to represent sea-urchins. This would have been tolerable enough, had it not been for a still more outlandish dish, such a horrible concoction, we would rather have died than touch it. Directly it was on the table—to all appearance a fatted goose, with fish and fowl of all kinds round it—"Friends," cried Trimalchio, "every single thing you see on that dish is made out of one substance." With my wonted perspicacity, I instantly guessed its nature, and said, "For my part, I shall be greatly surprised if it is not all made of filth, or at any rate mud. When I was in Rome at the Saturnalia, I saw some sham eatables of the same sort." I had not done speaking when Trimalchio explained, "As I hope to grow a bigger man—in fortune I mean, not fat—I declare my cook made it every bit out of a pig. Never was a more invaluable fellow! Give the word, he'll make you a fish of the paunch, a wood-pigeon of the lard, a turtledove of the forehand, and a hen of the hind legs! And that's why I very cleverly gave him such a fine and fitting name as Daedalus. And because he's such a good servant, I brought him a present from Rome, a set of knives of Noric steel." These he immediately ordered to be brought, and examined and admired them, even allowing us to try their edge on our cheeks.

All of a sudden in rushed two slaves, as if fresh from a quarrel at the fountain; at any rate they still had their water-pots hanging from the shoulder-yokes. Then when Trimalchio gave judgement upon their difference, they would neither of them accept his decision, but each smashed the other's pot with a stick. We were horrorstruck at the drunken scoundrels' insolence, and, looking hard at the combatants, we noticed oysters and scallops tumbling out of the broken pitchers, which another slave gathered up and handed round on a platter. This refinement was matched by the ingenious cook, who now brought in snails on a little silver gridiron, singing the while in a quavering, horribly rasping voice. I am really ashamed to relate what followed, it was so unheard-of a piece of luxury. Long-haired slave-boys brought in an unguent in a silver basin, and anointed our feet with it as we lay at table, after first wreathing our legs and ankles with garlands. Afterwards a small quantity of the same perfume was poured into the wine-jars and the lamps. . . .

The thing was getting positively sickening, when Trimalchio, now in a state of disgusting intoxication, commanded a new diversion, a company of horn-blowers, to be introduced; and then stretching himself out along the edge of a couch on a pile of pillows, "Make believe I am dead," he ordered. "Play something fine." Then the horn-blowers struck up a loud funeral dirge. In particular one of these undertaker's men, the most conscientious of the lot, blew so tremendous a fanfare that it roused the whole neighbourhood. Hereupon the watchmen in charge of the surrounding district, thinking Trimalchio's house was on fire, suddenly burst open the door, and, rushing in with water and axes, started the much-admired confusion usual under such circumstances. For our part, we seized the excellent opportunity thus offered . . . and ran away helter-skelter just as if we were escaping!

From *The Adventures of Peregrine Pickle* by Tobias Smollett, 1721–1771

The Doctor with an air of infinite satisfaction began:—This here, gentlemen, is a boiled goose, served up in a sauce composed of pepper, lovage, coriander, mint, rue, anchovies, and oil! I wish for your sakes, gentlemen, it was one of the geese of Ferrara, so much celebrated among the ancients for the magnitude of their livers, one of which is said to have weighed upwards of two pounds: with this food, exquisite as it was, did the tyrant Heliogabalus regale his hounds. But I beg pardon, I had almost forgotten the soup, which I hear is so necessary an article at all tables in France. At each end there are dishes of the *salacacabia* of the Romans; one is made of parsley, pennyroyal, cheese, pine-tops, honey, vinegar, brine, eggs, cucumbers, onions, and hen-livers; the other is much the same as the *soup-maigre* of this country. Then there is a loin of veal boiled with fennel and caraway seed, on a pottage composed of pickle, oil, honey, and flour, and a curious *hachis* of the lights, liver and blood of an hare, together with a dish of roasted pigeons. Monsieur le Baron, shall I help you to a plate of this soup?—The German, who did not at all approve of the ingredients, assented to the proposal, and seemed to relish the composition; while the marquis was in consequence of his desire accommodated with a portion of the *soup-maigre;* and the count supplied himself with a pigeon. . . .

The Frenchman, having swallowed the first spoonful, made a pause; his throat swelled as if an egg had stuck in his gullet, his eyes rolled, and his mouth underwent a series of involuntary contractions and dilations. Pallet, who looked steadfastly at this connoisseur, with a view of consulting his taste, before he himself would venture upon the soup, began to be disturbed at these emotions, and observed, with some concern, that the poor gentleman seemed to be going into a fit; when Peregrine assured him these were symptoms of ecstasy, and, for further confirmation, asked the marquis how he found the soup. It was with infinite difficulty that his complaisance could so far master his disgust, as to enable him to answer, "Altogether excellent, upon my honour!" And the painter, being certified of his approbation, lifted the spoon to his mouth without scruple; but far from justifying the eulogium of his taster, when this precious composition diffused itself upon his palate, he seemed to be deprived of all sense and motion, and sat like the leaden statue of some river god, with the liquor flowing out at both sides of his mouth. . . .

The Doctor, alarmed at this indecent phenomenon, earnestly inquired into the cause of it; and when Pallet recovered his recollection, and swore that he would rather swallow porridge made of burning brimstone, than such an infernal mess as that which he had tasted, the physician, in his own vindication, assured the company, that, except the usual ingredients, he had mixed nothing in the soup but some sal-ammoniac instead of the ancient nitrum, which could not now be procured; and appealed to the marquis, whether such a succedaneum was not an improvement of the whole. The unfortunate *petit-maître*, driven to the extremity of his condescension, acknowledged it to be a masterly refinement; and deeming himself obliged, in point of honour, to evince his sentiments by his practice, forced a few more mouthfuls of this disagreeable potion down his throat, till his stomach was so much offended that he was compelled to start up of a sudden; and, in the hurry of his elevation, overturned his plate into the bosom of the baron. The emergency of his occasions would not permit him to stay and make apologies for this abrupt behaviour; so that he flew into another apartment, where Pickle found him puking, and crossing himself with great devotion; and a chair, at his desire, being brought to the door, he slipped into it, more dead than alive.... When our hero returned to the dining-room the places were filled with two pyes, one of dormice liquored with syrup of white poppies which the Doctor had substituted in the room of toasted poppy-seed, formerly eaten with honey, as a dessert; and the other composed of a hock of pork baked in honey.

Pallet hearing the first of these dishes described, lifting up his hands and eyes, and with signs of loathing and amazement, pronounced, "A pye made of dormice and syrup of poppies—Lord in Heaven! What beastly fellows those Romans were!"

All the Doctor's invitations and assurances could not prevail upon his guests to honour the *hachis* and the goose; and that course was succeeded by another. "That which smokes in the middle," said he, "is a sow's stomach, filled with a composition of minced pork, hog's brains, eggs, pepper, cloves, garlick, aniseed, rue, oil, wine, and pickle. On the right-hand side are the teats and belly of a sow, just farrowed, fried with sweet wine, oil, flour, lovage, and pepper. On the left is a fricassee of snails, fed, or rather purged, with milk. At that end, next Mr. Pallet, are fritters of pompions, lovage, origanum, and oil; and here are a couple of pullets, roasted and stuffed in the manner of Apicius."

The painter, who had by wry faces testified his abhorrence of the sow's stomach, which he compared to a bag-pipe, and the snails which had undergone purgation, no sooner heard him mention the roasted pullets, than he eagerly solicited the wing of a fowl; but scarce were they set down before him, when the tears ran down his cheeks, and he called aloud in a manifest disorder, "Z———nds! This is the essence of a whole bed of garlic!" That he might not, however, disappoint or disgrace the entertainer, he applied his instruments to one of the birds, and when he opened up the cavity, was assailed by such an irruption of intolerable smells, that, without staying to disengage himself from the cloth, he sprung away, with an exclamation of "Lord Jesus!" and involved the whole table in havoc, ruin, and confusion.

Before Pickle could accomplish his escape, he was soused with the syrup of the dormouse-pye, which went to pieces in the general wreck; and as for the Italian count, he was overwhelmed by the sow's stomach, which bursting in the fall, discharged its contents upon his leg and thigh, and scalded him so miserably, that he shrieked with anguish, and grinned with a most ghastly and horrible aspect. . . .

The Doctor was confounded with shame and vexation. He expressed his sorrow for the misadventure and protested there was nothing in the fowls which could give offense to a sensitive nose, the stuffing being a mixture of pepper, lovage, and assafoetida, and the sauce consisting of wine and herring-pickle, which he had used instead of the celebrated garum of the Romans.

From *The Golden Ass* by Lucius Apuleius, circa 160 A.D.

As for me, I was ruled and handled by fortune, according to her pleasure: for the soldier which got me without a seller and paid never a penny for me, by the commandment of his captain was sent unto Rome in course of his duty to carry letters to the great Prince, and before he went he sold me for eleven pence to two of his companions, brothers, being servants to a man of worship and wealth, whereof one was a baker, that baked sweet bread and delicates; the other a cook, which dressed with rich sauces fine and excellent meats for his master. These two lived in common, and would drive me from place to place to carry such vessels as were necessary for their master when he travelled through divers countries. In this sort I was received by these two as a third brother and companion, and I thought I was never better placed than with them: for when night came and the lord's supper was done, which was always exceedingly rich and splendid, my masters would bring many good morsels into their chamber for themselves: one would bring large rests of pigs, chickens, fish, and other good meats; the other fine bread, pastries, tarts, custards, and other delicate junkets dipped in honey. And when before meat they had shut their chamber door and went to the baths; O Lord, how I would fill my guts with those goodly dishes: neither was I so much a fool, or so very an ass, as to leave the dainty meats and grind my teeth upon hard hay. In this sort I continued a great space in my artful thieving, for I played the honest ass, taking but a little of one dish and a little of another, whereby no man mistrusted me. In the end I was more hardier and more sure that I should not be discovered, and began to devour the whole messes of the sweetest delicates, which caused the baker and the cook to suspect not a little; howbeit they never mistrusted me, but searched about to apprehend the daily thief. At length they began to accuse one another of base theft, and to keep and guard the dishes more diligently, and to number and set them in order, one by another, because they would learn what was taken away: and at last one of them was compelled to throw aside all doubting and to say thus to his fellow: "Is it right or reason to break promise and faith in this sort, by stealing away the best meat and selling to augment thy private good, and yet nevertheless to have thy equal part of the residue that is left? If our partnership do displease thee, we will be partners and brothers in other things, but in this we will break off: for I perceive that the great loss which I sustain will at length grow from complaining to be a cause of great discord between us." Then answered the other: "Verily I praise thy great constancy and subtileness, in that thou (when thou hast secretly taken away the meat) dost begin to complain first; whereas I by long space of time have silently suffered thee, because I would not seem to accuse my brother of a scurvy theft. But I am right glad in that we are fallen into communication of this matter, to seek a remedy for it, lest by our silence like contention might arise between us as fortuned between Eteocles* and his brother." When they had reasoned and striven together in this sort, they sware both earnestly that neither of them stole or took away any jot of the meat, but that they must conclude to search out the thief by all kind of means in common. For they could not

---

* Eteocles and Polynices were the two sons of Oedipus who killed one another in the internecine strife at Thebes.

imagine or think that the ass, who stood alone there, would fancy any such meats, and yet every day the best parts thereof would utterly disappear; neither could they think that flies were so great or ravenous as to devour whole dishes of meat, like the birds harpies which carried away the meats of Phineus, king of Arcadia.

In the mean season, while I was fed with dainty morsels, and fattened with food fit for men, I gathered together my flesh, my skin waxed soft and juicy, my hair began to shine, and I was gallant on every part; but such fair and comely shape of my body was cause of my dishonour, for the baker and the cook marvelled to see me so sleek and fine, considering that my hay was every day left untouched. Wherefore they turned all their minds towards me, and on a time when at their accustomed hour they made as they would go to the baths and locked their chamber door, it fortuned that ere they departed away they espied me through a little hole how I fell roundly to my victuals that lay spread abroad. Then they marvelled greatly, and little esteeming the loss of their meat laughed exceedingly at the marvellous daintiness of an ass, calling the servants of the house, one by one and then more together, to shew them the greedy gorge and wonderful appetite of a slow beast. The laughing of them all was so immoderate that the master of the house passing by heard them, and demanded the cause of their laughter; and when he understood all the matter, he looked through the hole likewise, wherewith he took such a delectation that he had well nigh burst his guts with laughing and commanded the door to be opened, that he might see me at his pleasure. Then I, beholding the face of fortune altogether smiling upon me, was nothing abashed, but rather more bold for joy, whereby I never rested eating till such time as the master of the house commanded me to be brought out as a novelty, nay he led me into his own parlour with his own hands, and there caused all kinds of meats, which had been never before touched, to be set on the tables; and these (although I had eaten sufficiently before, yet to win the further favour of the master of the house) I did greedily devour, and made a clean riddance of the delicate meats. And to prove my mild and docile nature wholly, they gave me such meat as every ass doth greatly abhor, for they put before me beef and vinegar, birds and pepper, fish and sharp sauce. In the mean season, they that beheld me at the table did nothing but laugh; then one of the wits that was there said to his master: "I pray you, sir, give this feaster some drink to his supper." "Marry," quoth he, "I think thou sayest true, rascal; for so it may be that to his meat this our dinner-fellow would drink likewise a cup of wine. Oh, boy, wash yonder golden pot, and fill it with wine; which done, carry it to my guest, and say that I have drank to him." Then all the standers-by looked on, looking eagerly to see what would come to pass; but I (as soon as I beheld the cup) stayed not long, but at my leisure, like a good companion, gathering my lips together to the fashion of a man's tongue, supped up all the wine at one draught, while all who were there present shouted very loudly and wished me good health.

But no, not even a golden ass, so sleek and gay, can ease for us the revolting tightness of our spiritual belts. Bestial gluttony has tainted us, and there is the sour stink of indigestion everywhere.

Lucullus still stands proud and pure, if criminally wasteful, as the one Roman who fed his various hungers with finesse and delicacy, and would never have stooped to the ugliness of his admirers' table habits. But Lucullus is not enough. It takes more than one mortal man to atone for many.

That is why, as antidote to all this surfeit, I have chosen to end with two stories of the immortals.

The first one, by Ovid, is as fresh and sweet as the breezes that still move in the boughs of two trees that might be Baucis and Philemon, on any hill where love is.

And the second story, with a little piece in front of it by Rabelais of France, is of the death of Socrates.

Perhaps that seems a strange kind of feast to put in this book, but surely the bitter cup of hemlock was in its way important to men's souls, like the wine and the unleavened bread of a Passover feast in Jerusalem, shared in a room with twelve men other than Jesus. It is not only Christians who have been touched by the superhuman mystery of that Last Supper. And philosophers are not the only men whose lives have bent to the beauty and the dignity of Socrates' final cup with his friends, which he drank alone but which each one of them forever after tasted.

From *Philemon and Baucis* by Ovid, 43 B.C.–? 17 A.D.

In the Phrygian Hills an oak-tree stands by the side of a linden, both surrounded by a low wall; I have seen the place myself. Not far from this place there is a marsh, once habitable land, now water, haunted by divers and coots. To this place Jupiter came, once upon a time, in mortal guise, and with him Mercury, without his wings or wand. To a thousand homes they came, seeking a place for rest; and a thousand homes were bolted against them. Still, one house did receive them, a little cottage, to be sure, humble, thatched with straw and rushes. A good old woman, Baucis, and her old husband Philemon had been married in that house when they were young, and had grown old there together; they made their poverty light by admitting it, and by bearing it with no mean spirit. It would make no difference if you asked for masters or servants in that house; the two of them were the whole household; the two of them give the orders and obey them.

So when the gods came to this humble home, and, ducking their heads, came through the low doorway, the old man set out a bench, and bade them rest their limbs, while over the bench the old wife threw a rough covering. Then she raked aside the warm ashes on the hearth and fanned to life yesterday's fire, feeding it with leaves and dry bark, blowing them to flame with the breath of her old body. Then she took down from the roof some fine-split wood and dry twigs, broke them up, and placed them under the small copper kettle. From the well-watered garden her husband had brought in a head of cabbage, which she took and stripped of its outer leaves. In the meantime he took a forked stick and reached down a side of bacon which hung from the black beams, and he cut off a lean strip, and put it to cook in the boiling water. And they keep the talk going while these preparations are being made.

A mattress of soft sedge-grass was placed on a couch with frame and feet of willow. Over this they threw a spread, usually reserved for holiday occasions, but even this was poor and frayed, a very good match for the willow couch. Here the gods reclined. The old woman, her skirts tucked up, set the table with trembling hands. One of the legs was too short; she used a shell to prop it up and make it even. Then when it was level, she scoured the surface with a handful of green mint. Next she set on the table olives, green ones and ripe ones, and some autumnal wild cherries pickled in the lees of wine; endive, radishes, cottage cheese, and eggs, lightly turned in the warm ashes, all these being served in earthen dishes. After this course, a mixing bowl of the same . . . ware was set on the table, with beechwood cups, coated inside with yellow wax. There was a short wait, and then the steaming victuals were brought from the fire, and wine, none too old, was served, and the final course made ready. This time there were nuts and figs, dried dates, plums and apples in sweet-smelling baskets, purple grapes just picked from the vines, and in the center of the board a comb of clear white honey. And over and beyond all this, were kindly faces, and a good will neither sluggish nor poverty-stricken.

Meanwhile they saw that the wine-bowl, as often as it was drained, kept filling up of its own accord, and that the wine, all by itself, kept brimming up again. The two old folks were frightened and amazed; with upturned hands they prayed, begging pardon, trembling old things, for their scanty fare and meager entertainment. They had one goose, the guardian of their small estate, and now they decided to catch and kill him to please their divine guests. But the goose was swift of wing, and the slow old people almost ran out of breath in trying to catch him. For a long time he kept out of their reach, and finally seemed to flee for refuge to the feet of the gods themselves. Then the gods told them not to kill the goose.

"We are gods," they said, "and this wicked neighborhood shall be punished as it deserves; but you shall be saved and protected. Only leave your house and come with us and go with us to that tall mountain over there." They obeyed, and tottered along, using their staves, up the long mountain slope. They were almost at the summit, within arrow-shot, when they looked back and saw the whole countryside flooded with water, only their own house above the waves. And even while they were wondering at this, and grieving for the fate of their neighbors, their old house, small even for the two of them, turned into a temple. Marble columns took the place of the worked wooden props; the yellow straw turned yellow gold; the gates were richly carved, the ground was floored with marble. Then Jupiter calmly spoke: "O good old man, and wife, worthy of the good husband, tell us what you would like to have." Philemon spoke a few words with Baucis, then, turning to the gods, revealed their common decision: "We ask to be priests and to guard your temple; and since our years together have been happy ones, we pray that the same hour may carry us both off; let me never see the tomb of my wife, and let her never see mine."

Their request was granted. As long as they lived, they had charge of the temple. And at last, when they were very old indeed, and happened to be standing in front of the temple, talking of olden times, Baucis saw

Philemon putting forth leaves, and likewise Philemon saw Baucis so, and as the tree-top formed over their faces, they had time for one phrase only, "Farewell, my dear!", and the bark closed over and covered their mouths. Even to this day the local peasants point out the two trees standing close together, and growing from one double trunk. Sensible old men (and there was no reason why they should want to fool me) told me this story. And I saw votive garlands hanging from the boughs, and added fresh ones of my own, and hanging them, I made up a verse: "The gods look after the good, and those who cherish are cherished."

From the Prologue to *Gargantua and Pantagruel* by François Rabelais, 1483?–1553

Alcibiades [in the work of Plato's called *The Banquet*], praising his master Socrates (undoubtedly the prince of philosophers), happens, among other things, to liken him to sileni. Sileni, in the days of yore, were small boxes such as you may see nowadays at your apothecary's. They were named for Silenus, foster father to Bacchus. The outside of these boxes bore gay, fantastically painted figures of harpies, satyrs, bridled geese, hares with gigantic horns, saddled ducks, winged goats in flight, harts in harness, and many other droll fancies. They were pleasurably devised to inspire just the sort of laughter Silenus, Bacchus's master, inspired.

But inside these sileni, people kept priceless drugs such as balsam of Mecca, ambergris from the sperm whale, amomum from the cardamon, musk from the deer, and civet from the civet's arsehole—not to mention various sorts of precious stones, used for medical purposes, and other invaluable possessions.

Well, Alcibiades likened Socrates to these boxes, because, judging by his exterior, you would not have given an onion skin for him. He was ill-shaped, ridiculous in carriage, with a nose like a knife, the gaze of a bull, and the face of a fool. His ways stamped him a simpleton, his clothes a bumpkin. Poor in fortune, unlucky when it came to women, hopelessly unfit for all office in the republic, forever laughing, forever drinking neck to neck with his friends, forever hiding his divine knowledge under a mask of mockery. . . .

Yet had you opened this box, you would have found in it all sorts of priceless, celestial drugs: immortal understanding, wondrous virtue, indomitable courage, unparalleled sobriety, unfailing serenity, perfect assurance, and an heroic contempt for whatever moves humanity to watch, to bustle, to toil, to sail ships overseas, and to engage in warfare.

From *The Death of Socrates* by Plato, 427?–347 B.C.

When he had bathed, and his children had been brought to him—he had two sons quite little, and one grown up—and the women of his family were come, he spoke with them in Crito's presence, and gave them his last commands; then he sent the women and children away, and returned to us. By that time it was near the hour of sunset, for he had been a long while within. When he came back to us from the bath he sat down, but not much was said after that. Presently the servant of the Eleven came and stood before him and said, "I know that I shall not find you unreasonable like other men, Socrates. They are angry with me and curse me when I bid them drink the poison because the authorities make me do it. But I have found you all along the noblest and gentlest and best man that has ever come here; and now I am sure that you will not be angry with me, but with those who you know are to blame. And so farewell, and try to bear what must be as lightly as you can; you know why I have come." With that he turned away weeping, and went out.

Socrates looked up at him, and replied, "Farewell; I will do as you say." Then he turned to us and said, "How courteous the man is! And the whole time that I have been here, he has constantly come in to see me, and sometimes he has talked to me, and has been the best of men; and now, how generously he weeps for me! Come, Crito, let us obey him: let the poison be brought if it is ready, and if it is not ready, let it be prepared."

Crito replied: "Nay, Socrates, I think that the sun is still upon the hills; it has not set. Besides, I know that other men take the poison quite late, and eat and drink heartily, and even enjoy the company of their chosen friends, after the announcement has been made. So do not hurry; there is still time."

Socrates replied: "And those whom you speak of, Crito, naturally do so; for they think that they will be gainers by so doing. And I naturally shall not do so; for I think that I should gain nothing by drinking the poison a little later, but my own contempt for so greedily saving up a life which is already spent. So do not refuse to do as I say."

Then Crito made a sign to his slave who was standing by; and the slave went out, and after some delay returned with the man who was to give the poison, carrying it prepared in a cup. When Socrates saw him, he asked, "You understand these things, my good sir, what have I to do?"

"You have only to drink this," he replied, "and to walk about until your legs feel heavy, and then lie down; and it will act of itself." With that he handed the cup to Socrates, who took it quite cheerfully, Echecrates, without trembling, and without any change of colour or of feature, and looked up at the man with that fixed glance of his, and asked, "What say you to making a libation from this draught? May I, or not?" "We only prepare so much as we think sufficient, Socrates," he answered. "I understand," said Socrates. "But I suppose that I may, and must, pray to the gods that my journey hence may be prosperous: that is my prayer; be it so." With these words he put the cup to his lips and drank the poison calmly and cheerfully. Till then most of us had been able to control our grief fairly well; but when we saw him drinking, and then the poison finished, we could do so no longer; my tears came fast in spite of myself, and I covered my face and wept for myself: it was not for him, but at my own misfortune in losing such a friend. Even before that, Crito had been unable to restrain his tears, and had gone away; and Apollodorus, who had never once ceased weeping the whole time, burst into a loud cry, and made us one and all break down by his sobbing and grief, except only Socrates himself. "What are you doing, my friends?" he exclaimed. "I sent away the women chiefly in order that they might not offend in this way; for I have heard that a man should die in silence. So calm yourselves and bear up." When we heard that, we were ashamed, and we ceased from weeping. But he walked about, until he said that his legs were getting heavy, and then he lay down on his back, as he was told. And the man who gave the poison began to examine his feet and legs, from time to time: then he pressed his foot hard, and asked if there was any feeling in it, and Socrates said, "No": and then his legs, and so higher and higher, and showed us that he was cold and stiff. And Socrates felt himself, and said that when it came to his heart, he should be gone. He was already growing cold about the groin, when he uncovered his face, which had been covered, and spoke for the last time. "Crito," he said, "I owe a cock to Asclepius; do not forget to pay it." "It shall be done," replied Crito. "Is there anything else that you wish?" He made no answer to this question; but after a short interval there was a movement, and the man uncovered him, and his eyes were fixed. Then Crito closed his mouth and his eyes.

Such was the end, Echecrates, of our friend, a man, I think, who was the wisest and justest, and the best man that I have ever known.

V

ONE MAN'S MEAT

Cannibals and Poisoners

There are two aspects of gastronomy with somewhat the same peculiar fascination for human beings: poisoning and cannibalism.

Few men have actually eaten their fellows' flesh, but the possibility that sometime it might be necessary haunts every thoughtful creature, with varying degrees of perverse excitement. Stories of such grim nourishment, masterly or merely lurid, are inevitable in any collection of popular writings, and there is hardly one of us, I think, who will not admit to remembering this or that detail of them with a particular if unwilling vividness.

I was about eight years old when I read in an English newspaper an interview with a South Sea Islander studying at Oxford, and every startlingly casual word of it sticks in my mind and always will, although now for more clinical reasons than the innocent creepiness of my first thrill in it. "Myself, I do not care much for human meat," the princeling said in his precise impeccable accent. "However, my father the King has often prevailed upon me to enjoy with him his favorite tidbit, the tiny fillet from the ball of the thumb!"

My own feeling that I might one day be faced with some such parental or regal request is mixed less with spiritual aversion than with physical: I cannot believe that the average modern diet (a coke and a peanut-butter-on-white for lunch) is capable of producing particularly agreeable meat. A fat body would be too much so, a thin one stringy. Probably a well-rounded adolescent, of either sex but raised in the country on fresh apples and plenty of creamy milk, would make the best food, since the tasteless flesh of infancy would have ripened a little, but not enough to be toughened by the cholers and ardors of maturity. . . .

But there is no ignoring the fact that there is a tabu against cannibalism, and always has been almost everywhere in the world. Among heathens it is generally practiced in connection with one or another form of mystic religious rite, and is a complex and symbolical thing which has little if anything to do with pleasure. Among so-called civilized beings it is either a form of insanity or sexual perversion, or a question of starvation, which is in itself a madness.

Men who have been morally broken to the point of being able to eat their companions, and perhaps of murdering them first, are almost unclaimable again as decent creatures. They live always under an invisible web of horror, unless like one of the characters in a story by Joseph Conrad they find a good solid love to brush it away.

And people like the wealthy Parisian gourmet who always managed to eat some part of every criminal hanged or guillotined, which was brought to him by the well-paid executioner and prepared by his equally bribed chef; people like the man who hated the world so much that he finally contrived to invite his favorite enemies to an exquisite banquet and then damn them all forever by informing them at the last bite of it that they had dined on human flesh: such case histories are of small value to anything but the most juvenile editions of sensational "true story magazines,' " fit only to be read by children already inured to *Jack the Giant-Killer* with its "Fee-fi-fo-fum," or by pathetic perverts.

Human sacrifice has never figured in the Christian religion, except mystically in the communion with Christ through His body and blood, and gentlemen of the Church, especially its English branches, have long done their utmost to make cannibalism a heathen and disreputable thing. Most of them, however, have mercifully and conveniently forgotten the accounts of some of the earliest British feasts of the Druids!

The story D. H. Lawrence wrote called *The Woman Who Rode Away* is probably the best description I have ever read, the most inevitable and logical and real, of how a human victim is prepared for its ceremonial death. Of course the white-skinned fair woman in that haunting English prose-poem, which I wish I had room to quote here, may or may not have been eaten afterward; but it does not matter; she was sacrificed, after long rites much like those described by William H. Prescott:

From *History of the Conquest of Mexico* by William H. Prescott, 1796–1859
Human sacrifices were adopted by the Aztecs early in the fourteenth century, about two hundred years before the Conquest. Rare at first, they became more frequent with the wider extent of their empire; till, at length, almost every festival was closed with this cruel abomination. These religious ceremonials were generally arranged in such a manner as to afford a type of the most prominent circumstances in the character or history of the deity who was the object of them. A single example will suffice.

One of their most important festivals was that in honor of the god Tezcatlipoca, whose rank was inferior only to that of the Supreme Being. He was called "the soul of the world," and supposed to have been its creator. He was depicted as a handsome man, endowed with perpetual youth. A year before the intended sacrifice, a captive, distinguished for his personal beauty, and without a blemish on his body, was selected to represent this deity. Certain tutors took charge of him, and instructed him how to perform his new part with becoming grace and dignity. He was arrayed in a splendid dress, regaled with incense and with a profusion of sweet-scented flowers, of which the ancient Mexicans were as fond as their descendants at the present day. When he went abroad, he was attended by a train of the royal pages, and, as he halted in the streets to play some favorite melody, the crowd prostrated themselves before him, and did him homage as the representative of their good deity. In this way he led an easy, luxurious life, till within a month of his sacrifice. Four beautiful girls, bearing the names of the principal goddesses, were then selected to share the honors of his bed; and with them he continued to live in idle dalliance, feasted at the banquets of the principal nobles, who paid him all the honors of a divinity.

At length the fatal day of sacrifice arrived. The term of his short-lived glories was at an end. He was stripped of his gaudy apparel, and bade adieu to the fair partners of his revelries. One of the royal barges transported him across the lake to a temple which rose on its margin, about a league from the city. Hither the inhabitants of the capital flocked, to witness the consummation of the ceremony. As the sad procession wound up the sides of the pyramid, the unhappy victim threw away his gay chaplets of flowers, and broke in pieces the musical instruments with which he had solaced the hours of captivity. On the summit he was received by six priests, whose long and matted locks flowed disorderly over their sable robes, covered with hieroglyphic scrolls of mystic import. They led him to the sacrificial stone, a huge block of jasper, with its upper surface somewhat convex. On this the prisoner was stretched. Five priests secured his head and his limbs; while the sixth, clad in a scarlet mantle, emblematic of his bloody office, dexterously opened the breast of the wretched victim with a sharp razor of *itzli*—a volcanic substance, hard as flint—and, inserting his hand in the wound, tore out the palpitating heart. The minister of death, first holding this up towards the sun, an object of worship throughout Anahuac, cast it at the feet of the deity to whom the temple was devoted, while the multitudes below prostrated themselves in humble adoration. The tragic story of this prisoner was expounded by the priests as the type of human destiny, which, brilliant in its commencement, too often closes in sorrow and disaster.

Such was the form of human sacrifice usually practised by the Aztecs. It was the same that often met the indignant eyes of the Europeans, in their progress through the country, and from the dreadful doom of which they themselves were not exempted. There were, indeed, some occasions when preliminary tortures, of the most exquisite kind—with which it is unnecessary to shock the reader—were inflicted, but they always terminated with the bloody ceremony above described. It should be remarked, however, that such tortures were not the spontaneous suggestions of cruelty, as with the North American Indians; but were all rigorously prescribed in the Aztec ritual, and doubtless were often inflicted with the same compunctious visitings which a devout familiar of the Holy Office might at times experience in executing its stern decrees. Women, as well as the other sex, were sometimes reserved for sacrifice. On some occasions, particularly in seasons of drought, at the festival of the insatiable Tlaloc, the god of rain, children, for the most part infants, were offered up. As they were borne along in open litters, dressed in their festal robes, and decked with the fresh blossoms of spring, they moved the hardest heart to pity, though their cries were drowned in the wild chant of the priests, who read in their tears a favorable augury for their petition. These innocent victims were generally bought by the priests of parents who were poor, who stifled the voice of nature, probably less at the suggestions of poverty than of a wretched superstition.

The most loathsome part of the story—the manner in which the body of the sacrificed captive was disposed of—remains yet to be told. It was delivered to the warrior who had taken him in battle, and by him, after being dressed, was served up in an entertainment of his friends. This was not the coarse repast of famished cannibals, but a banquet teeming with delicious beverages and delicate viands, prepared with art, and attended by both sexes, who, as we shall see hereafter, conducted themselves with all the decorum of civilized life. Surely, never were refinement and the extreme of barbarism brought so closely in contact with each other!

Human sacrifices have been practised by many nations, not excepting the most polished nations of antiquity; but never by any on a scale to be compared with those in Anahuac. The amount of victims immolated on its accursed altars would stagger the faith of the least scrupulous believer. Scarcely any author pretends to estimate the yearly sacrifices throughout the empire at less than twenty thousand, and some carry the number as high as fifty!

It is possible to argue that forms of religious cannibalism are in their complex ways revenge-killings, done indirectly by the gods themselves in anger or ambition or desire. When men stoop to vengeance, however, by using the flesh of their victims as a weapon, they are far from godlike.

The story of a cuckold who feeds the lover's heart to his unfaithful wife is one of the oldest, and most continuously and horridly titillating, in the world. It has been told too many times, with too many variations, but since it is a part of the history of gastronomy, once more will not hurt. The version I have chosen, perhaps because its quaint language strips it of some of its revolting nature, is from Boccaccio's *Decameron*, and was written about 1350 A.D., based on an earlier account by one Nostrodamus in his *Lives of the Troubadours*:

From *The Decameron* by Giovanni Boccaccio, 1313–1375

You must know . . . that in Provence were two noble knights, who had each of them castles of their own, and vassals under their subjection; one of these knights was called Gulielmo Rossiglione, and the other, Gulielmo Guardastagno; and, being both persons of great prowess, they took a great delight in military exploits, and used to go together to all tilts and tournaments, and appeared always in the same colours. Though they lived ten miles asunder, yet it happened that, Rossiglione having a very beautiful wife, the other, notwithstanding the friendship that existed between them, became violently in love, and by one means or other he soon let her know it. He being a valiant knight, this was not at all displeasing to her, and she began to entertain the same respect for him, so that she wished for nothing so much as that he should speak to her upon that subject, which in some little time came to pass, and they were together more than once. They being not so discreet as they ought to have been, the husband soon perceived it, and he resented it to that degree, that the extreme friendship he had entertained for Guardastagno was turned into the most inveterate hatred; but he was more private with it than they had the prudence to be with their amour, and was fully bent upon putting him to death. Continuing in this resolution, it fell out that a public tilting match was proclaimed in France, which Rossiglione immediately signified to Guardastagno, and sent to desire his company at his castle, when they would confer together about going, and in what manner: Guardastagno was extremely pleased with the message, and sent word back that he would sup with him the next night without fail.

Rossiglione, hearing this, thought it a fit opportunity to effect his design, and arming himself the next day, with some of his servants he went on horseback into a wood about a mile from his castle, through which Guardastagno was to pass, where he lay in wait for him. After a long stay, he beheld him coming unarmed, with two servants unarmed likewise, as not apprehending any danger; and when he saw him in a fit place for his purpose, he ran with his lance at him, with the utmost malice and fury, saying, "Villain, thou art a dead man!" and the very instant he spoke the word, the lance passed out behind through his breast, and he fell down dead, without uttering a word. The servants not knowing who had done this, turned their horses, and fled with all possible haste to their lord's castle. Rossiglione now dismounted from his horse, and with a knife cut Guardastagno's breast open, and took out his heart, and, wrapping it in the streamer belonging to his lance, gave it to one of his servants to carry. Then commanding them not to dare to speak of it, he mounted his horse, and, it being now night, returned to his castle.

The lady, who had heard of Guardastagno's supping there that night, and longed much to see him, finding that he did not come, was a good deal surprised, and said to her husband, "Pray, what is the reason that Guardastagno is not here?" He replied, "I have just received a message from him that he cannot be with us till to-morrow"; at which she seemed very uneasy. As soon as he alighted from his horse, he sent for the cook, and said to him, "Here take this boar's heart, and be sure you make it as delicious as possible, and send it up to the table in a silver dish." Accordingly, he took and minced it very small, dressing it up with rich spices, and making it a sort of high-seasoned forced meat.

When supper-time came, they sat down, and the dishes were served up; but Rossiglione could not eat much for thinking of what he had done. At last the cook having sent up the forced meat, he set it before his lady, pretending himself to be out of order, but commending it to her as a nice dish. She, who was not at all squeamish, began to taste, and liked it so well that she ate it all up. When he saw that she had made an end, he said, "Madam, how do you like it?" She replied, "In good truth, Sir, I like it much."—"As God shall help me," quoth the knight, "I believe you; nor do I wonder that it pleases you so much now it is dead, which, when living, pleased you above all things." She made a pause at this, and then said— "Why, what is it that you have given me?" He replied, "It is really the heart of Guardastagno, whom you, base woman, loved so well: be assured it is the same, for these very hands took it out of his breast, a little time before I returned home."

When the lady heard this of him whom she loved above all the world, you may easily imagine what her anguish must have been. At last she replied, "You have acted like a base villain as you are; for if I granted him a favour of my own accord, and you were injured thereby, it was I, and not he, that ought to have been punished. But let it never be said that any other food ever came after such a noble repast as was the heart of so valiant and worthy a knight." Then, rising up, she instantly threw herself out of the window. It was a great height from the ground, and she was in a manner dashed to pieces. He, seeing this, was a good deal confounded, and being conscious of having done a base action, fearing also the country's resentment, he had his horses saddled, and fled directly away. The next morning the whole story was known all around the country, when the two bodies were taken and buried together with the utmost lamentation in one grave in the church which had belonged to the lady; and verses were written over them, signifying who they were, as well as the manner and cause of their deaths.

Poisoning, for some reason, has much of the same decadent phosphorescence as cannibalism about it, in the gastronomy of the mind. It fascinates; it tantalizes. It lacks the ultimate titillation of the tabu, but, to compensate, it is much more easily imaginable and, unfortunately, more practicable a form of crime.

Since all of us are potential murderers or murderees, each one of us is intrinsically capable of either poisoning another human being or being thus done away with by him. And it is almost too banal a fact to mention that undoubtedly a great many more of us are poisoners, and therefore murderers, than has yet been proved. . . .

The art of removing an undesirable person by putting death in his food or drink has been practiced for almost as many years as men have lived in the world, and of course has reached newer and newer heights of refinement. No matter how crude the method or the drug (Miss Lizzie Borden whacked her parents to death with an axe, but it has often been felt that such an end was really a *coup de grâce* after serving them bananas, cookies, and cold mutton soup for breakfast!), the crime itself is a much more intelligent one than most other kinds of murder. It takes premeditation, if of only a few seconds, and it usually calls for delicacy, skill, an iron courage, and the appalling ability to watch and wait, sometimes for months or years, for the end to announce itself. (Miss Borden could not wait, or perhaps could no longer endure to share the breakfast poison with her family!)

People like the Renaissance Borgias used it with such consummate autocracy that it became almost a social honor to taste their delicious brews—Max Beerbohm in his *Hosts and Guests* writes that "though you would often in the fifteenth century have heard the snobbish Roman say, in a would-be offhand tone, 'I am dining with the Borgias tonight,' no Roman was ever able to say, 'I dined last night with the Borgias' "—and the lethal subtleties they fed were, to my mind, much less ugly than are the spiritual poisons injected by modern political overlords into their victims' minds and hearts. A Huey Long, generous to voters with fish fries and burgoos, can spread death more than any wily Roman ruler ever did with his fine roasted ortolans and peacocks' tongues. . . .

That is the kind of murder William Blake wrote about in *A Poison Tree*, much more insidious than the honest arsenic and strychnine that were as dust to mighty Mithridates, or the loathsome brew the witches made, that "deed without a name":

A Poison Tree by William Blake, 1757–1827

I was angry with my friend:
I told my wrath, my wrath did end.
I was angry with my foe:
I told it not, my wrath did grow.

And I water'd it in fears,
Night and morning with my tears;
And I sunnèd it with smiles,
And with soft deceitful wiles.

And it grew both day and night,
Till it bore an apple bright;
And my foe beheld it shine,
And he knew that it was mine,

And into my garden stole
When the night had veil'd the pole:
In the morning glad I see
My foe outstretch'd beneath the tree.

From A Shropshire Lad by A. E. Housman, 1859–1936

There was a king reigned in the East:
There, when kings will sit to feast,
They get their fill before they think
With poisoned meat and poisoned drink.
He gathered all that springs to birth

From the many-venomed earth;
First a little, thence to more,
He sampled all her killing store;
And easy, smiling, seasoned sound,
Sate the king when healths went round.
They put arsenic in his meat
And stared aghast to watch him eat;
They poured strychnine in his cup
And shook to see him drink it up:
They shook, they stared as white's their shirt;
They it was their poison hurt.
—I tell the tale that I heard told.
Mithridates, he died old.

From Macbeth by William Shakespeare, 1564–1616

A cavern. In the middle, a cauldron boiling.

Thunder. Enter the three WITCHES.

1. WITCH. Thrice the brinded cat hath mew'd.

2. WITCH. Thrice and once the hedge-pig whin'd.

3. WITCH. Harpier cries; 'tis time, 'tis time.

1. WITCH. Round about the cauldron go;
    In the poison'd entrails throw.
    Toad, that under cold stone
    Days and nights has thirty-one
    Swelt'red venom sleeping got,
    Boil thou first i' th' charmed pot.

  ALL. Double, double, toil and trouble;
    Fire burn, and cauldron bubble.

2. WITCH. Fillet of a fenny snake,
    In the cauldron boil and bake;
    Eye of newt, and toe of frog,
    Wool of bat, and tongue of dog,
    Adder's fork, and blindworm's sting,
    Lizard's leg, and howlet's wing;
    For a charm of pow'rful trouble
    Like a hell-broth boil and bubble.

ALL. Double, double, toil and trouble;
 Fire burn, and cauldron bubble.

3. WITCH. Scale of dragon, tooth of wolf
 Witch's mummy, maw and gulf
 Of the ravin'd salt-sea shark,
 Root of hemlock, digg'd i' th' dark;
 Liver of blaspheming Jew,
 Gall of goat, and slips of yew
 Sliver'd in the moon's eclipse;
 Nose of Turk and Tartar's lips;
 Finger of birth-strangled babe
 Ditch-deliver'd by a drab:
 Make the gruel thick and slab.
 Add thereto a tiger's chaudron
 For th' ingredience of our cauldron.

ALL. Double, double, toil and trouble;
 Fire burn, and cauldron bubble.

2. WITCH. Cool it with a baboon's blood,
 Then the charm is firm and good.

VI

PARFIT GENTIL KNIGHTS

The Middle Ages

Every *wise* man, after *fifty*, ought to begin to lessen at least the quantity of his *aliment*, and if he would continue free of great and dangerous Distempers and preserve his Senses and Faculties clear to the last he ought every seven years to go abateing gradually and sensibly, and at last *descend* out of Life as he ascended into it, even unto the Child's Diet.

GEORGE CHEYNE

And this is as true of a man's literary hungers as those more easily identified with his body. At first the diet is light, a kind of pap of little jingles, of rhymes easy to sing and to remember. Gradually the taste-buds grow more demanding, and without realizing it a reader is deep in intrigue and fustian, just as in his adolescence he finds himself craving heavy sweetmeats and the high clash of pepper and spice.

Then comes the period of increasing subtlety, when novels give way to essays and canned tomato soup to *bisque d'écrevisse*.

Somewhere after this the reversal sets in, until finally an old man can sustain himself happily on remembered phrases and the occasional slow digestion of a poem, or a maxim from his youth, or a verse from the Psalms, as he sits a-sunning with his stomach carefully full of warmed milk and crumbs. . . ."

The high pace of an *Ivanhoe* read by a twelve-year-old may slow unbearably, in the next twenty years, to a ridiculous stuffy pompous jog, but there is one part of the Middle Ages, whether in Scott's novels or The Bodleian Manuscripts, that increases in its amusement and curiosity. That is almost any kind of cookbook from those far fusty days. Once read, their quirky phrases once interpreted, they are stuck fast in the mind's storeroom, along with a few limericks and some tag-ends of Shakespeare.

The Forme of Curye is a good example. It was compiled by the master-cooks of King Richard II of England in 1390 "aftir the conquest; the which was accounted the best and royallest viander [the nicest eater!] of all Christian kings. . . ."

Masters of physic and philosophy worked upon this assemblage of some hundred and ninety-six quaint recipes, which is perhaps one reason why it is such fun to read. The passage of time may have something to do with a modern reader's enjoyment, too: a kind of thanksgiving that he lives now instead of then, when he would have had to study how to make "grounden beans, rapes in pottage, and tarts of fish," and to prepare "common pottages and common meats for the household, as they should be made, craftily and wholesomely . . . curious soups for all manner of states, both high and low. . . ."

The little preamble to *The Forme* ends, straightforwardly, "So this little table, here following will teach a man without tarrying, to find what meat that he lusts for to have"! That is good. It makes a noble nincompoop like Ivanhoe seem more like a human being, suddenly, to see such proof that he did lust for anything but Rowena, in a decorously sublimated way. . . .

In the same vigorous fashion as the medieval books of cookery, or curye, the names of London streets make the people who trod them seem like good hungry fellow creatures instead of attenuated illuminations of an ancient manuscript. There was Pudding Lane. There was Pye Corner. They show that since the twelfth century Englishmen have tended their bellies with solicitude, and patronized a thousand cookshops which finally burned down in the great fire of 1666, and thus proved to all the righteous that gluttony could come to no cool end.

London was always a town of gourmandizing, and most of its mayors at one time or another have passed strict laws against luxuries, all soon ignored, just as they were in Rome a thousand and more years before.

It was probably the monasteries of medieval England that gave the Britons such a taste for the good things of the table. They served as a kind of chain of luxury hotels, the only ones in that whole country, and any man of any station was more than welcome to stop in them, for one night or a month.

The monks were bored stupid with their brothers, and with the limited intellectual and sensual scope of their lives. It was natural that they spend much thought and almost unlimited money on food and drink, and even the poorest of them kept troupes of musical gypsies and minstrels indefinitely lodged with them, rather than sit telling their own beads.

Carousal was inevitable, but so was limitless generosity. When an Abbot of Canterbury was installed in 1309, six thousand persons were fed, and three thousand dishes were prepared, which meant that the poor ate all the enormous leavings.

As for the Archbishop of that same cathedral town, he fed five thousand poor people daily, and great numbers of the bedridden in their homes, in addition to a loaf of good bread for anyone who asked for it. Besides this he made a distribution of one hundred and fifty pence on every feast-day, of which, needless to say, there were many.

Here is an account of a churchly festival in the time of Edward the Black Prince, in the middle of the fourteenth century:

The great feast at the intronization of the reverende father in God George Nevell, Archbishop of York, and Chauncelour of Englande in the vi. yere of the raigne of kyng Edwarde the fourth,

And first the goodly provision made for the same

In Wheate	300 quarters
In Ale	300 tunne
Wyne	100 tunne
of Ipocrasse	1 pipe
In Oxen	104
Wylde Bulles	6
Muttons	1000
Veales	304

Porkes	304
Swannes	400
Geese	2000
Capons	1000
Pygges	2000
Plovers	400
Quayles	100 dozen
Of the fowls called Rees	200 dozen
In Peacockes	104
Mallardes and Teales	4000
In Cranes	204
In Kyddes	204
In Chyckyns	2000
Pigeons	4000
Conyes	4000
In Bittors	204
Heronshawes	400
Fessauntes	200
Partriges	500
Woodcockes	400
Curlewes	100
Egrittes	1000
Stagges, Buckes, and Roes	500 plus
Pasties of Venison colde	4000
Parted dysshes of Gelly	1000
Cold Tartes baked	4000
Cold Custardes baked	3000
Hot pasties of Venison	1500
Hot Custardes	3000
Lypes and Breames	608
Porposes and seales	12
Playne dysshes of Gelly	3000
Spices, Sugared Delicates, and Wafers, plentie	

After this list in the plan of the "great feast" come the names of the important officers of it, such as Stewarde, Carver, Cupbearer, "kepers of the Cubborde" (that is, of all the silver, plate, and salt, laid out in the main hall on special tables and shelves), and all of them of very high rank.

Next are the names and ranks of the people seated at the high table, on down through all six tables in the Hall, three in the Chief Chamber (mostly ladies, with a few of the more gallant youths to keep them gay), two tables in the Second Chamber, three in the Great Chamber, and "In the lowe Hall

Gentlemen, Franklins, and head Yeomen, foure hundred and twelve, twyce filled and served."

Furthermore, in the Gallery were all the servants of the noblemen, four hundred and more, twice filled and served!

The Hall was hung with the Archbishop's canopy over the high table, and cushions of silk and cloth of gold were on all the chairs and benches. A huge fire burned in the middle of the main room, and probably in one or two of the others, and along the walls were the side-boards or "cubbordes," laden with plate and the all-important salt.

There was one broad sharp knife on each table, for the Carver's use, and the plates were wooden trenchers, but there were silver and pewter spoons and the napkins were of the finest silk.

The ceremony was intolerable, as complicated as any religious ritual, while the noble attendants went through an elaborate ballet of bowing and backing, tasting and then waiting for any poison to show itself, bowing more and more, presenting the salt and the dishes in a frenzy of proto-col. Hour after hour the dance went on, while musicians and jugglers kept boredom if not indigestion dutifully at bay, and a procession of set-pieces called subtleties lightened the gloom of the ceremony between the intermi-nable courses.

Each fantastic creation was carried slowly on its great tray through the rooms, in the order of their importance, and the guests laughed and cried out in admiration as they looked at the artful jellies, sugars, wires, gilt, feathers of the set-pieces, and recognized the Archbishop molded in almond paste upon his reverend golden throne, surrounded by his patron saints and his favorite prelates. Knights jousted on a field of spiced green aspic; angels flew on silver wires with spun-sugar wings; and in the final, most important piece of all, Mary Queen of Heaven and John the Baptist and three minor saints helped crown with a jewel-set mitre the new head of the Cathedral, while angels held torches burning with live flame amongst all the pastry.

With this the feast ended, and after the tablecloths had been removed in a last complex ballet by the noble waiters, the whole company stood for a final drink "and that done, every man departeth at his own good pleasure"!

Things had not always been so robustly gay and handsome in the British dining halls. It is true, though, that for some three hundred years at the be-ginning of the Christian era, the Romans lent a certain graciousness to the wild manners of the natives in England. They built roads and houses, and introduced many new delights to the primitive islanders.

(The fact that one early Gaul, Albinus the King, overate at a banquet in his honor proves that although his manners may have been gluttonous his taste for exotic dainties was excellent: it was one hundred peaches, ten melons, fifty large green figs, and three hundred oysters that finally forced him to excuse himself from the generous Latin board!)

But as soon as the conquerors had departed, to try to save Rome from the Goths, the Britons reverted to their old savage diet of nuts and pounded grain and an occasional orgy of half-raw meat.

The invasion of the Saxons did little to add finesse to the national manners: they were a hard-drinking crowd, and gauged their own strength and wealth by the amount of gorging they could do in the company of their equals. The "unsocial and gloomy" Round Table, so prettily idealized by Tennyson and other inspirers of modern youth, was a fine example of their boorishness, in that its very design prevented any one of the suspicious jealous chieftains from sitting in a position superior to that of the other banqueters. Men always ate with their daggers laid ready to hand on the board, and toasts were a matter of life-and-death drinking as the horn was passed.

Gradually a few refinements crept back, and by the time the Danes invaded England and brought an increased love of drinking and gluttonizing, there were such niceties as tablecloths, bowls, and dishes.

The Danish warriors' insane courage in battle resulted from their belief that when they died they would enjoy endless feastings in the hall of Odin, with unnumbered virgins and countless horns of strong drink; and their last king in England, Hardeknout, died in a fit after a brave life, from drinking a whole great goblet of wine without stopping for breath, at a wedding feast in Lambeth.

The Norman Conquest changed all this, by introducing a startling new theory to the brutish Saxons, that the quality of food rather than its quantity was a desirable thing. For the first time delicacy reared its outlandish head around the banquet table, and all kinds of sissified French mannerisms exasperated the muttering and defeated British.

King William brought his chefs with him, and three times a year gave a magnificent feast for all the noble Saxons as well as visiting foreign grandees and ambassadors. Christmas Day he was at Gloucester, and the traditional roasted boars' heads steamed on a hundred platters. At Easter-time he was in Winchester, and ate bacon with all his guests to show his scorn of the Jews, and then for Whitsunday he traveled to Westminster and made his people happy with the fruits of summer, and young roasted lambs, and white swans in their feathers, crowned with rosebuds.

At these feasts the terrible Conqueror made a vow to grant every request, and unbent to the point of out drinking most of his hardheaded guests, but for the rest of the year he was stern and insistent upon the decorum of a well-run court. Perhaps that is why his son Rufus was a debauched profligate, a gross stupid man who spent his subjects' money on such projects as Westminster Hall, built solely for his banquets.

It was two hundred and seventy feet long and seventy-four feet wide, with not a pillar in it to interfere with the swift heavy-laden servitors, and the ceiling was all of wood, better to send back the fine odors of the feasts. When people exclaimed at the size of the great room, Rufus snorted and replied that it was but a bedchamber compared with the one he planned to build next.

Perhaps fortunately for England he died of excesses before he had time for that: an angry chronicle of his day records that "the courtiers devoured the substance of the tenants; there the laying out of hair (in curls) and the superfluity of garments, was found, the tenderness of the body, and wrestling with women, nice going, with dissolute behaviour, was in use; there followed the court a number of effeminate persons, and great companies of ruffians, whereby the same court was not a place of majesty, but a brothel house of unlawful things, such as ought to be abolished."

Such refinements of bestiality continued through two or three more reigns, but as the pageantry of knighthood grew in popularity the manners of the courtiers improved, at least in public. Ladies like the fair Rowena were invited from their towers and silken tents to join the lords at table, and by their presence toned down the old roistering to what must have seemed very tame behavior indeed to the few staunch Saxons left to watch it.

Niceties of dress and actions and a new pomp brought from the Orient by the Crusaders changed the picture so rapidly that by the time Richard II ruled in England, it was not found extraordinary to see at one of his feasts a hollow marble pillar, tall and exquisitely wrought, standing in the middle of the banquet hall, wreathed with fresh lilies and roses and spouting free wine for any comer from four carven spigots at different levels, and a special wine from each spigot at that!

Ten thousand people ate each day at Richard's tables. It took two thousand cooks and almost that many serving-men to care for them, with a daily slaughter of twenty-eight oxen, three hundred sheep, incredible numbers of fowls and game. . . .

It was the old story of royal extravagances, like Solomon's and Darius' and Nero's, when if the king hungered for a stuffed quail then five hundred must be killed and stuffed, to feed the people who in one way or another did the killing and the stuffing.

The four feasts I have chosen to put here and now are not all taken from the tables of the mighty. There is the poignant ballad about the young Lord Randal, who ate eel soup with his true love and died from it. Then there are a few paragraphs from *The Bridal Wreath*, by Sigrid Undset. They tell how Kristin Lavransdatter ate her first meal in the convent, and they remind any person who can remember back into adolescence of the first painful echoing night in a new school, even though this was eight hundred years ago and not eighteen.

Next I have chosen a part of *The Cloister and the Hearth*, by Charles Reade, which is not about a feast at all but does tell all too vividly of the mixed blessings of supping at a medieval inn.

And last, there is one bit of nostalgic, high-blown prose from *Ivanhoe*, an echo from almost any reader's past, a flavor that was once pure excitement on the mind's palate.

Lord Randal, Anonymous, Middle Ages

"O where hae ye been, Lord Randal, my son?
O where hae ye been, my handsome young man?"
"I hae been to the wild wood; mother, make my bed soon,
For I'm weary wi' hunting, and fain wald lie down."

"Where gat ye your dinner, Lord Randal, my son?
Where gat ye your dinner, my handsome young man?"
"I din'd wi' my true-love; mother, make my bed soon,
For I'm weary wi' hunting, and fain wald lie down."

"What gat ye to your dinner, Lord Randal, my son?
What gat ye to your dinner, my handsome young man?"
"I gat eels boiled in broo; mother, make my bed soon,
For I'm weary wi' hunting, and fain wald lie down."

"What became of your bloodhounds, Lord Randal, my son?
What became of your bloodhounds, my handsome young man?"
"O they swell'd and they died; mother, make my bed soon,
For I'm weary wi' hunting, and fain wald lie down."

"O I fear ye are poison'd, Lord Randal, my son!
O I fear ye are poison'd, my handsome young man!"
"O yes! I am poison'd; mother, make my bed soon,
For I'm sick at the heart and I fain would lie down."

From *The Bridal Wreath* by Sigrid Undset, 1882–1949

The refectory was a great and fair room with a stone floor and pointed windows with glass panes. There was a doorway into another room, where, Kristin could see, there must be glass windows too, for the sun shone in.

The Sisters were already seated at the table waiting for their food— the elder nuns upon a cushioned stone-bench along the wall under the windows; the younger Sisters and the bareheaded maidens in light-hued wadmal dresses sat upon a wooden bench on the outer side of the board. In the next room a board was laid too; this was for the commoners and the lay-servants; there were a few old men amongst them. These folk did not wear the convent habit, but were none the less clad soberly in dark raiment.

Sister Potentia showed Kristin to a seat on the outer bench, but went and placed herself near to the Abbess's high-seat at the end of the board— the high-seat was empty to-day.

All rose, both in this room and in the side room, while the Sisters said grace. After that a fair, young nun went and stood at a lectern placed in the doorway between the two chambers. And while the lay-sisters in the greater room, and two of the youngest nuns in the side room, bore in food and drink, the nun read in a high and sweet voice, and without stopping or tripping at a single word, the story of St. Theodora and St. Didymus.

At first Kristin was thinking most of minding her table-manners, for she saw all the Sisters and the young maids bore them as seemly and ate as nicely as though they had been sitting at the finest feast. There was abundance of the best food and drink, but all helped themselves modestly, and dipped but the very tips of their fingers into the dishes; no one spilled the broth either upon the cloths or upon their garments, and all cut up the meat so small that they did not soil their mouths, and ate with so much care that not a sound was to be heard.

Kristin grew hot with fear that she might not seem as well-behaved as the others; she was feeling ill at ease, too, in her bright dress in the midst of all these women in black and white—she fancied that they were all looking at her. So when she had to eat a fat piece of breast of mutton, and was holding it by the bone with two fingers, while cutting morsels off with her right hand, and taking care to handle the knife lightly and neatly—suddenly the whole slipped from her fingers; her slice of bread and the meat flew onto the cloth, and the knife fell clattering on the stone flags.

The noise sounded fearfully in the quiet room. Kristin flushed red as fire and would have bent to pick up the knife, but a lay-sister came noiselessly in her sandals and gathered up the things.

But Kristin could eat no more. She found, too, that she had cut one of her fingers, and she was afraid of bleeding upon the cloth, so she sat with her hand wrapped in a corner of her skirt, and thought of how she was staining the goodly light-blue dress she had gotten for the journey to Oslo—and she did not dare to raise her eyes from her lap.

From *The Cloister and the Hearth* by Charles Reade, 1814–1884

That evening [Gerard] came to a small straggling town where was one inn. It had no sign; but being now better versed in the customs of the country he detected it at once by the coats of arms on its walls. These belonged to the distinguished visitors who had slept in it at different epochs since its foundation, and left these customary tokens of their patronage. At present it looked more like a mausoleum than a hotel. Nothing moved nor sounded either in it, or about it. Gerard hammered on the great oak door: no answer. He hallooed: no reply. After a while he hallooed louder, and at last a little round window, or rather hole in the wall, opened, a man's head protruded cautiously, like a tortoise's from its shell, and eyed Gerard stolidly, but never uttered a syllable.

"Is this an inn?" asked Gerard with a covert sneer.

The head seemed to fall into a brown study; eventually it nodded, but lazily.

"Can I have entertainment here?"

Again the head pondered and ended by nodding, but sullenly, and seemed a skull overburdened with catchpenny interrogatories.

"How am I to get within, an't please you?"

At this the head popped in, as if the last question had shot it; and a hand popped out, pointed round the corner of the building, and slammed the window.

Gerard followed the indication, and after some research discovered that the fortification had one vulnerable part, a small, low door on its flank. As for the main entrance, that was used to keep out thieves and customers, except once or twice in a year, when they entered together, i.e., when some duke or count arrived in pomp with his train of gaudy ruffians.

Gerard, having penetrated the outer fort, soon found his way to the stove (as the public room was called from the principal article in it), and sat down near the oven, in which were only a few live embers that diffused a mild and grateful heat.

After waiting patiently a long time, he asked a grim old fellow with a long white beard, who stalked solemnly in, and turned the hourglass and then was stalking out—when supper would be. The grisly Ganymede counted the guests on his fingers—"When I see thrice as many here as now." Gerard groaned.

The grisly tyrant resented the rebellious sound. "Inns are not built for one," said he; "if you can't wait for the rest, look out for another lodging."

Gerard sighed.

At this the greybeard frowned.

After a while company trickled steadily in, till full eighty persons of various conditions were congregated, and to our novice the place became a chamber of horrors; for here the mothers got together and compared ringworms, and the men scraped the mud off their shoes with their knives, and left it on the floor, and combed their long hair out, inmates included, and made their toilet, consisting generally of a dry rub. Water, however, was brought in ewers. Gerard pounced on one of these, but at sight of the liquid contents lost his temper and said to the waiter, "Wash you first your water, and then a man may wash his hands withal."

"An it likes you not, seek another inn!"

Gerard said nothing, but went quietly and courteously besought an old traveller to tell him how far it was to the next inn.

"About four leagues."

Then Gerard appreciated the grim pleasantry of th' unbending sire.

That worthy now returned with an armful of wood, and, counting the travellers, put on a log for every six, by which act of raw justice the hotter the room the more heat he added. Poor Gerard noticed this little flaw in the ancient man's logic, but carefully suppressed every symptom of intelligence, lest his feet should have to carry his brains four leagues farther that night.

When perspiration and suffocation were far advanced, they brought in the table-cloths; but oh, so brown, so dirty, and so coarse: they seemed like sacks that had been worn out in agriculture and come down to this, or like shreds from the mainsail of some worn-out ship. The Hollander, who had never seen such linen even in a nightmare, uttered a faint cry.

"What is to do?" inquired a traveller. Gerard pointed ruefully to the dirty sackcloth. The other looked at it with lack-lustre eye, and comprehended nought.

A Burgundian soldier with his arbalest at his back came peeping over Gerard's shoulder, and, seeing what was amiss, laughed so loud that the room rang again, then slapped him on the back and cried, "*Courage! le diable est mort.*"

Gerard stared: he doubted alike the good tidings and their relevancy: but the tones were so hearty and the arbalestrier's face, notwithstanding a formidable beard, was so gay and genial, that he smiled, and after a pause said drily, "*Il a bien fait: avec l'eau et linge du pays on allait le noircir à ne se reconnaître plus.*"

"*Tiens, tiens!*" cried the soldier, "*v'là qui parle le Français, peu s'en faut,*" and he seated himself by Gerard, and in a moment was talking volubly of war, women, and pillage, interlarding his discourse with curious oaths, at which Gerard drew away from him more or less.

Presently in came the grisly servant, and counted them all on his fingers superciliously, like Abraham telling sheep, then went out again and returned with a deal trencher and deal spoon to each.

Then there was an interval. Then he brought them a long mug apiece made of glass, and frowned. By and by he stalked gloomily in with a hunch of bread apiece, and exited with an injured air. Expectation thus raised, the guests sat for nearly an hour balancing the wooden spoons, and with their own knives whittling the bread. Eventually when hope was extinct, patience worn out, and hunger exhausted, a huge vessel was brought in with pomp, the lid was removed, a cloud of steam rolled forth, and behold some thin broth with square pieces of bread floating. This, though not agreeable to the mind, served to distend the body. Slices of Strasbourg ham followed, and pieces of salt fish, both so highly salted that Gerard could hardly swallow a mouthful. Then came a kind of gruel, and, when the repast had lasted an hour and more, some hashed meat highly peppered: and the French and Dutch being now full to the brim with the above dainties, and the draughts of beer the salt and spiced meats had provoked, in came roasted kids, most excellent, and carp and trout fresh from the stream. Gerard made an effort and looked angrily at them, but "could no more" as the poets say. The Burgundian swore, by the liver and pikestaff of the good centurion, the natives had outwitted him. Then turning to Gerard he said, "*Courage, l'ami, le diable est mort,*" as loudly as before, but not with the same tone of conviction. The canny natives had kept an internal corner for contingencies, and polished the kids' very bones.

The feast ended with a dish of raw animalcula in a wicker cage. A cheese had been surrounded with little twigs and strings; then a hole made in it and a little sour wine poured in. This speedily bred a small but numerous vermin. When the cheese was so rotten with them that only the twigs and string kept it from tumbling to pieces and walking off quadrivious, it came to table. By a malicious caprice of fate cage and menagerie were put down right under the Dutchman's organ of self-torture. He recoiled with a loud ejaculation, and hung to the bench by the calves of his legs.

"What is the matter?" said a traveller disdainfully. "Does the good cheese scare ye? Then put it hither, in the name of all the saints!"

"Cheese!" cried Gerard, "I see none. These nauseous reptiles have made away with every bit of it."

"Well," replied another, "it is not gone far. By eating of the mites we eat the cheese to boot."

"Nay, not so," said Gerard. "These reptiles are made like us, and digest their food and turn it to foul flesh even as we do ours to sweet: as well might you think to chew grass by eating of grass-fed beeves, as to eat cheese by swallowing these uncleanly insects."

Gerard raised his voice in uttering this, and the company received the paradox in dead silence, and with a distrustful air, like any other stranger, during which the Burgundian, who understood German but imperfectly, made Gerard Gallicise the discussion. He patted his interpreter on the back. "*C'est bien, mon gars: plus fin que toi n'est pas bête,*" and administered his formula of encouragement; and Gerard edged away from him; for next to ugly sights and ill odours the poor wretch disliked profaneness.

Meantime, though shaken in argument, the raw reptiles were duly eaten and relished by the company, and served to provoke thirst, a principal aim of all the solids in that part of Germany. So now the company drank "garausses" all around, and their tongues were unloosed, and oh the Babel! But above the fierce clamour rose at intervals, like some hero's war cry in battle, the trumpet-like voice of the Burgundian soldier shouting lustily, "*Courage, camarades, le diable est mort!*"

Entered grisly Ganymede holding in his hand a wooden dish with circles and semicircles marked on it in chalk. He put it down on the table and stood silent, sad, and sombre, as Charon by Styx waiting for his boat-load of souls. Then pouches and purses were rummaged, and each threw a coin into the dish. Gerard timidly observed that he had drunk next to no beer, and inquired how much less he was to pay than the others.

"What mean you?" said Ganymede roughly. "Whose fault is it you have not drunken? Are all to suffer because one chooses to be a milksop? You will pay no more than the rest and no less."

Gerard was abashed.

"*Courage, petit, le diable est mort,*" hiccoughed the soldier, and flung Ganymede a coin.

"You are as bad as he is," said the old man peevishly, "you are paying too much;" and the tyrannical old Aristides returned him some coin out of the trencher with a most reproachful countenance. And now the man whom Gerard had confuted an hour and a half ago awoke from a brown study, in which he had been ever since, and came to him and said, "*Yes:* but the honey is none the worse for passing through the bees' bellies."

Gerard stared. The answer had been so long on the road he hadn't an idea what it was an answer to. Seeing him dumbfoundered, the other concluded him confuted, and withdrew calmed.

From *Ivanhoe* by Sir Walter Scott, 1771–1832

Prince John held his high festival in the Castle of Ashby, ... and, seeking at present to dazzle men's eyes by his hospitality and magnificence, had given orders for great preparations, in order to render the banquet as splendid as possible.

The purveyors of the Prince, who exercised on this and other occasions the full authority of royalty, had swept the country of all that could be collected which was esteemed fit for their master's table. Guests also were invited in great numbers; and in the necessity in which he then found himself of courting popularity, Prince John had extended his invitation to a few distinguished Saxon and Danish families, as well as to the Norman nobility and gentry of the neighbourhood. However despised and degraded on ordinary occasions, the great numbers of the Anglo-Saxons must necessarily render them formidable in the civil commotions which seemed approaching, and it was an obvious point of policy to secure popularity with their leaders. . . .

. . . The guests were seated at a table which groaned under the quantity of good cheer. The numerous cooks who attended on the Prince's progress, having exerted all their art in varying the forms in which the ordinary provisions were served up, had succeeded almost as well as the modern professors of the culinary art in rendering them perfectly unlike their natural appearance. Besides these dishes of domestic origin, there were various delicacies brought from foreign parts, and a quantity of rich pastry, as well as of the simnel-bread and wastle cakes which were only used at the tables of the highest nobility. The banquet was crowned with the richest wines, both foreign and domestic.

But, though luxurious, the Norman nobles were not, generally speaking, an intemperate race. While indulging themselves in the pleasures of the table, they aimed at delicacy, but avoided excess, and were apt to attribute gluttony and drunkenness to the vanquished Saxons, as vices peculiar to their inferior station. Prince John, indeed, and those who courted his pleasure by imitating his foibles, were apt to indulge to excess in the pleasures of the trencher and the goblet; and indeed it is well known that his death was occasioned by a surfeit upon peaches and new ale. His conduct, however, was an exception to the general manners of his countrymen.

With sly gravity, interrupted only by private signs to each other, the Norman knights and nobles beheld the ruder demeanour of Athelstane and Cedric at a banquet to the form and fashion of which they were unaccustomed. And while their manners were thus the subject of sarcastic observation, the untaught Saxons unwittingly transgressed several of the arbitrary rules established for the regulation of society. Now it is well known that a man may with more impunity be guilty of an actual breach either of real good breeding or of good morals, than appear ignorant of the most minute point of fashionable etiquette. Thus Cedric, who dried his hands with a towel, instead of suffering the moisture to exhale by waving them gracefully in the air, incurred more ridicule than his companion Athelstane, when he swallowed to his own single share the whole of a large pasty composed of the most exquisite foreign delicacies, and termed at that time a *Karum-pie*. When, however, it was discovered, by a serious cross-examination, that the Thane of Coningsburgh (or Franklin, as the Normans termed him) had no idea what he had been devouring, and that he had taken the contents of the Karum-pie for larks and pigeons, whereas they were in fact beccaficoes and nightingales, his ignorance brought him in for an ample share of the ridicule which would have been more justly bestowed on his gluttony.

The long feast had at length its end; and, while the goblet circulated freely, men talked. . . .

VII

NOBLE AND ENOUGH

The Renaissance

Just as black night followed the perfumed twilight of the Roman Empire, that "period of insatiable veracity and the peacock's plume" so light was born after the Middle Ages, long dark and silent, slumbering.

The time now called the Renaissance, loosely located by historians between the fourteenth and sixteenth centuries, was one of such vital rebirth that its name is inevitable. It sprang like Gargantua from the loins of his mother Gargamelle, lustier and hungrier and fuller of excitement than possible. The accumulation of several hundred years of silent, almost secret thought in the dim cloisters of the Middle Ages burst suddenly into the light, and what men had been pondering on was there, formed, dazzling, ready for life.

All the arts flowered, and the sciences, and gastronomy was not the least of either of them. It more than most had survived the leanness of the past, mainly in order to keep monks fat; although strictures of their religion had imposed a thousand rules of fasting, for the good of their bodies if not their souls they had managed to evade them. Some of the greatest theological minds, it is safe to say, had lent themselves to studying the most artful ways of making red beef look like harmless turbot or salmon on the countless "meager" days, and the ingenious deceptions of the refectories did nothing to dull medieval brains.

By the time the warmth and richness of the Renaissance brightened the moderately holy convent kitchens, cookery was a mature art, ready to make the logical transition from priests' board to banquet-table. And the reverend fathers, tired of their cramped if well-fed lives, were more than ready to travel, wherever ships were going, to spread the word of God and sample a few exotic delicacies while their seamates looked for western gold or a new passage to India.

There was a great seething and restlessness everywhere. Everything that was good came to Italy and France and Spain, the center of the pot, like morsels in a soup-cauldron.

Potatoes and turkeys and crystallized sugar, as well as bullion, flowed back from the New World. Tea came from China. Explorers brought chocolate home from the fantastic palaces of Mexico. A hundred spices, hoarded like jewels by the returning Crusaders of the Middle Ages, became ordinary articles of trade with the sailors of the Renaissance.

And princesses married and moved to foreign countries, and they took the best and newest treasures with them, as when Catherine de' Medici went to France, armed with Italian sherbets and seeds of parsley. Either of these innovations has been counted more valuable than any of her diplomatic attributes by numberless gastronomers since she first marched into Paris with her bodyguard of cooks.

Chefs became as well known as the masters they served, so that their names were printed side by side on menus for the great dinners. The masters too grew impassioned about the arts of the kitchen, as a prerequisite to the pleasures of the table, and men like Richelieu and Soubise and Conti, as well as Louis XIV himself, bent knowingly over pots and casseroles in imitation of their cooks, while all the high-born ladies played at being milkmaids and scullions, sometimes most cannily.

Gastronomy became a prize subject for discussion, wittier than weighty, in the most intellectual salons of Europe, and the proper temperature of eggs for a mayonnaise a problem worthy of the period's greatest minds.

One of the gayest, liveliest records of Renaissance life is the rich collection called *The Decameron*, by Boccaccio. It is the story of how seven beautiful young ladies and three young men, handsome of course, fled the plague in Florence in 1348, and spent summer days eating and drinking and telling tales. They talked and talked and talked, and most of what they said is amusing in spite of the somewhat grimly moralistic tone that occasionally showed itself, in deference to the disease-ridden city they had escaped from. The fourth story in the book, for instance, is a good example of the robust, sensitive sunniness of the whole:

From *The Decameron* by Giovanni Boccaccio, 1313–1375

... Though ready wit and invention furnish people with words proper to their different occasions, yet sometimes does fortune, an assistant to the timorous, tip the tongue with a sudden, and yet a more pertinent, reply than the most mature deliberation could ever have suggested, as I shall now briefly relate to you.

Currado Gianfiliazzi, as most of you have both known and seen, was always esteemed a gallant and worthy citizen, delighting much in hounds and hawks, not to mention his other excellences, as no way relating to our present purpose. Having taken a crane one day with his hawk, and finding it to be young and fat, he sent it home to his cook, Chichibio, who was a Venetian, with orders to prepare it for supper. The cook, a poor simple fellow, trussed and spitted it, and when it was nearly roasted, and began to smell pretty well, it chanced that a woman of the neighbourhood, called Brunetta, with whom he was much enamoured, came into the kitchen, and, being taken with the high savour, earnestly begged of him to give her a leg. He replied very merrily, singing all the time, "Madam Brunetta, you shall have no leg from me." Nettled at this, she retorted, "As I hope to live, if you do not give it me, you need never expect any favour more from me." The dispute was carried to a great height between them, and to quiet her, at last, he was forced to give her one of the legs. Accordingly the crane was served up at supper, with only one leg, Currado having a friend along with him. Currado wondered at this, and, sending for the cook, demanded what was become of the other leg. He very foolishly replied, and without the least thought, "Cranes have only one leg, sir."—"What the devil does the man talk of?" cried Currado, in great wrath. "Only one leg! Rascal, dost think I never saw a crane before?" Chichibio still persisted in his denial. "Believe me, sir, it is as I say, and I will prove it to you whenever you please, upon living cranes."—"Well," said Currado, who did not choose to have any more words then out of regard to his friend, "as thou undertakest to show me a thing which I never saw or heard of before, I am content to make proof thereof tomorrow morning; but by all the saints, if I find it otherwise, I will make thee remember it the longest day thou hast to live."

There was an end to the matter for that night, and the next morning Currado, whose passion would scarcely suffer him to get any rest, rose betimes, ordered his horses, and took Chichibio along with him towards a river, where he used early in the morning to see plenty of cranes. "We shall soon see," said he, "whether you spoke truth or not, last night." Chichibio, finding his master's wrath not at all abated, and that he was now to make good his random words, rode on first with all the fear imaginable: gladly would he have made his escape, but he saw no possible means: and he was continually looking about him, expecting everything that appeared to be a crane with two legs. But being come near to the river, he chanced to see before anybody else, a number of cranes, each standing upon one leg, as they are used to do when they are sleeping; whereupon, showing them quickly to his master, he said, "Now, sir, yourself may see that I spoke nothing but truth, when I said that cranes have only one leg: look at those yonder, if you please." Currado, beholding the cranes, replied, "Yes, sirrah! but stay awhile, and I will show thee that they have two." Then, riding up to them, he cried out, "Shough! shough!" which made them set down the other foot, and after taking a step or two, they all flew away. Currado then turned to him, and said, "Well, thou lying knave, art thou now convinced that they have two legs?" Chichibio, quite at his wit's end, and scarcely knowing whether he was on his head or his heels, suddenly made answer, "Yes, sir; but you did not shout out 'Shough! shough!' to that crane last night, as you have done to these; if you had, it would have put down the other leg, as these did now." This pleased Currado so much, that, turning all wrath into mirth and laughter, he said, "Chichibio, thou sayest right, I should have done so indeed." By this sudden and comical answer, Chichibio escaped a sound drubbing, and made peace with his master.

It took a long time for the subtleties of Renaissance life to affect the stalwart British. It is true, however, that during the fifteenth century there was an increasing love of order in the rules of behavior in upper-class homes, so that cookbooks and pamphlets on good manners were popular among the young ladies of the nobility, and even the gentlemen heeded some of the newly discovered tenets.

Discipline in the management of a great house was strict, so that it is hard not to question how the poorly educated women of that period could cope with the intricacies of domestic protocol, and hard not to admire them for doing it at all, against great odds.

The sumptuary laws became much sterner in proportion to such interior order, too, and there were severe regulations about fasting and ordinary feasting, according to the age and rank of each inhabitant. Entertaining, however, which escaped all bans, was more lavish than ever, perhaps because of the limitations placed on ordinary nourishment, so that such traditional banquet-plates as the Christmas boar's head assumed an almost legendary importance.

Furnishings were still very simple, even in the greatest castles, but pewter was beginning to take the place of wood for plates and trenchers. The Carver was still chief figure at any large meal, since he must prepare the meats to be eaten with fingers: forks, called fursifers, were not to appear in England from Italy until the end of the seventeenth century.

Anthony Cooper, first Earl of Shaftesbury, who lived between 1621 and 1683, wrote a good round description of an English country gentleman. Although Cooper describes him as a throwback to Renaissance times in England, the fact that he could find him still in the flesh in his own day may suggest the slowness with which the British accepted the refinements long since considered essential to noble European living:

From *Texts and Pretexts*, edited by Aldous Huxley, 1894–1963

Mr. Hastings was an original in our age, or rather the copy of our nobility in ancient days, in hunting and not warlike times. He was low, very strong, and very active, of a reddish flaxen hair, his clothes always green cloth, and never all worth when new five pounds. His house was perfectly of the old fashion, in the midst of a large park well stocked with deer, and near the house rabbits to serve his kitchen, many fish-ponds, and great store of wood and timber; a bowling green in it, long but narrow, full of high ridges, it being never levelled since it was ploughed; they used round sand balls and it had a banqueting-house like a stand, a large one built in a tree. He kept all manner of sport-hounds that ran buck, fox, hare, otter, and badger, and hawks long and short winged; he had a walk in the New Forest and the manor of Christ Church. This last supplied him with red deer, sea and river fish; and indeed all his neighbours' grounds and royalties were open to him, who bestowed all his time in such sports, but what he borrowed to caress his neighbours' wives and daughters, there being not a woman in all his walks of the degree of a yeoman's wife or under, and under the age of forty, but it was extremely her fault if he were not intimately acquainted with her. This made him very popular, always speaking kindly to the husband, brother, or father, who was to boot very welcome to his house whenever he came; there he found beef pudding and small beer in great plenty, a house not so neatly kept as to shame him and his dirty shoes, the great hall strewed with marrow bones, full of hawks' perches, hounds, spaniels, and terriers, the upper sides of the hall hung with the fox-skins of this and the last year's skinning, here and there a polecat intermixed, guns and keepers' and huntsmen's poles in abundance. The parlour was a large long room as properly furnished; in a great hearth paved with brick lay some terriers and the choicest hounds and spaniels; seldom but two of the great chairs had litters of young cats in them which were not to be disturbed, he having always three or four attending him at dinner, and a little white round stick of fourteen inches long lying by his trencher that he might defend such meat as he had no mind to part with to them. The windows, which were very large, served for places to lay his arrows, cross-bows, stonebows, and other such like accoutrements; the corners of the room full of the best chose hunting and hawking poles; an oyster table at the lower end, which was of constant use twice a day all the year round, for he never failed to eat oysters before dinner and supper through all seasons; the neighboring town of Poole supplied him with them. The upper part of this room had two small tables and a desk, on the one side of which was a church Bible, on the other the *Book of Martyrs*; on the tables were hawks' hoods, bells, and such like, two or three old green hats with their crowns thrust in so as to hold ten or a dozen eggs, which were of a peasant kind of poultry he took much care of and fed himself; tables, dice, cards and boxes were not wanting. In the hole of the desk were store of tobacco pipes that had been used. On one side of this end of the room was the door of a closet, wherein stood the strong beer and the wine, which never came thence but in single glasses, that being the rule of the house exactly observed, for he never exceeded in drink or permitted it. On the other side was a door into an old chapel, not used for devotion; the pulpit, as the safest place, was never wanting of a cold chine of beef, pasty of venison, gammon of bacon, or great apple pie with thick crust extremely baked. His table cost him not much, though it was very good to eat at, his sports supplying all but beef and mutton, except Friday, when he had the best sea fish he could get, and was the day that his neighbours of best quality most visited him. He never wanted a London pudding, and always sung it in with "my part lies therein-a." He drank a glass of wine or two at meals, very often syrup of gilliflower in his sack, and had always a tun glass without feet stood by him holding a pint of small beer, which he often stirred with a great sprig of rosemary. He was well-natured, but soon angry, calling his servants bastard and cuckoldy knaves, in one of which he often spoke the truth to his own knowledge, and sometimes in both, though of the same man. He lived to a hundred, never lost his eyesight, but always writ and read without spectacles, and got to horse without help. Until past fourscore he rode to the death of a stag as well as any.

Londoners, always conscious of their stomachs, fared well enough if they had the necessary coins, and there were many little cook shops called "ordinaries" where for three pence and on up to twelve pence clerks and lawyers and merchants could eat a worthy equivalent of the modern cut-of the-joint-and-two-veg. And everywhere were public kitchens where good cooks, some of them refugees from foreign turmoil, turned out handsome pies and roasts and even such Parisian flim flammeries as little cakes coated with gold dust and artfully flavored with spices warranted to increase the already rampant Elizabethan vigor.

(Aphrodisiacs were much used in those days, and books of recipes for them sold everywhere. On the Continent a hundred such obvious ingredients as dried goat-testicles, bat's blood, and the hearts and tongues of vipers were most popular, but in England the prized remedy for real or imagined sexual fatigue was a simple mixture of sugar and powdered root of sea-holly called, aptly enough, "kissing comfits.")

Pamphlets dealing with all aspects of mass gastronomy were sold in the streets of London as fast as they could be printed: a good indication of the hungry interest people felt in their own hunger! One such, by "John Taylor, London, Printed by Anne Griffin, 1637" is typical of most of them. The title page, elaborately balanced in a dozen different types, says:

> Drinke and welcome: or the Famous Historie of the most part of Drinks,
> in use now in the Kingdomes of Great Brittaine and Ireland; with an
> especial declaration of the potency, vertue, and operation of our English
> Ale With a description of all sorts of Waters, from the Ocean sea, to the
> Teares of a Woman.

I cannot resist adding parts of one discussion from it, on Pomperkin: it was "the sixt sorte of Brittish drinkes . . . made of Apples . . . bruised and beaten to mash, with water put to them, which is a drinke of so weake a condition that it is no where acceptable but amongst the Rustickes and Plebeyans, being a heartlesse liquor much of the nature of Swillons in Scotland, or small Beere in England, such as is said to be made of the washings of the Brewers legges and aprons. . . ."

Another pamphlet I like very much, "By J. Marriott, of Grays-Inn, Gent.," was printed in London in 1652, and is a fair indication of the occasional bothers suffered by Elizabethan trenchermen.

On the first page is an engraving of an enormously fat "gent.," with a balloon floating from his blubbery lips saying

> Behold the Wonder of this Age.
> If thou observ'st these Rules, and Tak'st my Physick,
> 'Twill keep thee from the Pox, Plague, Cough, or Tysick,
> Consumptions, Dropsies; nay, the truth to tell ye,
> From all griefes either i' th' head, back, or belly.

The title page goes on:

> The English Mountebank: Or, a Physical Dispensatory, Wherein is prescribed, Many Strange and excellent Receits of Mr. MARRIOTT, the great Eater of Grays-Inn: With the manner how he makes his Cordial Broaths, Pills, Purgations, Julips, and Vomits, to keep his Body in temper, and free from SURFEITS. With Sundry directions,
>
> 1. How to make his Cordial Broath.
> 2. His Pills to appease Hunger.

3. His strange Purgations, never before practiced by any Doctor in England.

4. The manner and reason, why he swalows Bullets & Stones.

5. How he orders his baked meat, or rare Dish on Sunday.

6. How to make his new fasshion Fish-broth.

7. How to make his Sallet, for cooling of the Bloud.

8. How to make his new Dish, called a Frigazee: the operation whereof, expels all Sadness and melancholy.

While city mice lived thusly, beset by "grumbling in the Guts, or a wambling Stomack" as well as the pleasures antecedent to them, country mice in their cottages fared more simply on such suppers as milk and hot crabapples, which must have tasted fine indeed on a night when little birds brooded in the snow:

From *Love's Labour's Lost* by William Shakespeare, 1564–1616

When icicles hang by the wall,
　And Dick the shepherd blows his nail,
And Tom bears logs into the hall,
　And milk comes frozen home in pail,
When blood is nipp'd, and ways be foul,
Then nightly sings the staring owl:
　　　"Tu-who!
Tu-whit, tu-who!" a merry note,
While greasy Joan doth keel the pot.

When all aloud the wind doth blow,
　And coughing drowns the parson's saw,
And birds sit brooding in the snow,
　And Marian's nose looks red and raw;
When roasted crabs hiss in the bowl,
Then nightly sings the staring owl:
　　　"Tu-who!
Tu-whit, tu-who!" a merry note,
While greasy Joan doth keel the pot.

In the palaces, though, things grew stuffier with every reign. Henry VIII, finally, indulged his passion for masquerades and postprandial frolicking to such a degree that by Elizabeth's time his comparatively childish pageants of costumed and disguised courtiers had become a deadly routine of elaborate classical allusions and pedantic affectations.

In any country-house thrown open to the Queen on her frequent jaunts through England the servants were of necessity re-christened before her arrival, so that a messenger boy could answer to the name of Mercury, and the maids set to carrying pitchers-and-bowls would be called all the words applied to water nymphs by the ancients. The royal cooks learned to make confections inspired by Ovid's *Metamorphoses*, and thought nothing of decorating their banquet-cakes with sugared bas-reliefs of the Fall of Troy.

All this silliness was a part of the solemn and wasteful pomp expected by the Queen, but it is comforting to know that occasionally there were breaks for completely rowdy bear-baiting and "dawncing," which she enjoyed with the best of her subjects.

It is better, I think, to go down to the cottages, where "There's pippins and cheeses to come," or back to the ordinaries and the taverns of London.

> (Ah, Ben!
> Say how, or when
> Shall we thy guests
> Meet at those Lyric Feasts,
> Made at the Sun,
> The Dog, the Triple Tun?
> Where we such clusters had
> As made us nobly wild, not mad;
> And yet each Verse of thine
> Out-did the meat, out-did the frolic wine!)*

The best companion anyone could find for pub-crawling, at least as it was done in the seventeenth century, would to my mind be Samuel Pepys. He it was who on April 17, in 1661, went with three friends to The Dolphin, where they "did eat a barrel of oysters and two lobsters, which I did give them, and

---

* Robert Herrick, *An Ode for Ben Jonson.*

were very merry" . . . and probably did drink much more than Pepys had sworn to, after his last troubled head.

At the end of that year, on December 30, he gave a party at the Mitre, "whither I had invited all my old acquaintance of the Exchequer to a good chine of beef, which with three barrels of oysters and three pullets, and plenty of wine and mirth, was our dinner, and there was about twelve of us. I made them a foolish promise to give them one this day twelve-month, and so forever while I live; but I do not intend it." (A fine New Year's resolution, indeed!)

The amount of food prepared for a little dinner by Mrs. Pepys is staggering to anyone accustomed as we are now to offering our guests two or at most four simple courses: for fourteen people, as an example, she got ready "a dish of marrow bones; a leg of mutton; a loin of veal; a dish of fowl, three pullets, and two dozen larks all in a dish; a great tart, a neat's tongue, a dish of anchovies; a dish of prawns and cheese"!

Another time, in 1663, Pepys writes: "My poor wife rose by five in the morning, before day, and went to market and bought fowls and many other things for dinner, with which I was highly pleased; and the chine of beef was done also before six o'clock, and my own jack, of which I was doubtful, do carry it very well. Things being put in order, and the cook come, I went to the office. . . ."

At noon he returned home to meet his six guests: "I had for them, after oysters, as first course a hash of rabbits, a lamb, and a rare chine of beef. Next a great dish of roasted fowl, cost me about 30s., and a tart; and then fruit and cheese. My dinner was noble and enough. I had my house mighty clean and neat; my room below with a good fire in it; my dining room above, and my chamber being made a withdrawing chamber; and my wife's a good fire also. I find my new table very proper, and will hold nine or ten people well, but eight with great room."

The guests left at ten that night, "very merry at, before, and after dinner," having played cards and then been sustained by a late supper of cold meat and a good sack posset . . . "both them and myself highly pleased with our management of this day; I believe (it) will cost me near five pounds."

Not all of Pepys's meals were as fine as this. He hated untidiness, and food that was not decently fresh ("a damned venison pasty that stunk like the devil . . . Lord! so sorry a dinner, venison baked in pans . . . a damned bad dinner which did not please us at all"), but he recognized like a true gourmet the blessings of simplicity, as when, on March 25, 1669, on board *The Charles* off Chatham, "the Boatswain of the ship did bring us out of the kettle, a piece of hot salt beef and some brown bread and brandy; and there we did make a little meal, but so good as I would never desire to eat better meat while I live, only I would have cleaner plates."

One of Mr. Pepys's friends, and a charming one, was John Evelyn, who wrote about a slightly different type of banqueting, and with less intimacy but no less grace than his colleague.

He was one of the real "gentlemen" of his period, the kind that flowers rarely but deathlessly in the hothouse of British diplomacy, and he lived easily with kings and priests and common men. His learning was quiet but impressive, and he owned the voracious curiosity of a true scientist, which could make some fantastic experiment at the Royal Society more interesting to him than an ambassadorial feast, as he described in his *Diary* on April 12, in 1682:

From the *Diary* of John Evelyn, 1620–1706

I went this afternoon with several of the Royal Society to a supper which was all dressed, both fish and flesh, in Monsieur Papin's digestors, by which the hardest bones of beef itself, and mutton, were made as soft as cheese, without water or other liquor, and with less than eight ounces of coals, producing an incredible quantity of gravy; and for close of all, a jelly made of the bones of beef, the best for clearness and good relish, and the most delicious that I had ever seen, or tasted. We eat pike and other fish bones, and all without impediment; but nothing exceeded the pigeons, which tasted just as if baked in a pie, all these being stewed in their own juice, without any addition of water save what swam about the digestor, as *in balneo*; the natural juice of all these provisions acting on the grosser substances, reduced the hardest bones to tenderness; but it is best descanted, with more particulars for extracting tinctures, preserving and stewing fruit, and saving fuel, in Dr. Papin's book published and dedicated to our Society, of which he is a member. He is since gone to Venice with the late Resident here (and also a member of our Society), who carried this excellent mechanic, philosopher, and physician, to set up a philosophical meeting in that city. This philosophical supper caused much mirth amongst us, and exceedingly pleased all the company. I sent a glass of the jelly to my wife, to the reproach of all that the ladies ever made of their best hartshorn.

John Evelyn's palate was as fastidious and exploratory as his mind, so that he quite naturally gave serious consideration to tasting a new fruit; it occupied a relative importance in his life-plan with a diplomatic visit to the king, a new greenhouse for his rare saplings, or the publication of his book *The Perfection of Painting*. In 1668 he noted in his journal:

From the *Diary* of John Evelyn, 1620–1706

I saw the magnificent entry of the French Ambassador Colbert, received in the Banqueting House. I had never seen a richer coach than that which he came in to Whitehall. Standing by his Majesty at dinner in the presence, there was of that rare fruit called the King-pine, growing in Barbadoes and the West Indies; the first of them I had ever seen. His Majesty having cut it up, was pleased to give me a piece off his own plate to taste of; but, in my opinion, it falls short of those ravishing varieties of deliciousness described in Captain Ligon's History, and others; but possibly it might be, or certainly was, much impaired in coming so far; it has yet a grateful acidity, but tastes more like the quince and melon than of any other fruit he mentions.

So much of Evelyn's time was taken up in his rich political career with what was, perhaps rightly, considered the highest society of his day (he knew Charles II and James II well, and their ministers, and was visited by every eminent foreigner in England during his long life) that it seems fitting to quote what he said about one of the countless "great entertainments" he attended. It is hard to see how he managed to do and be so much, but he was typical of the whole Renaissance, vital and eager and full of a kind of spiritual elation at being free from the dark chains of ignorance of the Middle Ages.

On December 18, then, in 1685:

From the *Diary* of John Evelyn, 1620–1706

I dined at the great entertainment his Majesty gave the Venetian Ambassadors, Signors Zenno and Justiniani, accompanied with ten more noble Venetians of their most illustrious families, Cornaro, Maccenigo, &c., who came to congratulate their Majesties coming to the Crown. The dinner was most magnificent and plentiful, at four tables, with music, kettle-drums, and trumpets, which sounded upon a whistle at every health. The banquet [dessert] was twelve vast chargers piled up so high that those who sat one against another could hardly see each other. Of these sweetmeats, which doubtless were some days piling up in that exquisite manner, the Ambassadors touched not, but leaving them to the spectators who came out of curiosity to see the dinner, were exceedingly pleased to see in what a moment of time all that curious work was demolished, the comfitures voided, and the tables cleared. Thus his Majesty entertained them three days, which (for the table only) cost him £600, as the Clerk of the Green Cloth (Sir William Boreman) assured me. Dinner ended, I saw their procession, or cavalcade, to Whitehall, innumerable coaches attending. The two Ambassadors had four coaches of their own, and fifty footmen (as I remember), besides other equipage as splendid as the occasion would permit, the Court being still in mourning. Thence, I went to the audience which they had in the Queen's presence-chamber, the Banqueting House being full of goods and furniture till the galleries on the garden-side, council-chamber, and new chapel, now in building, were finished. They went to their audience in those plain black gowns and caps which they constantly wear in the city of Venice. I was invited to have accompanied the two Ambassadors in their coach to supper that night, returning now to their own lodgings, as no longer at the King's expense; but, being weary, I excused myself.

At about the same time (and what difference can a few years make now to all those well-fed ghosts, or even to us?), there took place in a village in Norfolk a merry festival, one long planned for and nobly prepared, which I must quote here for two reasons: its apt juxtaposition to the Venetian trappings in London and all such elegance, and its poignant last line.

A Bill of Ffare at the Christning of Mr. Constable's Child, Rector of Cockley Cley in Norfolk, Jan. 2, 1682, Anonymous

1. A whole hog's head, souc'd with carrotts in the mouth and pendants in the ears, with guilded oranges thick sett.
2. 2 ox.'s cheekes stewed, with 6 marrow bones.
3. A leg of veal larded, with 6 pullets.
4. A leg of mutton, with 6 rabbits.

5. A chine of bief, a chine of venison, chine of mutton, chine of veal, chine of pork, supported by 4 men.
6. A venison pasty.
7. A great minced pye, with 12 small ones about it.
8. A gelt fat turkey, with 6 capons.
9. A bustard, with 6 pluver.
10. A pheasant, with 6 woodcocks.
11. A great dish of tarts made all of sweetmeats.
12. A Westphalia hamm, with 6 tongues.
13. A jowle of sturgeon.
14. A great chargr of all sorts of sweetmeats, with wine and all sorts of liquors answerable.

The child, a girle; godfather, Mr. Green, a clergyman; godmothers, Mis Beddingfield of Sherson, and a sister-in-law of Mr. Constable's.

The guests, Mr. Green, Mr. Bagg and his daughter, and the godmothers.

The parishrs entertained at another house with rost and boil'd bief, geese, and turkeys. Soon after the child dy'd, and the funerall expences came to 6d.

The death of Mr. Constable's suckling makes me think, but with increased somberness, of another death, this time before the feast began instead of soon after. It was poor Vatel, chef to the Prince de Condé, who on April 11, 1671, stabbed himself until he died.

The popular and very sketchy rumor that he died from shame because his turbot did not arrive in time for the King's banquet is only partly true: he was a victim, if ever there was one, of the senseless extravagance and ostentation that has always seemed an inevitable part of a royal visit, in any land or epoch.

This time it was a long-heralded descent upon Chantilly of the King of France and his retinue of hunters and their ladies. Condé had but lately re-occupied the run-down old country estate, rented to careless tenants, and it fell upon his cherished steward Vatel to put the whole place in order in an almost impossibly short time. He had carpenters and drapers and repair-men from all that part of France, and meanwhile was training an enormous staff of bumpkins to do the countless menial tasks of keeping such an establishment operating, while he rehearsed the Prince's regular servants in their unaccustomed duties.

The entire plan for all the meals for every soul in Chantilly, from the King to the lowest scullion, was also a part of Vatel's Herculean job.

He had always been insomniac, and perhaps this was accentuated by his first love, which pounced upon him after almost forty celibate and serious years, for a lady-in-waiting in the château. Whatever the causes, the harried man went sleepless for twelve nights, so that by the time the King's party arrived his head was turning, and he begged Gourville, the Prince's friend and assistant, to help him.

Gourville reassured him as best he could, but it was evident that this peak of Vatel's whole studious and ambitious life was ill-fated: his eyes were like red coals, and he trembled in a fever that did not cease.

The first fabulously elaborate luncheon for the royal party went off smoothly, to all except poor Vatel, who saw that one or two tables lacked enough roasted meat. The Prince de Condé himself reassured his good friend, but Vatel would not be consoled even by the obvious reminder that twice as many guests had come as had been invited or prepared for.

That night he prowled the halls . . .

But Madame de Sévigné, in a letter to her confidante Madame de Grignan, tells it best. All I must add is that the poor distracted cook's body was hustled out of the château at dawn, still warm, and propped up to look as if he were merely drunk, and was buried in a suicide's grave most secretly, so that the gay hunting-party would not be too much disturbed at the thought of missing one of his famous sauces or ingenious confections of cream and spun sugar.

From the *Letters* of Madame de Sévigné, 1626–1696
Paris, Sunday, April 26th, 1671

I have just learned from Moreuil of what passed at Chantilly with regard to poor Vatel. I wrote to you last Friday, that he had stabbed himself; these are the particulars of the affair. The King arrived there on Thursday night; the walk, and the collation, which was served in a place set apart for the purpose, and strewed with jonquils, were just as they should be. Supper was served, but there was no roast meat at one or two of the tables, on account of Vatel's having been obliged to provide several dinners more than were expected. This affected his spirits, and he was heard to say several times, "I have lost my fame! I cannot bear this disgrace!" "My head is quite bewildered," he said to Gourville. "I have not had a wink of sleep these twelve nights, I wish you would assist me in giving orders." Gourville did all he could to comfort and assist him; but the failure of the roast meat (which, however, did not happen at the King's table, but at some of the other twenty-five) was always uppermost with him. Gourville mentioned it to the Prince, who went directly to Vatel's apartment, and said to him, "Everything is extremely well conducted, Vatel; nothing could be more admirable than His Majesty's supper." "Your highness's goodness," replied he, "overwhelms me; I am sensible that there was a deficiency of roast meat at two tables." "Not at all," said the Prince. "Do not perplex yourself, and all will go well." Midnight came: the fireworks did not succeed, they were covered with a thick cloud; they cost sixteen thousand francs. At four o'clock in the morning, Vatel went round, and found everybody asleep; he met one of the under-purveyors, who had just come in with only two loads of fish. "What!" said he. "Is this all?" "Yes, Sir," said the man, not knowing that Vatel had dispatched other people to all the seaports round. Vatel waited for some time, the other purveyors did not arrive; his head grew distracted; he thought that there was no more fish to be had; he flew to Gourville. "Sir," said he, "I cannot outlive this disgrace." Gourville laughed at him; Vatel, however, went to his apartment, and setting the hilt of his sword against the door, after two ineffectual attempts, succeeded in the third, in forcing the sword through his heart. At that instant the carriers arrived with the fish; Vatel was inquired after to distribute it; they ran to his apartment, knocked at the door, but received no answer; upon which they broke it open, and found him weltering in his blood. A messenger was immediately dispatched to acquaint the Prince with what had happened, who was like a man in despair. The Duke wept, for his journey to Burgundy depended upon Vatel. The Prince related the whole affair to His Majesty, with an expression of great concern: it was considered as the consequence of too nice a sense of honor; some blamed, others praised him for his sense of courage. The King said he had put off this excursion for more than five years, because he was aware that it would be attended with infinite trouble, and told the Prince that he ought to have had but two tables, and not have been at the expense of so many, and declared that he would never suffer him to do so again; but all this was too late for poor Vatel. However, Gourville endeavored to supply the loss of Vatel; which he did in great measure.

VIII

VANITY FAIR

Eighteenth- and Nineteenth-Century England

Two things that are especially memorable about the eighteenth century in England, both of them concerned with spirits: its letter writers were perhaps the wittiest and most urbane the world has yet seen, and its citizens, from the princeliest to the most miserable, were confirmed and bottomless drunkards.

It is true that the upper-class topers moved in what has since been idealized into a delicate ballet of suppers, balls, musical soirées, and endless brilliant conversations, where all the drawing rooms were filled with exquisitely epigrammatical mistresses of incredibly gallant and aristocratic diplomats. Certainly the letters of brittle gossip that flowed from the pens of practically every literate person above the rank of baronet in those chatty days would prove the point . . . if it were not for such a scathing comment as Thackeray made, a hundred or so years later, in his essay on Steele:

From *The English Humourists of the Eighteenth Century* by William Makepeace Thackeray, 1811–1863
There exists a curious document descriptive of the manners of the last age, which describes most minutely the amusements and occupations of persons of fashion in London at the time of which we are speaking; the time of Swift, and Addison, and Steele.

When Lord Sparkish, Tom Neverout, and Colonel Alwit, the immortal personages of Swift's polite conversation, came to breakfast with my Lady Smart, at eleven o'clock in the morning, my Lord Smart was absent at the levee. His lordship was at home to dinner at three o'clock to receive his guests; and we may sit down to this meal, like the Barmecide's, and see the fops of the last century before us. Seven of them sat down at dinner, and were joined by a country baronet who told them they kept Court hours. These persons of fashion began their dinner with a sirloin of beef, fish, a shoulder of veal, and a tongue. My Lady Smart carved the sirloin, my Lady Answerall helped the fish, and the gallant Colonel cut the shoulder of veal. All made a considerable inroad on the sirloin and the shoulder of veal with the exception of Sir John, who had no appetite, having already partaken of a beefsteak and two mugs of ale, besides a tankard of March beer as soon as he got out of bed. They drank claret, which the master of the house said should always be drunk after fish; and my Lord Smart particularly recommended some excellent cider to my Lord Sparkish, which occasioned some brilliant remarks from that nobleman. When the host called for wine, he nodded to one or other of his guests, and said, "Tom Neverout, my service to you."

After the first course came almond-pudding, fritters, which the Colonel took with his hands out of the dish, in order to help the brilliant Miss Notable; chickens, black puddings, and soup; and Lady Smart, the elegant mistress of the mansion, finding a skewer in a dish, placed it in her plate with directions that it should be carried down to the cook and dressed for the cook's own dinner. Wine and small beer were drunk during the second course; and when the Colonel called for beer, he called the butler Friend, and asked whether the beer was good. Various jocular remarks passed from the gentlefolks to the servants; at breakfast several persons had a word and a joke for Mrs. Betty, my lady's maid, who warmed the cream and had charge of the canister (the tea cost thirty shillings a pound in those days). When my Lady Sparkish sent her footman out to my Lady Match to come at six o'clock and play at quadrille, her ladyship warned the man to follow his nose, and if he fell by the way not to stay to get up again. And when the gentleman asked the hall-porter if his lady was at home, that functionary replied, with manly waggishness, "She was at home just now, but she's not gone out yet."

After the puddings, sweet and black, the fritters, and soup, came the third course, of which the chief dish was a hot venison pasty, which was put before Lord Smart, and carved by that nobleman. Besides the pasty there was a hare, a rabbit, some pigeons, partridges, a goose, and a ham. Beer and wine were freely imbibed during this course, the gentlemen always pledging somebody with every glass which they drank; and by this time the conversation between Tom Neverout and Miss Notable had grown so brisk and lively, that the Derbyshire baronet began to think the young gentlewoman was Tom's sweetheart: on which Miss remarked, that she loved Tom "like pie." After the goose, some of the gentlemen took a dram of brandy, "which was very good for the wholesomes," Sir John said; and now having had a tolerably substantial dinner, honest Lord Smart bade the butler bring up the great tankard full of October to Sir John. The great tankard was passed from hand to hand and mouth to mouth, but when pressed by the noble host upon the gallant Tom Neverout, he said, "No, faith, my lord; I like your wine, and won't put a churl upon a gentleman. Your honour's claret is good enough for me." And so, the dinner over, the host said, "Hang saving, bring us up a ha'porth of cheese."

The cloth was now taken away, and a bottle of burgundy was set down, of which the ladies were invited to partake before they went to their tea. When they withdrew, the gentlemen promised to join them in an hour: fresh bottles were brought; the "dead men," meaning the empty bottles, removed; and "D'you hear, John! bring clean glasses," my Lord Smart said. On which the gallant Colonel Alwit said, "I'll keep my glass; for wine is the best liquor to wash glasses in."

After an hour the gentlemen joined the ladies, and then they all sat and played quadrille until three o'clock in the morning, when the chairs and the flambeaux came, and this noble company went to bed.

Such were manners six or seven score years ago. I draw no inference from this queer picture—let all moralists here present deduce their own. Fancy the moral condition of that society in which a lady of fashion joked with a footman, and carved a sirloin, and provided besides a great shoulder of veal, a goose, hare, rabbit, chickens, partridges, black puddings, and a ham for a dinner for eight Christians. What—what could have been the condition of that polite world in which people openly ate goose after almond-pudding, and took their soup in the middle of dinner? Fancy a

Colonel in the Guards putting his hand into a dish of *beignets d'abricot* and helping his neighbour, a young lady *du monde*! Fancy a noble lord calling out to the servants, before the ladies at his table, "Hang expense, bring us a ha'porth of cheese!" Such were the ladies of St. James's—such were the frequenters of "White's Chocolate-House," when Swift used to visit it, and Steele described it as the centre of pleasure, gallantry, and entertainment, a hundred and forty years ago!

Perhaps this basic coarseness in the behavior of their period forced such people as Lady Mary Wortley Montagu and Horace Walpole and a hundred more to escape to other lands, willy-nilly, or bury themselves in an abyss of politics and intrigue at home.

Whatever the cause, the result was good, and the correspondence that has been preserved from those sharp-tongued intelligent snobs of two centuries ago is one of the great delights, a leaven in the mighty dough of literature.

The one letter from Lady Mary that I have chosen to print is at best a tantalizing snippet from her fat correspondence, but a good sample, I think, of the astounding woman's energy and hungry curiosity about life.

The thought of giving birth to a child in Constantinople in 1718 is disturbing enough, in spite of Lady Mary's calm statement that the Turks were much more progressive about such things than the English; and her little jaunt to interview the Sultana a month later is downright exhausting to look back on. And then her sharp, sharp eyes!

How could she manage, in her short visit, to count each diamond in the fastenings of pearls around the royal *talpoche*? How did she know that there were two hundred emeralds in each of the three necklaces, emeralds "close joined together, of the most lively green, perfectly matched, every one as large as a half-crown piece, and as thick as three crown pieces"?

And the fifty dishes of meat, each served separately! And every detail of the service itself: what was in china, what in silver, what in gold!

Lady Mary must have had the mind of a tabulating machine ... and the unmitigated gall of a Hollywood society-columnist, unafraid of impudence in any of her questionings about the thises-and-thats of such a closed subject as the seraglio and its special etiquette of fornication. The thing, of course, that separates her forever from being either machinelike or merely obnoxious is that she wrote like a witty, charming aristocrat, which is what she was.

From the *Letters* of Lady Mary Wortley Montagu, 1689–1762

Pera of Constantinople, March 10, O.S. [1718]

To the Countess of ——

I have not written to you, dear sister, these many months:—a great piece of self-denial. But I know not where to direct, or what part of the world you were in. I have received no letter from you since that short note of April last, in which you tell me that you are on the point of leaving England, and promise me a direction for the place you stay in; but I have in vain expected it till now: and now I only learn from the gazette, that you are returned, which induces me to venture this letter to your house at London. I had rather ten of my letters should be lost, than you imagine I don't write; and I think it is hard fortune if one in ten don't reach you. However, I am resolved to keep the copies, as testimonies of my inclination to give you, to the utmost of my power, all the diverting part of my travels, while you are exempt from all the fatigues and inconveniences.

In the first place, I wish you joy of your niece; for I was brought to bed of a daughter five weeks ago. I don't mention this as one of my diverting adventures; though I must own that it is not half so mortifying here as in England, there being as much difference as there is between a little cold in the head, which sometimes happens here, and the consumptive cough, so common in London. Nobody keeps their house a month for lying in; and I am not so fond of any of our customs to retain them when they are not necessary. I returned my visits at three weeks' end; and about four days ago crossed the sea, which divides this place from Constantinople, to make a new one, where I had the good fortune to pick up many curiosities.

I went to see the Sultana Hafitén, favourite of the late Emperor Mustapha, who, you know (or perhaps you don't know) was deposed by his brother, the reigning Sultan Achmet, and died a few weeks after, being poisoned, as it was generally believed. This lady was, immediately after his death, saluted with an absolute order to leave the seraglio, and choose herself a husband from the great men at the Porte. I suppose you may imagine her overjoyed at this proposal. Quite contrary: these women, who are called, and esteem themselves, queens, look upon this liberty as the greatest disgrace and affront that can happen to them. She threw herself at the Sultan's feet, and begged him to poignard her, rather than use his brother's widow with that contempt. She represented to him, in agonies of sorrow, that she was privileged from this misfortune, by having brought five princes into the Ottoman family; but all the boys being dead, and only one girl surviving, this excuse was not received, and she [was] compelled to make her choice. She chose Bekir Effendi, then secretary of state, and above fourscore years old, to convince the world that she firmly intended to keep the vow she had made, of never suffering a second husband to approach her bed; and since she must honour some subject so far as to be called his wife, she would choose him as a mark of her gratitude, since it was he that had presented her, at the age of ten years old, to her last lord. But she has never permitted him to pay her one visit; though it is now fifteen years she has been in his house, where she passes her time in uninterrupted mourning, with a constancy very little known in Christendom, especially in a widow of twenty-one, for she is now but thirty-six. She has no black eunuchs for her guard, her husband being obliged to respect her as a queen, and not inquire at all into what is done in her apartment, where I was led into a large room, with a sofa the whole length of it, adorned with white marble pillars like a *ruelle,* covered with pale blue figured velvet on a silver ground, w ith cushions of the same, where I was desired to repose till the Sultana appeared, who had contrived this manner of reception to avoid rising up at my entrance, though she made me an inclination of her head, when I rose up to her. I was very glad to observe a lady that had been distinguished by the favour of an emperor, to whom beauties were every day presented from all parts of the world. But she did not seem to me to have ever been half so beautiful as the fair Fatima I saw at Adrianople; though she had the remains of a fine face, more decayed by sorrow than time. But her dress was something so surprisingly rich, I cannot forbear describing it to you. She wore a vest called *donalma,* and which differs from a *caftán* by longer sleeves, and folding over at the bottom. It was of purple cloth, straight to her shape, and thick set, on each side, down to her feet, and round the sleeves, with pearls of the best water, of the same size as their buttons commonly are. You must not suppose I mean as large as those of my Lord ———, but about the bigness of a pea; and to these buttons large loops of diamonds, in the form of those gold loops so common upon birthday coats. This habit was tied, at the waist, with two large tassels of smaller pearl, and round the arms embroidered with large diamonds: her shift fastened at the bottom with a great diamond, shaped like a lozenge; her girdle as broad as the broadest English ribbon, entirely covered with diamonds. Round her neck she wore three chains, which reached to her knees: one of large pearl, at the bottom of which hung a fine coloured emerald, as big as a turkey-egg; another, consisting of two hundred emeralds, close joined together, of the most lively green, perfectly matched, every one as large as a half-crown piece, and as thick as three crown pieces; and another of small emeralds, perfectly round. But her ear-rings eclipsed all the rest. They were two diamonds, shaped exactly like pears, as large as a big hazel-nut. Round her talpoche she had four strings of pearl, the whitest and most perfect in the world, at least enough to make four necklaces, every one as large as the Duchess of Marlborough's, and of the same size, fastened with two roses, consisting of a large ruby for the middle stone, and round them twenty drops of clean diamonds to each. Besides this, her headdress was covered with bodkins of emeralds and diamonds. She wore large diamond bracelets, and had five rings on her fingers, all single diamonds, (except Mr. Pitt's) the largest I ever saw in my life. It is for jewellers to compute the value of these things; but, according to the common estimation of jewels in our part of the world, her whole dress must be worth above a hundred thousand pounds sterling. This I am very sure of, that no European queen has half the quantity; and the empress's jewels, though very fine, would look very mean near hers.

She gave me a dinner of fifty dishes of meat, which (after their fashion) were placed on the table but one at a time, and was extremely tedious. But the magnificence of her table answered very well to that of her dress. The knives were of gold, the hafts set with diamonds. But the piece of luxury that grieved my eyes was the table-cloth and napkins, which were all tiffany, embroidered with silks and gold, in the finest manner, in natural flowers. It was with the utmost regret that I made use of these costly napkins, as finely wrought as the finest handkerchiefs that ever came out of this country. You may be sure that they were entirely spoiled before dinner was over. The sherbet (which is the liquor they drink at meals) was served in china bowls; but the covers and salvers massy gold. After dinner, water was brought in a gold basin, and towels of the same kind of the napkins, which I very unwillingly wiped my hands upon; and coffee was served in china, with gold *soucoupes*.

The Sultana seemed in a very good humour, and talked to me with the utmost civility. I did not omit this opportunity of learning all that I possibly could of the seraglio, which is so entirely unknown among us. She assured me, that the story of the Sultan's throwing a handkerchief is altogether fabulous; and the manner upon that occasion, no other but that he sends the *kyslár agá,* to signify to the lady the honour he intends her. She is immediately complimented upon it by the others, and led to the bath, where she is perfumed and dressed in the most magnificent and becoming manner. The Emperor precedes his visit by a royal present, and then comes into her apartment: neither is there any such thing as her creeping in at the bed's foot. She said, that the first he made choice of was always after the first in rank, and not the mother of the eldest son, as other writers would make us believe. Sometimes the Sultan diverts himself in the company of all his ladies, who stand in a circle round him. And she confessed that they were ready to die with jealousy and envy of the happy she that he distinguished by any appearance of preference. But this seemed to me neither better nor worse than the circles in most courts, where the glance of the monarch is watched, and every smile waited for with impatience, and envied by those who cannot obtain it.

Horace Walpole wrote to everybody who was "anybody" in Great Britain and Europe, probably; and in a period when the ability to produce an urbane, polished, perfectly constructed letter was a prerequisite to social standing, his shine out as by far the best of their kind.

Candor was as much a part of gentlemanly manners then as common sense, and the picture that Walpole paints of himself is not always agreeable; but in the main it is easy to see why he was one of the most desirable men alive in the eighteenth century, whether as correspondent, dinner guest, lover, or architect of Strawberry Hill, his fabulous Gothic country-house.

His letter to the Earl of Hertford, written April 7, 1765, is typical of him and of the society in which he was happiest to move. And it reminds me of one of Brillat-Savarin's aphorisms, written some fifty years later, but eternally true as all of his are bound to be: "A man who keeps a good dinner waiting for a tardy friend commits an outrage upon all the other guests."

From the *Letters* of Horace Walpole, 1717–1797

. . . I was to dine at Northumberland-house, and went a little after four: there I found the Countess, Lady Betty Mackenzie, Lady Strafford; my

Lady Finlater, who was never out of Scotland before; a tall lad of fifteen, her son; Lord Drogheda, and Mr. Worseley. At five, arrived Mr. Mitchell, who said the Lords had begun to read the Poor-bill, which would take at least two hours, and perhaps would debate it afterwards. We concluded dinner would be called for, it not being very precedented for ladies to wait for gentlemen:—no such thing. Six o'clock came—seven o'clock came—our coaches came—well! we sent them away, and excuses were, we were engaged. Still the Countess's heart did not relent, nor uttered a syllable of apology. We wore out the wind and the weather, the Opera and the Play, Mrs. Cornelys's and Almack's, and every topic that would do in a formal circle. We hinted, represented—in vain. The clock struck eight; my Lady, at last, said, she would go and order dinner; but it was a good half-hour before it appeared. We then sat down to a table for fourteen covers: but instead of substantials, there was nothing but a profusion of plates striped red, green, and yellow, gilt plate, blacks, and uniforms! My Lady Finlater, who had never seen these embroidered dinners, nor dined after three, was famished. The first course stayed as long as possible, in hopes of the Lords: so did the second. The dessert at last arrived, and the middle dish was actually set on when Lord Finlater and Mr. Mackay arrived!—would you believe it?—the dessert was remanded, and the whole first course brought back again!— Stay, I have not done:—just as this second first course had done its duty, Lord Northumberland, Lord Strafford, and Mackenzie came in, and the whole began a third time! Then the second course and the dessert! I thought we should have dropped from our chairs with fatigue and fumes! When the clock struck eleven, we were asked to return to the drawing-room, and drink tea and coffee, but I said I was engaged to supper, and came home to bed. My dear lord, think of four hours and a half in a circle of mixed company, and three great dinners, one after another, without interruption. . . .

And here, as fillip for Horace Walpole's horrid dinner, and to end his letter as I began it with a quotation from Brillat-Savarin, is my translation of one of that wise old master's typical "anecdotes":

From *The Physiology of Taste* by Anthelme Brillat-Savarin, 1755–1826

I was invited, this day, to the home of an important official. The card read five thirty, and at that precise hour all the guests had arrived, because it was common knowledge that the host loved punctuality and sometimes scolded his lazier friends.

I was struck, on my arrival, by an air of alarm which I saw everywhere: the guests whispered among themselves, or peeked through the window-panes into the courtyard, and some of their faces showed plain stupefaction. Obviously something extraordinary had occurred.

I went up to the one of the guests I felt would be best able to satisfy my curiosity, and asked him what had happened. "Alas!" he answered in a voice of the deepest suffering, "his lordship has been summoned to a conference of state. He just this moment left for it, and who knows when he will be back again?"

"Is that all ?" I replied, in an insouciant way which was far from genuine. "It's a question of a quarter-hour at the most; some information they needed; everyone knows that an official banquet is taking place here today; there is absolutely no reason to make us fast at it." I continued to talk this way; but in the bottom of my heart I was not without anxiety, and I should have loved to be safely out of the whole business.

The first hour passed well enough, with the guests seated next to their preferred friends; conversational banalities were soon exhausted, and we amused ourselves by guessing the reasons why our good host had been thus summoned to the Tuileries.

During the second hour a few signs of impatience began to show themselves: the guests looked at each other worriedly, and the first ones who complained aloud were three or four of the company who, not having found places to sit down and wait, were especially uncomfortable.

By the third hour, discontent was general, and everyone complained. "When will he be back?" one of them asked. "What can he be thinking of?" another said. "This is murderous!" said a third, and everywhere it was demanded, with never a satisfactory reply, "Should we go? Should we not go?"

By the fourth hour all the symptoms had grown worse: the guests stretched themselves, at the risk of knocking into their neighbors; the room was filled with the singsong of helpless yawns; every face was flushed with concentration; and not a soul listened to me when I risked remarking that our host was without doubt the most miserable of any of us.

At one point our attention was riveted by a ghostly sight. One of the guests, more familiar to the house than some of us, roamed as far as the kitchens; he came back completely out of breath; his face looking as if the end of the world were upon us, and he burst out in an almost unintelligible voice, in that heavy tone which betrays both a fear of being heard and a wish to be listened to: "His lordship left without giving any orders, and no matter how long he is gone, nothing will be served until he comes back!" He had spoken: the horror which his announcement roused could not possibly be outdone by the trumpet of the last judgment.

Among all these martyrs, the unhappiest was the good d'Aigrefeuille, well-known to all of Paris in those days; his body was the personification of misery, and the agony of a Laocoön showed in his face. Pale, distracted, sightless, he hunched himself into a chair, crossed his little hands over his generous belly, and closed his eyes, not to sleep, but to wait for his own death.

It was not Death, however, who came. About ten o'clock there was the sound of carriage-wheels in the courtyard. Everyone jumped to his feet. Gaiety took the place of sadness, and five minutes later we were seated at the table.

But the time of appetite had passed. There was a feeling of astonishment at beginning a dinner at this unfamiliar hour; our jaws could not attain that synchronized chewing which is a guarantee of perfect digestion, and I learned later that several of the guests were inconvenienced by it.

The procedure indicated in such a situation is not to eat immediately after the enforced fast has ended, but to drink a glass of sugared water, or a cup of broth, to comfort the stomach; and then to wait another twelve or fifteen minutes, since otherwise the abused organ will find too oppressive the weight of the foods with which it has been overstuffed.

One of the least read and most quoted writers of the eighteenth century, gastronomically, is Thomas Walker.

It is not easy to find much about him, except through occasional references in other people's letters, and from his own unconscious self-portraits in *The Original*, which he wrote and published weekly for twenty-nine weeks before his death in 1836.

Each number of this periodical, whose title might well serve as a description of its author, contains a number of short articles on a variety of subjects:

"Whatever is most interesting and important in Religion and Politics, in Morals and Manners, and in our Habits and Customs." Mr. Walker added that he hoped to be able to treat these matters "as forcibly, perspicuously, and concisely," as they and his own ability would allow, and although much of what he wrote seems somewhat pompous now, there is through the whole of *The Original* a special flavor, a serious but amiable spirit.

His was a true lawyer's mind, orderly and logical, and yet permitting a tolerantly sensual enjoyment of the more refined pleasures of life. He described whatever subject he was considering with much more than the force, perspicuity, and conciseness he promised to strive for, and some such little picture as the one of his famous whitebait dinner has a real charm about it, in spite of its sententious lack of humor:

From *The Original* by Thomas Walker, ?-1836

I will give you, dear reader, an account of a dinner I have ordered this very day at Lovegrove's at Blackwell. . . . The party will consist of seven men beside myself, and every guest is asked for some reason—upon which good fellowship mainly depends, for people brought together unconnectedly had, in my opinion, better be kept separate. . . .

The dinner is to consist of turtle followed by no other fish but whitebait, which is to be followed by no other meat but grouse, which are to be succeeded simply by apple fritters and jelly, pastry on such occasions being quite out of place. With the turtle of course there will be punch, with the whitebait, champagne, and with the grouse, claret . . . I shall permit no other wines, unless perchance a bottle of port. . . . With respect to the adjuncts, I shall take care that there is cayenne, with lemon cut in halves, not in quarters, within reach of everyone, for the turtle, and that brown bread and butter in abundance is set upon the table for the whitebait. It is no trouble to think of these little matters beforehand, but they make a vast difference in convivial contentment. The dinner will be followed by ices and a good dessert, and after which, coffee and one glass of liqueur each and no more; so that the present may be enjoyed rationally without introducing retrospective regrets. If the master of a feast wishes his party to succeed he must know how to command, and not let his guests run riot each according to his own wild fancy. Such, reader, is my idea of a dinner, of which I hope you approve.

Just as opinions vary about the table manners of Brillat-Savarin (some have him a gross boor and others a polished and delightful supper-companion), so the picture of Samuel Johnson, Gourmand, changes with the artist who paints it. There is no use pretending, however, even for the sake of variety, that anyone observed him more thoroughly than Boswell.

"The big man," as Oliver Goldsmith called him, had strong if somewhat contradictory ideas about gastronomy, and invented a word connected with it for his dictionary: *gulosity*, meaning greediness, gluttony, voracity.

A few years before his death in 1772, Johnson said, after a supper which apparently left him in a mellow state, "Some people have a foolish way of not minding, or pretending not to mind, what they eat. For my part, I mind my belly very studiously, and very carefully; for I look upon it, that he who does not mind his belly will hardly mind anything else."

And Boswell goes on to say, in this characteristic excerpt from his biography of Johnson:

From *The Life of Johnson* by James Boswell, 1740–1795

He now appeared to me *Jean Bull philosophe*, and he was, for the moment, not only serious but vehement. Yet I have heard him, upon other occasions, talk with great contempt of people who were anxious to gratify their palates; and the 206th number of his *Rambler* is a masterly essay against gulosity. His practice indeed, I must acknowledge, may be considered as casting the balance of his different opinions upon this subject; for I never knew any man who relished good eating more than he did. When at table, he was totally absorbed in the business of the moment; his looks seemed rivetted to his plate; nor would he, unless when in very high company, say one word, or even pay the least attention to what was said by others, till he had satisfied his appetite, which was so fierce, and indulged with such intenseness, that while in the act of eating, the veins of his forehead swelled, and generally a strong perspiration was visible. To those whose sensations were delicate, this could not but be disgusting; and it was doubtless not very suitable to the character of a philosopher, who should be distinguished by self-command. But it must be owned, that Johnson, though he could be rigidly *abstemious*, was not a *temperate* man either in eating or drinking. He could refrain, but he could not use moderately. He told me that he had fasted two days without inconvenience, and that he had never been hungry but once. They who beheld with wonder how much he eat upon all occasions when his dinner was to his taste, could not easily conceive what he must have meant by hunger; and not only was he remarkable for the extraordinary quantity which he eat, but he was, or affected to be, a man of very nice discernment in the science of cookery. He used to descant critically on the dishes which had been at table where he had dined or supped, and to recollect very minutely what he had liked. I remember, when he was in Scotland, his praising *"Gordon's palates"* (a dish of palates at the Honourable Alexander Gordon's) with a warmth of expression which might have done honour to more important subjects. "As for Maclaurin's imitation of a *made dish,* it was a wretched attempt." He about the same time was so much displeased with the performances of a nobleman's French cook, that he exclaimed with vehemence, "I'd throw such a rascal into the river"; and he then proceeded to alarm a lady at whose house he was to sup, by the following manifesto of his skill: "I, Madam, who live at a variety of good tables, am a much better judge of cookery, than any person who has a very tolerable cook, but lives much at home; for his palate is gradually adapted to the taste of his cook; whereas, Madam, in trying by a wider range, I can more exquisitely judge." When invited to dine, even with an intimate friend, he was not pleased if something better than a plain dinner was not prepared for him. I have heard him say on such an occasion, "This was a good dinner enough, to be sure; but it was not a dinner to *ask* a man to." On the other hand, he was wont to express, with great glee, his satisfaction when he had been entertained quite to his mind. One day when we had dined with his neighbor and landlord in Bolt-court, Mr. Allen, the printer, whose old housekeeper had studied his taste in everything, he pronounced this eulogy: "Sir, we could not have had a better dinner had there been a *Synod of Cooks.*"

There are some people in the world who cannot read with any true enjoyment the long story of the lexicographer, or perhaps have not yet matured enough to find it anything but weighty. In the same way the books by Jane Austen are for some of us a robust delicacy to be savored long after the literary pangs of adolescence, at no matter what age, have been satisfied by less subtle dishes. Once fully tasted, though, and with the proper seasoning of leisure, they can arouse a hunger never again quite to be sated, at least by them.

Here is one fair sample of the things that Jane Austen did with words: the satirical self-betrayal of Miss Lutterel, when she writes to her dear friend Miss Lesley:

From *Lesley Castle* by Jane Austen, 1775–1817

Glenford, February 12th

I have a thousand excuses to beg for having so long delayed thanking you my dear Peggy for your agreeable Letter, which believe me I should not have deferred doing, had not every moment of my time during the last five weeks been so fully employed in the necessary arrangements for my sister's marriage. . . . And now what provokes me more than anything else is that the Match is broke off, and all my Labour thrown away. Imagine how great the Disappointment must be to me, when you consider that after having laboured both by Night and by Day, in order to get the Wedding dinner ready by the time appointed, after having Roasted Beef, Broiled Mutton, and Stewed Soup enough to last the new-married Couple through the Honey-moon, I had the mortification of finding that I had been Roasting, Broiling, and Stewing both the Meat and Myself to no purpose. Indeed, my dear Friend, I never remember suffering any vexation equal to what I experienced on last Monday when my sister came running to me in the storeroom with her face as White as a Whipt Syllabub and told me that Henry had been thrown from his Horse, had fractured his Scull and was pronounced by his surgeon to be in the most emminent Danger. "Good God (said I) you don't say so? Why what in the name of Heaven will become of all the Victuals? We shall never be able to eat it while it is good. However, we'll call in the Surgeon to help us. I shall be able to manage the Sirloin myself, my Mother will eat the Soup, and You and the Doctor must finish the rest." Here I was interrupted, by seeing my poor Sister fall down to all appearance Lifeless upon one of the Chests, where we keep our table linen. I immediately called my Mother and the Maids, and at last we brought her to herself again . . . we laid her upon the Bed, and she continued for some Hours in the most dreadful Convulsions. My Mother and I continued in the room with her, and when any intervals of tolerable composure in Eloisa would allow us, we joined heartfelt lamentations on the dreadful Waste in our provisions which the Event must occasion, and in concerting some plan for getting rid of them. We agreed that the best thing we could do was to begin eating them immediately, and accordingly we ordered up the cold Ham and Fowls, and instantly began our Devouring Plan on them with great Alacrity. We would have persuaded Eloisa to have taken a wing of Chicken, but she would not be persuaded. . . . We endeavored to rouse her by every means in our power, but to no purpose. I talked to her of Henry. "Dear Eloisa (said I) there's no occasion for your crying so much about such a trifle. (For I was willing to make light of it in order to comfort her.) I beg you would not mind it— You see it does not vex me in the least; though perhaps *I* may suffer most from it after all; for I shall not only be obliged to eat up all the Victuals I have dressed already, but must if Henry should recover (which however is not very likely) dress as much for you again; or should he die (as I suppose he will) I shall still have to prepare a Dinner for you whenever you marry anyone else. . . . Yet I daresay he'll die soon, and then his pain will be over and you will be easy, whereas my Trouble will last much longer, for work as hard as I may, I am certain that the pantry cannot be cleared in less than a fortnight."

A man is no more desirable a companion because he can write well, and often the opposite seems true: few authors make their readers eager to know them as human beings. The Reverend Sydney Smith is one of the exceptions.

He might have risen as high as mortal could in the Church, if he had held his tongue or used it less amusingly (his idea of Heaven was eating *pâté de foie gras* to the sound of trumpets!). But his letters are probably more spiritually stimulating to his fellow men than any archiepiscopal prayers could have been a century ago, and he would not have had the time to write them anyway, wearing a mitre.

There is no proof that he actually said of strawberries, "Doubtless God could have made a better berry, but doubtless he never did," but in one of his letters he wrote, "What is real piety? What is true attachment to the Church? How are these fine feelings best evinced? The answer is plain: by sending strawberries to a clergyman. Many thanks."

Another time he wrote, "If there is a pure and elevated pleasure in this world it is roast pheasant and bread sauce. Barn-door fowls for Dissenters, but for the real Churchman, the thirty-nine times articled clerk, the pheasant, the pheasant!"

As for his much-quoted recipe in rhyme, it is not much more than a curiosity, gastronomically. It is because Sydney Smith wrote it, and not because it could possibly make a good salad dressing, that I put it here:

Recipe for Salad by Sydney Smith, 1771–1845
To make this condiment your poet begs
The pounded yellow of two hard-boil'd eggs;
Two boiled potatoes, passed through kitchen sieve,
Smoothness and softness to the salad give.
Let onion atoms lurk within the bowl,
And, scarce suspected, animate the whole.
Of mordant mustard add a single spoon,
Distrust the condiment that bites so soon;
But deem it not, thou man of herbs, a fault
To add a double quantity of salt.
Four times the spoon with oil from Lucca crown,
And twice with vinegar procured from town;
And, lastly, o'er the flavour'd compound toss
A magic soupçon of anchovy sauce.
Oh, green and glorious! Oh, herbaceous treat!
'T would tempt the dying anchorite to eat;
Back to the world he'd turn his fleeting soul,
And plunge his fingers in the salad bowl.
Serenely full, the epicure would say,
"Fate cannot harm me, I have dined today."

It is very hard to find *A Story Without a Tail*. Few people have read it, or even heard of it, and yet it is probably one of the best things of its kind in all literature: a masterpiece of gastronomical writing, of jollity and good-fellowship, of hearty appetites and deep thirsts well satisfied, of humorous subtle characterization. It is fun to read, and then read again.

William Maginn, as any respectable encyclopedia will tell but few people know or care, was an Irish poet and journalist and writer of short stories.

He was of what Saintsbury calls "the second order of genius," with a charming wit and an acute critical sense. He wrote for *Blackwood's* and then *Frazer's* magazines for years, and knew every other writer of his time. He was the kind of comet which now and then flashes through a literary heaven, so that other less brilliant if more important minds were a little awed by his. Thackeray put him in *Pendennis*, and when he died one epitaph recalled him as "the bright broken Maginn," a subtly envious phrase.

Here is most of his *Story Without a Tail*, which he wrote in 1832:

From A Story Without a Tail by William Maginn, 1793-1842

It was finally agreed upon that we should dine at Jack Ginger's chambers in the Temple. . . . There were, besides our host, Tom Meggot, Joe Macgillicuddy, Humpy Harlow, Bob Burke, Antony Harrison, and myself. As Jack Ginger had little coin and no credit we contributed each our share to the dinner. He himself provided room, fire, candles, tables, chairs, tablecloth, napkins—no, not napkins; on second thought, we did not bother ourselves with napkins—plates, dishes, knives, forks, spoons (which he borrowed from the wig-maker), tumblers, lemons, sugar, water, glasses, decanters—by the by, I am not sure that there were decanters—salt, pepper, vinegar, mustard, bread, butter (plain and melted), cheese, radishes, potatoes, and cookery. Tom Meggot was a cod's head and shoulders, and oysters to match; Joe Macgillicuddy, a boiled leg of pork and peas-pudding; Humpy Harlow, a sirloin of beef roast, with horse-radish; Bob Burke, a gallon of half-and-half, and four bottles of whisky, of prime quality; . . . Antony Harrison, half a dozen of port, he having tick to that extent at some unfortunate wine merchant's; and I supplied cigars *à discrétion,* and a bottle of rum, which I borrowed from a West-Indian friend of mine as I passed by. So that, on the whole, we were in no danger of suffering from any of the extremes of hunger and thirst for the course of that evening.

We met at five o'clock sharp, and very sharp. Not a man was missing when the clock of the Inner Temple struck the last stroke. Jack Ginger had done everything to admiration. Nothing could be more splendid than his turn-out. He had superintended the cooking of every individual dish with his own eyes, or rather eye, he having but one, the other having been lost in a skirmish when he was midshipman on board a pirate in the Brazilian service. "Ah!" said Jack often and often, "those were my honest days. Gad! did I ever think when I was a pirate that I was at the end to turn rogue, and study the law?" All was accurate to the utmost degree. The tablecloth, to be sure, was not exactly white, but it had been washed last week, and the collection of plates was miscellaneous, exhibiting several of the choicest patterns of delf. We were not of the silver-fork school of poetry, but steel is not to be despised. If the table was somewhat rickety, the inequality in the legs was supplied by clapping a volume of Vesey under the short one. As for the chairs—but why weary about details, chairs being made to be sat upon?— it is sufficient to say that they answered their purposes, and whether they had backs or not, whether they were cane-bottomed or hair-bottomed or rush-bottomed, is nothing to the present inquiry.

Jack's habit of discipline made him punctual, and dinner was on the table in less than three minutes after five. Down we sat, hungry as hunters, and eager for the prey.

"Is there a parson in the company?" said Jack Ginger from the head of the table.

"No," responded I from the foot.

"Then, thank God," said Jack, and proceeded, after this pious grace, to distribute the cod's head and shoulders to the hungry multitude.

The history of that cod's head and shoulders would occupy but little space to write. Its flakes, like the snow-flakes on a river, were for one moment bright, then gone for ever; it perished unpitiable. "Bring hither," said Jack with a firm voice, "the leg of pork." It appeared, but soon to disappear again. Not a man of the company but showed his abhorrence to the Judaical practice of abstaining from the flesh of swine. Equally clear was it in a few minutes that we were truly British in our devotion to beef. The sirloin was impartially destroyed on both sides, upper and under. Dire was the clatter of the knives, but deep the silence of the guests. Jerry Gallagher, Jack's *valet-de-chambre,* footman, cook, clerk, shoeblack, *aide-de-camp,* scout, confidant, dun-chaser, bum-defyer, and many other offices *in commendam,* toiled like a hero. He covered himself with glory and gravy every minute. In a short time a vociferation arose for fluid, and the half-and-half . . . was inhaled with the most savage satisfaction.

"The pleasure of a glass of wine with you, Bob Burke," said Joe Macgillicuddy, wiping his mouth with the back of his hand.

"With pleasure, Joe," replied Bob. "What wine do you choose? You may as well say port, for there is no other; but attention to manners always becomes a gentleman."

"Port, then, if you please," cried Joe, "as the ladies of Limerick say when a man looks at them across the table."

"Hobnobbing wastes time," said Jack Ginger, laying down the pot out of which he had been drinking for the last few minutes; "and besides, it is not necessary now in genteel society to pass the bottle about."

(I here pause in my narrative to state on more accurate recollection, that we had not decanters. We drank from the black bottle, which Jack declared was according to the fashion of the Continent.)

So the port was passed round, and declared to be superb. Antony Harrison received the unanimous applause of the company; and, if he did not blush at all the fine things that were said in his favour, it was because his countenance was of that peculiar hue that no addition of red could be visible upon it. A blush on Antony's face would be like gilding refined gold.

Whether cheese is prohibited or not in the higher circles of the West End, I cannot tell; but I know it was not prohibited in the very highest chambers of the Temple.

"It's double Gloucester," said Jack Ginger; "prime, bought at the corner. Heaven pay the cheesemonger, for I shan't; but, as he is a gentleman, I give you his health."

"I don't think," said Joe Macgillicuddy, "that I ought to demean myself to drink the health of a cheesemonger; but I'll not stop the bottle."

And, to do Joe justice, he did not. Then we attacked the cheese, and in an incredibly short period we battered in a breach of an angle of forty-five degrees in a manner that would have done honour to any engineer that directed the guns at San Sebastian.

"Clear the decks," said Jack Ginger to Jerry Gallagher. "Gentlemen, I did not think of getting pastry, or puddings, or dessert, or ices, or jellies, or blancmange, or anything of the sort for men of sense like you."

We all unanimously expressed our indignation at being supposed even for a moment guilty of any such weakness; but a general suspicion seemed to arise among us that a dram might not be rejected with the same marked scorn. Jack Ginger accordingly uncorked one of Bob Burke's bottles. Whop! went the cork, and the potteen soon was seen meandering round the table.

"For my part," said Antony Harrison, "I take this dram because I ate pork, and fear it might disagree with me."

"I take it," said Bob Burke, "chiefly by reason of the fish."

"I take it," said Joe Macgillicuddy, "because the day was warm, and it is very close in these chambers."

"I take it," said Tom Meggot, "because I have been very chilly all the day."

"I take it," said Humpy Harlow, "because it is such strange weather that one does not know what to do."

"I take it," said Jack Ginger, "because the rest of the company takes it."

"And I take it," said I, winding up the conversation, "because I like a dram."

So we all took it for one reason or another, and there was an end of that.

"Be off, Jerry Gallagher," said Jack. "I give to you, your heirs and assigns, all that and those which remain in the pots of half-and-half—item, for your own dinners what is left of the solids; and when you have pared the bones clean, you may give them to the poor. Charity covers a multitude of sins. Brush away like a shoeblack, and levant."

"Why, thin, God bless your honour," said Jerry Gallagher, "it's a small liggacy he would have that would dippind for his daily bread for what is left behind any of ye in the way of the drink, and this blessed hour there's not as much as would blind the left eye of a midge in one of them pots, and may it do ye all good, if it a'n't the blessing of Heaven to see ye eating. By my sowl, he that has to pick a bone after you won't be much troubled with the mate. Howsomever—"

"No more prate," said Jack Ginger. "Here's two pence for you to buy some beer; but no," he continued, drawing his empty hand from that breeches-pocket into which he had most needlessly put it; "no," said he, "Jerry, get it on credit wherever you can, and bid them score it to me."

"If they will," said Jerry.

"Shut the door," said Jack Ginger in a peremptory tone, and Jerry retreated.

"That Jerry," said Jack, "is an uncommonly honest fellow, only he is the damnedest rogue in London. But all this is wasting time, and time is life. Dinner is over, and the business of the evening is about to begin. So bumpers, gentlemen, and get rid of this wine as fast as we can. Mr. Vice, look to your bottles."

And on this Jack Ginger gave a bumper toast.

This being done, every man pulled in his chair close to the table, and prepared for serious action. It was plain that we all, like Nelson's sailors at

Trafalgar, felt called upon to do our duty. The wine circulated with considerable rapidity; and there was no flinching on the part of any individual of the company. It was quite needless for our president to remind us of the necessity of bumpers, or the impropriety of leaving heel-taps. We were all too well trained to require the admonition or to fall into the error. On the other hand, the chance of any man obtaining more than his share in the round was infinitesimally small. The Sergeant himself, celebrated as he is, could not have succeeded in obtaining a glass more than his neighbours. Just to our friends, we were also just to ourselves; and a more rigid circle of philosophers never surrounded a board.

The wine was really good, and its merits did not appear the less striking from the fact that we were not habitually wine-bibbers, our devotion generally being paid to fluids more potent or heavy than the juice of the grape, and it soon excited our powers of conversation. Heavens! What a flow of soul! More good things were said in Jack Ginger's chambers that evening than in the House of Lords and Commons in a month. We talked of everything—politics, literature, the fine arts, drama, high life, low life, the opera, the cockpit—everything from the heavens above to the hells in St. James's Street. There was not an article in a morning, evening, or weekly paper for the week before which we did not repeat. It was clear that our knowledge of things in general was drawn in a vast degree from these recondite sources. . . . We spoke, in fact, articles that would have made the fortunes of half a hundred magazines, if the editors of these works would have had the perspicacity to insert them; and this we did with such ease to ourselves that we never for a moment stopped the circulation of the bottle, which kept running on its round rejoicing, while we settled the affairs of the nation. . . .

"I perceive this is the last bottle of port," said Jack Ginger; "so I suppose that there cannot be any harm in drinking bad luck to Antony Harrison's wine-merchant, who did not make it the dozen."

"Yes," said Harrison, "the skinflint thief would not stand more than the half, for which he merits the most infinite certainty of non-payment."

(You may depend upon it that Harrison was as good as his word, and treated the man of bottles according to his deserts.)

The port was gathered to its fathers, and potteen punch reigned in its stead. . . . "I'll clear away these marines," [said Jack Ginger] "and do you,

Bob Burke, make the punch. I think you will find the lemons good, the sugar superb, and the water of the Temple has been famous for centuries."

"And I'll back the potteen against any that ever came from the Island of Saints," said Bob, proceeding to his duty, which all who have the honour of his acquaintance will admit him to be well qualified to perform. He made it in a couple of big blue water-jugs, observing that making punch in small jugs was nearly as great a bother as ladling from a bowl; and, as he tossed the steamy fluid from jug to jug to mix it kindly, he sang the pathetic ballad of Hugger-mo-fane:

"I wish I had a red herring's tail," etc.

The punch being made, and the jug revolving, the conversation continued as before. But it may have been observed that I have not taken any notice of the share which one of the party, Humpy Harlow, took in it. The fact is that he had been silent for almost all the evening, being outblazed and overborne by the brilliancy of the conversation of his companions. We were all acknowledged wits in our respective lines, whereas he had not been endowed with the same talents. How he came among us I forget, nor did any of us know well who or what he was. Some maintained he was a drysalter in the City; others surmised he might be a pawnbroker in the West End. Certain it is that he had some money, which perhaps might have recommended him to us, for there was not a man in the company who had not occasionally borrowed from him a sum too trifling, in general, to permit any of us to think of repaying it. He was a broken-backed little fellow, as vain of his person as a peacock, and accordingly we always called him Humpy Harlow, with the spirit of gentlemanlike candour which characterised all our conversation. With a kind feeling towards him, we in general permitted him to pay our bills for us whenever we dined together at tavern or chop-house, merely to gratify the little fellow's vanity, which I have already hinted to be excessive.

He had this evening made many ineffective attempts to shine, but was at last obliged to content himself with opening his mouth for the admission, not for the utterance, of good things. He was evidently unhappy, and a rightly constituted mind could not avoid pitying his condition. As jug, however, succeeded jug, he began to recover his self-possession; and it was clear, about eleven o'clock, when the fourth bottle of potteen was converting into punch, that he had a desire to speak. We had been for some time busily employed in smoking cigars, when, all on a sudden, a shrill and sharp voice was heard from the midst of a cloud, exclaiming, in a high treble key:

"Humphries told me—"

We all puffed our Havannahs with the utmost silence, as if we were so many Sachems at a palaver, listening to the narration which issued from the misty tabernacle in which Humpy Harlow was enveloped. He unfolded a tale of wondrous length, which we never interrupted. No sound was heard save that of the voice of Harlow, narrating the story which had to him been confided by the unknown Humphries, or the gentle gliding of the jug, an occasional tingle of a glass, or the soft suspiration of the cigar. On moved the story in its length, breadth, and thickness, for Harlow gave it to us in its full dimensions. He abated it not a jot. The firmness which we displayed was unequalled since the battle of Waterloo. We sat with determined countenances, exhaling smoke and inhaling punch, while the voice still rolled onward. At last Harlow came to an end; and a babel of conversation burst from lips in which it had long been imprisoned. Harlow looked proud of his feat, and obtained the thanks of the company, grateful that he had come to a conclusion. How we finished the potteen, converted my bottle of rum into a bowl . . . how Jerry Gallagher, by super-human exertions, succeeded in raising a couple of hundred oysters for supper; how the company separated each to get to his domicile as best he could—all this must be left to other historians to narrate.

At three o'clock [the next day] Antony Harrison and I found ourselves eating bread and cheese, part of the cheese, at Jack Ginger's. We recapitulated the events of the preceding evening, and expressed ourselves highly gratified with the entertainment. Most of the good things we had said were revived, served up again, and laughed at once more. We were perfectly satisfied with the parts we had respectively played, and talked ourselves into excessive good-humour. All on a sudden, Jack Ginger's countenance clouded. He was evidently puzzled; and sat for a moment in thoughtful silence. We asked him, with Oriental simplicity of sense, "Why art thou troubled?" and . . . he answered:

"What was the story which Humpy Harlow told us about eleven o'clock last night, just as Bob Burke was teeming the last jug?"

"It began," said I, "with 'Humphries told me.'"

"It did," said Antony Harrison, cutting a deep incision into the cheese.

"I know it did," said Jack Ginger; "but what was it that Humphries told him? I cannot recollect it if I was to be made Lord Chancellor."

Antony Harrison and I mused in silence, and racked our brains, but to no purpose. On the tablet of our memories no trace had been engraved, and the tale of Humphries, as reported by Harlow, was as if it were not so far as we were concerned.

While we were in this perplexity Joe Macgillicuddy and Bob Burke entered the room.

"We have been just taking a hair of the same dog," said Joe. "It was a pleasant party we had last night. Do you know what Bob and I have been talking of for the last half hour?"

We professed our inability to conjecture.

"Why, then," continued Joe, "it was about the story that Harlow told last night."

"The story begins with 'Humphries told me,'" said Bob.

"And," proceeded Joe, "for our lives we cannot recollect what it was."

"Wonderful!" we all exclaimed. "How inscrutable are the movements of the human mind!"

And we proceeded to reflect on the frailty of our memories, moralising in a strain that would have done honour to Dr. Johnson.

"Perhaps," said I, "Tom Meggot may recollect it."

Idle hope! dispersed to the winds almost as soon as it was formed. For the words had scarcely passed the "bulwark of my teeth" when Tom appeared, looking excessively bloodshot in the eye. On inquiry it turned out that he, like the rest of us, remembered only the cabalistic words which introduced the tale, but of the tale itself nothing.

Tom had been educated in Edinburgh, and was strongly attached to what he calls metapheesicks; and, accordingly, after rubbing his forehead, he exclaimed:

"This is a psychological curiosity which deserves to be developed. I happen to have half a sovereign about me" (an assertion which, I may remark in passing, excited considerable surprise in his audience); "and I'll ask Harlow to dine with me at the Rainbow. I'll get the story out of the humpy rascal, and no mistake."

We acquiesced in the propriety of this proceeding; and Antony Harrison, observing that by chance he happened to be disengaged, hooked himself on Tom, who seemed to have a sort of natural antipathy to such a ceremony, with a talent and alacrity that proved him to be a veteran warrior, or what, in common parlance, is called an old soldier.

Tom succeeded in getting Harlow to dinner, and Harrison succeeded in making him pay the bill, to the great relief of Meggot's half-sovereign, and they parted at an early hour in the morning. The two Irishmen and myself were at Ginger's shortly after breakfast; we had been part occupied in tossing halfpence to decide which of us was to send out for ale, when Harrison and Meggot appeared. There was conscious confusion written in their countenances. "Did Humpy Harlow tell you that story?" we all exclaimed at once.

"It cannot be denied that he did," said Meggot. "Precisely as the clock struck eleven, he commenced, 'Humphries told me.'"

"Well, and what then?"

"Why, there it is," said Antony Harrison. "May I be drummed out if I can recollect another word."

"Nor I," said Meggot.

The strangeness of this singular adventure made a deep impression on us all. We were sunk in silence for some minutes, during which Jerry Gallagher made his appearance with the ale, which I omitted to mention had been lost by Joe Macgillicuddy. We sipped that British beverage, much abstracted in deep thought. The thing appeared to us perfectly inscrutable. At last I said: "This will never do; we cannot exist much longer in this atmosphere of doubt and uncertainty. We must have it out of Harlow tonight, or there is an end of all the grounds and degrees of belief, opinion, and assent. I have credit," said I, "at the widow's in St. Martin's Lane. Suppose we all meet there tonight, and get Harlow there if we can?"

"That I can do," said Antony Harrison, "for I quartered myself to dine with him today, as I saw him home, poor little fellow, last night. I promise that he figures at the widow's tonight at nine o'clock."

So we separated. At nine every man of the party was in St. Martin's Lane, seated in the little back parlour; and Harrison was as good as his word, for he brought Harlow with him. He ordered a sumptuous supper of mutton kidneys interspersed with sausages, and we set to. At eleven o'clock the eyes of Humpy Harlow brightened; and, putting his pipe down, he commenced in a shrill voice:

"Humphries told me—"

"Aye," said we all with one accord, "here it is—now we shall have it—take care of it this time."

"What do you mean?" said Humpy Harlow, performing that feat which by the illustrious Mr. John Reeve is called "flaring up."

"Nothing," we replied, "nothing: but we are anxious to hear that story."

"I understand you," said our broken-backed friend. "I now recollect that I did tell it once or so before in your company, but I shall not be a butt any longer for you or anybody else."

"Don't be in a passion, Humpy," said Jack Ginger.

"Sir," replied Harlow, "I hate nicknames. It is a mark of a low mind to use them; and, as I see I am brought here only to be insulted, I shall not trouble you any longer with my company."

Saying this the little man seized his hat and umbrella and strode out of the room.

"His back is up," said Joe Macgillicuddy, "and there's no use of trying to get it down. I am sorry he is gone, because I should have made him pay for another round."

But he was gone, not to return again, and the story remains unknown; yea, as undiscoverable as the hieroglyphical writings of the ancient Egyptians. It exists, to be sure, in the breast of Harlow; but there it is buried, never to emerge into the light of day. It is lost to the world, and means of recovering it there, in my opinion, exist none. The world must go on without it; and states and empires must continue to flourish and to fade without the knowledge of what it was that Humphries told Harlow. Such is the inevitable course of events.

There is nothing yes-and-no about liking Jorrocks. You either do or you don't. You either think he is very funny and delightful, and forgive any such small irritations as his custard-pie-comedy pronunciations of foreign words, or you are bored by the whole insensate mess of low jokes and tack-room vulgarities.

Jorrocks, "the sporting Falstaff," after whom Charles Dickens modeled Mr. Pickwick (himself!), was born in 1831 in the pages of *The New Sporting*

Magazine, from the pen of its owner and editor, Robert Smith Surtees. The series of sketches of this hearty, horsey little man was called *Jorrocks's Jaunts and Jollities*, as it is today, but with the additional title: "or the Hunting, Shooting, Racing, Driving, Sailing, Eating, Eccentric and Extravagant Exploits of that renowned Sporting Citizen, Mr. John Jorrocks of St. Botolph Lane and Great Coram Corner," and it was illustrated by Phiz.

Robert Surtees was not only a sensitive reporter of all the idioms and habits of his time, and a trained watcher of his fellows; he was a born sportsman. It was inevitable that his character's hilarious adventures should immediately become as much a part of English life as Pickwick's were to be a little later. Everything he said, as it appeared in the magazine, was quoted in hunting-stables and dining rooms all over the Empire, and people felt about him as Thackeray did when he wrote to Mr. Surtees, "Jorrocks has long been a dear and intimate friend of mine."

He was, and is still, one of the great fool-heroes, infectiously and ridiculously and lovably absurd. He ate and talked and drank with irresistible gusto.

That is, he did if he is irresistible to you. If he is not, then he seems a stupid uncouth lout, a coarse fool. And if he is that, then do not read these pages I have taken from his *Jaunts and Jollities*, for the food in them, and the heel-taps of stout liquor, and all the silliness, will be worse than dull. (They either will be . . . or suddenly they won't!)

From *Jorrocks's Jaunts and Jollities* by Robert Smith Surtees, 1803–1864

"Now tell me," [asked Mr. Jorrocks] "have you any objection to breakfasting in the kitchen?—more retired, you know, besides which you get every thing hot and hot, which is what I call doing a bit of plisure." "Not at all," said the Yorkshireman, "so lead the way"; and down they walked to the lower regions.

It was a nice comfortable-looking place, with a blazing fire, half the floor covered with an old oil-cloth, and the rest exhibiting the cheerless aspect of the naked flags. About a yard and a half from the fire was placed the breakfast table; in the centre stood a magnificent uncut ham, with a great quartern loaf on one side and a huge Bologna sausage on the other; beside these there were nine eggs; two pyramids of muffins, a great deal of toast, a dozen ship-biscuits, and a half a pork-pie, while a dozen kidneys were spluttering on a spit before the fire, and Betsy held a gridiron covered with mutton-chops on the top; altogether there was as much as would have served ten people. "Now, sit down," said Jorrocks, "and let us be doing, for I am as hungry as a hunter. Hope you are peckish too; what shall I give you? tea or coffee?—but take both—coffee first and tea after a bit. If I can't give you them good, don't know who can. You must pay your devours, as we say in France, to the 'am, for it is an especial fine one, and do take a few eggs with it; there, I've not given you above a pound of 'am, but you can come again, you know—'waste not, want not.' Now take some muffins, do, pray. Batsay, bring some more cream, and set the kidneys on the table, the Yorkshireman is getting nothing to eat. Have a chop with your kidney, werry luxterous—I could eat an elephant stuffed with grenadiers, and wash them down with a ocean of tea; but pray lay in to the breakfast, or I shall think you don't like it. There, now take some tea and toast, or one of those biscuits, or whatever you like; would a little more 'am be agreeable? Batsay, run into the larder and see if your Missis left any of that cold chine of pork last night—and hear, bring the cold goose, and any cold flesh you can lay hands on, there are really no wittles on the table. I am quite ashamed to set you down to such a scanty fork breakfast; but this is what comes of not being master of your own house. Hope your hat may long cover your family: rely upon it, it is 'cheaper to buy your bacon than to keep a pig.'"

And, as "Major Appleby" says in his introduction, "That was for two heroes who were starting out from St. Botolph's Lane for a day with Surrey hounds!"

The other excerpt about John Jorrocks, his dinner party in honor of the great sportsman Happerley Nimrod, is my favorite.

Needless to say, the preparations for it were almost endless, and then it went on long after the host's final perfunctory grace, through increasingly muddled toasts and "healths all 'round." All we can read here is the actual dinner, so generous and confused and honest, with spots on the cloth and red faces no doubt, but lightened always with kindness.

It begins with the hasty departure from the drawing room of Mrs. Jorrocks, who returns on the heels of her husband's forthright explanation of her genteel evasions about the calls of nature with a half-pint smelling-bottle held to her nose, to prove that she left for nothing less ladylike than a slight faintness. . . .

From *Jorrocks's Jaunts and Jollities* by Robert Smith Surtees, 1803–1864

Benjamin followed immediately after, and throwing open the door proclaimed, in a half-fledged voice, that "dinner was sarved," upon which the
party all started on their legs.

"Now, Mr. Happerley Nimrod," cried Jorrocks, "you'll trot Mrs. J——
down—according to the book of etiquette, you know, giving her the wall
side. Sorry, gentlemen, I haven't ladies apiece for you, but my sally-manger,
as we say in France, is rayther small, besides which I never like to dine more
than eight. Stubbs, my boy, Green and you must toss up for Belinda—here's
a half-penny, and let be 'Newmarket' if you please. Wot say you? a voman!
Stubbs wins!" cried Mr. Jorrocks, as the halfpenny fell head downwards.
"Now, Spiers, couple up with Crane, and James and I will whip in to you.
But stop, gentlemen!" cried Mr. Jorrocks, as he reached the top of the stairs,
"let me make one request—that you von't eat the windmill you'll see on the
centre of the table. Mrs. Jorrocks has hired it for the evening, of Mr. Farrell, the confectioner, in Lamb's Conduit Street, and it's engaged to two
or three evening parties after it leaves this." "Lauk, John! how wulgar you
are. What matter can it make to your friends where the windmill comes
from!" exclaimed Mrs. Jorrocks in an audible voice from below, Nimrod,
with admirable skill, having piloted her down the straights and turns of
the staircase. Having squeezed herself between the backs of the chairs and
the wall, Mrs. Jorrocks at length reached the head of the table, and with
a bump of her body and wave of her hand motioned Nimrod to take the
seat on her right. Green then pushed past Belinda and Stubbs, and took
the place on Mrs. Jorrocks's left, so Stubbs, with a dexterous manoeuvre,
placed himself in the centre of the table, with Belinda between himself and
her uncle. Crane and Spiers then filled the vacant places on Nimrod's side,
Mr. Spiers facing Mr. Stubbs.

The dining-room was the breadth of the passage narrower than the
front drawing-room, and, as Mr. Jorrocks truly said, was rayther small—
but the table being excessively broad, made the room appear less than it
was. It was lighted up with spermaceti candles in silver holders, one at
each corner of the table, and there was a lamp in the wall between the
red-curtained windows, immediately below a brass nail, on which Mr. Jorrocks's great hunting-whip and a bunch of boot garters were hung. Two
more candles in the hands of bronze Dianas on the marble mantelpiece

lighted up a coloured copy of Barraud's picture of John Warde on Blue Ruin; while Mr. Ralph Lambton, on his horse Undertaker, with his hounds and men, occupied a frame on the opposite wall. The old-fashioned cellaret sideboard, against the wall at the end, supported a large bright-burning brass lamp, with raised foxes round the rim, whose effulgent rays shed a brilliant halo over eight black hats and two white ones, whereof the four middle ones were decorated with evergreens and foxes' brushes. The dinner table was crowded, not covered. There was scarcely a square inch of cloth to be seen on any part. In the centre stood a magnificent finely spun barley-sugar windmill, two feet and a half high, with a spacious sugar foundation, with a cart and horses and two or three millers at the door, and a she-miller working a ball-dress flounce at a lower window.

The whole dinner, first, second, third, fourth course—everything, in fact, except dessert—was on the table, as we sometimes see it at ordinaries and public dinners. Before both Mr. and Mrs. Jorrocks were two great tureens of mock-turtle soup, each capable of holding a gallon, and both full up to the brim. Then there were two sorts of fish; turbot and lobster sauce, and a great salmon. A round of boiled beef and an immense piece of roast occupied the rear of these, ready to march on the disappearance of the fish and soup—and behind the walls formed by the beef of old England came two dishes of grouse, each dish holding three brace. The side dishes consisted of a calf's head hashed, a leg of mutton, chickens, ducks, and mountains of vegetables; and round the windmill were plum-puddings, tarts, jellies, pies, and puffs.

Behind Mrs. Jorrocks's chair stood "Batsay" with a fine brass-headed comb in her hair, and stiff ringlets down her ruddy cheeks. She was dressed in a green silk gown, with a coral necklace, and one of Mr. Jorrocks's lavender and white coloured silk pocket-handkerchiefs made into an apron. "Binjimin" stood with the door in his hand, as the saying is, with a towel twisted round his thumb, as though he had cut it.

"Now, gentlemen," said Mr. Jorrocks, casting his eye up the table, as soon as they had all got squeezed and wedged round it, and the dishes were uncovered, "you see your dinner, eat whatever you like except the windmill—hope you'll be able to satisfy nature with what's on—would have had more but Mrs. J—— is so werry fine, she won't stand two joints of the same sort on the table."

Mrs. J. Lauk, John, how can you be so wulgar! Who ever saw two rounds of beef, as you wanted to have? Besides, I'm sure the gentlemen will excuse any little defishency, considering the short notice we have had, and that this is not an elaborate dinner.

Mr. Spiers. I'm sure, ma'm, there's no de*fish*ency at all. Indeed, I think there's as much fish as would serve double the number—and I'm sure you look as if you had your soup "on sale or return," as we say in the magazine line.

Mr. J. Haw! haw! haw! werry good, Mr. Spiers. I owe you one. Not bad soup though—had it from Birch's. Let me send you some; and pray lay into it, or I shall think you don't like it. Mr. Happerley, let me send you some—and, gentlemen, let me observe, once for all, that there's every species of malt liquor under the side table. Prime stout, from the Marquess Cornwallis, hard by. Also ale, table, and what my friend Crane there calls lamen*table*—he says, because it's so werry small—but, in truth, because I don't buy it of him. There's all sorts of drench, in fact, except water—a thing I never touch—rots one's shoes, don't know what it would do with one's stomach if it was to get there. Mr. Crane, you're eating nothing. I'm quite shocked to see you; you don't surely live upon hair? Do help yourself, or you'll faint from werry famine. Belinda, my love, does the Yorkshireman take care of you? Who's for some salmon?—bought at Luckey's, and there's both Tally ho and Tantivy sarce to eat with it. Somehow or other I always fancies I rides harder after eating these sarces with fish. Mr. Happerley Nimrod, you are the greatest man at table, consequently I axes you to drink wine first, according to the book of etiquette—help yourself, sir. Some of Crane's particklar, hot and strong, real stuff, none of your wan de bones [*vin de beaume*] or rot-gut French stuff—hope you like it—if you don't, pray speak your mind freely, now that we have Crane among us. Binjimin, get me some of that duck before Mr. Spiers, a leg and wing, if you please, sir, and a bit of the breast.

Mr. Spiers. Certainly, sir, certainly. Do you prefer a right or left wing, sir?

Mr. Jorrocks. Oh, either. I suppose it's all the same.

Mr. Spiers. Why no, sir, it's not exactly all the same; for it happens there is only one remaining, therefore it must be the *left* one.

Mr. J. (chuckling). Haw! haw! haw! Mr. S——, werry good that—werry good indeed. I owes you two.

"I'll trouble you for a little, Mr. Spiers, if you please," says Crane, handing his plate round the windmill.

"I'm sorry, sir, it is all gone," replies Mr. Spiers, who had just filled Mr. Jorrocks's plate; "there's nothing left but the neck," holding it up on the fork.

"Well, send it," rejoins Mr. Crane; "neck or nothing, you know, Mr. Jorrocks, as we say with the Surrey."

"Haw! haw! haw!" grunts Mr. Jorrocks, who is busy sucking a bone; "haw! haw! haw! werry good, Crane, werry good—owes you one. Now, gentlemen," added he, casting his eye up the table as he spoke, "let me adwise ye, before you attack the grouse, to take the hedge [edge] off your appetites, or else there won't be enough, and, you know, it does not do to eat the farmer after the gentlemen. Let's see, now—three and three are six, six brace among eight—oh, dear, that's nothing like enough. I wish, Mrs. J——, you had followed my adwice, and roasted them all. And now, Binjimin, you're going to break the windmill with your clumsiness, you little dirty rascal! Why von't you let Batsay arrange the table? Thank you, Mr. Crane, for your assistance—your politeness, sir, exceeds your beauty." [A barrel organ strikes up before the window, and Jorrocks throws down his knife and fork in an agony.] "Oh dear, oh dear, there's that cursed horgan again. It's a regular annihilator. Binjimin, run and kick the fellow's werry soul out of him. There's no man suffers so much from music as I do. I wish I had a pocketful of sudden death, that I might throw one at every thief of a musicianer that comes up the street. I declare the scoundrel has set all my teeth on edge. Mr. Nimrod, pray take another glass of wine after your roast beef.—Well, with Mrs. J—— if you choose, but I'll join you— always says that you are the werry cleverest man of the day—read all your writings—anny-tommy [anatomy] of gaming, and all. Am a hauthor my- self, you know—once set to, to write a werry long and elaborate harticle on scent, but after cudgelling my brains, and turning the thing over and over again in my mind, all that I could brew on the subject was, that scent was a werry rum thing; nothing rummer than scent, except a woman."

"Pray," cried Mrs. Jorrocks, her eyes starting as she spoke, "don't let us have any of your low-lifed stable conversation here—you think to show off before the ladies," added she, "and flatter yourself you talk about what we don't understand. Now, I'll be bound to say, with all your fine sporting hinformation, you carn't tell me whether a mule brays or neighs!"

"Vether a mule brays or neighs?" repeated Mr. Jorrocks, considering. "I'll lay I can!"

"Which, then?" inquired Mrs. Jorrocks.

"Vy, I should say it brayed."

"Mule bray!" cried Mrs. Jorrocks, clapping her hands with delight. "There's a cockney blockhead for you! It brays does it?"

Mr. Jorrocks. I meant to say, neighed.

"Ho! ho! ho!" grinned Mrs. J——, "neighs, does it? You are a nice man for a fox-'unter—a mule neighs—thought I'd catch you some of these odd days with your wain conceit."

"Vy, what does it do then?" inquired Mr. Jorrocks, his choler rising as he spoke. "I hopes, at all ewents, he don't make the 'orrible noise you do."

"Wy, it screams, you great hass!" rejoined his loving spouse.

A single, but very resolute knock at the street door, sounding quite through the house, stopped all further ebullition, and Benjamin, slipping out, held a short conversation with someone in the street, and returned.

"What's happened now, Binjimin?" inquired Mr. Jorrocks, with anxiety on his countenance, as the boy re-entered the room; "the 'osses arn't amiss, I 'ope?"

"Please, sir, Mr. Farrell's young man has come for the windmill—he says you've had it two hours," replied Benjamin.

"The deuce be with Mr. Farrell's young man! he does not suppose we can part with the mill before the cloth's drawn—tell him to mizzle, or I'll mill him. 'Now's the day and now's the hour'; who's for some grouse? Gentlemen, make your game, in fact. But first of all let's have a round robin. Pass the wine, gentlemen. What wine do you take, Stubbs?"

"Why, champagne is good enough for me."

Mr. Jorrocks. I dare say; but if you wait till you get any here, you will have a long time to stop. Shampain, indeed! had enough of that nonsense abroad—declare you young chaps drink shampain like hale. There's red and wite port, and sherry, in fact, and them as carn't drink, they must go without.

X. was expensive and soon became poor,

Y. was the wise man and kept want from the door.

"Now for the grouse!" added he, as the two beefs disappeared, and they took their stations at the top and bottom of the table. "Fine birds, to be sure! Hope you havn't burked your appetites, gentlemen, so as not to be able to do justice to them—smell high—werry good—gamey, in fact. Binjimin, take an 'ot plate to Mr. Nimrod—sarve us all round with them."

The grouse being excellent, and cooked to a turn, little execution was done upon the pastry, and the jellies had all melted long before it came to their turn to be eat. At length everyone, Mr. Jorrocks and all, appeared satisfied, and the noise of knives and forks was succeeded by the din of tongues and the ringing of glasses, as the eaters refreshed themselves with wine or malt liquors. Cheese and biscuit being handed about on plates, according to the *Spirit of Etiquette*, Binjimin and Batsay at length cleared the table, lifted off the windmill, and removed the cloth. Mr. Jorrocks then delivered himself of a most emphatic grace.

William Makepeace Thackeray knew good food and drink, and wrote about them lovingly, not as a separate thing but as one part, inextricable and important, of his characters and himself.

The supper menus for George II, in *The Four Georges*, are as dissolute as the king; Doctor Warner "revels in the thoughts of ox-cheek and burgundy—he is a boisterous, uproarious parasite, licks his master's shoes with explosions of laughter and cunning smack and gusto, and likes the taste of that blacking as much as the best claret"; in Newgate Prison, "You need not be particular about the sauce for Mr. Rice's fowl," says one turnkey, "for you know he's to be hanged in the morning." "Yes," the second answers, "but the chaplain sups with him, and he is a terrible fellow for melted butter."

The oft-quoted jingles about bouillabaisse and curry are nice enough, but not particularly important, to my mind. I much prefer some such straight forward recipe as the one of Thackeray's which starts out, "This ragout should be cooked in a stewpan rather broad than deep," and then goes on with the matter-of-fact precision of a good cook to give proper measurements and weights and procedure.

And out of the whole interminable comedy of *A Little Dinner at Timmins's* I like best the description, almost an "aside," of the "grand cook and confectioner of the Brobdingnag quarter," Fubsby's:

From A *Little Dinner at Timmins's* by William Makepeace Thackeray, 1811–1863

[Fubsby's was] a shop into which [Fitzroy Timmins] had often cast a glance of approbation as he passed; for there are not only the most wonderful and delicious cakes and confections in the window, but at the counter there are almost sure to be three or four of the prettiest women in the whole of this world, with little darling caps of the last French make, with beautiful wavy hair, and the neatest possible waists and aprons.

Yes, there they sit; and others, perhaps, besides Fitz have cast a sheep's-eye through those enormous plate-glass window panes. I suppose it is the fact of perpetually living among such a quantity of good things that makes those young ladies so beautiful. They come into the place, let us say, like ordinary people, and gradually grow handsomer and handsomer, until they grow out into the perfect angels you see. It can't be otherwise: if you and I, my dear fellow, were to have a course of that place, we should become beautiful too. They live in an atmosphere of the most delicious pine-apples, blanc-manges, creams (some whipt, and some so good that of course they don't want whipping), jellies, tipsy-cakes, cherry-brandy—one hundred thousand sweet and lovely things. Look at the preserved fruits, look at the golden ginger, the outspreading ananas, the darling little rogues of China oranges, ranged in the gleaming crystal cylinders. *Mon Dieu!* Look at the strawberries in the leaves. Each of them is as large nearly as a lady's reticule, and looks as if it had been brought up in a nursery to itself. One of those strawberries is a meal for those young ladies behind the counter: they nibble off a little from the side; and if they are very hungry, which can scarcely ever happen, they are allowed to go to the crystal canisters and take out a rout-cake or macaroon. In the evening they sit and tell each other little riddles out of the bonbons; and when they wish to amuse themselves, they read the most delightful remarks, in the French language, about Love, and Cupid, and Beauty, before they place them inside the crackers. They always are writing down good things into Mr. Fubsby's ledgers. It must be a perfect feast to read them. Talk of the Garden of Eden! I believe it was nothing to Mr. Fubsby's house; and I have no doubt that after those young ladies have been there a certain time, they get to such a pitch of loveliness at last that they become complete angels, with wings sprouting out of their lovely

shoulders, when (after giving just a preparatory balance or two) they fly up
to the counter and perch there for a minute, hop down again, and affectionately kiss the other young ladies, and say, "Good-bye, dears! We shall
meet again *là haut*." And then, with a whirr of their deliciously-scented
wings, away they fly for good, whisking over the trees of Brobdingnag
Square, and up into the sky, as the policeman touches his hat.

It is up there that they invent the legends for the crackers, and the
wonderful riddles and remarks on the bonbons. No mortal, I am sure,
could write them.

It is only because I know that my butchery can do no real harm to anything
as inviolate as *Vanity Fair* that I dare snip pieces from it. There are many more
as apt as the ones I have chosen, because Thackeray used what and how his
characters ate to prove their actuality.

"Tell me what a man eats . . . ," the old saw says, and old saws are perforce
right.

These cuttings give, then, a faint hint of the various states of Becky's fortunes, from the first hot bite of curry with fat Joseph Sedley to her last sordid,
hidden snack before he rescued her, so long after, from the tawdry end that
seemed inevitable.

They leave out all the gay little suppers with her cuckold Rawdon and his
brother officers, where Becky played and sang above the noise of the cred-
itors, and served tidbits from the silver hot-dishes with her own exquisite
hands, and kept one eye on the omnipresent Lord Steyne, protector of her
extramarital chastity.

Perhaps it is wrong, truly, to try to cut into such tissue . . . but when it is
as magical as this, it grows whole again while I think of it. . . .

From *Vanity Fair* by William Makepeace Thackeray, 1811–1863

Downstairs . . . they went, Joseph very red and blushing, Rebecca very
modest, and holding her green eyes downwards. She was dressed in white,
with bare shoulders as white as snow—the picture of youth, unprotected
innocence, and humble virgin simplicity. "I must be very quiet," thought
Rebecca, "and very much interested about India."

Now we have heard how Mrs. Sedley had prepared a fine curry for her
son, just as he liked it, and in the course of dinner a portion of this dish

was offered to Rebecca. "What is it?" said she, turning an appealing look to Mr. Joseph.

"Capital," said he. His mouth was full of it; his face quite red with the delightful exercise of gobbling. "Mother, it's as good as my own curries in India."

"Oh, I must try some, if it is an Indian dish," said Miss Rebecca. "I am sure everything must be good that comes from there."

"Give Miss Sharp some curry, my dear," said Mr. Sedley, laughing.

Rebecca had never tasted the dish before.

"Do you find it as good as everything else from India?" said Mr. Sedley.

"Oh, excellent!" said Rebecca, who was suffering tortures with the cayenne pepper.

"Try a chili with it, Miss Sharp," said Joseph, really interested.

"A chili," said Rebecca, gasping. "Oh yes!" She thought a chili was something cool, as its name imported, and was served with some. "How fresh and green they look!" she said, and put one into her mouth. It was hotter than the curry; flesh and blood could bear it no longer. She laid down her fork. "Water, for Heaven's sake, water!" she cried. Mr. Sedley burst out laughing (he was a coarse man, from the Stock Exchange, where they love all sorts of practical jokes). "They are real Indian, I assure you," said he. "Sambo, give Miss Sharp some water."

The paternal laugh was echoed by Joseph, who thought the joke capital. The ladies only smiled a little. They thought poor Rebecca suffered too much. She would have liked to choke old Sedley, but she swallowed her mortification as well as she had the abominable curry before it, and, as soon as she could speak, said, with a comical, good-humoured air—

"I ought to have remembered the pepper which the Princess of Persia puts in the cream-tarts in the *Arabian Nights.* Do you put cayenne into your cream-tarts in India, sir?"

Old Sedley began to laugh, and thought Rebecca was a good-humoured girl. Joseph simply said—"Cream-tarts, Miss? Our cream is very bad in Bengal. We generally use goats' milk; and, 'gad, do you know, I've got to prefer it!"

"You won't like *everything* from India now, Miss Sharp," said the old gentleman; but when the ladies had retired after dinner, the wily old fellow said to his son, "Have a care, Joe; that girl is setting her cap at you."

Miss Rebecca Sharp to Miss Amelia Sedley, Russell Square,
London. (Free.—Pitt Crawley.)

"My dearest, sweetest Amelia—With what mingled joy and sorrow do I take up the pen to write to my dearest friend! Oh, what a change between today and yesterday! . . . I will not tell you in what tears and sadness I passed the fatal night in which I separated from you. . . . I was awakened at day-break by the charwoman, and having arrived at the inn, was at first placed inside the coach. But when we got to a place called Leakington, where the rain began to fall very heavily—will you believe it?—I was forced to come outside; for Sir Pitt is a proprietor of the coach, and as a passenger came at Mudbury, who wanted an inside place, I was obliged to go outside in the rain, where, however, a young gentleman from Cambridge College sheltered me very kindly in one of his *several* greatcoats. . . .

"A carriage and four splendid horses, covered with armorial bearings, however, awaited us at Mudbury, four miles from Queen's Crawley, and we made our entrance to the baronet's park in state. There is a fine avenue of a mile long leading to the house, and the woman at the lodge-gate (over the pillars of which are a serpent and a dove, the supporters of the Crawley arms), made us a number of curtsies as she flung open the old iron carved doors. . . .

"Half an hour after our arrival the great dinner-bell was rung, and I came down with my two pupils (they are very thin, insignificant little chits of ten and eight years old). I came down in your *dear* muslin gown . . . for I am to be treated as one of the family, except on company days, when the young ladies and I are to dine upstairs. . . .

"'My lady is served,' says the Butler in black, in an immense white shirt-frill, that looked as if it had been one of the Queen Elizabeth's ruffs depicted in the hall. . . .

"Sir Pitt was already in the room with a silver jug. He had just been to the cellar, and was in full dress too—that is, he had taken his gaiters off, and showed his little dumpy legs in black worsted stockings. The sideboard was covered with glistening old plate—old cups, both gold and silver; old salvers and cruet-stands, like Rundell and Bridge's shop. Everything on the table was in silver too, and two footmen, with red hair and canary-coloured liveries, stood on either side of the sideboard.

"Mr. Crawley said a long grace, and Sir Pitt said Amen, and the great silver dish-covers were removed.

"'What have we for dinner, Betsy?' said the Baronet.

"'Mutton broth, I believe, Sir Pitt,' answered Lady Crawley.

"'*Mouton aux navets*,' added the Butler gravely (pronounce, if you please, moutongonavvy); 'and the soup is *potage de mouton à l'Ecossaise.* The side-dishes contain *pommes de terre au naturel*, and *choufleur à l'eau.*'

"'Mutton's mutton,' said the Baronet, 'and a devilish good thing. What *ship* was it, Horrocks, and when did you kill?'

"'One of the black-faced Scotch, Sir Pitt; we killed on Thursday.'

"'Who took any?'

"'Steel, of Mudbury, took the saddle and two legs, Sir Pitt; but he says the last was too young and confounded woolly, Sir Pitt.'

"'Will you take some *potage*, Miss ah—Miss Blunt?' said Mr. Crawley.

"'Capital Scotch broth, my dear,' said Sir Pitt, 'though they call it by a French name.'

"'I believe it is the custom, sir, in decent society,' said Mr. Crawley haughtily, 'to call the dish as I have called it;' and it was served to us on silver soup-plates by the footmen in the canary coats, with the *mouton aux navets*. Then 'ale and water' were brought, and served to us young ladies in wine-glasses. I am not a judge of ale, but I can say with a clear conscience I prefer water.

"While we were enjoying our repast, Sir Pitt took occasion to ask what had become of the shoulders of the mutton.

"'I believe they were eaten in the servants' hall,' said my lady humbly.

"'They was, my lady,' said Horrocks; 'and precious little else we get there neither.'

"Sir Pitt burst into a horse-laugh, and continued his conversation with Mr. Horrocks. 'That there little black pig of the Kent sow's breed must be uncommon fat now.'

"'It's not quite busting, Sir Pitt,' said the Butler with the gravest air, at which Sir Pitt, and with him the young ladies this time, began to laugh violently.

"'Miss Crawley, Miss Rose Crawley,' said Mr. Crawley, 'your laughter strikes me as being exceedingly out of place.'

"'Never mind my lord,' said the Baronet, 'we'll try the porker on Saturday. Kill un on Saturday morning, John Horrocks. Miss Sharp adores pork, don't you, Miss Sharp?'

"And I think this is all the conversation that I remember at dinner. When the repast was concluded, a jug of hot water was placed before Sir Pitt, with a case-bottle containing, I believe, rum. Mr. Horrocks served myself and my pupils with three little glasses of wine, and a bumper was poured out for my lady. When we retired, she took from her work-drawer an enormous interminable piece of knitting; the young ladies began to play at cribbage with a dirty pack of cards. We had but one candle lighted, but it was in a magnificent old silver candlestick; and after a very few questions from my lady, I had my choice of amusement between a volume of sermons, and a pamphlet on the corn-laws, which Mr. Crawley had been reading before dinner.

"So we sat for an hour . . . and then we went to bed. . . .

"*Saturday.*—This morning, at five, I heard the shrieking of the little black pig. Rose and Violet introduced me to it yesterday; and to the stables, and to the kennel, and to the gardener, who was picking fruit to send to market, and from whom they begged hard a bunch of hothouse grapes; but he said that Sir Pitt had numbered every single 'Man Jack' of them, and it would be as much as his place was worth to give any away. . . .

"Lady Crawley is always knitting the worsted. Sir Pitt is always tipsy, every night; and, I believe, sits with Horrocks, the butler. . . .

"A hundred thousand grateful loves to your dear papa and mamma. Is your poor brother recovered of his rack punch? O dear! O dear! How men should beware of wicked punch!

"Ever and ever thine own

"Rebecca."

. . . Jos had himself arrayed with unusual care and splendour; and without thinking it necessary to say a word to any member of his family . . . or asking for their company in his walk, he sallied forth at an early hour, and was presently seen making inquiries at the door of the Elephant Hotel. In consequence of the *fêtes* the house was full of company, the tables in the street were already surrounded by persons smoking and drinking the national small-beer, the public rooms were in a cloud of smoke, and Mr. Jos having, in his pompous way and with his clumsy German, made inquiries for the person of whom he was in search, was directed to the very top of the house, above the first-floor rooms, where some travelling pedlars had lived, and were exhibiting their jewellery and brocades; above the second-floor apartments, occupied by the *état major* of the gambling firm; above the third-floor rooms, tenanted by the band of renowned Bohemian vaulters and tumblers; and so on to the little cabins of the roof, where, among students, bagmen, small tradesmen, and country-folk, come in for the festival, Becky had found a little nest—as dirty a little refuge as ever beauty lay hid in.

Becky liked the life. She was at home with everybody in the place— pedlars, punters, tumblers, students, and all. She was of a wild, roving nature, inherited from father and mother, who were both Bohemians by taste and circumstance. If a lord was not by, she would talk to his courier with the greatest pleasure; the din, the stir, the drink, the smoke, the tattle of the Hebrew pedlars, the solemn, braggart ways of the poor tumblers, the *sournois* talk of the gambling-table officials, the songs and swagger of the students, and the general buzz and hum of the place had pleased and tickled the little woman, even when her luck was down, and she had not wherewithal to pay her bill. . . .

As Jos came creaking and puffing up the final stairs, and was speechless when he got to the landing, and began to wipe his face and then to look for No. 92, the room where he was directed to seek for the person he wanted, the door of the opposite chamber, No. 90, was open, and a student, in jackboots and a dirty *schlafrock*, was lying on the bed smoking a long pipe, whilst another student, in long yellow hair and a braided coat, exceeding smart and dirty too, was actually on his knees at No. 92, bawling through the keyhole supplications to the person within.

"Go away," said a well-known voice, which made Jos thrill; "I expect somebody—I expect my grandpapa. He mustn't see you there."

"Angel Englanderinn!" bellowed the kneeling student with the whity-brown ringlets and the large finger-ring, "do take compassion upon us. Make an appointment. Dine with me and Fritz at the inn in the park. We will have roast pheasants and porter, plum-pudding and French wine. We shall die if you don't."

"That we will," said the young nobleman on the bed. And this colloquy Jos overheard, though he did not comprehend it, for the reason that he had never studied the language in which it was carried on.

"Newmero kattervang dooze, si vous plait," Jos said, in his grandest manner, when he was able to speak.

"Quater fang tooce!" said the student, starting up, and he bounced into his own room, where he locked the door, and where Jos heard him laughing with his comrade on the bed.

The gentleman from Bengal was standing disconcerted by this incident, when the door of the 92 opened of itself, and Becky's little head peeped out full of archness and mischief. She lighted on Jos. "It's you," she said, coming out. "How I have been waiting for you! Stop! not yet; in one minute you shall come in." In that instant she put a rouge-pot, a brandy-bottle, and a plate of broken meat into the bed, gave one smooth to her hair, and finally let in her visitor.

She had, by way of morning robe, a pink domino, a trifle faded and soiled, and marked here and there with pomatum; but her arms shone out from the loose sleeves of the dress very white and fair, and it was tied round her little waist so as not ill to set off the trim little figure of the wearer. She led Jos by the hand into her garret. "Come in," she said—"come, and talk to me; sit yonder on the chair," and she gave the Civilian's hand a little squeeze, and laughingly placed him upon it. As for herself, she placed herself on the bed—not on the bottle and plate, you may be sure—on which Jos might have reposed, had he chosen that seat; and so there she sate and talked with her old admirer.

"How little years have changed you!" she said, with a look of tender interest. "I should have known you anywhere. What a comfort it is amongst strangers to see once more the frank, honest face of an old friend!"

The frank, honest face, to tell the truth, at this moment bore any expression but one of openness and honesty; it was, on the contrary, much perturbed and puzzled in look. Jos was surveying the queer little apartment in which he found his old flame. One of her gowns hung over the bed, another depending from a hook of the door; her bonnet obscured half the looking-glass, on which, too, lay the prettiest little pair of bronze boots; a French novel was on the table by the bedside, with a candle not of wax. Becky thought of popping that into the bed too, but she only put in the little paper nightcap with which she had put the candle out on going to sleep. "I should have known you anywhere," she continued; "a woman never forgets some things. And you were the first man I ever—I ever saw."

"Was I, really?" said Jos. "God bless my soul, you—you don't say so."

"When I came with your sister from Chiswick, I was scarcely more than a child," Becky said. "How is that dear love? Oh, her husband was a sad, wicked man, and of course it was of me that the poor dear was jealous. As if I cared about him, heigh-ho! when there was somebody—but no— don't let us talk of old times;" and she passed her handkerchief with the tattered lace across her eyelids.

"Is not this a strange place," she continued, "for a woman, who has lived in a very different world too, to be found in? I have had so many griefs and wrongs, Joseph Sedley, I have been made to suffer so cruelly, that I am almost made mad sometimes. I can't stay still in any place, but wander about always restless and unhappy. All my friends have been false to me—all. There is no such thing as an honest man in the world. I was the truest wife that ever lived, though I married my husband out of pique, because somebody else—but never mind that. I was true, and he trampled upon me and deserted me. I was the fondest mother. I had but one child, one darling, one hope, one joy, which I held to my heart with a mother's affection, which was my life, my prayer, my—my blessing; and they—they tore it from me—tore it from me;" and she put her hand to her heart with a passionate gesture of despair, burying her face for a moment on the bed.

The brandy-bottle inside clinked up against the plate which held the cold sausage. Both were moved, no doubt, by the exhibition of so much grief. Max and Fritz were at the door, listening with wonder to Mrs. Becky's sobs and cries. Jos, too, was a good deal frightened and affected at seeing his old flame in this condition. And she began forthwith to tell her story—a tale so neat, simple, and artless, that it was quite evident from hearing her that if ever there was a white-robed angel escaped from heaven to be subject to the infernal machinations and villainy of fiends here below, that spotless being, that miserable unsullied martyr, was present on the bed before Jos—on the bed, sitting on the brandy-bottle. . . .

Jos went away, convinced that she was the most virtuous as she was one of the most fascinating of women, and revolving in his mind all sorts of benevolent schemes for her welfare. Her persecutions ought to be ended; she ought to return to the society of which she was an ornament. He would see what ought to be done. . . . He would go and settle about it. . . . She wept tears of heartfelt gratitude as she parted from him, and pressed his hand as the gallant stout gentleman stooped down to kiss hers.

So Becky bowed Jos out of her little garret with as much grace as if it was a palace of which she did the honours; and that heavy gentleman having disappeared down the stairs, Max and Fritz came out of their hole, pipe in mouth, and she amused herself by mimicking Jos to them as she munched her cold bread and sausage and took draughts of her favourite brandy-and-water.

Charles Dickens's books are much easier to cut into than Thackeray's, but it is hard to say why. Dickens wrote more directly and less by implication, so that although both men used their characters' gastronomical habits as an intrinsic part of their being, his meals (or lack of them) are less involved in the past and future development of the story than they would be in anything by Thackeray.

Both men had a deep scorn for human venality and evil, but Dickens's satire is angrier than his contemporary's. However, there is always in his writings a pity and tenderness which may seem downright mawkish at times but which is in reassuring contrast to Thackeray's ruthless dissection of his fellows, and is in evidence even when he is most scathing and bitter, as in *Oliver Twist*.

There, for instance, he describes how the workhouse directors discover that the inmates actually like living there, and set about to change things at once:

From *Oliver Twist* by Charles Dickens, 1812–1870

So, they established the rule, that all poor people would have the alternative (for they would compel nobody, no, not they), of being starved by a gradual process in the house, or by a quick one out of it. With this view, they contracted with the water-works to lay on an unlimited supply of water; and with a corn-factor to supply periodically small quantities of oatmeal; and issued three meals a day of thin gruel, with an onion twice a week, and half a roll on Sundays. ... It was rather expensive at first, in consequence of the undertaker's bill, and the necessity of taking in the clothes of all the paupers, which fluttered loosely on their wasted, shrunken forms, after a week or two's gruel. But the number of workhouse inmates got thin as well as the paupers; and the board were in ecstacies.

Here I must give a recipe from *A Handbook of Cookery for Irish Workhouses*. It was published in 1911, but I feel there had been few changes made in it since little Oliver ate his gruel in such a place.

> *SOWANS OR FLUMMERY*
> 6 ounces unsifted oatmeal
> 1 gallon water
> Soak meal in lukewarm water 24 hours, press the mixture through a fine
> sieve, boil until thick, let stand 15 minutes, and serve.

And *that* reminds me of a brutal proverb of the very poor in France: *Tout fait ventre, pourvu que ça entre* . . . (Anything that can be swallowed is food . . . Food is anything you can get down without gagging.)

From *Oliver Twist* by Charles Dickens, 1812-1870

The room in which the boys were fed was a large stone hall, with a copper at one end: out of which the master, dressed in an apron for the purpose, and assisted by one or two women, ladled the gruel at meal-times. Of this festive composition each boy had one porringer, and no more—except on occasions of great public rejoicing, when he had two ounces and a quarter of bread besides. The bowls never wanted washing. The boys polished them with their spoons till they shone again; and when they had performed this operation (which never took very long, the spoons being nearly as large as the bowls), they would sit staring at the copper with such eager eyes as if they could have devoured the very bricks of which it was composed; employing themselves, meanwhile, in sucking their fingers most assiduously, with the view of catching up any stray splashes of gruel that might have been cast thereon. Boys have generally excellent appetites. Oliver Twist and his companions suffered the tortures of slow starvation for three months: at last they got so voracious and wild with hunger, that one boy, who was tall for his age, and hadn't been used to that sort of thing (for his father had kept a small cook-shop), hinted darkly to his companions, that unless he had another basin of gruel *per diem*, he was afraid he might some night happen to eat the boy who slept next him, who happened to be a weakly youth of tender age. He had a wild, hungry eye; and they implicitly believed him. A council was held; lots were cast who should walk up to the master after supper that evening, and ask for more; and it fell to Oliver Twist.

The evening arrived; the boys took their places. The master, in his cook's uniform, stationed himself at the copper; his pauper assistants ranged themselves behind him; the gruel was served out; and a long grace was said over the short commons. The gruel disappeared; the boys whispered each other, and winked at Oliver; while his next neighbours nudged him. Child as he was, he was desperate with hunger and reckless with misery. He rose from the table; and advancing to the master, basin and spoon in hand, said, somewhat alarmed at his own temerity:

"Please, sir, I want some more."

The master was a fat, healthy man; but he turned very pale. He gazed in stupefied astonishment on the small rebel for some seconds, and then clung for support to the copper. The assistants were paralyzed with wonder; the boys with fear.

"What!" said the master at length, in a faint voice.

"Please, sir," replied Oliver, "I want some more."

The master aimed a blow at Oliver's head with the ladle; pinioned him in his arms; and shrieked aloud for the beadle.

The board were sitting in solemn conclave when Mr. Bumble rushed into the room in great excitement, and, addressing the gentleman in the high chair, said,

"Mr. Limbkins, I beg your pardon, sir! Oliver Twist has asked for more!"

There was a general start. Horror was depicted on every countenance.

"For *more!*" said Mr. Limbkins. "Compose yourself, Bumble, and answer me distinctly. Do I understand that he asked for more, after he had eaten the supper allotted by the dietary?"

"He did, sir," replied Bumble.

"That boy will be hung," said the gentleman in the white waistcoat. "I know that boy will be hung."

Nobody controverted the prophetic gentleman's opinion. An animated discussion took place. Oliver was ordered into constant confinement; and a bill was next morning pasted on the outside of the gate, offering a reward of five pounds to anybody who would take Oliver Twist off the hands of the parish. In other words, five pounds and Oliver Twist were offered to any man or woman who wanted an apprentice to any trade, business, or calling.

"I never was more convinced of anything in my life," said the gentleman in the white waistcoat, as he knocked at the gate and read the bill next morning: "I never was more convinced of anything in my life, than I am that that boy will come to be hung."

It was hard to cut pieces out of *A Christmas Carol*: the whole foolish moving story is one of food, physical and spiritual, and I would have liked to put it here as I best like to read it, uncut from the first wonderful line, "Marley was dead: to begin with," to the last happy, moist-eyed "God bless us, every one!"

It hurts to leave out a single phrase, and I wince at the thought of not being able to print some such unforgettable description as the one of Marley's ghost, whose face "had a dismal light about it, like a bad lobster in a dark cellar." And old Scrooge, "secret, and self-contained, and solitary as an oyster," taking "his melancholy dinner in his usual melancholy tavern."

But it is impossible: *A Christmas Carol* must and can be read properly, the whole thing, again and again, and meanwhile here are crumbs of it, to whet the appetite:

From A Christmas Carol by Charles Dickens, 1812–1870

The people who were shovelling away on the housetops were jovial and full of glee; calling out to one another from the parapets, and now and then exchanging a facetious snowball—better-natured missile far than many a wordy jest—laughing heartily if it went right and not less heartily if it went wrong. The poulterers' shops were still half open, and the fruiterers' were radiant in their glory. There were great, round, pot-bellied baskets of chestnuts, shaped like the waistcoats of jolly old gentlemen, lolling at the doors, and tumbling out into the street in their apoplectic opulence. There were ruddy, brown-faced, broad-girthed Spanish onions, shining in the fatness of their growth like Spanish friars, and winking from their shelves in wanton slyness at the girls as they went by and glanced demurely at the hung-up mistletoe. There were pears and apples, clustered high in blooming pyramids; there were bunches of grapes, made, in the shopkeepers' benevolence, to dangle from conspicuous hooks, that people's mouths might water gratis as they passed; there were piles of filberts, mossy and brown, recalling, in their fragrance, ancient walks among the woods, and pleasant shufflings ankle deep through withered leaves; there were Norfolk Biffins, squat and swarthy, setting off the yellow of the oranges and lemons, and, in the great compactness of their juicy persons, urgently entreating and beseeching to be carried home in paper bags and eaten after dinner. The very gold and silver fish, set forth among these choice fruits in a bowl, though members of a dull and stagnant-blooded race, appeared to know that there was something going on; and, to a fish, went gasping round and round their little world in slow and passionless excitement.

The Grocers'! Oh, the Grocers'! Nearly closed, with perhaps two shutters down, or one; but through those gaps such glimpses! It was not alone that the scales descending on the counter made a merry sound, or that the twine and roller parted company so briskly, or that the canisters were rattled up and down like juggling tricks, or even that the blended scents of tea and coffee were so grateful to the nose, or even that the raisins were so plentiful and rare, the almonds so extremely white, the sticks of cinnamon so long and straight, the other spices so delicious, the candied fruits so caked and spotted with molten sugar as to make the coldest lookers-on feel faint and subsequently bilious. Nor was it that the figs were moist and pulpy, or that the French plums blushed in modest tartness from their highly-decorated boxes, or that everything was good to eat and in its Christmas dress: but the customers were all so hurried and so eager in the hopeful promise of the day, that they tumbled up against each other at the door, clashing their wicker baskets wildly, and left their purchases upon the counter, and came running back to fetch them, and committed hundreds of the like mistakes in the best humour possible; while the Grocer and his people were so frank and fresh that the polished hearts with which they fastened their aprons behind might have been their own, worn outside for general inspection, and for Christmas daws to peck at if they chose.

But soon the steeples called good people all, to church and chapel, and away they came, flocking through the streets in their best clothes, and with their gayest faces. And at the same time there emerged from scores of byestreets, lanes, and nameless turnings, innumerable people, carrying their dinners to the bakers' shops.

Up rose Mrs. Cratchit, Cratchit's wife, dressed out but poorly in a twice-turned gown, but brave in ribbons, which are cheap and make a goodly show for sixpence; and she laid the cloth, assisted by Belinda Cratchit, second of her daughters, also brave in ribbons; while Master Peter Cratchit plunged a fork into the saucepan of potatoes, and getting the corners of his monstrous shirt collar (Bob's private property, conferred upon his son and heir in honour of the day) into his mouth, rejoiced to find himself so gallantly attired, and yearned to show his linen in the fashionable Parks. And now two smaller Cratchits, boy and girl, came tearing in, screaming that outside the baker's they had smelt the goose, and known it for their own; and, basking in luxurious thoughts of sage-and-onion, these young Cratchits danced about the table, and exalted Master Peter Cratchit to the skies, while he (not proud, although his collars nearly choked him) blew the fire until the slow potatoes, bubbling up, knocked loudly at the saucepan-lid to be let out and peeled.

"What has ever got your precious father then?" said Mrs. Cratchit. "And your brother, Tiny Tim! And Martha warn't as late last Christmas Day by half-an-hour!"

"Here's Martha, mother!" said a girl, appearing as she spoke.

"Here's Martha, mother!" cried the two young Cratchits. "Hurrah! There's *such* a goose, Martha!"

"Why, bless your heart alive, my dear, how late you are!" said Mrs. Cratchit, kissing her a dozen times, and taking off her shawl and bonnet for her with officious zeal.

"We'd a deal of work to finish up last night," replied the girl, "and had to clear away this morning, mother!"

"Well! Never mind so long as you are come," said Mrs. Cratchit. "Sit ye down before the fire, my dear, and have a warm, Lord bless ye!"

"No, no! There's father coming," cried the two young Cratchits, who were everywhere at once. "Hide, Martha, hide!"

So Martha hid herself, and in came little Bob, the father, with at least three feet of comforter, exclusive of the fringe, hanging down before him; and his threadbare clothes darned up and brushed, to look seasonable; and Tiny Tim upon his shoulder. Alas for Tiny Tim, he bore a little crutch, and had his limbs supported by an iron frame!

"Why, where's our Martha?" cried Bob Cratchit, looking round.

"Not coming," said Mrs. Cratchit.

"Not coming!" said Bob, with a sudden declension in his high spirits;

for he had been Tim's blood horse all the way from church, and had come home rampant. "Not coming upon Christmas Day!"

Martha didn't like to see him disappointed, if it were only in joke; so she came out prematurely from behind the closet door, and ran into his arms, while the two young Cratchits hustled Tiny Tim, and bore him off into the wash-house, that he might hear the pudding singing in the copper.

"And how did little Tim behave?" asked Mrs. Cratchit, when she had rallied Bob on his credulity, and Bob had hugged his daughter to his heart's content.

"As good as gold," said Bob, "and better. Somehow he gets thoughtful, sitting by himself so much, and thinks the strangest things you ever heard. He told me, coming home, that he hoped the people saw him in the church, because he was a cripple, and it might be pleasant to them to remember upon Christmas Day, who made lame beggars walk and blind men see."

Bob's voice was tremulous when he told them this, and trembled more when he said that Tiny Tim was growing strong and hearty.

His active little crutch was heard upon the floor, and back came Tiny Tim before another word was spoken, escorted by his brother and sister to his stool before the fire; and while Bob, turning up his cuffs—as if, poor fellow, they were capable of being made more shabby—compounded some hot mixture in a jug with gin and lemons, and stirred it round and round and put it on the hob to simmer; Master Peter and the two ubiquitous young Cratchits went to fetch the goose, with which they soon returned in high procession.

Such a bustle ensued that you might have thought a goose the rarest of all birds; a feathered phenomenon, to which a black swan was a matter of course—and in truth it was something very like it in that house. Mrs. Cratchit made the gravy (ready beforehand in a little saucepan) hissing hot; Master Peter mashed the potatoes with incredible vigour; Miss Belinda sweetened up the applesauce; Martha dusted the hot plates; Bob took Tiny Tim beside him in a tiny corner at the table; the two young Cratchits set chairs for everybody, not forgetting themselves, and mounting guard upon their posts, crammed spoons into their mouths, lest they should shriek for goose before their turn came to be helped. At last the dishes were set on, and grace was said. It was succeeded by a breathless pause, as Mrs. Cratchit, looking slowly all along the carving knife, prepared to plunge it in the breast; but when she did, and when the long-expected gush of stuffing issued forth, one murmur of delight arose all round the board, and even Tiny Tim, excited by the two young Cratchits, beat on the table with the handle of his knife, and feebly cried Hurrah!

There never was such a goose. Bob said he didn't believe there ever was such a goose cooked. Its tenderness and flavour, size and cheapness, were the themes of universal admiration. Eked out by the applesauce and mashed potatoes, it was a sufficient dinner for the whole family; indeed, as Mrs. Cratchit said with great delight (surveying one small atom of a bone upon the dish), they hadn't ate it all at last! Yet everyone had had enough, and the youngest Cratchits, in particular, were steeped in sage and onion to the eyebrows! But now, the plates being changed by Miss Belinda, Mrs. Cratchit left the room alone—too nervous to bear witnesses—to take the pudding up and bring it in.

Suppose it should not be done enough! Suppose it should break in turning out! Suppose somebody should have got over the wall of the back yard, and stolen it, while they were merry with the goose—a supposition at which the two young Cratchits became livid! All sorts of horrors were supposed.

Hallo! A great deal of steam! The pudding was out of the copper. A smell like a washing-day! That was the cloth. A smell like an eating-house and a pastry cook's next door to each other, with a laundress's next door to that! That was the pudding! In half a minute Mrs. Cratchit entered—flushed, but smiling proudly—with the pudding like a speckled cannon-ball so hard and firm blazing in half of half-a-quartern of ignited brandy, and bedight with Christmas holly stuck into the top.

Oh, a wonderful pudding! Bob Cratchit said, and calmly too, that he regarded it as the greatest success achieved by Mrs. Cratchit since their marriage. Mrs. Cratchit said that now the weight was off her mind, she would confess she had had her doubts about the quantity of flour. Everybody had something to say about it, but nobody said or thought it was at all a small pudding for a large family. It would have been flat heresy to do so. Any Cratchit would have blushed to hint at such a thing.

At last the dinner was all done, the cloth was cleared, the hearth swept, and the fire made up. The compound in the jug being tasted, and considered perfect, apples and oranges were put upon the table, and a shovel-full of chestnuts on the fire. Then all the Cratchit family drew round the hearth, in what Bob Cratchit called a circle, meaning half a one; and at Bob Cratchit's elbow stood the family display of glass. Two tumblers, and a custard-cup without a handle.

These held the hot stuff from the jug, however, as well as golden goblets would have done; and Bob served it out with beaming looks, while the chestnuts on the fire sputtered and cracked noisily. Then Bob proposed:

"A Merry Christmas to us all, my dears. God bless us!"

Which all the family re-echoed.

"God bless us every one!" said Tiny Tim, the last of all.

THE POSTHUMOUS PAPERS OF THE PICKWICK CLUB are full of fantastic meals eaten lustily by fantastic people . . . for instance, the one after Mr. Pickwick's hat blew off at the military show, and came to rest at the very wheels of a fat gentleman's open barouche. The barouche, naturally, since it was within Mr. Pickwick's world, was loaded with young and old ladies, admirers of the former, a servant boy named Joe who slept except when he was eating, and "a hamper of spacious dimensions—one of those hampers which always awakens in a contemplative mind associations connected with cold fowls, tongues, and bottles of wine":

From *The Posthumous Papers of the Pickwick Club* by Charles Dickens, 1812–1870

After a great many jokes about squeezing the ladies' sleeves, and a vast quantity of blushing at sundry jocose proposals that the ladies should sit in the gentlemen's laps, the whole party were stowed down in the barouche; and the stout gentleman proceeded to hand the things from the fat boy (who had mounted up behind for the purpose) into the carriage.

"Now, Joe, knives and forks." The knives and forks were handed in, and the ladies and gentlemen inside, and Mr. Winkle on the box, were each furnished with those useful instruments.

"Plates, Joe, plates." A similar process employed in the distribution of the crockery.

"Now, Joe, the fowls. Damn that boy; he's gone to sleep again. Joe! Joe!" (Sundry taps on the head with a stick, and the fat boy, with some difficulty, roused from his lethargy.) "Come, hand in the eatables."

There was something in the sound of the last word which roused the unctuous boy. He jumped up; and the leaden eyes which twinkled behind his mountainous cheeks, leered horribly upon the food as he unpacked it from the basket.

"Now make haste," said Mr. Wardle; for the fat boy was hanging fondly over a capon, which he seemed wholly unable to part with. The boy sighed deeply, and, bestowing an ardent gaze upon its plumpness, unwillingly consigned it to his master.

"That's right—look sharp. Now the tongue—now the pigeon-pie. Take care of that veal and ham—mind the lobsters—take the salad out of the cloth—give me the dressing." Such were the hurried orders which issued from the lips of Mr. Wardle, as he handed in the different articles described, and placed dishes in everybody's hands, and on everybody's knees, in endless number.

"Now an't this capital?" inquired that jolly personage, when the work of destruction had commenced.

"Capital!" said Mr. Winkle, who was carving a fowl on the box.

"Glass of wine?"

"With the greatest pleasure."

"You'd better have a bottle to yourself, up there, hadn't you?"

"You're very good."

"Joe!"

"Yes, sir." (He wasn't asleep this time, having just succeeded in abstracting a veal patty.)

"Bottle of wine to the gentleman on the box. Glad to see you, sir."

"Thank'ee." Mr. Winkle emptied his glass, and placed the bottle on the coach-box, by his side.

"Will you permit me to have the pleasure, sir?" said Mr. Trundle to Mr. Winkle.

"With great pleasure," replied Mr. Winkle to Mr. Trundle: and then the two gentlemen took wine, after which they took a glass of wine round, ladies and all.

In fact, they all took a great deal of wine, and the party was very gay, and the fat gentleman asked the whole Pickwick Club to come and spend a week with him in Dingley Dell. It was a typical adventure, that is to say, for those wonderful silly delightful souls.

Of another, greater book, Dickens wrote, "Of all my books, I like this best. It will be easily believed that I am a fond parent to every child of my fancy, and that no one can ever love that family as I love them. But, like many fond parents, I have in my heart of hearts a favourite child. And his name is David Copperfield."

It was first published in 1850, illustrated by Phiz, with the satisfying title *The Personal History, Experience, and Observations of David Copperfield the Younger, of Blunderstone Rookery, Which He Never Meant to be Published on Any Account.* It is hard to imagine literature without it.

From *David Copperfield* by Charles Dickens, 1812–1870

The coach was in the yard, shining very much all over, but without any horses to it as yet; and it looked in that state as if nothing was more un-likely than its ever going to London. I was thinking this, and wondering what would ultimately become of my box, which Mr. Barkis had put down on the yard-pavement by the pole (he having driven up the yard to turn his cart), and also what would ultimately become of me, when a lady looked out of a bow-window where some fowls and joints of meat were hanging up, and said:

"Is that the little gentleman from Blunderstone?"

"Yes, ma'am," I said.

"What name?" inquired the lady.

"Copperfield, ma'am," I said.

"That won't do," returned the lady. "Nobody's dinner is paid for here in that name."

"Is it Murdstone, ma'am?" I said.

"If you're Master Murdstone," said the lady, "why do you go and give another name first?"

I explained to the lady how it was, who then rang a bell, and called out, "William! show the coffee-room!" upon which a waiter came running out of a kitchen on the opposite side of the yard to show it, and seemed a good deal surprised when he found he was only to show it to me.

It was a large long room, with some large maps in it. I doubt if I could have felt much stranger if the maps had been real foreign countries, and I cast away in the middle of them. I felt it was taking a liberty to sit down, with my cap in my hand, on the corner of the chair nearest the door; and when the waiter laid a cloth on purpose for me, and put a set of casters on it, I think I must have turned red all over with modesty.

He brought me some chops and vegetables, and took the covers off in such a bouncing manner that I was afraid I must have given him some offence. But he greatly relieved my mind by putting a chair for me at the table, and saying very affably, "Now, six-foot! come on!"

I thanked him, and took my seat at the board; but found it extremely difficult to handle my knife and fork with anything like dexterity, or to avoid splashing myself with the gravy, while he was standing opposite, staring so hard, and making me blush in the most dreadful manner every time I caught his eye. After watching me into the second chop, he said:

"There's half a pint of ale for you. Will you have it now?"

I thanked him, and said, "Yes." Upon which he poured it out of a jug into a large tumbler, and held it up against the light, and made it look beautiful.

"My eye!" he said. "It seems a good deal, don't it?"

"It does seem a good deal," I answered with a smile. For it was quite delightful to me to find him so pleasant. He was a twinkling-eyed, pimple-faced man, with his hair standing upright all over his head; and as he stood with one arm akimbo, holding up the glass to the light with the other hand, he looked quite friendly.

"There was a gentleman here yesterday," he said—"a stout gentleman, by the name of Topsawyer—perhaps you know him?"

"No," I said, "I don't think—"

"In breeches and gaiters, broad-brimmed hat, grey coat, speckled choker," said the waiter.

"No," I said bashfully, "I haven't the pleasure—"

"He came in here," said the waiter, looking at the light through the tumbler, "ordered a glass of this ale—*would* order it—I told him not—drank it, and fell dead. It was too old for him. It oughtn't to be drawn; that's the fact."

I was very much shocked to hear of this melancholy accident, and said I thought I had better have some water.

"Why, you see," said the waiter, still looking at the light through the tumbler, with one of his eyes shut up, "our people don't like things being ordered and left. It offends 'em. But *I'll* drink it, if you like. I'm used to it, and use is everything. I don't think it'll hurt me, if I throw my head back, and take it off quick. Shall I?"

I replied that he would much oblige me by drinking it, if he thought he could do it safely, but by no means otherwise. When he did throw his head back, and take it off quick, I had a horrible fear, I confess, of seeing him meet the fate of the lamented Mr. Topsawyer, and fall lifeless on the carpet. But it didn't hurt him. On the contrary, I thought he seemed the fresher for it.

"What have we got here?" he said, putting a fork into my dish. "Not chops?"

"Chops," I said.

"Lord bless my soul!" he exclaimed, "I didn't know they were chops. Why, a chop's the very thing to take off the bad effects of that beer! Ain't it lucky?"

So he took a chop by the bone in one hand, and a potato in the other, and ate away with a very good appetite, to my extreme satisfaction. He afterwards took another chop, and another potato; and after that another chop, and another potato. When he had done, he brought me a pudding, and having set it before me, seemed to ruminate, and to become absent in his mind for some moments.

"How's the pie?" he said, rousing himself.

"It's a pudding," I made answer.

"Pudding!" he exclaimed. "Why, bless me, so it is! What!" looking at it nearer, "you don't mean to say it's a batter-pudding?"

"Yes, it is indeed."

"Why, a batter-pudding," he said, taking up a tablespoon, "is my favourite pudding! Ain't that lucky? Come on, little 'un, and let's see who'll get most."

The waiter certainly got most. He entreated me more than once to come in and win; but what with his tablespoon to my teaspoon, his dispatch to my dispatch, and his appetite to my appetite, I was left far behind at the first mouthful, and had no chance with him. I never saw any one enjoy a pudding so much, I think; and he laughed, when it was all gone, as if his enjoyment of it lasted still.

Finding him so very friendly and companionable, it was then that I asked for the pen and ink and paper, to write to Peggotty. He not only brought it immediately, but was good enough to look over me while I wrote the letter. When I had finished it, he asked me where I was going to school.

I said, "Near London," which was all I knew.

"Oh! my eye!" he said, looking very low-spirited, "I am sorry for that."

"Why?" I asked him.

"Oh, Lord!" he said, shaking his head, "that's the school where they broke the boy's ribs—two ribs—a little boy he was. I should say he was—let me see—how old are you, about?"

I told him between eight and nine.

"That's just his age," he said. "He was eight years and six months old when they broke his first rib; eight years and eight months old when they broke his second, and did for him."

I could not disguise from myself, or from the waiter, that this was an uncomfortable coincidence, and inquired how it was done. His answer was not cheering to my spirits, for it consisted of two dismal words, "With whopping."

The blowing of the coach-horn in the yard was a seasonable diversion, which made me get up and hesitatingly inquire, in the mingled pride and diffidence of having a purse (which I took out of my pocket), if there were anything to pay.

"There's a sheet of letter-paper," he returned. "Did you ever buy a sheet of letter-paper?"

I could not remember that I ever had.

"It's dear," he said, "on account of the duty. Three-pence. That's the way we're taxed in this country. There's nothing else except the waiter. Never mind the ink; *I* lose by that."

"What should you—what should I—how much ought I to—what would it be right to pay the waiter, if you please?" I stammered, blushing.

"If I hadn't a family, and that family hadn't the cowpock," said the waiter, "I wouldn't take a sixpence. If I didn't support a aged pairint, and a lovely sister"—here the waiter was greatly agitated—"I wouldn't take a farthing. If I had a good place, and was treated well here, I should beg acceptance of a trifle, instead of taking of it. But I live on broken wittles, and I sleep on the coals"—here the waiter burst into tears.

I was very much concerned for his misfortunes, and felt that any recognition short of nine pence would be mere brutality and hardness of heart.

Therefore I gave him one of my three bright shillings, which he received with much humility and veneration, and spun up with his thumb, directly afterwards to try the goodness of.

It was a little disconcerting to me to find, when I was being helped up behind the coach, that I was supposed to have eaten all the dinner without any assistance. I discovered this from overhearing the lady in the bow-window say to the guard, "Take care of that child, George, or he'll burst!" and from observing that the women-servants who were about the place came out to look and giggle at me as a young phenomenon. My unfortunate friend the waiter, who had quite recovered his spirits, did not appear to be disturbed by this, but joined in the general admiration without being at all confused. If I had any doubt of him, I suppose this half awakened it; but I am inclined to believe that with the simple confidence of a child, and the natural reliance of a child upon superior years (qualities I am very sorry any children should prematurely change for worldly wisdom), I had no serious mistrust of him on the whole, even then.

I felt it rather hard, I must own, to be made, without deserving it, the subject of jokes between the coachman and guard as to the coach drawing heavy behind, on account of my sitting there, and as to the greater expediency of my travelling by wagon. The story of my supposed appetite getting wind among the outside passengers, they were merry upon it likewise, and asked me whether I was going to be paid for at school as two brothers or three, and whether I was contracted for, or went upon the regular terms, with other pleasant questions. But the worst of it was, that I knew I should be ashamed to eat anything when an opportunity offered, and that, after a rather light dinner, I should remain hungry all night; for I had left my cakes behind, at the hotel, in my hurry. My apprehensions were realized. When we stopped for supper I couldn't muster courage to take any, though I should have liked it very much, but sat by the fire and said I didn't want anything.

Until the day arrived on which I was to entertain my newly-found old friends, I lived principally on Dora and coffee. In my love-lorn condition, my appetite languished; and I was glad of it, for I felt as though it would have been an act of perfidy towards Dora to have a natural relish for my dinner. The quantity of walking exercise I took was not in this respect attended with its usual consequence, as the disappointment counteracted the fresh air. I have my doubts, too, founded on the acute experience acquired at this period of my life, whether a sound enjoyment of animal food can develop itself freely in any human subject who is always in torment from tight boots. I think the extremities require to be at peace before the stomach will conduct itself with vigour.

On the occasion of this domestic little party, I . . . provided a pair of soles, a small leg of mutton, and a pigeon-pie. . . . [Then,] having laid in the materials for a bowl of punch, to be compounded by Mr. Micawber; having provided a bottle of lavender water, two wax candles, a paper of mixed pins, and a pincushion, to assist Mrs. Micawber in her toilette, at my dressing-table; having also caused the fire in my bedroom to be lighted for Mrs. Micawber's convenience; and having laid the cloth with my own hands, I awaited the result with composure.

At the appointed time my three visitors arrived together—Mr. Micawber with more shirt collar than usual, and a new ribbon to his eye-glass; Mrs. Micawber with her cap in a whity-brown paper parcel; Traddles carrying the parcel, and supporting Mrs. Micawber on his arm. They were all delighted with my residence. When I conducted Mrs. Micawber to my dressing-table, and she saw the scale on which it was prepared for her, she was in such raptures that she called Mr. Micawber to come in and look.

"My dear Copperfield," said Mr. Micawber, "this is luxurious. This is a way of life which reminds me of the period when I was myself in a state of celibacy, and Mrs. Micawber had not yet been solicited to plight her faith at the Hymeneal altar."

"He means, solicited by him, Mr. Copperfield," said Mrs. Micawber archly. "He cannot answer for others." . . .

To divert his thoughts . . . I informed Mr. Micawber that I relied upon him for a bowl of punch, and led him to the lemons. His recent despondency, not to say despair, was gone in a moment. I never saw a man so thoroughly enjoy himself amid the fragrance of lemon-peel and sugar, the odour of burning rum, and the steam of boiling water, as Mr. Micawber did that afternoon. It was wonderful to see his face shining at us out of a thin cloud of these delicate fumes, as he stirred, and mixed, and tasted, and looked as if he were making, instead of punch, a fortune for his family down to the latest posterity. As to Mrs. Micawber, I don't know whether it was the effect of the cap, or the lavender water, or the pins, or the fire, or the wax candles, but she came out of my room, comparatively speaking, lovely. And the lark was never gayer than that excellent woman.

I suppose—I never ventured to inquire, but I suppose—that Mrs. Crupp, after frying the soles, was taken ill. Because we broke down at that point. The leg of mutton came up very red within, and very pale without; besides having a foreign substance of a gritty nature sprinkled over it, as if it had had a fall into the ashes of that remarkable kitchen fire-place. But we were not in a condition to judge of this fact from the appearance of the gravy, forasmuch as the "young gal" had dropped it all upon the stairs— where it remained, by-the-by, in a long train, until it was worn out. The pigeon-pie was not bad, but it was a delusive pie; the crust being like a disappointing head, phrenologically speaking—full of lumps and bumps, with nothing particular underneath. In short, the banquet was such a failure that I should have been quite unhappy—about the failure, I mean, for I am always unhappy about Dora—if I had not been relieved by the great good-humour of my company, and by a bright suggestion from Mr. Micawber.

"My dear friend Copperfield," said Mr. Micawber, "accidents will occur in the best-regulated families; and in families not regulated by that pervading influence which sanctifies while it enhances the—a—I would say, in short, by the influence of Woman, in the lofty character of Wife, they may be expected with confidence, and must be borne with philosophy. If you will allow me to take the liberty of remarking that there are few comestibles better, in their way, than a devil, and that I believe, with a little division of labour, we could accomplish a good one if the young person in attendance could produce a gridiron, I would put it to you that this little misfortune may be easily repaired."

There was a gridiron in the pantry, on which my morning rasher of bacon was cooked. We had it in, in a twinkling, and immediately applied ourselves to carrying Mr. Micawber's idea into effect. The division of labour to which he had referred was this: Traddles cut the mutton into slices; Mr. Micawber (who could do anything of this sort to perfection) covered them with pepper, mustard, salt, and cayenne; I put them on the gridiron, turned them with a fork, and took them off, under Mr. Micawber's direction; and Mrs. Micawber heated, and continually stirred, some mushroom ketchup in a little saucepan. When we had slices enough done to begin upon, we fell to, with our sleeves still tucked up at the wrists, more slices sputtering and blazing on the fire, and our attention divided between the mutton on our plates and the mutton then preparing.

What with the novelty of this cookery, the excellence of it, the bustle of it, the frequent starting up to look after it, the frequent sitting down to dispose of it as the crisp slices came off the gridiron hot and hot, the being so busy, so flushed with the fire, so amused, and in the midst of such a tempting noise and savour, we reduced the leg of mutton to the bone. My own appetite came back miraculously. I am ashamed to record it, but I really believe I forgot Dora for a little while. I am satisfied that Mr. and Mrs. Micawber could not have enjoyed the feast more, if they had sold a bed to provide it. Traddles laughed as heartily, almost the whole time, as he ate and worked. Indeed we all did, all at once; and I dare say there never was a greater success.

One of our first feats in the housekeeping way was a little dinner to Traddles. I met him in town, and asked him to walk out with me that afternoon. He readily consenting, I wrote to Dora, saying I would bring him home. It was pleasant weather, and on the road we made my domestic happiness the theme of conversation. Traddles was very full of it; and said that, picturing himself with such a home, and Sophy waiting and preparing for him, he could think of nothing wanting to complete his bliss.

I could not have wished for a prettier little wife at the opposite end of the table, but I certainly could have wished, when we sat down, for a little more room. I did not know how it was, but though there were only two of us, we were at once always cramped for room, and yet had always room enough to lose everything in. I suspect it may have been because nothing had a place of its own, except Jip's pagoda, which invariably blocked up the main thoroughfare. On the present occasion, Traddles was so hemmed in by the pagoda and the guitar-case and Dora's flower-painting, and my writing-table, that I had serious doubts of the possibility of his using his knife and fork; but he protested, with his own good-humour, "Oceans of room, Copperfield! I assure you, oceans!"

There was another thing I could have wished—namely, that Jip had never been encouraged to walk about the table-cloth during dinner. I began to think there was something disorderly in his being there at all, even if he had not been in the habit of putting his foot in the salt or the melted butter. On this occasion he seemed to think he was introduced expressly to keep Traddles at bay, and he barked at my old friend, and made short runs at his plate, with such undaunted pertinacity, that he may be said to have engrossed the conversation.

However, as I knew how tender-hearted my dear Dora was, and how sensitive she would be to any slight upon her favourite, I hinted no objection. For similar reasons I made no allusion to the skirmishing plates upon the floor; or to the disreputable appearance of the castors, which were all at sixes and sevens, and looked drunk; or to the further blockade of Traddles by wandering vegetable dishes and jugs. I could not help wondering in my own mind, as I contemplated the boiled leg of mutton before me, previous to carving it, how it came to pass that our joints of meat were of such extraordinary shapes, and whether our butcher contracted for all the deformed sheep that came into the world; but I kept my reflections to myself.

"My love," said I to Dora, "what have you got in that dish?"

I could not imagine why Dora had been making tempting little faces at me, as if she wanted to kiss me.

"Oysters, dear," said Dora timidly.

"Was that *your* thought?" said I, delighted.

"Ye-yes, Doady," said Dora.

"There never was a happier one!" I exclaimed, laying down the carving knife and fork. "There is nothing Traddles likes so much!"

"Ye-yes, Doady," said Dora, "and so I bought a beautiful little barrel of them, and the man said they were very good. But I—I am afraid there's something the matter with them. They don't seem right." Here Dora shook her head, and diamonds twinkled in her eyes.

"They are only opened in both shells," said I. "Take the top one off, my love."

"But it won't come off," said Dora, trying very hard, and looking very much distressed.

"Do you know, Copperfield," said Traddles, cheerfully examining the dish, "I think it is in consequence—they are capital oysters, but I *think* it is in consequence—of their never having been opened."

They never had been opened; and we had no oyster-knives, and couldn't have used them if we had; so we looked at the oysters, and ate the mutton. At least we ate as much of it as was done, and made up with capers. If I had permitted him, I am satisfied that Traddles would have made a perfect savage of himself, and eaten a plateful of raw meat, to express enjoyment of the repast. But I would hear of no such immolation on the altar of friendship; and we had a course of bacon instead—there happening, by good fortune, to be cold bacon in the larder.

My poor little wife was in such affliction when she thought I should be annoyed, and in such a state of joy when she found I was not, that the discomfiture I had subdued very soon vanished, and we passed a happy evening—Dora sitting with her arm on my chair while Traddles and I discussed a glass of wine, and taking every opportunity of whispering in my ear that it was so good of me not to be a cruel, cross old boy. By-and-by she made tea for us; which it was so pretty to see her do, as if she was busying herself with a set of doll's tea-things, that I was not particular about the quality of the beverage. Then Traddles and I played a game or two at cribbage; and Dora singing to the guitar the while, it seemed to me as if our courtship and marriage were a tender dream of mine, and the nights when I first listened to her voice were not yet over.

IX

A CONFUSION OF TONGUES

Russia, France, Germany, and England

In every kind of feast written about in Russia during the nineteenth century, there is much the same feeling of timelessness as in Chinese gastronomy. It does not matter what author describes what feast: you know that poor people ate one way, the age-old way of bread and soup, when they ate at all, and that in the fat kitchens of the landowners the only variations on the rich exotic theme were caused by political problems of importation, so that at one time it might be chic to serve German hocks, while at another nothing but French champagnes would do.

That is why I think it is all right to skip nonchalantly forward and back and forward again in this part of the book, although I shall begin it properly in 1804 with excerpts from *The Russian Journals of Martha and Catherine Wilmot.*

They were English girls who visited Moscow, and wrote voluminous un-gainly letters and notes about their life there which prove them to be aston-ishingly healthy young creatures, if not particularly sensitive to anything but the food and drink and bustle of the moment:

From *The Russian Journals of Martha and Catherine Wilmot*, 1804
Yesterday we went at twelve o'clock to Count Ostrowman's. . . . Immedi-ately on entering we were led to a table where what is called a Breakfast was

displayed—that is little odds and ends of dried fish, or Caviar, of Cheese, Bread, etc., and *eau de vie* were presented to us to give an appetite for dinner which was announced almost immediately. We assembled in the Hall, surrounded by a sort of gallery which was filled with Men, Women, Dwarfs, children, Fools, and enraged musicians who sang and played with such powerful effect as to deafen those whom Heaven had spared. . . .

A Trumpet sounded and "blew a blast so loud and dread" that every tongue was silenced. A crystal vase filled with champagne was presented to the Master of the Castle. He stood up and quaffed the sparkling draft to the health of the Lady of the feast. The Trumpet sounded a second time, the Goblet was presented to Princess Dashkaw who went thro' the same ceremony. A third time the Trumpet sounded and a third person quaffed from the same crystal vase to the same toast. In short the ceremony was repeated for every individual, and as there were a party of 46 you may judge the time which the parade and pomp took up.

Many a bad dinner I made from the mere fatigue of being offered fifty or sixty different dishes by servants who come out one after the other and flourish ready carv'd fish, flesh, fowl, Vegetables, fruits, soups of fish, etc., before your eyes, wines, Liqueurs, etc., in their turn. Seriously the profusion is beyond anything I ever saw. . . .

Yesterday we dined at Mr. Kissilof's where the only thing worth telling you about was a little Calmuck boy from the confines of China. He was brought in together with a little Circassian and an Indian to amuse the company, each dressed according to the fashion of his country. The two latter were not very remarkable, but the little Chineese was critically like the figures on old Indian serenes, cups and saucers, fans etc.. . . His dress was trousers of white Indian calico, a shawl sewed for shirt waistcoat, and all the rest of his dress, except a little spencer of scarlet cashimere, edged with silver spangles. . . . 'Tis here quite the custom to bring in men, or women or children, or fools, or anything that can amuse the company.

At a very agreeable sledging party . . . which was given nominally for the Princess (Dashkaw) we were a few minutes late, and could scarcely gain admittance for the number of Traineaus that were in the court and afterwards for the number of guests that were in the apartments. Soon after chocolate and cakes were handed, and then breakfast opened on our astonished optics in another room, which consisted of hot and cold soups, meat, fish, fowls, Ices, fruits, etc. The dessert was in another room, dry'd fruits, Cakes, and *eau de vie*. At length forty Traineaus, each drawn by six horses at least, quitted the House. In each Traineau were four people, two ladies and two gentlemen attended by two footmen and two or three postillions etc. The *coup d'oeil* was superb. We drove like lightning round the Town, each animating his coachman to unheard of exertions to pass the Traineau which was before him. . . . We were dressed in all our best array; but don't figure to yourself fur caps, etc.—not at all—white satin on some, pink on others, etc.—black beaver on a few, and amongst that number was your humble servant. Shawls and pelisses protected us from the cold, which, however, was not very intense that day. After parading with indefatigable speed for two hours and a half we returned to M. Kumberline's, arranged our Dresses as well as we could, drank tea, and then danced to conclude the evening. . . .

It is easy enough to talk of "sad, black Russia" and to find countless quotations by her writers to prove, even gastronomically, how black and sad she was in those far past days.

A typical one, from *Yama* by Alexander Kuprin, tells of the feast eaten by little Yerka, who has escaped from the brothel with her silly weak lover. He is about to be arrested for stealing government funds, so they decide to die together, and "although he had in his pockets only eleven kopecks, all in all, he gave orders sweepingly, like a habitual, downright prodigal; he ordered sturgeon stew, double snipes, and fruits; and, in addition to all this, coffee, liqueurs, and two bottles of frosted champagne."

And then, of course, after they have dined well in the expensive hotel-room, and he has killed the loving Yerka, this "hypocrite, coward, and blackguard" loses his nerve and fakes a wound upon the skin over his quaking ribs. . . .

Oh, sad black Russia!

It is good to turn to Gogol's monumental laughter, to his impious, unflinching mockery of everything weak and limited about the people of this country. He wrote *Dead Souls* in 1842, ten years before he died.

He meant to write two more parts of it, but a mystical remorse overwhelmed him in his last years, a feeling that he had betrayed Russia by laughing at her. He destroyed what he had completed of the second part of the book, but the first one was enough to influence many great writers since then, with its humanity and realism, and its clear-eyed irony.

From *Dead Souls* by Nikolai Gogol, 1809-1852

"Well, my love, shall we go in to dinner?" said Madame Sobakevitch to her husband.

"Please!" said Sobakevitch. Whereupon the two gentlemen, going up to the table which was laid with savouries, duly drank a glass of vodka each; they took a preliminary snack as is done all over the vast expanse of Russia, throughout the towns and villages, that is, tasted various salt dishes and other stimulating dainties; then all proceeded to the dining-room; the hostess sailed in at their head like a goose swimming. The small table was laid for four. In the fourth place there very shortly appeared—it is hard to say definitely who—whether a married lady, or a girl, a relation, a housekeeper or simply someone living in the house—a thing without a cap, about thirty years of age, in a bright-coloured handkerchief. There are persons who exist in the world not as primary objects but as incidental spots or specks on objects. They sit in the same place and hold their head immovably; one is almost tempted to take them for furniture and imagine that no word has ever issued from those lips; but in some remote region, in the maids' quarters or the storeroom, it is quite another story!

"The cabbage soup is particularly good today," said Sobakevitch, taking spoonfuls of the soup and helping himself to an immense portion of a well-known delicacy which is served with cabbage soup and consists of sheep's stomach, stuffed with buckwheat, brains, and sheep's trotters. "You won't find a dish like this in town," he went on, addressing Tchitchikov, "the devil only knows what they give you there!"

"The governor keeps a good table, however," said Tchitchikov.

"But do you know what it is all made of ? You won't eat it when you do know."

"I don't know how the dishes were cooked, I can't judge of that; but the pork chops and the stewed fish were excellent."

"You fancy so. You see I know what they buy at the market. That scoundrelly cook who has been trained in France buys a cat and skins it and sends it up to the table for a hare."

"Faugh, what unpleasant things you say!" said his wife.

"Well, my love! That's how they do things; it's not my fault, that's how they do things, all of them. All the refuse that our Alkulka throws, if I may be permitted to say so, into the rubbish pail, they put into the soup, yes, into the soup! In it goes!"

"You always talk about such things at table," his wife protested again.

"Well, my love," said Sobakevitch, "if I did the same myself, you might complain, but I tell you straight that I am not going to eat filth. If you sprinkle frogs with sugar I wouldn't put them into my mouth, and I wouldn't taste oysters, either: I know what oysters are like. Take some mutton," he went on, addressing Tchitchikov. "This is saddle of mutton with grain, not the fricassees that they make in gentlemen's kitchens out of mutton which has been lying about in the market-place for days. The French and German doctors have invented all that; I'd have them all hanged for it. They have invented a treatment too, the hunger cure! Because they have a thin-blooded German constitution, they fancy they can treat the Russian stomach too. No, it's all wrong, it's all their fancies, it's all . . ." Here Sobakevitch shook his head wrathfully. "They talk of enlightenment, enlightenment, and this enlightenment is . . . faugh! I might use another word for it but it would be improper at the dinner table. It is not like that in my house. If we have pork we put the whole pig on the table, if it's mutton, we bring in the whole sheep, if it's a goose, the whole goose! I had rather eat only two dishes, and eat my fill of them." Sobakevitch confirmed this in practice; he put half a saddle of mutton on his plate and ate it all, gnawing and sucking every little bone.

"Yes," thought Tchitchikov, "the man knows what's what."

"It's not like that in my house," said Sobakevitch, wiping his fingers on a dinner napkin, "I don't do things like a Plyushkin: he has eight hundred souls and he dines and sups worse than any shepherd."

"Who is this Plyushkin?" inquired Tchitchikov.

"A scoundrel," answered Sobakevitch. "You can't fancy what a miser he is. The convicts in prison are better fed than he is: he has starved all his servants to death . . ."

"Really," Tchitchikov put in with interest. "And do you actually mean that his serfs have died in considerable numbers?"

"They die off like flies."

"Really, like flies? Allow me to ask how far away does he live?"

"Four miles."

"Four miles!" exclaimed Tchitchikov and was even aware of a slight palpitation of the heart. "But when one drives out of your gate, is it to the right or to the left?"

"I don't advise you even to learn the road to that cur's," said Sobakevitch. "There is more excuse for visiting the lowest haunt than visiting him."

"Oh, I did not ask for any special . . . but simply because I am interested in knowing all about the locality," Tchitchikov replied.

The saddle of mutton was followed by curd cheese-cakes, each one of which was much larger than a plate, then a turkey as big as a calf, stuffed with all sorts of good things: eggs, rice, kidneys, and goodness knows what. With this the dinner ended, but when they had risen from the table Tchitchikov felt as though he were two or three stones heavier. They went into the drawing-room, where they found a saucer of jam already awaiting them—not a pear, nor a plum, nor any kind of berry—and neither of the gentlemen touched it. The lady of the house went out of the room to put out some more on other saucers.

Taking advantage of her absence, Tchitchikov turned to Sobakevitch, who, lying in an easy-chair, was merely gasping after his ample repast and emitting from his throat undefinable sounds while he crossed himself and continually put his hand before his mouth.

Tchitchikov addressed him as follows: "I should like to have a few words with you about a little matter of business."

"Here is some more jam," said the lady of the house, returning with a saucer, "it's very choice, made with honey!"

"We will have some of it later on," said Sobakevitch. "You go to your own room now. Pavel Ivanitch and I will take off our coats and have a little nap."

The lady began suggesting that she should send for feather beds and pillows, but her husband said, "There's no need, we can doze in our easy-chairs," and she withdrew.

Sobakevitch bent his head slightly, and prepared to hear what the business might be.

And then Tchitchikov proceeded to outline to Sobakevitch his astounding scheme for buying up the tax-rights on all the serfs who, since the last census, were, as he discreetly phrased it, "nonexistent": the dead souls of Russia.

It was a proposition couched in the most altruistic language, and could have been made only by a Tchitchikov, who, Gogol said, he had "taken as a type to show forth the vices and failings, rather than the merits and virtues, of the commonplace Russian individual; and the characters which revolve around him have also been selected for the purpose of demonstrating our national weaknesses and shortcomings."

The steady overeating of the rich country people in *Dead Souls* grows tiresome, but I cannot resist giving two more examples of it, at the risk of being repetitive as far as digestive snores may go. In both of them Tchitchikov is staying with Piotr Petrovitch, a fat generous man who loves company. He serves a noonday dinner, to chase away the habitual boredom of one of the company, and then after they have awakened from the stupor it throws them into he takes them for a boat-ride. He swims naked like a great fish in the chilly water, and develops a fine appetite for tea, while the others watch him enviously . . . and then they go home across the waters, in an unforgettably beautiful moment, and pick up their forks again.

From *Dead Souls* by Nikolai Gogol, 1809–1852

. . . "Run quickly to the kitchen, Alexasha, and tell the cook to send in the fish pies as soon as she can. But where's that sluggard Emelyan and that thief Antoshka? Why don't they bring the savouries?"

But the door opened. The sluggard Emelyan and the thief Antoshka made their appearance with table napkins, laid the table, set a tray with six decanters of various coloured homemade wines; soon round the trays and decanters there was a necklace of plates—caviare, cheese, salted mushrooms of different kinds, and something was brought in from the kitchen covered with a plate, under which could be heard the hissing of butter. The sluggard Emelyan and the thief Antoshka were quick and excellent fellows. Their master gave them those titles because to address them without nicknames seemed tame and flat, and he did not like anything to be so; he was a kind-hearted man, but liked to use words of strong flavour. His servants did not resent it, however.

The savouries were followed by dinner. The good-hearted fat gentleman showed himself now a regular ruffian. As soon as he saw one piece on a visitor's plate he would put a second piece beside it, saying: "It is not good for man or bird to live alone." If the visitor finished the two pieces, he would foist a third on him, saying: "What's the good of two, God loves a trinity." If the guest devoured all three he would say: "Where's the cart with three wheels? Who built a three-cornered hut?" For four he had another saying and for five, too.

Tchitchikov ate nearly a dozen slices of something and thought: "Well, our host won't force anything more upon me." But he was wrong; without a word the master of the house laid upon his plate a piece of ribs of veal roasted on a spit, the best piece of all with the kidney, and what veal it was!

"We kept that calf for two years on milk," said the fat gentleman. "I looked after him as if he were my son!"

"I can't," said Tchitchikov.

"You try it, and after that say you can't!"

"It won't go in, there's no room for it."

"Well, you know, there was no room in the church, but when the mayor arrived, room was made; and yet there was such a crush that an apple couldn't have fallen to the floor. You just try it: that morsel's like the mayor."

Tchitchikov did try it, it certainly might be compared with the mayor; room was made for it though it had seemed that it could not have been got in.

It was the same thing with the wines. When he had received the money from the mortgage of his estate Pyotr Petrovitch had laid in a supply of wine for the next ten years. He kept on filling up the glasses; what the guests would not drink he poured out for Alexasha and Nikolasha, who simply tossed off one glass after another, and yet got up from the table as though nothing had happened, as though they had only drunk a glass of water. It was not the same with the visitors. They could hardly drag themselves to the verandah, and were only just able to sink into armchairs; as soon as the master of the house had settled himself in his, an armchair that would have held four, he dropped asleep. His corpulent person was transformed into a blacksmith's bellows: from his open mouth and from his nose he began to emit sounds such as are not found even in the newest music. All the instruments were represented, the drum, the flute, and a strange abrupt note, like the yap of a dog. . . .

. . . The sun had set; the sky remained clear and tranparent. There was the sound of shouting. In place of the fishermen there were groups of boys bathing on the banks; splashing and laughter echoed in the distance. The oarsmen, after plying their twenty-four oars in unison, suddenly raised them all at once into the air and the long-boat, light as a bird, darted of itself over the motionless, mirror-like surface. A fresh-looking sturdy lad, the third from the stern, began singing in a clear voice; five others caught it up, and the other six joined in and the song flowed on, endless as Russia; and putting their hands to their ears the singers themselves seemed lost in its endlessness. Listening to it one felt free and at ease, and Tchitchikov thought: "Ah, I really shall have a country place of my own one day." . . .

It was dusk as they returned. In the dark the oars struck the water which no longer reflected the sky. Lights were faintly visible on both sides of the river. The moon rose just as they were touching the bank. On all sides fishermen were boiling soups of perch and still quivering fish on tripods. Everything was at home. The geese, the cows, and the goats had been driven home long before, and the very dust raised by them was laid again by now, and the herdsmen who had driven them were standing by the gates waiting for a jug of milk and an invitation to partake of fish soup. Here and there came the sound of talk and the hum of voices, the loud barking of the dogs of their village and of other villages far away. The moon had risen and had begun to light up the darkness; and at last everything was bathed in light—the lake and the huts; the light of the fires was paler; the smoke from the chimneys could be seen silvery in the moonlight. Alexasha and Nikolasha flew by them, racing after each other on spirited horses; they raised as much dust as a flock of sheep.

"Oh, I really will have an estate of my own one day!" thought Tchitchikov. A buxom wife and little Tchitchikovs rose before his imagination again. Whose heart would not have been warmed by such an evening!

At supper they over-ate themselves again. When Pavel Ivanovitch had retired to the room assigned to him, and had got into bed, he felt his stomach: "It's as tight as a drum!" he said; "no mayor could possibly get in." As luck would have it, his host's room was the other side of the wall; the wall was a thin one and everything that was said was audible. On the pretence of an early lunch he was giving the cook directions for a regular dinner, and what directions! It was enough to give a dead man an appetite. He licked and smacked his lips. There were continually such phrases as: "But roast it well, let it soak well." While the cook kept saying in a thin high voice: "Yes sir, I can, I can do that too."

"And make a four-cornered fish pasty; in one corner put a sturgeon's cheeks and the jelly from its back, in another put buckwheat mush, mushrooms and onions and sweet roe, and brains and something else—you know . . ."

"Yes sir, I can do it like that."

"And let it be just a little coloured on one side, you know, and let it be a little less done on the other. And bake the underpart, you understand, that it may be all crumbling, all soaked in juice, so that it will melt in the mouth like snow."

"Confound him," thought Tchitchikov, turning over on the other side, "he won't let me sleep."

"Make me a haggis and put a piece of ice in the middle, so that it may swell up properly. And let the garnishing for the sturgeon be rich. Garnish it with crayfish and little fried fish, with a stuffing of little smelts, add fine mince, horse radish and mushrooms and turnips, and carrots and beans, and is there any other root?"

"I might put in kohlrabi and beetroot cut in stars," said the cook.

"Yes, put in kohlrabi, and beetroot, and I'll tell you what garnish to serve with the roast . . ."

"I shall never get to sleep," said Tchitchikov. Turning over on the other side, he buried his head in the pillow and pulled the quilt up over it, that he might hear nothing, but through the quilt he heard unceasingly: "And roast it well," and "Bake it thoroughly." He fell asleep over a turkey.

Next day the guests over-ate themselves to such a degree that Platonov could not ride home; his horse was taken back by one of Pyetuh's stable boys. They got into the carriage: Platonov's dog Yarb followed the carriage lazily, he too had over-eaten himself.

"No, it is really too much," said Tchitchikov, as soon as the carriage had driven out of the yard. "It's positively piggish. Aren't you uncomfortable, Platon Mihailitch? The carriage was so very comfortable and now it seems uncomfortable all at once. Petrushka, I suppose you have been stupidly rearranging the luggage? There seem to be baskets sticking up everywhere!"

Platonov laughed. "I can explain that," he said, "Pyotr Petrovitch stuffed them in for the journey."

"To be sure," said Petrushka, turning round from the box. "I was told to put them all in the carriage—pasties and pies."

"Yes indeed, Pavel Ivanovitch," said Selifan, looking round from the box in high good humour. "A most worthy gentleman, and most hospitable! He sent us out a glass of champagne each, and bade them let us have the dishes from the table, very fine dishes, most delicate flavour. There never was such a worthy gentleman."

I should have liked to print here, among many more things, the whole chapter called "Dinner at the Rostovs'" from *War and Peace*: it is charming and complex and serene, a picture of a world that is forever gone. But I have compromised between space and my own wishes by limiting myself to parts of two other chapters, perhaps more significant ones.

The first is a description of a dinner arranged by old Count Ilya Rostov in honor of the great hero Bagration, and the second, in good contrast to it, is about the gay, fresh, unplanned evening of the young hunters with "Uncle" in the country:

From *War and Peace* by Leo Tolstoy, 1828–1910

At the beginning of March, old Count Ilya Rostov was very busy arranging a dinner in honor of Prince Bagration at the English club.

The count walked up and down the hall in his dressing gown, giving orders to the club steward and to the famous Feoktist, the Club's head cook, about asparagus, fresh cucumbers, strawberries, veal, and fish for this dinner. The count had been a member and on the committee of the Club from the day it was founded. To him the Club entrusted the arrangement of the festival in honor of Bagration, for few men knew so well how to arrange a feast on an openhanded, hospitable scale, and still fewer men would be so well able and willing to make up out of their own resources what might be needed for the success of the fete. The club cook and the steward listened to the count's orders with pleased faces, for they knew that under no other management could they so easily extract a good profit for themselves from a dinner costing several thousand rubles.

"Well then, mind and have cock's combs in the turtle soup, you know!"

"Shall we have three cold dishes then?" asked the cook.

The count considered.

"We can't have less—yes, three ... the mayonnaise, that's one," said he, bending down a finger.

"Then am I to order those large sterlets?" asked the steward.

"Yes, it can't be helped if they won't take less. Ah, dear me! I was forgetting. We must have another entree. Ah, goodness gracious!" he clutched at his head. "Who is going to get me the flowers? Dmitri! Eh, Dmitri! Gallop off to our Moscow estate," he said to the factotum who appeared at his call. "Hurry off and tell Maksim, the gardener, to set the serfs to work. Say that everything out of the hothouses must be brought here well wrapped up in felt. I must have two hundred pots here on Friday."

Having given several more orders, he was about to go to his "little countess" to have a rest, but remembering something else of importance, he returned again, called back the cook and the club steward, and again began giving orders. A light footstep and the clinking of spurs were heard at the door, and the young count, handsome, rosy, with a dark little mustache, evidently rested and made sleeker by his easy life in Moscow, entered the room.

"Ah, my boy, my head's in a whirl!" said the old man with a smile, as if he felt a little confused before his son. "Now, if you would only help a bit! I must have singers too. I shall have my own orchestra, but shouldn't we get the gypsy singers as well? You military men like that sort of thing."

"Really, Papa, I believe Prince Bagration worried himself less before the battle of Schön Grabern than you do now," said his son with a smile.

The old count pretended to be angry.

"Yes, you talk, but try it yourself!"

And the count turned to the cook, who, with a shrewd and respectful expression, looked observantly and sympathetically at the father and son.

"What have the young people come to nowadays, eh, Feoktist?" said he. "Laughing at us old fellows!"

"That's so, your excellency, all they have to do is to eat a good dinner, but providing it and serving it all up, that's not their business!"

"That's it, that's it!" exclaimed the count, and gaily seizing his son by both hands, he cried, "Now I've got you, so take the sleigh and pair at once, and go to Bezukhov's, and tell him 'Count Ilya has sent you to ask for strawberries and fresh pineapples.' We can't get them from anyone else. He's not there himself, so you'll have to go in and ask the princesses; and from there go on to the Rasgulyay—the coachman Ipatka knows—and look up the gypsy Ilyushka, the one who danced at Count Orlov's, you remember, in a white Cossack coat, and bring him along to me."

"And am I to bring the gypsy girls along with him?" asked Nicholas, laughing. "Dear, dear!" ...

On that third of March, all the rooms in the English Club were filled with a hum of conversation, like the hum of bees swarming in springtime. The members and guests of the Club wandered hither and thither, sat, stood, met and separated, some in uniform and some in evening dress, and a few here and there with powdered hair and in Russian *kaftans*. Powdered footmen, in livery with buckled shoes and smart stockings, stood at every door anxiously noting the visitors' every movement in order to offer their services. Most of those present were elderly, respected men with broad, self-confident faces, fat fingers, and resolute gestures and voices. This class of guests and members sat in certain habitual places and met in certain habitual groups. A minority of those present were casual guests—chiefly young men, among whom were Denisov, Rostov, and Dolokhov, who was now again an officer in the Semenov regiment. The faces of these young people, especially those who were military men, bore that expression of condescending respect for their elders which seems to say to the older generation, "We are prepared to respect and honor you, but all the same remember that the future belongs to us." ...

Count Ilya Rostov, hurried and preoccupied, went about in his soft boots between the dining and drawing rooms, hastily greeting the important and unimportant, all of whom he knew, as if they were all equals, while his eyes occasionally sought out his fine well-set-up young son, resting on him and winking joyfully at him. Young Rostov stood at a window with Dolokhov, whose acquaintance he had lately made and highly valued. The old count came up to them and pressed Dolokhov's hand.

"Please come and visit us ... you know my brave boy ... been together out there ... both playing the hero ... Ah, Vasili Ignatovich ... How d'ye do, old fellow?" he said, turning to an old man who was passing, but before he had finished his greeting there was a general stir, and a footman who had run in announced, with a frightened face: "He's arrived!"

Bells rang, the stewards rushed forward, and—like rye shaken together in a shovel—the guests who had been scattered about in different rooms came together and crowded in the large drawing room by the door of the ballroom.

Bagration appeared in the doorway of the anteroom without hat or sword, which, in accord with the Club custom, he had given up to the hall porter. He had no lambskin cap on his head, nor had he a loaded whip over his shoulder, as when Rostov had seen him on the eve of the battle of Austerlitz, but wore a tight new uniform with Russian and foreign Orders, and the Star of St. George on his left breast. Evidently just before coming to the dinner he had had his hair and whiskers trimmed, which changed his appearance for the worse. There was something naively festive in his air, which, in conjunction with his firm and virile features, gave him a rather comical expression. . . .

It was at first impossible to enter the drawing-room door for the crowd of members and guests jostling one another and trying to get a good look at Bagration over each other's shoulders, as if he were some rare animal. Count Ilya Rostov, laughing and repeating the words, "Make way, dear boy! Make way, make way!" pushed through the crowd more energetically than anyone, led the guests into the drawing room, and seated them on the center sofa. The bigwigs, the most respected members of the Club, beset the new arrivals. Count Ilya, again thrusting his way through the crowd, went out of the drawing room and reappeared a minute later with another committeeman, carrying a large silver salver which he presented to Prince Bagration. On the salver lay some verses composed and printed in the hero's honor. Bagration, on seeing the salver, glanced around in dismay, as though seeking help. But all eyes demanded that he should submit. Feeling himself in their power, he resolutely took the salver with both hands and looked sternly and reproachfully at the count who had presented it to him. Someone obligingly took the dish from Bagration (or he would, it seemed, have held it till evening and have gone in to dinner with it) and drew his attention to the verses.

"Well, I will read them, then!" Bagration seemed to say, and, fixing his weary eyes on the paper, began to read them with a fixed and serious expression. But the author himself took the verses and began reading them aloud. Bagration bowed his head and listened:

> Bring glory then to Alexander's reign
> And on the throne our Titus shield.
> A dreaded foe be thou, kindhearted as a man,
> A Rhipheus at home, a Caesar in the field!
> E'en fortunate Napoleon

Knows by experience, now, Bagration,

And dare not Herculean Russians trouble....

But before he had finished reading, a stentorian major-domo announced that dinner was ready! The door opened, and from the dining room came the resounding strains of the polonaise:

Conquest's joyful thunder waken,

Triumph, valiant Russians, now! ...

and Count Rostov, glancing angrily at the author, who went on reading his verses, bowed to Bagration. Everyone rose, feeling that dinner was more important than verses, and Bagration, again preceding all the rest, went in to dinner. He was seated in the place of honor between two Alexanders—Bekleshev and Naryshkin—which was a significant allusion to the name of the sovereign. Three hundred persons took their seats in the dining room, according to their rank and importance: the more important nearer to the honored guest, as naturally as water flows deepest where the land lies lowest....

Count Ilya Rostov with the other members of the committee sat facing Bagration and, as the very personification of Moscow hospitality, did the honors to the prince.

His efforts had not been in vain. The dinner, both the lenten and the other fare, was splendid, yet he could not feel quite at ease till the end of the meal. He winked at the butler, whispered directions to the footmen, and awaited each expected dish with some anxiety. Everything was excellent. With the second course, a gigantic sterlet (at sight of which Ilya Rostov blushed with self-conscious pleasure), the footmen began popping corks and filling the champagne glasses. After the fish, which made a certain sensation, the count exchanged glances with the other committeemen. "There will be many toasts, it's time to begin," he whispered, and taking up his glass, he rose. All were silent, waiting for what he would say.

"To the health of our Sovereign, the Emperor!" he cried, and at the same moment his kindly eyes grew moist with tears of joy and enthusiasm. The band immediately struck up "Conquest's joyful thunder waken ..." All rose and cried "Hurrah!" Bagration also rose and shouted "Hurrah!" in exactly the same voice in which he had shouted it on the field at Schön Grabern. Young Rostov's ecstatic voice could be heard above the three hundred others. He nearly wept. "To the health of our Sovereign, the Emperor!" he roared, "Hurrah!" and emptying his glass at one gulp he dashed it to the floor. Many followed his example, and the loud shouting continued for a long time. When the voices subsided, the footmen cleared away the broken glass and everybody sat down again, smiling at the noise they had made and exchanging remarks. The old count rose once more, glanced at a note lying beside his plate, and proposed a toast, "To the health of the hero of our last campaign, Prince Peter Ivanovich Bagration!" and again his blue eyes grew moist. "Hurrah!" cried the three hundred voices again, but instead of the band a choir began singing a cantata composed by Paul Ivanovich Kutuzov:

> Russians! O'er all barriers on!
> Courage conquest guarantees;
> Have we not Bagration?
> He brings foemen to their knees, . . . etc.

As soon as the singing was over, another and another toast was proposed and Count Ilya Rostov became more and more moved, more glass was smashed, and the shouting grew louder. They drank to Bekleshev, Naryshkin, Uvarov, Dolgorukov, Apraksin, Valuev, to the committee, to all the Club members and to all the Club guests, and finally to Count Ilya Rostov separately, as the organizer of the banquet. At that toast, the count took out his handkerchief and, covering his face, wept outright.

Toward evening [Nicholas found] they were so far from home that he accepted "Uncle's" offer that the hunting party should spend the night in his little village of Mikhaylovna.

"And if you put up at my house that will be better still. That's it, come on!" said "Uncle." "You see it's damp weather, and you could rest, and the little countess could be driven home in a trap."

"Uncle's" offer was accepted. A huntsman was sent to Otradnoe for a trap, while Nicholas rode with Natasha and Petya to "Uncle's" house.

Some five male domestic serfs, big and little, rushed out to the front porch to meet their master. A score of women serfs, old and young, as well as children, popped out from the back entrance to have a look at the hunters who were arriving. The presence of Natasha—a woman, a lady, and on horseback—raised the curiosity of the serfs to such a degree that many of them came up to her, stared her in the face, and unabashed by her presence made remarks about her as though she were some prodigy on show and not a human being able to hear or understand what was said about her.

"Arinka! Look, she sits sideways! There she sits and her skirt dangles. . . . See, she's got a little hunting horn!"

"Goodness gracious! See her knife? . . ."

"Isn't she a Tartar!"

"How is it you didn't go head over heels?" asked the boldest of all, addressing Natasha directly.

"Uncle" dismounted at the porch of his little wooden house which stood in the midst of an overgrown garden and, after a glance at his retainers, shouted authoritatively that the superfluous ones should take themselves off and that all necessary preparations should be made to receive the guests and the visitors.

The serfs all dispersed. "Uncle" lifted Natasha off her horse and taking her hand led her up the rickety wooden steps of the porch. The house, with its bare, unplastered log walls, was not overclean—it did not seem that those living in it aimed at keeping it spotless—but neither was it noticeably neglected. In the entry there was a smell of fresh apples, and wolf and fox skins hung about.

"Uncle" led the visitors through the anteroom into a small hall with a folding table and red chairs, then into the drawing room, with a round birchwood table and a sofa, and finally into his private room, where there was a tattered sofa, a worn carpet, and portraits of Suvorov, of the host's father and mother, and of himself in military uniform. The study smelt strongly of tobacco and dogs. "Uncle" asked his visitors to sit down and make themselves at home, and then went out of the room. Rugay [the dog], his back still muddy, came into the room and lay down on the sofa, cleaning himself with his tongue and teeth. Leading from the study was a passage in which a partition with ragged curtains could be seen. From behind this came women's laughter and whispers. Natasha, Nicholas, and Petya took off their wraps and sat down on the sofa. Petya, leaning on his elbow, fell asleep at once. Natasha and Nicholas were silent. Their faces glowed, they were hungry and very cheerful. They looked at one another (now that the hunt was over and they were in the house, Nicholas no longer considered it necessary to show his manly superiority over his sister), Natasha gave him a wink, and neither refrained long from bursting into a peal of ringing laughter even before they had a pretext ready to account for it.

After a while "Uncle" came in, in a Cossack coat, blue trousers, and small top boots. And Natasha felt that this costume, the very one she had regarded with surprise and amusement at Otradnoe, was just the right thing and not at all worse than a swallowtail or frock coat. "Uncle" too was in high spirits and, far from being offended by the brother's and sister's laughter (it could never enter his head that they might be laughing at his way of life), he himself joined in the merriment.

"That's right, young countess, that's it, come on! I never saw anyone like her!" said he, offering Nicholas a pipe with a long stem and, with a practiced motion of three fingers, taking down another that had been cut short. "She's ridden all day like a man, and is as fresh as ever!"

Soon after "Uncle's" reappearance the door was opened, evidently from the sound by a barefooted girl, and a stout, rosy, good-looking woman of about forty, with a double chin and full red lips, entered carrying a large loaded tray. With hospitable dignity and cordiality in her glance and in every motion, she looked at the visitors and, with a pleasant smile, bowed respectfully. In spite of her exceptional stoutness, which caused her to protrude her chest and stomach and throw back her head, this woman (who was "Uncle's" housekeeper) trod very lightly. She went to the table, set down the tray, and with her plump white hands deftly took from it the bottles and various *hors-d'oeuvres* and dishes and arranged them on the table. When she had finished, she stepped aside and stopped at the door with a smile on her face. "Here I am. I am she! Now do you understand 'Uncle'?" her expression said to Rostov. How could one help understanding? Not only Nicholas, but even Natasha, understood the meaning of his puckered brow and the happy complacent smile that slightly puckered his lips when Anisya Fedorovna entered. On the tray was a bottle of herb wine, different kinds of vodka, pickled mushrooms, rye cakes made with buttermilk, honey in the comb, still mead and sparkling mead, apples, nuts (raw and roasted), and nut-and-honey sweets. Afterwards she brought a freshly roasted chicken, ham, preserves made with honey, and preserves made with sugar.

All this was the fruit of Anisya Fedorovna's housekeeping, gathered and prepared by her. The smell and taste of it all had a smack of Anisya Fedorovna herself: a savor of juiciness, cleanliness, whiteness, and pleasant smiles.

"Take this, little Lady-Countess!" she kept saying, as she offered Natasha first one thing and then another.

Natasha ate of everything and thought she had never seen or eaten such buttermilk cakes, such aromatic jam, such honey-and-nut sweets, or such a chicken anywhere. Anisya Fedorovna left the room.

After supper, over their cherry brandy, Rostov and "Uncle" talked of past and future hunts, of Rugay and Ilagin's dogs, while Natasha sat upright on the sofa and listened with sparkling eyes. She tried several times to wake Petya that he might eat something, but he only muttered incoherent words without waking up. Natasha felt so lighthearted and happy in these novel surroundings that she only feared the trap would come for her too soon. After a casual pause, such as often occurs when receiving friends for the first time in one's own house, "Uncle," answering a thought that was in his visitors' minds, said:

"This, you see, is how I am finishing my days. . . . Death will come. That's it, come on! Nothing will remain. Then why harm anyone?"

"Uncle's" face was very significant and even handsome as he said this. Involuntarily Rostov recalled all the good he had heard about him from his father and the neighbors. Throughout the whole province "Uncle" had the reputation of being the most honorable and disinterested of cranks. They called him in to decide family disputes, chose him as executor, confided secrets to him, elected him to be a justice and to other posts; but he always persistently refused public appointments, passing the autumn and spring in the fields on his bay gelding, sitting at home in winter, and lying in his overgrown garden in summer.

"Why don't you enter the service, Uncle?"

"I did once, but gave it up. I am not fit for it. That's it, come on! I can't make head or tail of it. That's for you—I haven't brains enough. Now, hunting is another matter—that's it, come on! Open the door, there!" he shouted. "Why have you shut it?"

The door at the end of the passage led to the huntsmen's room, as they called the room for the hunt servants.

There was a rapid patter of bare feet, and an unseen hand opened the door into the huntsmen's room, from which came the clear sounds of a balalayka on which someone, who was evidently a master of the art, was playing. Natasha had been listening to those strains for some time and now went out into the passage to hear better.

"That's Mitka, my coachman. . . . I have got him a good balalayka. I'm fond of it," said "Uncle."

It was the custom for Mitka to play the balalayka in the huntsmen's room when "Uncle" returned from the chase. "Uncle" was fond of such music.

"How good! Really very good!" said Nicholas with some unintentional superciliousness, as if ashamed to confess that the sounds pleased him very much.

"Very good?" said Natasha reproachfully, noticing her brother's tone. "Not 'very good'—it's simply delicious!"

Just as "Uncle's" pickled mushrooms, honey, and cherry brandy had seemed to her the best in the world, so also that song, at that moment, seemed to her the acme of musical delight.

"More, please, more!" cried Natasha at the door as soon as the balalayka ceased.

I am a valiant flea indeed, thus to have nipped at the lion Tolstoy! And I shall make one more small nibble, and copy here a prayer I can never forget. It is the one simple Platon the soldier said every night, before he turned over and fell peacefully asleep, whether at home or on the battlefield:

> Lord Jesus Christ, have mercy and
> save me! Let me lie down like a stone,
> O God, and rise up like new bread.

It is inevitable that morsels from Brillat-Savarin's *Physiology of Taste* be scattered through this or any other book about feasting and the pleasures of the table. His collection of gastronomical anecdotes and observations took perhaps twenty-five years to write, at the peaceful pace he chose after long wanderings as a political refugee from France, but it is probable that in ten times that many years, or a hundred, it will still do much to feed men's intellectual hunger. It is elegant, witty, subtly sly, the kind of writing that clears fustiness from the tongue of the mind like dry champagne.

Brillat-Savarin himself, in the last third of his life, became a legend of mild eccentricity in the law-courts and salons of Paris. Wits of the period who frequented the drawing room of his cousins the Récamiers found him "amiable, delicate, highly fashionable." The Marquis de Cussy, a gastronomical rival, wrote of him that "he ate copiously and ill; he chose little, talked dully, had no vivacity in his looks, and was absorbed at the end of a repast." His colleagues at the Court of Cassation shunned him more than once for the smell of the game that he carried in his warm coat-pockets to get high! He was, it is safe to guess even in the face of the Marquis, a charming, gay old man ... he had, one of his friends said, "a stylish mind and stomach."

It is hard to choose any special morsel from his book, but there follows one which seems to hold everything that is delicious about them: a teasing, satirical pedantry in the first part, wisdom, and a smooth, light, almost affectionate artfulness in the little story at the end:

From *The Physiology of Taste* by Anthelme Brillat-Savarin, 1755–1826

But, the impatient reader may exclaim, how can one possibly assemble, in this year of grace 1825, a meal which will meet all the conditions necessary to attain the ultimate in the pleasures of the table?

I am about to answer that question. Draw near, Reader, and pay heed: it is Gasterea, the loveliest of the muses, who inspires me; I shall speak more clearly than an oracle, and my precepts will live throughout the centuries.

"Let the number of guests be no more than twelve, so that conversation may always remain general;

"Let them be so chosen that their professions will be varied, their tastes analogous, and that there be such points of contact that the odious formality of introductions will not be needed;

"Let the dining room be more than amply lighted, the linen of dazzling cleanliness, and the temperature maintained at from sixty to sixty-eight degrees Fahrenheit;

"Let the gentlemen be witty without pretension, and the ladies charming without too much coquetry;

"Let the dishes be of exquisite quality, but limited in their number, and the wines of the first rank also, each according to its degree;

"Let the progression of the former be from the most substantial to the lightest, and of the latter from the simplest wines to the headiest;

"Let the tempo of eating be moderate, the dinner being the last affair of the day: the guests should behave like travellers who must arrive together at the same destination;

"Let the coffee be piping hot, and the liqueurs of the host's especial choice;

"Let the drawing room which awaits the diners be large enough to hold a card table for those who cannot do without it, with enough space left for after-dinner conversations;

"Let the guests be disciplined by the restraints of polite society and animated by the hope that the evening will not pass without its rewarding pleasures;

"Let the tea be not too strong, the toast artfully buttered, and the punch made with care;

"Let the leavetakings not begin before eleven o'clock, but by midnight let every guest be home and abed."

If anyone has attended a party combining all these virtues, he can boast that he has known perfection, and for each one of them which has been forgotten or ignored he will have experienced the less delight.

I have already said that the pleasures of the table, as I conceive of them, can go on for a rather long period of time; I am going to prove this now by giving a detailed and faithful account of the lengthiest meal I ever ate in my life; it is a little bonbon which I shall pop into my reader's mouth as a reward for having read me thus far with such agreeable politeness. Here it is:

I used to have, at the end of the Rue du Bac, a family of cousins composed of the following: Doctor Dubois, seventy-eight years old; the captain, seventy-six; their sister Jeannette, who was seventy-four. I went now and then to pay them a visit, and they always received me very graciously.

"By George!" the doctor said one day to me, standing on tiptoe to slap me on the shoulder. "For a long time now you've been boasting of your *fondues* (eggs scrambled with cheese), and you always manage to keep our mouths watering. It's time to stop all this. The captain and I are coming soon to have breakfast with you, to see what it's all about." (It was, I believe, in 1801 that he thus teased me.)

"Gladly," I replied. "You'll taste it in all its glory, for I myself will make it. Your idea is completely delightful to me. So . . . tomorrow at ten sharp, military style!"

At the appointed hour I saw my guests arrive, freshly shaved, their hair carefully arranged and well-powdered: two little old men who were still spry and healthy.

They smiled with pleasure when they saw the table ready, spread with white linen, three places laid, and at each of them two dozen oysters and a gleaming golden lemon.

At both ends of the table rose up bottles of Sauterne, carefully wiped clean except for the corks, which indicated in no uncertain way that it was a long time that the wine had rested there.

Alas, in my life-span I have almost seen the last of those oyster breakfasts, so frequent and so gay in the old days, where the molluscs were swallowed by the thousands! They have disappeared with the abbés, who never ate less than a gross apiece, and with the chevaliers, who went on eating them forever. I regret them, in a philosophical way: if time can change governments, how much more influence has it over our simple customs!

After the oysters, which were found to be deliciously fresh, grilled skewered kidneys were served, a deep pastry shell of truffled *foie gras,* and finally the *fondue.*

All its ingredients had been mixed in a casserole, which was brought to the table with an alcohol lamp. I performed on this battlefield, and my cousins did not miss a single one of my gestures.

They exclaimed with delight on the charms of the whole procedure, and asked for my recipe, which I promised to give them, the while I told the two anecdotes on the subject which my reader will perhaps find further on.

After the *fondue* came seasonable fresh fruits and sweetmeats, a cup of real Mocha made *à la Dubelloy,* a method which was then beginning to be known, and finally two kinds of liqueurs, one sharp for refreshing the palate and the other oily for soothing it.

The breakfast being well-ended, I suggested to my guests that we take a little exercise, and that it consist of inspecting my apartment, quarters which are far from elegant but which are spacious and comfortable, and which pleased my company especially since the ceilings and gildings date from the middle of the reign of Louis XV.

I showed them the clay original of the bust of my lovely cousin Mme. Récamier by Chinard, and her portrait in miniature by Augustin; they were so delighted by these that the doctor kissed the portrait with his full fleshy lips, and the captain permitted himself to take such liberty with the statue that I slapped him away; for if all the admirers of the original did likewise, that breast so voluptuously shaped would soon be in the same state as the big toe of Saint Peter in Rome, which pilgrims have worn to a nubbin with their kisses.

Then I showed them a few casts from the works of the best antique sculptors, some paintings which were not without merit, my guns, my musical instruments, and a few fine first editions, as many of them French as foreign.

In this little excursion into such varied arts they did not forget my kitchen. I showed them my economical stockpot, my roastingshell, my clockwork spit, and my steamcooker. They inspected everything with the most finicky curiosity, and were all the more astonished since in their own kitchens everything was still done as it had been during the Regency.

At the very moment we re-entered my drawing room, the clock struck two. "Bother!" the doctor exclaimed. "Here it is dinner time, and sister Jeannette will be waiting for us! We must hurry back to her. I must confess I feel no real hunger, but still I must have my bowl of soup. It is an old habit with me, and when I go for a day without taking it I have to say with Titus, *Diem perdidi.*"

"My dear doctor," I said to him, "why go so far for what is right here at hand? I'll send someone to the kitchen to give warning that you will stay awhile longer with me, and that you will give me the great pleasure of accepting a dinner toward which I know you will be charitable, since it will not have all the finish of such a meal prepared with more leisure."

A kind of oculary consultation took place at this point between the two brothers, followed by a formal acceptance. I then sent a messenger posthaste to the Faubourg Saint-Germain, and exchanged a word or two with my master cook; and after a remarkably short interval, and thanks partly to his own resources and partly to the help of neighboring restaurants, he served us a very neatly turned out little dinner, and a delectable one to boot.

It gave me deep satisfaction to observe the poise and aplomb with which my two friends seated themselves, pulled nearer to the table, spread out their napkins, and prepared for action.

They were subjected to two surprises which I myself had not intended for them; for first I served them Parmesan cheese with the soup, and then I offered them a glass of dry Madeira. These were novelties but lately imported by Prince Talleyrand, the leader of all our diplomats, to whom we owe so many witticisms, so many epigrams and profundities, and the man so long followed by the public's devout attention, whether in the days of his power or of his retirement.

Dinner went off very well in both its accessory and its main parts, and my cousins reflected as much pleasure as gaiety.

Afterwards I suggested a game of piquet, which they refused; they preferred the sweet siesta, the *far niente*, of the Italians, the captain told me; and therefore we made a little circle close to the hearth.

In spite of the delights of a postprandial doze, I have always felt that nothing lends more calm pleasure to the conversation than an occupation of whatever kind, so long as it does not absorb the attention. Therefore I proposed a cup of tea.

Tea in itself was an innovation to the old die-hard patriots. Nevertheless it was accepted. I made it before their eyes, and they drank down several cups of it with all the more pleasure since they had always before considered it a remedy.

Long practice has taught me that one pleasure leads to another, and that once headed along this path a man loses the power of refusal. Therefore it was that in an almost imperative voice I spoke of finishing the afternoon with a bowl of punch.

"But you will kill us!" the doctor said.

"Or at least make us tipsy!" the captain added.

To all this I replied only by calling vociferously for lemons, for sugar, for rum.

I concocted the punch then, and while I was busy with it, I had made for me some beautifully thin, delicately buttered, and perfectly salted slices of zwiebach (TOAST).

This time there was a little protest. My cousins assured me that they had already eaten very well indeed, and that they would not touch another thing; but since I am acquainted with the temptations of this completely simple dish, I replied with only one remark, that I hoped I had made enough of it. And sure enough, soon afterwards the captain took the last slice, and I caught him peeking to see if there were still a little more or if it was really the last. I ordered another plateful immediately.

During all this, time had passed, and my watch showed me it was past eight o'clock.

"We must get out of here!" my guests exclaimed. "We are absolutely obliged to go home and eat at least a bit of salad with our poor sister, who has not set eyes on us today!"

I had no real objection to this; faithful to the duties of hospitality when it is concerned with two such delightful old fellows, I accompanied them to their carriage, and watched them be driven away.

Someone may ask if boredom did not show itself now and then in such a long séance.

I shall reply in the negative: the attention of my guests was fixed by my making the *fondue*, by the little trip around the apartment, by a few things which were new to them in the dinner, by the tea, and above all by the punch, which they had never before tasted.

Moreover the doctor knew the genealogy and the bits of gossip of all Paris; the captain had passed part of his life in Italy, both as a soldier and as an envoy to the Parman court; I myself have traveled a great deal; we chatted without affectation, and listened to one another with delight. Not even that much is needed to make time pass with grace and rapidity.

The next morning I received a letter from the doctor; he wished to inform me that the little debauch of the night before had done them no harm at all; quite to the contrary, after the sweetest of sleeps, the two old men had arisen refreshed, feeling both able and eager to begin anew.

One of the most entertaining characters in nineteenth-century French literature is Doctor Gasterini, the fabulous Parisian gourmet who wanders in and out of several novels by Eugène Sue. It is a pity that the books themselves are so labored and ridiculous: the idea of making a cynical society-doctor into a kind of Robin Hood of the morals of the period is amusing, and in spite of the ridiculous plots his adventures, especially with the fat clergy, are fun to read. The novel I have chosen to cut into for this present collection is, for obvious reasons, *Gluttony*, one of Sue's "exposés" of the seven cardinal sins.

In it he manages to prove, in an ingenious and lively way, that intelligent gourmandizing can be a virtue rather than a sin ... and that virtue, as always, will triumph!

The story is one of the silliest ever written, probably. Doctor Gasterini rescues a beautiful Spanish girl from a convent and his handsome sea-captain nephew from prison and sees them properly blessed by the dastardly and conniving priests, all to the tune of the sardonic blackmailing of a gluttonous old canon who has arranged the whole foul plot in order to get his lovely ward's money into the hands of the Church, and so on and so on and so on.

The canon, who for the first time in his life has lost his appetite, is tortured by Gasterini disguised as a cook. The poor priest eats one miraculous meal and then is given nothing but ordinary food until, desperate, he promises to release the beautiful señorita from the convent and give her his holiest blessing. All is well, and Gasterini, unmasked and sardonically virtuous, cooks another incredibly delicious meal for the hungry old pig.

Here is the first one, just for fun:

From *Gluttony* by Eugène Sue, 1804–1857

There was a resignation full of doubt, of curiosity, of anguish, and of vague hope, in the accent with which Dom Diégo uttered the words, "I am waiting."

Soon the major-domo reappeared.

He walked with a solemn air, bearing on a tray a little chafing-dish of silver, the size of a plate, surmounted with its stew-pan. On the side of the tray was a small crystal flagon, filled with a limpid liquid, the colour of burnt topaz.

Pablo, as he approached, several times held his nose to the edge of the stew-pan to inhale the appetising exhalations which escaped from it; finally, he placed on the table the little chafing-dish, the flagon, and a small card.

"Pablo," asked the canon, pointing to the chafing-dish, surmounted with its pan, "what is that silver plate?"

"It belongs to M. Appetite, sir; under this pan is a dish with a double bottom, filled with boiling water, because this great man says the food must be eaten burning hot."

"And that flagon, Pablo?"

"Its use is marked on the card, sir, which informs you of all the dishes you are going to eat."

"Let me see this card," said the canon, and he read:

" 'Guinea fowl eggs fried in the fat of quails, relieved with a gravy of crabs.

" 'N. B. Eat burning hot, make only one mouthful of each egg, after having softened it well with the gravy.

" 'Masticate *pianissimo.*

" 'Drink after each egg two fingers of Madeira wine of 1807, which has made five voyages from Rio Janeiro to Calcutta. (It is needless to say that certain wines are vastly improved by long voyages.)

" 'Drink this wine with meditation.

" 'It is impossible for me not to take the liberty to accompany each dish which I have the honour of serving Lord Dom Diégo with a flagon of wine appropriate to the particular character of the aforesaid dish.' ". . .

The canon, whose agitation was increasing, lifted the top of the silver dish with a trembling hand.

Suddenly a delicious odour spread itself through the atmosphere. Pablo clasped his hands, dilating his wide nostrils and looking at the dish with a greedy eye.

In the middle of the silver dish, half steeped in an unctuous, velvety gravy of a beautiful rosy hue, the major-domo saw four little round soft eggs, that seemed still to tremble with their smoking, golden frying.

The canon, struck like his major-domo with the delicious fragrance of the dish, literally ate it with his eyes, and for the first time in two months a sudden desire of appetite tickled his palate. Nevertheless, he still doubted, believing in the deceitful illusion of a false hunger. Taking in a spoon one of the little eggs, well impregnated with gravy, he shovelled it into his large mouth.

"Masticate *pianissimo,* my lord!" cried Pablo, who followed every motion of his master with a beating heart. "Masticate slowly, the magician said, and afterwards drink this, according to the directions."

And Pablo poured out two fingers of the Madeira wine of 1807, in a glass as thin as the peel of an onion, and presented it to Dom Diégo.

Oh, wonder! Oh, marvel! Oh, miracle! The second movement of the mastication *pianissimo* was hardly accomplished when the canon threw his head gently back, and, half shutting his eyes in a sort of ecstasy, crossed his two hands on his breast, still holding in one hand the spoon with which he had just served himself. . . .

Each service was accompanied with an "order," as Pablo called it, and a new flagon of wine, drawn, no doubt, from the cellar of this wonderful cook.

A collection of these culinary bulletins will give an idea of the varied delights enjoyed by Dom Diégo.

After the note which announced the Guinea fowl eggs, the following menu was served, in the order in which we present it:

"Trout from the lake of Geneva with Montpellier butter, preserved in ice.

"Envelope each mouthful of this exquisite fish, hermetically, in a layer of this highly spiced seasoning.

"Masticate *allegro.*

"Drink two glasses of this Bordeaux wine, Sauterne of 1834, which has made the voyage from the Indies three times.

"This wine should be *meditated.*"

"A painter or a poet would have made an enchanting picture of this trout with Montpellier butter preserved in ice," said the canon to Pablo. "See there, this charming little trout, with flesh the colour of a rose, and a head like mother-of-pearl, voluptuously lying on this bed of shining green, composed of fresh butter and virgin oil congealed by ice, to which tarragon, chive, parsley, and watercresses have given this bright emerald colour! And what perfume! How the freshness of this seasoning contrasts with the pungency of the spices which relieve it! How delicious! And this wine of Sauterne! As the great man of the kitchen says, how admirably this ambrosia is suited to the character of this divine trout which gives me a growing appetite!"

After the trout came another dish, accompanied with this bulletin:

"Fillets of grouse with white Piedmont truffles, minced raw.

"Enclose each mouthful of grouse between two slices of truffle, and moisten the whole well with sauce à la Perigueux, with which black truffles are mingled.

"Masticate *forte*, as the white truffles are raw.

"Drink two glasses of this wine of Château-Margaux 1834—it also has made a voyage from the Indies.

"This wine reveals itself in all its majesty only in the aftertaste."

These fillets of grouse, far from appeasing the growing appetite of the canon, excited it to violent hunger, and, in spite of the profound respect which the orders of the great man had inspired in him, he sent Pablo, before another ringing of the bell, in search of a new culinary wonder.

Finally the bell sounded.

The major-domo returned with this note, which accompanied another dish:

"Salt marsh rails roasted on toast à la Sardanapalus.

"Eat only the legs and rump of the rails; do not cut the leg, take it by the foot, sprinkle it lightly with salt, then cut it off just above the foot, and chew the flesh and the bone.

"Masticate *largo* and *fortissimo*; eat at the same time a mouthful of the hot toast, coated over with an unctuous condiment made of the combination of snipe liver and brains and fat livers of Strasburg, roebuck marrow, pounded anchovy, and pungent spices.

"Drink two glasses of Clos Vougeot of 1817.

"Pour out this wine with emotion, drink it with religion."

After this roast, worthy of Lucullus or Trimalcyon, and enjoyed by the canon with all the intensity of unsatisfied hunger, the major-domo reappeared with two side-dishes that the menu announced thus:

"Mushrooms with delicate herbs and the essence of ham; let this divine mushroom soften and dissolve in the mouth.

"Masticate *pianissimo.*

"Drink a glass of the wine Côte-Rôtie 1829, and a glass of Johannisberg of 1729, drawn from municipal vats of the burgomasters of Heidelberg.

"No recommendation to make for the advantage of the wine, Côte-Rôtie; it is a proud, imperious wine, it asserts itself. As for the old Johannisberg, one hundred and forty years old, approach it with the veneration which a centenarian inspires; drink it with compunction.

"Two sweet side-dishes.

"Morsels à la duchesse with pineapple jelly.

"Masticate *amoroso.*

"Drink two or three glasses of champagne dipped in ice, dry Sillery the year of the comet.

"Dessert.

"Cheese from Brie made on the farm of Estonville, near Meaux. This house had for forty years the honour of serving the palate of Prince Talleyrand, who pronounced the cheese of Brie the king of cheeses—the only royalty to which this great diplomatist remained faithful unto death.

"Drink a glass or two of Port wine drawn from a hogshead recovered from the great earthquake of Lisbon.

"Bless Providence for this miraculous salvage, and empty your glass piously.

"N. B. Never fruits in the morning; they chill, burden, and involve the stomach at the expense of the repose of the evening; simply rinse the mouth with a glass of cream from the Barbadoes of Madame Amphoux, 1780, and take a light siesta, dreaming of dinner."

It is needless to say that all the prescriptions of the cook were followed literally by the canon, whose appetite, now a prodigious thing, seemed to increase in proportion as it was fed; finally, having exhausted his glass to the last drop, Dom Diégo, his ears scarlet, his eyes softly closed, and his cheeks flushed, commenced to feel the tepid moisture and light torpor of a happy and easy digestion; then, sinking into his armchair with a delicious languor, he said to his major-domo:

"If I were not conscious of a tiger's hunger, which threatens explosion too soon, I would believe myself in Paradise. So, Pablo, go at once for this great man of the kitchen, this veritable magician; tell him to come and enjoy his work; tell him to come and judge of the ineffable beatitude in which he has plunged me, and above all, Pablo, tell him that if I do not go myself to testify my admiration, my gratitude, it is because—"

The canon was interrupted by the sight of the culinary artist, who suddenly entered the room, and stood face to face with Diégo, staring at him with a strange expression of countenance.

There is one man, more than any other among Frenchmen written about by Frenchmen, who counteracts all of Sue's indigestible flim-flam: Tartarin of Tarascon. He is as innocent as cool water after too many sauces. He is light and gay and silly after the affectations and excesses of more worldly gluttons. He is a lovable little braggart, with such an appetite for life that he makes us hungry too, whether he is lying about his trips to fabulous countries or is upsetting the routine in a stuffy Swiss pension by refusing to touch either the boiled rice or the boiled prunes for dessert.

From *Tartarin on the Alps* by Alphonse Daudet, 1840–1897

A sight indeed is the *salle-à-manger* of the Rigi-Kulm.

Six hundred guests seated around an immense horse-shoe table on which dishes of rice and prunes alternate in long files with green plants, reflecting in their clear or brown sauce the lights of the lustres or the gilding of the panelled ceiling.

As at all Swiss *tables d'hôte,* this rice and these prunes divide the diners into two rival factions, and the looks of hatred or covetousness bestowed upon the dessert dishes is quite sufficient to enable the spectator to divine to which party the guests belong. The Rice Party betray themselves by their pallor, the Prunes by their congested appearance.

On this particular evening the latter were in the majority, and included all the most important personages, quite European celebrities, such as the great historian Astier-Réhu of the French Academy; the Baron de Stolz, an old Austro-Hungarian diplomatist; Lord Chippendale, a member of the Jockey Club with his niece (?) (hum!); the illustrious Professor Schwanthaler, of Bonn University; a Peruvian general and his eight daughters.

To all these the Rice faction could only oppose as *vedettes* a Belgian senator and his family; Madame Schwanthaler, the wife of the Professor aforesaid; and an Italian tenor on his way from Russia, exhibiting upon the tablecloth a pair of sleeve-links as large as saucers.

These double and opposing currents no doubt gave an air of lassitude and stiffness to the *table d'hôte.* How otherwise can we account for the silence of these six hundred persons, stiff, surly, defiant, with that supreme contempt which they affected to possess one for the other? A superficial observer would have attributed it to the stupid Anglo-Saxon reserve which now gives the tone to the travelling world.

But no! Human beings do not thus hate each other at first sight; turning up their noses at each other; sneering, and glancing superciliously at one another in the absence of introductions. There must have been something else!

Rice and Prunes, I tell you. There you have the explanation of the mournful silence that weighed down upon the dinner at the Rigi-Kulm, which, considering the number and the varied nationalities of the guests, ought to have been very animated and noisy; something like what one would imagine a meal at the foot of the Tower of Babel might have been.

The mountaineer entered the room—a little perplexed in this assembly of Trappists beneath the glare of the lustres—coughed loudly without anyone taking any notice of him, and seated himself in his place next the last comer, at the end of the table. Unaccoutred now, he was simply an ordinary tourist, but of a very amiable appearance; bald, rotund, his beard thick and pointed, a fine nose, thick and somewhat fierce eyebrows, with a pleasant manner and appearance.

Rice or Prune! No one knew yet.

Scarcely had he seated himself when quitting his place with a bound, he exclaimed, *"Outre!* a draught!" and rushed to an empty chair turned down at the centre of the table.

He was stopped by one of the Swiss female attendants, a native of the canton of Uri, wearing little silver chains and white stomacher.

"Monsieur, that is engaged."

Then, from the table, a young lady, of whom he could see nothing but a mass of fair hair relieved by a neck white as virgin snow, said, without turning round, and with a foreign accent:

"This seat is at liberty; my brother is not well, and will not come down to dinner."

"Ill?" asked the mountaineer, with an interested, almost affectionate, manner, as he seated himself. "Ill? Not dangerously, *au moins?"*

He pronounced the last words *au mouain,* and they reasserted themselves with some other vocal parasites, *"hé, qué, té, zou, vé, vaï, allons,"* &c., that still further accentuated his southern tongue, which was no doubt displeasing to the youthful blonde; for she only replied to him with a stony stare—from eyes of deep, dark blue.

The neighbour on his right was not encouraging either. He was the Italian tenor, with a low forehead, very moist eyes, and Hectoring moustaches which he twirled in an irritable manner, for had he not been separated from his pretty neighbour? But the good mountaineer had a habit of talking while he was eating—he thought it good for his digestion.

"Vé! What pretty buttons," he remarked aloud to himself, as he glanced at the Italian's sleeve-studs. "Those notes of music, inlaid with the jasper, have a charming effect"—*"un effet charmain!"*

His strident tones rang through the silent *salle,* without producing the least echo.

"Surely monsieur is a singer, *qué?"*

"Non capisco," growled the Italian through his moustache.

For a moment the man devoted himself to his dinner without speaking—but the food choked him. At length, as his opposite neighbour, the Austro-Hungarian diplomatist, attempted to reach the mustard-pot with his small, aged, shaking hands, enveloped in mittens, our hero passed it politely to him, saying, "*A votre service, monsieur le baron,*" for he had heard him thus addressed.

Unfortunately poor M. de Stolz, notwithstanding the cunning and ingenious air which he had contracted in the pursuit of Chinese diplomacy, had long ago lost his speech and his ideas, and was travelling around the mountains with the view of finding them again. He opened his eyes wide and gazed at the unknown face, and then shut them again without saying anything. It would have taken ten old diplomats of his intellectual power to find the formula of acknowledgment.

At this new failure the mountaineer made a grimace, and the rough manner in which he seized the bottle gave one the idea that he was going to break, with it, the cracked head of the old diplomatist. But no such thing. It was merely to offer his neighbour a glass of wine, but she did not hear him, being lost in a murmured conversation—a chirping, sweet and lively, in an unknown tongue—with two young people close by. She leaned forward, she became animated. He could see her little curls shimmer in the light against a tiny ear, transparent and rosy-tinted. Polish? Russian? Norwegian? Well, certainly Northern; and a pretty little song of his native district escaped the lips of the Southerner, who quietly began to hum:

> *O coumtesso gènto,*
> *Estelo dou Nord*
> *Qué la neu argento,*
> *Qu' Amour friso en or.*

Everybody at table turned round: they all thought he had gone mad. He blushed and kept himself quiet in his place, not moving except to push violently away the dish of sacred fruit which they passed to him.

"Prunes! Never in my life!"

This was too much.

There was a great movement of chairs. The Academician, Lord Chippendale, the Professor of Bonn, and some other notables of the party, rose and quitted the room by way of protest.

The Rice Party almost immediately followed them when they perceived the stranger push away from him the other dessert dish as violently as the former.

Neither Rice nor Prune! What then?

All the guests retired, and the silence was truly glacial as the people, with bowed heads and with the corners of their mouths disdainfully drawn down, passed in front of the unhappy individual who remained alone in the immense dining-room, inclined *de faire une trempette* after the manner of his country, but kept down by the universal disdain!

J. K. Huysmans, who wrote *Against the Grain*, has often been called "a prince of gastronomes," and "the father of present-day table sybaritism," with a complete inaccuracy which would have displeased and astonished him. He was never a gastronomer, in the quasi-professional sense attributed to that term, although his was a fastidious and intelligent appetite which could teach much to the self-styled "gourmets" of the world.

His friend and doctor, de Lézinier, wrote of him, "The frugality of his stomach and the austerity of his appetite had refined the aristocracy of his palate ... he chose his food and wines primarily for their taste, and then for their health-sustaining properties."

He was a man ever conscious of the "distressing absurdity of human affairs," and yet his constant shuddering disgust was always tolerant, patient, and even a little amused, so that, as one English critic has written of him in the *Wine and Food Quarterly*, "Like Robert Louis Stevenson he believed that to detect the flavor of an olive is no less a piece of human perfection than to find beauty in the colors of the sunset."

The three short excerpts I have chosen from *Against the Grain* give, perhaps as well as any could, an idea of the jaded young Des Esseintes's extravagantly futile life in Paris, just before he fled to the country; the way he lived there, in his equally futile attempt at simplicity; and finally, how he spent his last evening in Paris, on his way to London and freedom from satiety:

From *Against the Grain* by J. K. Huysmans, 1848–1907

He acquired the reputation of an eccentric, which he enhanced by wearing costumes of white velvet, and gold-embroidered waistcoats, by inserting, in place of a cravat, a Parma bouquet in the opening of his shirt, by giving famous dinners to men of letters, one of which, a revival of the eighteenth century, celebrating the most futile of his misadventures, was a funeral repast.

In the dining room, hung in black and opening on the transformed garden with its ash-powdered walks, its little pool now bordered with basalt and filled with ink, its clumps of cypresses and pines, the dinner had been served on a table draped in black, adorned with baskets of violets and scabiouses, lit by candelabra from which green flames blazed, and by chandeliers from which wax tapers flared.

To the sound of funeral marches played by a concealed orchestra, nude Negresses, wearing slippers and stockings of silver cloth with patterns of tears, served the guests.

Out of black-edged plates they had drunk turtle soup and eaten Russian rye bread, ripe Turkish olives, caviar, smoked Frankfort black pudding, game with sauces that were the color of licorice and blacking, truffle gravy, chocolate cream puddings, nectarines, grape preserves, mulberries, and black-heart cherries; they had sipped, out of dark glasses, wines from Limagnes, Roussillon, Tenedos, Val de Penas, and Porto, and after the coffee and walnut brandy had partaken of kvas and porter and stout.

The farewell dinner to a temporarily dead virility—this was what he had written on invitation cards designed like bereavement notices.

. . . It occurred to him that he needed a cordial to revive his flagging spirits.

He went to the dining room where, built in one of the panels, was a closet containing a number of tiny casks, ranged side by side, and resting on small stands of sandalwood.

This collection of barrels he called his mouth organ.

A stem could connect all the spigots and control them by a single movement, so that once attached, he had only to press a button concealed in the woodwork to turn on all the taps at the same time and fill the mugs placed underneath.

The organ was now open. The stops labelled flute, horn, celestial voice, were pulled out, ready to be placed. Des Esseintes sipped here and there, enjoying the inner symphonies, succeeded in procuring sensations in his throat analogous to those which music gives to the ear.

Moreover, each liquor corresponded, according to his thinking, to the sound of some instrument. Dry curaçao, for example, to the clarinet, whose tone is sourish and velvety; *kümmel* to the oboe, whose sonorous notes snuffle; mint and anisette to the flute, at once sugary and peppery, puling and sweet; while, to complete the orchestra, *kirschwasser* has the furious ring of the trumpet; gin and whiskey burn the palate with their strident crashing of trombones and cornets; brandy storms with the deafening hubbub of tubas; while the thunder-claps of the cymbals and the furiously beaten drum roll in the mouth by means of the *rakis de Chio*.

He also thought that the comparison could be continued, that quartets of string instruments could play under the palate, with the violin simulated by old brandy, fumous and fine, piercing and frail; the tenor violin by rum, louder and more sonorous; the cello by the lacerating and lingering ratafia, melancholy and caressing; with the double-bass, full-bodied, solid and dark as the old bitters. If one wished to form a quintet, one could even add a fifth instrument with the vibrant taste, the silvery detached and shrill note of dry cumin imitating the harp.

The comparison was further prolonged. Tone relationships existed in the music of liquors; to cite but one note, benedictine represents, so to speak, the minor key of that major key of alcohols which are designated, in commercial scores, under the name of green Chartreuse.

These principles once admitted, he succeeded, after numerous experiments, in enjoying silent melodies on his tongue, mute funeral marches, in hearing, in his mouth, solos of mint, duos of ratafia and rum.

He was even able to transfer to his palate real pieces of music, following the composer step by step, rendering his thought, his effects, his nuances, by combinations or contrasts of liquors, by approximative and skilled mixtures.

At other times, he himself composed melodies, executed pastorals with mild black-currant which evoked, in his throat, the trillings of nightingales; with the tender chouva cocoa which sang saccharine songs like "The romance of Estelle" and the "Ah! Shall I tell you, mama," of past days.

But on this evening Des Esseintes was not inclined to listen to this music. He confined himself to sounding one note on the keyboard of his organ, by swallowing a little glass of genuine Irish whiskey.

The fiacre stopped in front of the tavern. Once more, Des Esseintes alighted and entered a long dark plain room, divided into partitions as high as a man's waist—a series of compartments resembling stalls. In this room, wider towards the door, many beer pumps stood on a counter, near hams having the color of old violins, red lobsters, marinated mackerel, with onions and carrots, slices of lemon, bunches of laurel and thyme, juniper berries and long peppers swimming in thick sauce.

One of these boxes was unoccupied. He took it and called a young black-suited man who bent forward, muttering something in a jargon he could not understand. While the cloth was being laid, Des Esseintes viewed his neighbors. They were islanders ... with cold *faïence* eyes, crimson complexions, thoughtful or haughty airs. They were reading foreign newspapers. The only ones eating were unescorted women in pairs, robust English women with boyish faces, large teeth, ruddy apple cheeks, long hands and legs. They attacked, with genuine ardor, a rumpsteak pie, a warm meat dish cooked in mushroom sauce and covered with a crust, like a pie.

After having lacked appetite for such a long time, he remained amazed in the presence of these hearty eaters whose voracity whetted his hunger. He ordered oxtail soup and enjoyed it heartily. Then he glanced at the menu for the fish, ordered a haddock and, seized with a sudden pang of hunger at the sight of so many people relishing their food, he ate some roast beef and drank two pints of ale, stimulated by the flavor of a cowshed which this fine, pale beer exhaled.

His hunger persisted. He lingered over a piece of blue Stilton cheese, made quick work of a rhubarb tart, and to vary his drinking quenched his thirst with porter, that dark beer which smells of Spanish licorice but which does not have its sugary taste.

He breathed deeply. Not for years had he eaten and drunk so much. This change of habit, this choice of unexpected and solid food had awakened his stomach from its long sleep. He leaned back in his chair, lit a cigarette and prepared to sip his coffee, into which gin had been poured.

The rain continued to fall. He heard it patter on the panes which formed a ceiling at the end of the room; it fell in cascades down the spouts. No one was stirring in the room. Everybody, utterly weary, was indulging himself in front of his wine glass.

Tongues were now wagging freely. As almost all the English men and women raised their eyes as they spoke, Des Esseintes concluded that they were talking of the bad weather; not one of them laughed. He threw a delighted glance on their suits, whose color and cut did not perceivably differ from that of others, and he experienced a sense of contentment in not being out of tune in this environment, of being, in some way, though superficially, a naturalized London citizen.

There were two revolutions in French and therefore international gastronomy: the Revolution itself, and the almost equally drastic accident of César Ritz's first hotel, with Escoffier in the kitchen.

From "From Esau to Escoffier" by André Simon, *Wine and Food Quarterly,* Spring 1940

In France, during the reigns of Louis XV and Louis XVI, gastronomy flourished under royal patronage; courtiers and courtesans, financiers and church dignitaries paid lavishly for the services of gifted chefs who had to provide quantities of victuals, prepare them in the most novel ways and present them in the most spectacular manner possible, in order to provoke the admiration of guests, many of whom were not merely exacting, but *blasés.* Unfortunately, whilst the *Grande Cuisine* had never been "grander," the people had never been poorer nor so poorly fed, and starvation brought in the Revolution.

The great chefs of the day, whose noble or wealthy masters had shared the fate of the King, or else had fled the country, had no hope of finding anybody anxious to secure their services or able to reward them. The best thing they could do was to give the benefit of their skill to *"la nation"* and *"les citoyens"*; it is what many of them did. They opened restaurants where all and sundry could and did seek better fare than they had at home. Véry, Méot, Beauvilliers, and others soon became famous as restaurateurs. Simple and inexpensive as was the fare which they offered to the public, at least at the beginning of their new career, it had the artist's touch and must have been excellent. Chefs became very popular and their former association with hated aristocratic "ci-devants" was forgiven and forgotten, even when their charges rose with their fortunes and when their cuisine became too dear for any but the *nouveaux riches* of the *nouveau régime.* Food, more food and better food was the cry of the hour; the cook's head was more sacred than that of his king, and the chef's calling became one of the most important as well as one of the best paid: many of the more intelligent youths of the day, attracted by the success of those who made it their business to feed the people, rushed forth as willing apprentices of the great chefs. They were taught and trained in the right tradition, and, in time, they taught and trained others. By becoming more democratic, in France, gastronomy lost nothing: on the contrary, it gained a great deal. When it ceased to be the privilege of a comparatively few extravagant idlers, it brought to the mass of the people the glad tidings that food is not to man what fodder is to his horse, merely a necessity, but that it could be and that it should be a joy as well. This happy realization came about gradually: its dawn, as brilliant and sudden as that of the tropical sun, came in during the first decade of the nineteenth century, with Câreme, and it reached its zenith a hundred years later, with Escoffier. Both ... were remarkable men, skilled artisans, who possessed the great and rare gift of expression; men of taste both, and of great courage; men of faith and vision both, but, of course, men of their own generation. Câreme, in spite of being—or maybe because he had been—brought up on a starvation diet, was the apostle of majesty; his dishes are rich, his cakes are works of art. But Escoffier, in spite of—or perhaps because of—his long association with Ritz and having cooked for all the European crowned heads, at a time when they were numerous and brilliant, was always the apostle of simplicity.

In the siege of Paris, during the Franco-Prussian War of 1870–71, César Ritz was already a waiter at Voisin's, and Escoffier was a rising young chef at a minor restaurant called Le Petit Moulin Rouge. As the enemy tightened the walls of hunger and anxiety around Paris, Voisin's became almost another government headquarters, as one of the few restaurants whose owners had thought to store up extra provisions ... "sides of beef, carcasses of mutton, rows of hams, of sausages, tanks of trout, cages of rabbits and poultry," Marie Louise Ritz writes in the biography of her husband.

From César Ritz, 1938, by Marie Louise Ritz

... Nevertheless, by the end of November the catering problem was acute. For a time—probably for much longer than any other Paris restaurant—Voisin's stood out against the newest culinary innovations. But in December beef was unprocurable, horse meat was growing scarce, and well-dressed bourgeois citizens were glad to join the queues of people outside groceries where a few tinned foods might still be found. The business of preserving foods was given quite an impetus by the Franco-German war, when more than one French town suffered a prolonged siege and the mortality from malnutrition exceeded the mortality from wounds in battle. Escoffier told me that his experience in Metz, where he was *chef de cuisine* at General Headquarters, gave him the first idea of the possibility and of the dire necessity the world had for tinned foods. And he was the first great chef to study seriously the preservation of meats, vegetables, and sauces and to manufacture them in quantities. Only the other day an Englishman who had lived many years in India told me, "Thanks to Escoffier's tinned and bottled foods, I was able for many years to enjoy good French cooking in the wilds." Tinned foods now became a rare and much appreciated luxury.

Rats were being sold openly in the market for from one franc to one franc fifty, depending upon their size. Ragout of rabbit and saddle of lamb still figured on restaurant menus, but stray cats and dogs had become mysteriously rare! Roast donkey was a gourmet's luxury. The small lake in the Luxembourg Gardens had been dragged for tiny fish. The banks of the Seine were crowded with earnest fishermen, in respectable bourgeois black, in army red, in workmen's blouses. And one by one the animals in the Jardin des Plantes were killed. . . .

Both Escoffier and Ritz used to torment me with descriptions of the food they had eaten at this time. In Metz the cavalry horses had eventually all been slaughtered and before the end of the siege there even the teams for heavy artillery had been sacrificed. "Horse meat," thus Escoffier would hold forth, his eyes twinkling, "is delicious, when you are in the right condition to appreciate it!" "A little sweet, perhaps," César would add. "I found, too, that it is hard to digest. But cat-meat! Now, there is a gourmet's dish! The best ragout of rabbit I ever ate was made of alley-cat." "And as to rat-meat, it approaches in delicacy the taste of roast pig!" "But you should taste a stew of elephant trunk! A little oily—but with marvellous flavour—" Etc., etc., until they saw I could stand no more!

Bellenger* stood out as long as possible, then he had to capitulate. One day he had a consultation with the chef, and the following menu was the result—the first of a long series of such menus:

---

* The proprietor.

Purée de lentilles

Sardines à l'huile

Vol-au-vent

Selle d'Epagneul

Haricots blancs et rouges

Oranges

The chef complained most bitterly of the lack of butter, coco-butter being but a poor substitute in cooking for the real thing. The clients did not worry about such details, but they did, for the most part, object to the saddle of spaniel. But according to César, the worst feature of the menu was the quite rightly anonymous *vol-au-vent*.

Before the siege was over, the chef had an opportunity to prepare more exotic dishes. Castor and Pollux, the two elephants of the Zoo, were killed and their carcasses fetched good prices. The trunks were considered tidbits, and the price for them was accordingly high. Bellenger put in a supply of elephant; and Voisin's soon became famous for its "elephant trunk, *sauce chasseur*," and elephant blood-pudding was pronounced by people of cultivated taste to be most excellent.

It is not inappropriate to note here that human curiosity, as well as human hunger, has made men taste and furthermore enjoy many more exotic foods than elephant and spaniel.

Fried new-born mice in China, the hump of the white rhino roasted in its skin in South Africa, crocodile eggs (which Theodore Roosevelt preferred scrambled); narwhal skin ("When fresh, the flavor is delicious and reminds one of nuts or mushrooms. It is about half an inch thick and looks like linoleum. When one bites it, it has the same consistency as celery. . . ."); bats and flying foxes in Australia; hedgehogs roasted in clay by English gypsies at Michaelmas, when the little beasts have had their fill of windfalls and crabapples and their flesh is white and tender; termites in Africa "like pineapple, but there is a knack in popping them into the mouth and synchronizing the bite" before the tongue is nipped in return; bees plucked of their wings and fried in butter in Asia: few if any men have ever died from or even been sickened by such outlandish dishes.

I hope never to have to eat the saddle of a little dog, and yet I do not see why I should be any more averse to that than to chops cut from the tender lightsome body of a young spring-bok. Gastronomy is influenced by both geography and behaviorism.

The miraculous combination of César Ritz's exquisite taste as a restaurateur and Escoffier's masterly skill as a chef created the first Ritz Hotel, and then many other such luxurious, fashionable, and above all *proper* gathering-places. For the first time ladies as well as demi-mondaines, on both sides of the Atlantic, enjoyed all the pleasures of fine food and wine in public, and gentlemen came out from the rich alcoholic shadows of their clubs to join them. Everywhere in high society there was a new interest in the amenities of the table, and quality, not quantity, became the order, just as it had so long ago when the Normans first taught the vanquished Saxons not to snarl over their banquet-bones.

"More simplicity, as well as greater refinement, became the law," André Simon writes, but when we read a typical Ritz menu, following in the great chef's tradition although served as late as 1930, it is difficult to think with anything but amusement of what he believed was gastronomical restraint! Here, as his wife reports it, is what was produced from the kitchens and cellars of the Ritz in Paris, to celebrate a successful financial deal made by one of the postwar brokers:

From *César Ritz*, 1938, by Marie Louise Ritz

There were ten guests, all men, all world-known financiers, German, French, and Belgian. The host consulted with Rey, with Olivier, with Gimon. "Money doesn't count," he said to Rey. "I only want you to see that the food and wine are perfect, regardless of cost. Here's a little to go on with." And the great financier produced ten crisp one-thousand-franc notes! The ten thousand francs were, as it turned out, not enough to cover the costs, and before the day arrived Rey asked for and received a couple of thousand more.

Here is the menu that was finally decided upon:

Consommé de Faisan en Tasse
Mousseline de Sole Empire
Cassolette de Queues d'Ecrevisses
Escalope de Foie gras au Beurre noisette

Velouté de Petits Poisfrais

Carré de Veau braisé à la crême

Pommes de Terre Anna

Pointes d'Asperges

Sorbets au Montrachet

Bécasses au Fumet

Salade de Laitue

Truffes en Papillotes

Mandarines de Nice givrées

Friandises

Le splus beaux Fruits de France

Now, that is a good menu, it is even an excellent menu, and Rey, Olivier, and Gimon are to be complimented upon its composition. Fresh peas and asparagus in December, and truffles and woodcock at any time, are apt to be expensive. But why should this dinner, no matter how exquisitely prepared, cost more than one thousand francs per person? Ah, but I have not yet mentioned the wines. The host, a famous connoisseur, knew the type of wine which he wished to be served with each course—as did Rey. And he insisted that Rey should furnish from the Ritz cellars or elsewhere just the right wines, vintage wines all of them, and of the best years.

Here is the list of wines which were served, in their correct order:

Sherry Carta Oro Viejo

Meursault Goutte d'Or 1915

Magnum de Château Léonville Barton 1878

Jeroboam de Château Lafitte 1870

Pommery 1911

Grand Chambertin 1906

Romanée 1881

Giesler 1906

Château Yquem 1869

Cognac Hennessy (Réservée Privée)

To procure these wines was not in every case easy. The Jeroboam of Château Lafitte 1870 and the Château Yquem 1869 had to be brought specially from Bordeaux by messenger! The messenger sat up all night with his precious package, never let it leave his hand for a moment, was careful to see that it received the minimum of shock in movement. Both messenger and wine were heavily insured, and their arrival was awaited with much tenseness on the part of all concerned. As to the Romanée 1881, that was "found" by Rey in the private cellars of a princely friend. The Château Yquem, served with the dessert, tasted, Rey assures me, "like flowers."

The liqueur, Cognac Hennessy, from our private stock, and of which there is still a small supply in our cellars, was entirely worthy of the wines that had preceded it. Guyot, our present chief cellarer, who is young, but who knows his *métier* if anyone does (this would amaze Julian Street, who maintained in one of his books that "a *sommelier* must be grey-haired"), assures me that it is "priceless." Three-star Hennessy, bearing no date whatever, not cobwebbed in the least—our cellarmen scorn factitious spiderwebs—yet it is wondrous old and wondrous good, and could follow, with no loss of dignity, a list of wines which is almost incomparable.

If the assembling of these wines had caused trouble, their serving did likewise. Aside from the business of bringing them all to the exact, the absolutely exact temperatures required, there was the business of the glasses. Not the finding of the correct shapes and sizes or the perfect thinness and fragility, for our glasses were designed with care and beautifully made by Baccarat; but with such wines with which to fill them, Rey took especial pains that they should be polished to an unheard-of degree. And he personally supervised their washing, adding lemon to the water in which they were rinsed.

At last the tables were set, the waiters held themselves ready, and Rey took one last look to see that all was well. He had emphasised the importance of keeping the glasses in their polished state, and a waiter, in an agony of zeal, had—oh, tragedy!—covered them lightly with clean table-napkins. Rey lifted a glass towards his nose. Horrors! There was a smell—a faint smell, but still, enough!—of fresh laundry! Back to the kitchens went those glasses, to be washed, rinsed, and polished anew. This at the last minute.

Well, the dinner was a success. The guests sat down to it at half past eight, and coffee was not served until eleven o'clock! When Rey saw that the guests intended to sit long over their coffee, liqueurs and cigars—and I wonder what momentous conversation?—he skilfully had arm-chairs substituted for the chairs. The guests continued to sit in comfort. And the party did not break up until two o'clock in the morning.

But as a test of the perfection of that menu, the superb quality of the food and wine, Rey always adds when he recites the epic story of this dinner: "And none of the guests felt in the least indisposed on the following morning." The host, in fact, telephoned next day to each of his guests, and put to them the same questions: Had they slept well? Were they feeling well? And the report in each case was favourable.

Are such efforts worthwhile to achieve so transient a work of art as a dinner? The host and the guests in this case, all connoisseurs, all gourmets, apparently thought so. Rey, Olivier, and Gimon still think so. Our chief cellarer, Guyot, who presides over his domains with the zeal of a priest guarding sacred altars, thinks so, and thinks so passionately.

The one thing I have chosen to print from German literature, the housewarming dinner in *Buddenbrooks* by Thomas Mann, I have also chosen to place as a kind of spiritual link between the gastronomy of the Continent and England. It has all the exotic, subtle overtones, down to the last little glass of "sweet, golden-yellow Malmsey," of a moral heritage from old Europe, with its infinity of behavior-patterns carried from the Orient, and the South, and the hard North. And at the same time it has the solidity, and the accustomed gracefulness, often monotonously smug at the moment it is most admirable, of the well-fed bourgeoisie which probably came to its full flower in England under Queen Victoria.

It is at once sophisticated and full of hard common sense, just as its table-talk ranges from poetical outbursts to business details, and its fare from carp in red wine to cabbage soup.

We are in the drawing room of the renovated and newly furnished townhouse of the Buddenbrooks', in a German shipping center, in October 1835. Most of the family, and the oldest friends, are there for the housewarming:

From *Buddenbrooks* by Thomas Mann, 1875–1955

The company had for the most part seated themselves on the chairs and the sofa. They talked with the children or discussed the unseasonable cold and the new house. Herr Hoffstede admired a beautiful Sèvres inkstand, in the shape of a black and white hunting dog, that stood on the secretary. Doctor Grabow, a man of about the Consul's age, with a long mild face between thin whiskers, was looking at the table, set out with cakes and currant bread and salt-cellars in different shapes. This was the "bread and salt" that had been sent by friends for the housewarming; but the "bread" consisted of rich, heavy pastries, and the salt came in dishes of massive gold, that the senders might not seem to be mean in their gifts.

"There will be work for me here," said the Doctor, pointing to the sweetmeats and threatening the children with his glance. . . .

The guests did not sit down, but stood about awaiting the principal event of the evening and passing the time in casual talk. At length, Johann Buddenbrook the older offered his arm to Madame Köppen and said in an elevated voice, "Well, *mesdames et messieurs,* if you are hungry . . ."

Mamsell Jungmann and the servant had opened the folding-doors into the dining-room; and the company made its way with studied ease to table. One could be sure of a good square meal at the Buddenbrooks'. . . . [Madame Buddenbrook] sat down between Pastor Wunderlich and the elder Kröger, who presided on the window side.

"*Bon appétit!*" she said, with her short, quick, hearty nod, flashing a glance down the whole length of the table till it reached the children at the bottom.

"Our best respects to you, Buddenbrook—I repeat, our best respects!" Herr Köppen's powerful voice drowned the general conversation as the maid-servant, in her heavy striped petticoat, her fat arms bare and a little white cap on the back of her head, passed the cabbage soup and toast, as-sisted by Mamsell Jungmann and the Frau Consul's maid from upstairs. The guests began to use their soup-spoons.

"Such plenty, such elegance! I must say, you know how to do things!—I must say—" Herr Köppen had never visited the house in its former owner's time. He did not come of a patrician family, and had only lately become a man of means. He could never quite get rid of certain vulgar tricks of speech—like the repetition of "I must say"; and he said "respecks" for "re-specks." . . .

As far as possible, ladies and gentlemen had been paired off, and members of the family placed between friends of the house. But the arrangement could not be carried out in every case; the two Overdiecks were sitting, as usual, nearly on each other's laps, nodding affectionately at one another. The elder Kröger was bolt upright, enthroned between Madame Antoinette and Frau Senator Langhals, dividing his pet jokes and his flourishes between the two ladies.

"When was the house built?" asked Herr Hoffstede diagonally across the table of old Buddenbrook, who was talking in a gay chaffing tone with Madame Köppen.

"Anno . . . let me see . . . about 1680, if I am not mistaken. My son is better at dates than I am."

"Eighty-two," said the Consul, leaning forward. He was sitting at the foot of the table, without a partner, next to Senator Langhals. "It was finished in the winter of 1682. Ratenkamp and Company were just getting to the top of their form. . . . Sad, how the firm broke down in the last twenty years!"

A general pause in the conversation ensued, lasting for half a minute, while the company looked down at their plates and pondered on the fortunes of the brilliant family who had built and lived in the house and then, broken and impoverished, had left it. . . .

The Consul rather absently lifted his glass to his father. Lebrecht Kröger broke in: "Let's stick by the jolly present!" He took up a bottle of white wine that had a little silver stag on the stopper; and with one of his fastidious, elegant motions he held it on its side and examined the label. "C. F. Köppen," he read, and nodded to the wine-merchant. "Ah, yes, where should we be without you?"

Madame Antoinette kept a sharp eye on the servants while they changed the gilt-edged Meissen plates; Mamsell Jungmann called orders through the speaking-tube into the kitchen, and the fish was brought in. Pastor Wunderlich remarked, as he helped himself:

"This 'jolly present' isn't such a matter of course as it seems, either. The young folk here can hardly realize, I suppose, that things could ever have been different from what they are now. But I think I may fairly claim to have had a personal share, more than once, in the fortunes of the Buddenbrook family. Whenever I see one of these, for instance—" he picked up one of the heavy silver spoons and turned to Madame Antoinette— "I can't help wondering whether they belong to the set that our friend the philosopher Lenoir, Sergeant under His Majesty the Emperor Napoleon, had in his hands in the year 1806—and I think of our meeting in Alf Street, Madame."

Madame Buddenbrook looked down at her plate with a smile half of memory, half of embarrassment. Tom and Tony, at the bottom of the table, cried out almost with one voice, "Oh, yes, tell about it, Grandmama!" They did not want the fish, and they had been listening attentively to the conversation of their elders. But the Pastor knew that she would not care to speak herself of an incident that had been rather painful to her. He came to her rescue and launched out once more upon the old story. It was new, perhaps, to one or two of the present company. As for the children, they could have listened to it a hundred times.

"Well, imagine a November afternoon, cold and rainy, a wretched day; and me coming back down Alf Street from some parochial duty. I was thinking of the hard times we were having. Prince Blücher had gone, and the French were in the town. There was little outward sign of the excitement that reigned everywhere: the streets were quiet, and people stopped close in their houses. Prahl the master-butcher had been shot through the head, just for standing at the door of his shop with his hands in his pockets and making a menacing remark about its being hard to stand. Well, thought I to myself, I'll just have a look in at the Buddenbrooks'. Herr Buddenbrook is down with erysipelas, and Madame has a great deal to do, on account of the billeting.

"At that very moment, whom should I see coming towards me but our honored Madame Buddenbrook herself? What a state she was in! hurrying through the rain hatless, stumbling rather than walking, with a shawl flung over her shoulders, and her hair falling down—yes, Madame, it is quite true, it *was* falling down!

" 'This is a pleasant surprise,' I said. She never saw me, and I made bold to lay my hand on her sleeve, for my mind misgave me about the state of things. 'Where are you off to in such a hurry, my dear?' She realized who I was, looked at me, and burst out: 'Farewell, farewell! All is over—I'm going into the river!'

" 'God forbid,' cried I—I could feel that I went white. 'That is no place for you, my dear.' And I held her as tightly as decorum permitted. 'What has happened?' 'What has happened!' she cried, all trembling. 'They've got at the silver, Wunderlich! That's what has happened! And Jean lies there with erysipelas and can't do anything—he couldn't even if he were up. They are stealing my spoons, Wunderlich, and I am going into the river!'

"Well, I kept holding her, and I said what one would in such cases: 'Courage, dear lady. It will be all right. Control yourself, I beg of you. We will go and speak with them. Let us go.' And I got her to go back up the street to her house. The soldiers were up in the dining-room, where Madame had left them, some twenty of them, at the great silver-chest.

" 'Gentlemen,' I say politely, 'with which one of you may I have the pleasure of a little conversation?' They begin to laugh, and they say: 'With all of us, Papa.' But one of them steps out and presents himself, a fellow as tall as a tree, with a black waxed moustache and big red hands sticking out of his braided cuffs. 'Lenoir,' he said, and saluted with his left hand, for he had five or six spoons in his right. 'Sergeant Lenoir. What can I do for you?'

" 'Herr Officer,' I say, appealing to his sense of honour, 'after your magnificent charge, how can you stoop to this sort of thing? The town has not closed its gates to the Emperor.'

" 'What do you expect?' he answered. 'War is war. The people need these things. . . .'

" 'But you ought to be careful,' I interrupted him, for an idea had come into my head. 'This lady,' I said—one will say anything at a time like that—'the lady of the house, she isn't a German. She is almost a compatriot of yours—she is a Frenchwoman. . . .' 'Oh, a Frenchwoman,' he repeated. And then what do you suppose he said, this big swashbuckler? 'Oh, an *emigrée?* Then she is an enemy of philosophy!'

"I was quite taken aback, but I managed not to laugh. 'You are a man of intellect, I see,' said I. 'I repeat that I consider your conduct unworthy.' He was silent for a moment. Then he got red, tossed his half-dozen spoons back into the chest, and exclaimed, 'Who told you I was going to do anything with these things but look at them? It's fine silver. If one or two of my men take a piece as a souvenir . . .'

"Well, in the end, they took plenty of souvenirs, of course. No use appealing to justice, either human or divine. I suppose they knew no other god than that terrible little Corsican. . . ."

"Did you ever see him, Herr Pastor?"

The plates were being changed again. An enormous brick-red boiled ham appeared, strewn with crumbs and served with a sour brown onion sauce, and so many vegetables that the company could have satisfied their appetites from that one vegetable-dish. Lebrecht Kröger undertook the carving, and skilfully cut the succulent slices, with his elbows slightly elevated and his two long forefingers laid out along the back of the knife and fork. With the ham went the Frau Consul's celebrated "Russian jam," a pungent fruit conserve flavoured with spirits.

No, Pastor Wunderlich regretted to say that he had never set eyes on Bonaparte. Old Buddenbrook and Jean Jacques Hoffstede had both seen him face to face, one in Paris just before the Russian campaign, reviewing the troops at the Tuileries; the other in Danzig.

"I must say, he wasn't a very cheerful person to look at," said the poet, raising his eyebrows, as he disposed of a forkful of ham, potato, and sprouts. "But they say he was in a lively mood, at Danzig. There was a story they used to tell, about how he would gamble all day with the Germans, and make them pay up too, and then spend the evening playing with his generals. Once he swept a handful of gold off the table, and said: *'Les Allemands aiment beaucoup ces petits Napoléons, n'est-ce pas, Rapp?' 'Oui, Sire, plus que le Grand!'* Rapp answered."

There was general laughter—Hoffstede had told the story very prettily, even mimicking the Emperor's manner. . . .

. . . Herr Köppen had grown more and more crimson from eating, and puffed audibly as he spoke. Pastor Wunderlich had not changed colour; he looked as pale, refined, and alert as ever, while drinking down glass after glass of wine.

The candles burned down slowly in their sockets. Now and then they flickered in a draught and dispersed a faint smell of wax over the table.

There they all sat, on heavy, high-backed chairs, consuming good heavy food from good heavy silver plate, drinking full-bodied wines and expressing their views freely on all subjects. When they began to talk shop, they slipped unconsciously more and more into dialect, and used the clumsy but comfortable idioms that seemed to embody to them the business efficiency and the easy well-being of their community. Sometimes they even used an over-drawn pronunciation by way of making fun of themselves and each other, and relished their clipped phrases and exaggerated vowels with the same heartiness as they did their food.

The ladies had not long followed the discussion. Madame Kröger gave them the cue by setting forth a tempting method of boiling carp in red wine. "You cut it into nice pieces, my dear, and put it in the saucepan, add some cloves, and onions, and a few rusks, a little sugar, and a spoonful of butter, and set it on the fire. . . . But don't wash it, on any account. All the blood must remain in it."

The elder Kröger was telling the most delightful stories; and his son Justus, who sat with Dr. Grabow down at the bottom of the table, near the children, was chaffing Mamsell Jungmann. She screwed up her brown eyes and stood her knife and fork upright on the table and moved them back and forth. Even the Overdiecks were very lively. Old Frau Overdieck had a new pet name for her husband: "You good old bell-wether," she said, and laughed so hard that her cap bobbed up and down. . . .

"Krishan, don't eat too much," [old man Buddenbrook] suddenly called out, in dialect. "Never mind about Tilda—it doesn't hurt her. She can put it away like a dozen harvest hands, that child!"

And truly it was amazing, the prowess of this scraggy child with the long, old-maidish face. Asked if she wanted more soup, she answered in a meek drawling voice: "Ye-es, ple-ase." She had two large helpings both of fish and ham, with piles of vegetables; and she bent short-sightedly over her plate, completely absorbed in the food, which she chewed ruminantly, in large mouthfuls. "Oh, Un-cle," she replied, with amiable simplicity, to the old man's gibe, which did not in the least disconcert her. She ate: whether it tasted good or not, whether they teased her or not, she smiled and kept on, heaping her plate with good things, with the instinctive, insensitive voracity of a poor relation—patient, persevering, hungry, and lean.

And now came, in two great cut-glass dishes, the "Plettenpudding." It was made of layers of macaroons, raspberries, ladyfingers, and custard. At the same time, at the other end of the table, appeared the blazing plum-pudding which was the children's favourite sweet.

"Thomas, my son, come here a minute," said Johann Buddenbrook, taking his great bunch of keys from his trousers pocket. "In the second cellar to the right, the second bin, behind the red Bordeaux, two bottles— you understand?" Thomas, to whom such orders were familiar, ran off and soon came back with the two bottles, covered with dust and cobwebs; and the little dessert-glasses were filled with sweet, golden-yellow Malmsey from these unsightly receptacles. Now the moment came when Pastor Wunderlich rose, glass in hand, to propose a toast; and the company fell silent to listen. He spoke in the pleasant, conversational tone which he liked to use in the pulpit; his head a little on one side, a subtle, humorous smile on his pale face, gesturing easily with his free hand. "Come, my honest friends, let us honour ourselves by drinking a glass of this excellent liquor to the health of our host and hostess in their beautiful new home. Come, then—to the health of the Buddenbrook family, present and absent! May they live long and prosper!" . . .

Broker Gratjens got up next, and his speech was rather long-winded; he ended by proposing in his high-pitched voice a health to the firm of Johann Buddenbrook, that it might continue to grow and prosper and do honour to the town.

Johann Buddenbrook thanked them all for their kindness, first as head of the family and then as senior partner of the firm—and sent Thomas for another bottle of Malmsey. It had been a mistake to suppose that two would be enough.

Lebrecht Kröger spoke too. He took the liberty of remaining seated, because it looked less formal, and gestured with his head and hands most charmingly as he proposed a toast to the two ladies of the family, Madame Antoinette and the Frau Consul. As he finished, the Plettenpudding was nearly consumed, and the Malmsey nearing its end; and then, to a universal, long-drawn "Ah-h!" Jean Jacques Hoffstede rose up slowly, clearing his throat. The children clapped their hands with delight.

"*Excusez!* I really couldn't help it," he began. He put his finger to his long sharp nose and drew a paper from his coat pocket. . . . A profound silence reigned throughout the room.

His paper was gaily parti-coloured. On the outside of it was written, in an oval border surrounded by red flowers and a profusion of gilt flourishes:

> On the occasion of my friendly participation in a delightful housewarming party given by the Buddenbrook family. October 1835.

He read this aloud first; then turning the paper over, he began, in a voice that was already somewhat tremulous:

> Honoured friends, my modest lay
> Hastes to greet you in these walls:
> May kind Heaven grant to-day
> Blessing on their spacious halls. . . .

The general merriment had now reached its height. Herr Köppen felt a great need to unfasten a few buttons of his waistcoat; but it obviously wouldn't do, for not even the elderly gentlemen were permitting themselves the liberty. Lebrecht Kröger sat up as straight as he did at the beginning; Pastor Wunderlich's face was as pale as ever, his manner as correct. The elder Buddenbrook had indeed sat back a little in his chair, but he maintained perfect decorum. There was only Justus Kröger—he was plainly a little overtaken.

But where was Dr. Grabow? The butter, cheese, and fruit had just been handed round; and the Frau Consul rose from her chair and unobtrusively followed the waitress from the room; for the Doctor, Mamsell Jungmann, and Christian were no longer in their places, and a smothered wail was proceeding from the hall. There in the dim light, little Christian was half lying, half crouching on the round settee that encircled the central pillar. He was uttering heart-breaking groans. Ida and the Doctor stood beside him.

"Oh dear, oh dear," said she, "the poor child is very bad!"

"I'm ill, Mamma, damned ill," whimpered Christian, his little deep-set eyes darting back and forth, and his big nose looking bigger than ever. The "damned" came out in a tone of utter despair; but the Frau Consul said: "If we use such words, God will punish us by making us suffer still more!"

Doctor Grabow felt the lad's pulse. His kindly face grew longer and gentler.

"It's nothing much, Frau Consul," he reassured her. "A touch of indigestion." He prescribed in his best bed-side manner: "Better put him to bed and give him a Dover powder—perhaps a cup of camomile tea, to bring out the perspiration. . . . And a rigorous diet, you know, Frau Consul. A little pigeon, a little French bread . . ."

"I don't want any pigeon," bellowed Christian angrily. "I don't want to eat anything, ever any more. I'm ill, I tell you, damned ill!" The fervour with which he uttered the bad word seemed to bring him relief.

Doctor Grabow smiled to himself—a thoughtful, almost a melancholy smile. He would soon eat again, this young man. He would do as the rest of the world did—his father, and all their relatives and friends: he would lead a sedentary life and eat four good, rich, satisfying meals a day. Well, God bless us all! He, Friedrich Grabow, was not the man to upset the habits of these prosperous, comfortable tradesmen and their families. He would come when he was sent for, prescribe a few days' diet—a little pigeon, a slice of French bread—yes, yes, and assure the family that it was nothing serious this time. Young as he was, he had held the head of many an honest burgher who had eaten his last joint of smoked meat, his last stuffed turkey, and, whether overtaken unaware in his counting-house or after a brief illness in his solid old four-poster, had commended his soul to God. Then it was called paralysis, a "stroke," a sudden death. And he, Friedrich Grabow, could have predicted it, on all of these occasions when it was "nothing serious this time"—or perhaps at the times when he had not even been summoned, when there had only been a slight giddiness after luncheon. Well, God bless us all! He, Friedrich Grabow, was not the man to despise a roast turkey himself. That ham with onion sauce had been delicious, hang it! And the Plettenpudding, when they were already stuffed full—macaroons, raspberries, custard . . . "A rigorous diet, Frau Consul, as I say. A little pigeon, a little French bread. . . ."

They were rising from table.

"Well, ladies and gentlemen, *gesegnete Mahlzeit!* Cigars and coffee in the next room, and a liqueur if Madame feels generous. . . . Billiards for whoever chooses. Jean, you will show them the way back to the billiard-room? Madame Köppen, may I have the honour?"

Full of well-being, laughing and chattering, the company trooped back through the folding doors into the landscape-room. The Consul remained behind, and collected about him the gentlemen who wanted to play billiards.

"You won't try a game, Father?"

No, Lebrecht Kröger would stop with the ladies, but Justus might go if he liked. . . . Senator Langhals, Köppen, Gratjens, and Doctor Grabow went with the Consul, and Jean Jacques Hoffstede said he would join them later. "Johann Buddenbrook is going to play the flute," he said. "I must stop for that. *Au revoir, messieurs.*"

As the gentlemen passed through the hall, they could hear from the landscape-room the first notes of the flute, accompanied by the Frau Consul on the harmonium: an airy, charming little melody that floated sweetly through the lofty rooms. The Consul listened as long as he could. He would have liked to stop behind in an easy-chair in the landscape-room and indulge the reveries that the music conjured up; but his duties as host . . .

"Bring some coffee and cigars into the billiard-room," he said to the maid whom he met in the entry.

The dates of a group of stories and essays all written within the past ninety years certainly cannot matter very much, at least gastronomically, in a collection which starts somewhere behind the twenty centuries of the Christian era. What is more important, I think, is that they were all written by Britons, about themselves or their fellows, and that they all ate, after their own fashions.

Only a few days ago I heard a man who has read more than any human being should, say with unfeigned wistfulness, "How I envy anybody who is meeting Mr. Pooter for the first time!" And that is probably the way everyone feels who has ever read the imaginary diary written by two brothers in 1892, about Mr. Pooter the Nobody, who miraculously is everybody as he sets down the daily story of his life with Carrie and their troublesome son Lupin, of his little puns, his triumphs and misadventures, verbal and otherwise. He is an 1890 fuddydud for sure, but he is every gentle well-meaning respectable man who has ever lived in a suburban villa called "The Laurels" or "The Cedars" or "The Poplars," then or in 1996, near London or near Kansas City. His name is Pooter, and the book about him is called *The Diary of a Nobody*, beyond argument, but I know him well indeed, and so does anyone who has read even one page of the journal and then looked about him:

From *The Diary of a Nobody*, 1892, by George and Weedon Grossmith
November 12, Sunday.
Coming home from church Carrie and I met Lupin, Daisy Mutlar, and her brother. Daisy was introduced to us, and we walked home together, Carrie

walking on with Miss Mutlar. We asked them in for a few minutes, and I had a good look at my future daughter-in-law. My heart quite sank. She is a big young woman, and I should think at least eight years older than Lupin. I did not even think her good-looking. Carrie asked her if she could come in on Wednesday next with her brother to meet a few friends. She replied that she would only be too pleased.

November 13.

Carrie sent out invitations to Gowing, the Cummings, to Mr. and Mrs. James (of Sutton), and Mr. Stillbrook. I wrote a note to Mr. Franching, of Peckham. Carrie said we may as well make it a nice affair, and why not ask our principal, Mr. Perkupp? I said I feared we were not quite grand enough for him. Carrie said there was "no offence in asking him." I said: "Certainly not," and I wrote him a letter. Carrie confessed she was a little disappointed with Daisy Mutlar's appearance, but thought she seemed a nice girl.

November 14.

Everybody so far has accepted for our quite grand little party for tomorrow. Mr. Perkupp, in a nice letter which I shall keep, wrote that he was dining in Kensington, but if he could get away, he would come up to Holloway for an hour. Carrie was busy all day, making little cakes and open jam puffs and jellies. She said she felt quite nervous about her responsibilities tomorrow evening. We decided to have some light things on the table, such as sandwiches, cold chicken and ham, and some sweets, and on the sideboard a nice piece of cold beef and a Paysandu tongue for the more hungry ones to peg into if they liked.

Gowing called to know if he was to put on "swallow-tails" tomorrow. Carrie said he had better dress, especially as Mr. Franching was coming, and there was a possibility of Mr. Perkupp also putting in an appearance.

Gowing said: "Oh, I only wanted to know; for I have not worn my dress-coat for some time, and I must send it to have the creases pressed out."

After Gowing left, Lupin came in, and, in his anxiety to please Daisy Mutlar, carped at and criticised the arrangements, and, in fact, disapproved of everything, including our having asked our old friend Cummings, who, he said, would look in evening dress like a green-grocer engaged to wait, and who must not be surprised if Daisy took him for one.

I fairly lost my temper, and said: "Lupin, allow me to tell you Miss Daisy Mutlar is not the Queen of England. I gave you credit for more wisdom than to allow yourself to be inveigled into an engagement with a woman considerably older than yourself. I advise you to think of earning your living before entangling yourself with a wife whom you will have to support, and, in all probability, her brother also, who appeared to be nothing but a loafer."

Instead of receiving this advice in a sensible manner, Lupin jumped up and said: "If you insult the lady I am engaged to, you insult me. I will leave the house and never darken your doors again."

He went out of the house, slamming the hall-door. But it was all right. He came back to supper, and we played bezique till nearly twelve o'clock.

November 15.

A red-letter day. Our first important party since we have been in this house. I got home early from the City. Lupin insisted on having a hired waiter, and stood a half-dozen of champagne. I think this an unnecessary expense, but Lupin said he had had a piece of luck, having made three pounds out of a private deal in the City. I hope he won't gamble in his new situation. The supper-room looked so nice, and Carrie truly said: "We need not be ashamed of its being seen by Mr. Perkupp, should he honour us by coming."

I dressed early in case people should arrive punctually at eight o'clock, and was much vexed to find my new dress-trousers much too short. Lupin, who is getting beyond his position, found fault with my wearing ordinary boots instead of dress-boots.

I replied satirically: "My dear son, I have lived to be above that sort of thing."

Lupin burst out laughing, and said: "A man generally was above his boots."

This may be funny, or it may *not;* but I was gratified to find he had not discovered the coral had come off one of my studs. Carrie looked a picture, wearing the dress she wore at the Mansion House. The arrangement of the drawing-room was excellent. Carrie had hung muslin curtains over the folding-doors, and also over one of the entrances, for we had removed the door from its hinges.

Mr. Peters, the waiter, arrived in good time, and I gave him strict orders not to open another bottle of champagne until the previous one was empty. Carrie arranged for some sherry and port wine to be placed on the drawing-room sideboard, with some glasses. By-the-by, our new enlarged and tinted photographs look very nice on the walls, especially as Carrie has arranged some Liberty silk bows on the four corners of them.

The first arrival was Gowing, who, with his usual taste, greeted me with: "Hulloh, Pooter—why, your trousers are too short!"

I simply said: "Very likely, and you will find my temper 'short' also."

He said: "That won't make your trousers longer, juggins. You should get your missus to put a flounce on them."

I wonder I waste my time entering his insulting observations in my diary.

The next arrivals were Mr. and Mrs. Cummings. The former said: "As you didn't say anything about dress, I have come 'halfdress.'" He had on a black frock-coat and white tie. The James', Mr. Merton, and Mr. Stillbrook arrived, but Lupin was restless and unbearable till his Daisy Mutlar and Frank arrived.

Carrie and I were rather startled at Daisy's appearance. She had a bright-crimson dress on, cut very low in the neck. I do not think such a style modest. She ought to have taken a lesson from Carrie, and covered her shoulders with a little lace. Mr. Nackles, Mr. Sprice-Hogg and his four daughters came; so did Franching, and one or two of Lupin's new friends, members of the "Holloway Comedians." Some of these seemed rather theatrical in their manner, especially one, who was posing all the evening, and leant on our little round table and cracked it. Lupin called him "our Henry," and said he was "our lead at the H.C.'s," and was quite as good in that department as Harry Mutlar was as the low-comedy merchant. All this is Greek to me.

We had some music, and Lupin, who never left Daisy's side for a moment, raved over her singing of a song called "Some Day." It seemed a pretty song, but she made such grimaces, and sang, to my mind, so out of tune, I would not have asked her to sing again; but Lupin made her sing four songs right off, one after the other.

At ten o'clock we went down to supper, and from the way Gowing and Cummings ate you would have thought they had not had a meal for a month. I told Carrie to keep something back in case Mr. Perkupp should come by mere chance. Gowing annoyed me very much by filling a large tumbler of champagne, and drinking it straight off. He repeated this action, and made me fear our half-dozen of champagne would not last out. I tried to keep a bottle back, but Lupin got hold of it, and took it to the side-table with Daisy and Frank Mutlar.

We went upstairs, and the young fellows began skylarking. Carrie put a stop to that at once. Stillbrook amused us with a song, "What have you done with your Cousin John?" I did not notice that Lupin and Frank had disappeared. I asked Mr. Watson, one of the Holloways, where they were, and he said: "It's a case of 'Oh, what a surprise!'"

We were directed to form a circle—which we did. Watson then said: "I have much pleasure in introducing the celebrated Blondin Donkey." Frank and Lupin then bounded into the room. Lupin had whitened his face like a clown, and Frank had tied round his waist a large hearthrug. He was supposed to be the donkey, and he looked it. They indulged in a very noisy pantomime, and we were all shrieking with laughter.

I turned round suddenly, and then I saw Mr. Perkupp standing halfway in the door, he having arrived without our knowing it. I beckoned to Carrie, and we went up to him at once. He would not come right into the room. I apologised for the foolery, but Mr. Perkupp said: "Oh, it seems amusing." I could see he was not a bit amused.

Carrie and I took him downstairs, but the table was a wreck. There was not a glass of champagne left—not even a sandwich. Mr. Perkupp said he required nothing, but would like a glass of seltzer or soda water. The last syphon was empty. Carrie said: "We have plenty of port wine left." Mr. Perkupp said with a smile: "No, thank you. I really require nothing, but I am most pleased to see you and your husband in your own home. Goodnight, Mrs. Pooter—you will excuse my very short stay, I know." I went with him to his carriage, and he said: "Don't trouble to come to the office till twelve tomorrow."

I felt despondent as I went back to the house, and I told Carrie I thought the party was a failure. Carrie said it was a great success, and I was only tired, and insisted on my having some port myself. I drank two glasses and felt much better, and we went into the drawing-room, where they had commenced dancing. Carrie and I had a little dance, which I said reminded me of old days. She said I was a spooney old thing.

Few people have bothered to record the daily lives of the Pooters, in England or anywhere, but it is easy to find countless descriptions of life among the easier, plumper, more fortunate classes still referred to as "middle" but usually amplified as "upper middle"—a designation almost totally concerned with financial brackets. Most of the accounts are either poorly made or are intellectualized by professional writers.

That is why George Saintsbury's story of some of the dinner parties he gave during the last thirty years of the nineteenth century is so agreeable: it is written by a man who knew too much about both himself and the English language to be anything but good.

His *Notes on a Cellar-Book* appeared in 1920, after a long rich life when he was one of the foremost critics and scholars in a long rich period in British letters. His menus, thus "recollected in tranquillity," may seem strangely overelaborate now, but in a day of heavy abundance they stood out as gems of austerity.

A good proof of that is a quick glance at *Breakfasts, Luncheons, and Ball Suppers*, a book published anonymously in London in 1887. It attempted, with some success, to debunk the well-heeled Englishman's ambitions to outspend his club members in the three most popular forms of entertaining . . . and gives now a horrendous picture of what stark simplicity meant in that vanished epoch.

The writer, who cautiously signed himself "Major L——," perhaps to prove to his readers that although he urged embarrassingly low-class economy in his suggestions he was after all "one of them" in his rank and requisite breeding, wrote daringly on the subject of ball suppers: "I shall give only four bills of fare. Anyone who gives more than four balls in one year will probably be in a lunatic asylum before the next, so will not require more."

He goes on, after a lecture on saving time as well as nervous energy in such plans: "Ball suppers, like other repasts, require some care, some management, some taste to be displayed, to be really nice. In the winter a clever cutlet is a luxury, but unless the establishment is large I should almost advise that everything should be cold, soups of course excepted . . . a hot meal so soon after dinner is hardly required. . . ."

Then, as an example of his revolutionary and yet completely "acceptable" theories, he suggests the following basic menu for a little ball to be given in June:

Consommé

Purée of Chicken à la Crême

Chaufroix of Sole

Chaufroix of Salmon

Prawns in Aspic

Stuffed Quails

Chicken and Tongue

Mayonnaise of Lobster

Galantines in Aspic

Chaufroix of Chicken

Pâté of Chicken and Tongue

Cold Ham

Macédoine of Fruits

Compôte of Strawberries

Ices: Strawberry Cream, Raspberry Water

Cakes, Grapes, Strawberries

Oh, Mr. Pooter, how stingy was your party for Miss Daisy Mutlar! Oh, Professor Saintsbury, how niggardly was some such little "contrast of simplicity" as your third menu in *Notes on a Cellar-Book*!

And how agreeable it is to read about fine food, and beautiful bottles, in prose that is knowingly simple and honest, like the writer himself and the feasts he served to his friends!

Here are too few pages, and three bills of fare, from Saintsbury's book:

From *Notes on a Cellar-Book* by George Saintsbury, 1845–1933

It is good to have read Walz's *Rhetores Graeci* and the *Grand Cyrus,* and nearly all the English poets that anybody has ever heard of; also to find *The Earthly Paradise,* at a twentieth reading in 1920, as delightful as it was at a first in 1868. It is good to have heard Sims Reeves flood St. James's Hall with "Adelaida," till you felt as if you were being drowned, not in a bath but in an ocean of musical malmsey; and to have descanted on the beauties of your first Burne-Jones, without knowing that a half-puzzled, half-amused don stood behind you. Many other things past, and some present, have been and are—for anything, once more, that has been is—good.

But I do not feel the slightest shame in ranking as good likewise and very good, those voyages to the Oracle of the Bottle and those obediences to its utterance, taken literally as well as allegorically, which are partially chronicled here. If I subjoin a few examples of menus, and some wine-lists, it is chiefly for the purpose of illustrating the doctrines laid down and the practices recommended in this book. They are all records of meals and wines discussed in my own houses, and mostly devised by ourselves. Some great authorities have pronounced such things not bad reading, Barmecidal as they are. I know that I found them comfortable in the days of rationing, when there were other calls, even on the absurd modicum of meat that was allotted to one in common with babies, dead men, and vegetarians, and when one had to be content with sprats and spaghetti. I wish I could imitate the Barmecide himself in following up these ghostly banquets with real ones. But I hope that all good men and all fair ladies who read me will accept the assurance that I would, if I could, minister unto them, even as I was privileged to do to others of their kind from fifty to five years ago, when "we drank it as the Fates ordained it," and took, as cheerfully as we drank it, what else the Fates ordained.

Let us begin with two specimens of a kind of dinner which I now think over-elaborated. Two entrées are quite enough. But the fact was that at the time when they and others like them were given (the opening years of the Cellar-Book, 1884–6), both my wife and I were rather fascinated by a French chef named Grégoire, who in those days both sent out and superintended dishes, less impossibly than poor Rosa Timmins's volunteer assistant, and very admirably. Alas! he died. His soufflés were sublime.

By one of these may hang a little tale. At a dinner of the usual "sonnet" or "fourteener" number, the lady on my left refused it; the man next her, who was busy talking to his other neighbour, did ditto; so did his accomplice; and what a seventeenth-century Puritan pamphleteer, picturesquely anticipating later slang, calls "a rot among the Bishops" set in. My wife might have stopped it, but didn't: and the dish came back to me virgin. I helped myself, observed gravely, "I'm sorry to keep you all waiting," and ate. Thereupon my lady said, "It looks very good: may I change my mind?" And the man next her changed *his* mind; and his damsel followed; and they all followed—the whole dozen of them (omitting my wife, who is sometimes *propositi tenax*). I said nothing aloud: but murmured to myself and the *soufflé,* "Sheep!"

I.

Montilla	Consommé aux Pointcs d'Asperges
Johannisberg Claus Auslese, 1874	John Dory Sauce Livournaise
Ch. Grillet, 1865	Filets de Saumon à la gelée
Champagne Jeroboam. Dagonet, 1874 Romanée Conti, 1858 Ch. Margaux, 1868	Côtelettes à la Joncourt Plovers' Eggs Aspic de Volaille à la Reine Haunch of Mutton Mayonnaise de Homard
Port, 1853	Soufflé glacé au Marasquin
Pedro Ximénès	Canapés de Crevettes

III.

As a contrast of simplicity take the following, long afterwards (some twenty years) constructed as an endeavour to carry out, for a single guest, the admirable combination of *ordre et largeur* in Foker's prescription, "a bottle of sherry, a bottle of sham, a bottle of port, and a shass-caffy."

Sherry "Titania"	Clear Soup
	Fried Trout
Champagne Moët, 1893 Port Cockburn's, 1881	Filets de Bœuf à la St. Aubyn Roast Duckling Apricots à la Rosebery Sardines Dieu-sait-Comment
Green Chartreuse	Coffee

It would be foolish to make any kind of collection of recent English writing, even gastronomical, without having something by Somerset Maugham in it. Whether he writes about food or love or the weather, there is an epicurean detachment in what he says, epicurean in the true sense of intelligent and deliberate restraint, which is so often and easily forgotten by the gourmands of life.

The reason I have chosen such a simple thing as the story of the Vicar's egg, out of a wealth of possibilities, is that it is one of my favorite meals in all literature, unforgettable in its downright selfish hatefulness.

From *Of Human Bondage* by W. Somerset Maugham, 1874–1965

Philip parted from Emma with tears, but the journey to Blackstable amused him, and when they arrived he was resigned and cheerful. Blackstable was sixty miles from London. Giving their luggage to a porter, Mr. Carey set out to walk with Philip to the vicarage; it took them little more than five minutes, and when they reached it, Philip suddenly remembered the gate. It was red and five-barred: it swung both ways on easy hinges; and it was possible, though forbidden, to swing backwards and forwards on it. They walked through the garden to the front-door. This was only used by visitors and on Sundays, and on special occasions, as when the Vicar went up to London or came back. The traffic of the house took place through a side-door, and there was a back door as well for the gardener and for beggars and tramps. It was a fairly large house of yellow brick, with a red roof, built about five and twenty years before in an ecclesiastical style. The front-door was like a church porch, and the drawing-room windows were gothic.

Mrs. Carey, knowing by what train they were coming, waited in the drawing-room and listened for the click of the gate. When she heard it she went to the door.

"There's Aunt Louisa," said Mr. Carey, when he saw her. "Run and give her a kiss."

Philip started to run, awkwardly, trailing his club-foot, and then stopped. Mrs. Carey was a little, shrivelled woman of the same age as her husband, with a face extraordinarily filled with deep wrinkles, and pale blue eyes. Her gray hair was arranged in ringlets according to the fashion of her youth. She wore a black dress, and her only ornament was a gold chain, from which hung a cross. She had a shy manner and a gentle voice.

"Did you walk, William?" she said, almost reproachfully, as she kissed her husband.

"I didn't think of it," he answered, with a glance at his nephew.

"It didn't hurt you to walk, Philip, did it?" she asked the child.

"No, I always walk."

He was a little surprised at their conversation. Aunt Louisa told him to come in, and they entered the hall. It was paved with red and yellow tiles, on which alternately were a Greek Cross and the Lamb of God. An imposing staircase led out of the hall. It was of polished pine, with a peculiar smell, and had been put in because fortunately, when the church was reseated, enough wood remained over. The balusters were decorated with emblems of the Four Evangelists.

"I've had the stove lighted as I thought you'd be cold after your journey," said Mrs. Carey.

It was a large black stove that stood in the hall and was only lighted if the weather was very bad and the Vicar had a cold. It was not lighted if Mrs. Carey had a cold. Coal was expensive. Besides, Mary Ann, the maid, didn't like fires all over the place. If they wanted all them fires they must keep a second girl. In the winter Mr. and Mrs. Carey lived in the dining-room so that one fire should do, and in the summer they could not get out of the habit, so the drawing-room was used only by Mr. Carey on Sunday afternoons for his nap. But every Saturday he had a fire in the study so that he could write his sermon.

Aunt Louisa took Philip upstairs and showed him into a tiny bedroom that looked out on the drive. Immediately in front of the window was a large tree, which Philip remembered now because the branches were so low that it was possible to climb quite high up it.

"A small room for a small boy," said Mrs. Carey. "You won't be frightened at sleeping alone?"

"Oh, no."

On his first visit to the vicarage he had come with his nurse, and Mrs. Carey had had little to do with him. She looked at him now with some uncertainty.

"Can you wash your own hands, or shall I wash them for you?"

"I can wash myself," he answered firmly.

"Well, I shall look at them when you come down to tea," said Mrs. Carey.

She knew nothing about children. After it was settled that Philip should come down to Blackstable, Mrs. Carey had thought much how she should treat him; she was anxious to do her duty; but now he was there she found herself just as shy of him as he was of her. She hoped he would not be noisy and rough, because her husband did not like rough and noisy boys. Mrs. Carey made an excuse to leave Philip alone, but in a moment came back and knocked at the door; she asked him, without coming in, if he could pour out the water himself. Then she went downstairs and rang the bell for tea.

The dining-room, large and well-proportioned, had windows on two sides of it, with heavy curtains of red rep; there was a big table in the middle; and at one end an imposing mahogany sideboard with a looking-glass in it. In one corner stood a harmonium. On each side of the fireplace were chairs covered in stamped leather, each with an antimacassar; one had arms and was called the husband, and the other had none and was called the wife. Mrs. Carey never sat in the arm-chair: she said she preferred a chair that was not too comfortable; there was always a lot to do, and if her chair had had arms she might not be so ready to leave it.

Mr. Carey was making up the fire when Philip came in, and he pointed out to his nephew that there were two pokers. One was large and bright and polished and unused, and was called the Vicar; and the other, which was much smaller and had evidently passed through many fires, was called the Curate.

"What are we waiting for?" said Mr. Carey.

"I told Mary Ann to make you an egg. I thought you'd be hungry after your journey."

Mrs. Carey thought the journey from London to Blackstable very tiring. She seldom travelled herself, for the living was only three hundred a year, and, when her husband wanted a holiday, since there was not money for two, he went by himself. He was very fond of Church Congresses and usually managed to go up to London once a year; and once he had been to Paris for the exhibition, and two or three times to Switzerland. Mary Ann brought in the egg, and they sat down. The chair was much too low for Philip, and for a moment neither Mr. Carey nor his wife knew what to do.

"I'll put some books under him," said Mary Ann.

She took from the top of the harmonium the large Bible and the prayer-book from which the Vicar was accustomed to read prayers, and put them on Philip's chair.

"Oh, William, he can't sit on the Bible," said Mrs. Carey, in a shocked tone. "Couldn't you get him some books out of the study?"

Mr. Carey considered the question for an instant.

"I don't think it matters this once if you put the prayer-book on the top, Mary Ann," he said. "The book of Common Prayer is the composition of men like ourselves. It has no claim to divine authorship."

"I hadn't thought of that, William," said Aunt Louisa.

Philip perched himself on the books, and the Vicar, having said grace, cut the top off his egg.

"There," he said, handing it to Philip, "you can eat my top if you like."

Philip would have liked an egg to himself, but he was not offered one, so took what he could.

"How have the chickens been laying since I went away?" asked the Vicar.

"Oh, they've been dreadful, only one or two a day."

"How did you like that top, Philip?" asked his uncle.

"Very much, thank you."

"You shall have another one on Sunday afternoon."

Mr. Carey always had a boiled egg at tea on Sunday, so that he might be fortified for the evening service.

The report of a Christmas dinner served in the midst of war in London for a group of penniless old French refugees is one of the most touching things I have ever read, in spite of its far from literary polish. I am printing it just as it appeared in the *Wine and Food Quarterly*, firmly resisting all temptations to turn it into a story, or at least a withers-wringing anecdote. It could not be better done than it is here.

"Memorable Meals, No. 1"

From *Wine and Food Quarterly*, Spring, 1942

    The place: Soho

    The date: 25 December 1941

    The hostess: Mademoiselle Chicou d'Argences

    The guests: Forty-three destitute old French men and women

The fare: *Crème de tomates*

Dindonneau farci à la mode de chez nous

Haricots verts

Pêche de mes rêves

Café

The wines: *Un doigt de porto*

La piquette de la cigale

Les cerises de la fourmi

Mademoiselle Chicou d'Argences was born in 1858 and she has been an honoured guest at many rich men's tables in her native France as well as in the United States, where she had once upon a time many friends, most of them dead by now and the others unaware of the fact that she has no income whatever today. Her old ship is at the bottom of the sea but she is not downhearted! Like the rest of the company on that happy Christmas Day, she still lives and bobs up and down on the choppy sea of misfortune, safe enough on that old raft, the French Benevolent Society in London. And she still has "*le sourire*"; she also has "*le mot pour rire*." She was the most lively and delightful hostess imaginable when she presided over a *déjeuner de Noël*, provided by a generous French Restaurateur, who does not wish his name nor that of his restaurant to be mentioned.

The restaurant was closed to the public on that occasion and the little band of aged and poor French people, stranded in London, were given a meal such as they had lost all hope ever to enjoy again. The welcoming *verre de porto* which awaited them on arrival set everybody at ease and set tongues wagging. Then the steaming hot soup, the chestnut-stuffed turkey, and the *haricots verts* tossed in butter were so good that a hush fell upon the babel of tongues whilst jaws were busy. *La piquette* was unstinted, and what a joy it was for all these old French people to see once again wine in a glass before them; most of them looked at it with moist eyes before drinking it. To be penniless in a strange land and to be given wine when wine is so difficult to buy, even when you are as rich as rich can be! "*Quel miracle!*" Toasts began to be drunk before coffee was served, and with the coffee there was another miracle. "*Des cerises à l'eau-de-vie, ma chère! Tout comme chez ma grand'mère,*" confided a guest of close upon ninety years to her neighbour.

When the company dispersed, not without gentle hints that it was time to be making for home before black-out time, some of the old legs may have been a little less steady than before lunch, but all the hearts were younger. And they all promised the kind host to come again next Christmas, when he took leave of them with *"A llannée prochaine!"* as a parting gift. Was there ever a more memorable meal?

Possibly the nicest thing about G. B. Stern's jolly little book *Bouquet* is the final barbaric fillip to it when she admits, after a serious-minded albeit gay wine tour through France, that a dry Martini will taste very good indeed!

She and her husband are saying a last word to their two companions, who are motoring on to the Riviera with the luggage. She calls to them to have her tipple ready when she arrives at Antibes the day after tomorrow: "And suddenly a little thrill shot through my being, a thrill flavoured with Angostura and iced gin, as my imagination prophetically tasted this first most wonderful, most delicious cocktail, after the five weeks' haughty abstinence which connoisseurship had exacted of us."

I shall always admire Miss Stern for admitting to such a heathenish desire at the end of a book filled with so many sincerely appreciated bottles of fine wines!

Almost every page of *Bouquet* pleases in some such way as the last, even if one has not tasted quite so many noble vintages, nor known the delight of finding an "inn of legend" and proving the *Guide Michelin* a goose for once:

From *Bouquet* by G. B. Stern, 1890–1973

We had no idea, when we left Tain-l'Hermitage, that the rather dull, straight, white roads and poplars of my conventional imagination were to be exchanged for the enchantment of an unknown mountain region. When we left Le Puy the next morning, we saw by Michelin that it was a run of forty-five kilometres to Saugues; there, at the Hôtel de France, marked only with an egg-cup and spoon, we might be able to get a tolerable lunch. We had no idea that we were to be served with a lunch which is the dream of all who sojourn haphazard through France. There were no stars in Michelin to lure us to the Hôtel de France; and nothing on the outside of the hotel itself—plain walls and a plain sign, an open courtyard onto the village street, and an outside staircase to the steep front-door.

We asked if we could eat. We were taken through the kitchen by another dark winding scaircase into a small dining-room. At once, however, on entering it, we felt grateful, though it took a minute or two before we discovered why. . . . Ah yes, they had had the sense to keep their jalousies closed. The room was cool and dim in the green light filtering through; the blinding glare outside was blocked out, and there were no flies. Good! We asked the waiter, an efficient-looking man in white linen, what we could eat. "Trout and partridge," he replied, with humility. Well, yes, *faute de mieux*, trout and partridge. . . . We should have liked the worst-end-of-the-neck with some winter greens, but nevertheless—be it so! And the wine-list? Chablis, 1918, was our choice, and *vin ordinaire* to begin with.

The waiter quickly brought us some home-cured ham as an hors-d'oeuvre. It was not very good. Only when the trout arrived, perfectly cooked, brown and delicious, with just the right accompaniment of butter and gravy, did we begin to suspect that our lunch might be above the egg-cup-and-spoon level.

After the trout, and without any waiting, *champignons* appeared, a big dish, crisp and brown and succulent, far too good for any remnants to be left upon our plates. Humphrey began to remind us gloomily that his surname was "Petit-Panche," and that he had very little room left for partridge! And then the waiter, who appeared to know by magic just when we were ready for each course, brought in, *not* the partridge, but what was probably the most tender rabbit in the world, cooked with tomato sauce; because he said that Madame feared we would not have enough with partridge alone! I have eaten the breast of chicken which has tasted like rabbit, but I have never yet eaten rabbit which tasted so like the breast of chicken.

When the partridges appeared, we reminded the waiter that he had murmured something about potatoes, and could we have them at the same time? He agreed, but was genuinely distressed at our wish. "You will see," he said, arriving with the potatoes, "that the flavours do not mingle well."

That man was an artist. He was quite right. The potato savoury, with its delicate crust of cheese, was spoilt by being eaten with the partridge. We left it till afterwards.

The next course was *écrevisses,* delicate little river crayfish, cooked in brandy. I had given in by now, and Humphrey was sobbing bitterly; but Johnny plodded on; and Rosemary, in whom the gourmet had for once triumphed over indigestion, came in a good second.

The waiter cleared away the *écrevisses* rapidly and silently, and produced—*flan,* he called it: a delicious pudding of white of egg and cream beaten up, and sponge fingers to eat with it. Doubtless Madame was afraid that we might still be hungry! After that, we merely had to cope with cream-cheese, fruit, coffee, and four *fines.*

The bill for the four of us, complete with wine, mineral water, coffee, brandies, and service, amounted to one hundred and eighteen francs, fifty centimes. At the then rate of exchange, that is between fourteen and fifteen shillings, roughly, in English money. With the exception of the home-cured ham, not a single one of the nine courses or so but was as delicately and intelligently cooked—created, one might say—as a meal at any of the most famous five-star restaurants of Paris or London.

When we went down, we spoke a few dazed words of thanks and praise to Mme Anglade, the proprietress, a thin, quiet wisp of a woman. "Ah, madame," she replied, "I was perhaps a good enough cook once, *mais on devient vieille, et on perd le courage!*"

"But one gets old, and one loses courage. . . ." We wondered, not unnaturally, with what sort of a dinner Madame would have served us *before* she lost courage! . . .

Mrs. Ramsay, in Virginia Woolf's story *To the Lighthouse*, may not have been the author's mother, any more than Mr. Pooter was George and Weedon Grossmith themselves; but she is all exhausted beautiful fertile women who must feed their children and the people they choose to love. The story of the dinner party she gave one summer night is hard to cut into, as anything good must be. Nothing much was said or done, there in the shadowy dining room, but human beings suddenly seemed what they were, which is magic when it happens on paper.

Everything was wrong for Mrs. Ramsay: her husband the scholar had laughed at the plan to go next day to the lighthouse with their eight children; Mr. Bankes was a difficult prissy man who fussed about what he ate; two of her young guests were much in love and very late; she was tired . . .

From *To the Lighthouse* by Virginia Woolf, 1882–1941
. . . Again she felt alone in the presence of her old antagonist, life.

Jasper and Rose said that Mildred wanted to know whether she should wait dinner.

"Not for the Queen of England," said Mrs. Ramsay emphatically.

"Not for the Empress of Mexico," she added, laughing at Jasper; for he shared his mother's vice: he, too, exaggerated.

And if Rose liked, she said, while Jasper took the message, she might choose which jewels she was to wear. When there are fifteen people sitting down to dinner, one cannot keep things waiting for ever. She was now beginning to feel annoyed with them for being so late; it was inconsiderate of them, and it annoyed her on top of her anxiety about them, that they should choose this very night to be out late, when, in fact, she wished the dinner to be particularly nice, since William Bankes had at last consented to dine with them; and they were having Mildred's masterpiece—Bœuf en Daube. Everything depended upon things being served up to the precise moment they were ready. The beef, the bay-leaf, and the wine—all must be done to a turn. To keep it waiting was out of the question. Yet of course tonight, of all nights, out they went, and they came in late, and things had to be sent out, things had to be kept hot; the Bœuf en Daube would be entirely spoilt.

Jasper offered her an opal necklace; Rose a gold necklace. Which looked best against her black dress? Which did indeed, said Mrs. Ramsay absent-mindedly looking at her neck and shoulders (but avoiding her face) in the glass.

. . . There was a smell of burning. Could they have let the Bœuf en Daube overboil? she wondered, pray heaven not! when the great clangour of the gong announced solemnly, authoritatively, that all those scattered about, in attics, in bedrooms, on little perches of their own, reading, writing, putting the last smooth to their hair, or fastening dresses, must leave all that, and the little odds and ends on their washing-tables and dressing-tables, and the novels on the bed-tables, and the diaries which were so private, and assemble in the dining-room for dinner.

But what have I done with my life? thought Mrs. Ramsay, taking her place at the head of the table, and looking at all the plates making white circles on it. "William, sit by me," she said. "Lily," she said, wearily, "over there." They had that—Paul Rayley and Minta Doyle—she, only this—an infinitely long table and plates and knives. At the far end was her husband, sitting down, all in a heap, frowning. What at? She did not know. She did not mind. She could not understand how she had ever felt any emotion or affection for him. She had a sense of being past everything, through everything, out of everything, as she helped the soup, as if there was an eddy—there—and one could be in it, or one could be out of it, and she was out of it. It's all come to an end, she thought, while they came in one after another, Charles Tansley—"Sit there, please," she said—Augustus Carmichael—and sat down. And meanwhile she waited, passively, for some one to answer her, for something to happen. But this is not a thing, she thought, ladling out soup, that one says.

Raising her eyebrows at the discrepancy—that was what she was thinking, this was what she was doing—ladling out soup—she felt, more and more strongly, outside that eddy; or as if a shade had fallen, and, robbed of colour, she saw things truly. The room (she looked round it) was very shabby. There was no beauty anywhere. She forbore to look at Mr. Tansley. Nothing seemed to have merged. They all sat separate. And the whole of the effort of merging and flowing and creating rested on her. . . . [She] wished, looking at her husband at the other end of the table, that he would say something. One word, she said to herself. For if he said a thing, it would make all the difference. He went to the heart of things. He cared about fishermen and their wages. He could not sleep for thinking of them. It was altogether different when he spoke; one did not feel then, pray heaven you don't see how little I care, because one did care. Then, realising that it was because she admired him so much that she was waiting for him to speak, she felt as if somebody had been praising her husband to her and their marriage, and she glowed all over without realising that it was she herself who had praised him. She looked at him thinking to find this in his face; he would be looking magnificent. . . . But not in the least! He was screwing his face up, he was scowling and frowning, and flushing with anger. What on earth was it about? she wondered. What could be the matter? Only that poor old Augustus had asked for another plate of soup—that was all. It was unthinkable, it was detestable (so he signalled to her across the table) that Augustus should be beginning his soup over again. He loathed people eating when he had finished. She saw his anger fly like a pack of hounds into his eyes, his brow, and she knew that in a moment something violent would explode, and then—thank goodness! she saw him clutch himself and clap a brake on the wheel, and the whole of his body seemed to emit sparks but not words. He sat there scowling. He had said nothing, he would have her observe. Let her give him the credit for that! But why after all should poor Augustus not ask for another plate of soup? He had merely touched Ellen's arm and said:

"Ellen, please, another plate of soup," and then Mr. Ramsay scowled like that.

And why not? Mrs. Ramsay demanded. Surely they could let Augustus have his soup if he wanted it. He hated people wallowing in food, Mr. Ramsay frowned at her. He hated everything dragging on for hours like this. But he had controlled himself, Mr. Ramsay would have her observe, disgusting though the sight was. But why show it so plainly, Mrs. Ramsay demanded (they looked at each other down the long table sending these questions and answers across, each knowing exactly what the other felt). Everybody could see, Mrs. Ramsay thought. There was Rose gazing at her father, there was Roger gazing at his father; both would be off in spasms of laughter in another second, she knew, and so she said promptly (indeed it was time):

"Light the candles," and they jumped up instantly and went and fumbled at the sideboard. . . .

Now eight candles were stood down the table, and after the first stoop the flames stood upright and drew with them into visibility the long table entire, and in the middle a yellow and purple dish of fruit. What had she done with it, Mrs. Ramsay wondered, for Rose's arrangement of the grapes and pears, of the horny pink-lined shell, of the bananas, made her think of a trophy fetched from the bottom of the sea, of Neptune's banquet, of the bunch that hangs with vine leaves over the shoulder of Bacchus (in some picture), among the leopard skins and the torches lolloping red and gold. . . . Thus brought up suddenly into the light it seemed possessed of great size and depth, was like a world in which one could take one's staff and climb hills, she thought, and go down into valleys, and to her pleasure (for it brought them into sympathy momentarily) she saw that Augustus too feasted his eyes on the same plate of fruit, plunged in, broke off a bloom there, a tassel here, and returned, after feasting, to his hive. That was his way of looking, different from hers. But looking together united them.

Now all the candles were lit up, and the faces on both sides of the table were brought nearer by the candle light, and composed, as they had not been in the twilight, into a party round a table, for the night was now shut off by panes of glass, which, far from giving any accurate view of the outside world, rippled it so strangely that here, inside the room, seemed to be order and dry land; there, outside, a reflection in which things wavered and vanished, waterily.

Some change at once went through them all, as if this had really happened, and they were all conscious of making a party together in a hollow, on an island; had their common cause against that fluidity out there. Mrs. Ramsay, who had been uneasy, waiting for Paul and Minta to come in, and unable, she felt, to settle to things, now felt her uneasiness changed to expectation. . . . They must come now, [she] thought, looking at the door, and at that instant Minta Doyle, Paul Rayley, and a maid carrying a great dish in her hands came in together. . . . "Put it down there," she said, helping the Swiss girl to place gently before her the huge brown pot in which was the Bœuf en Daube. . . . An exquisite scent of olives and oil and juice rose from the great brown dish as Marthe, with a little flourish, took the cover off. The cook had spent three days over that dish. And she must take great care, Mrs. Ramsay thought, diving into the soft mass, to choose a specially tender piece for William Bankes. And she peered into the dish, with its shiny walls and its confusion of savoury brown and yellow meats and its bay leaves and its wine, and thought. . . .

"It is a triumph," said Mr. Bankes, laying his knife down for a moment. He had eaten attentively. It was rich; it was tender. It was perfectly cooked. How did she manage these things in the depths of the country? he asked her. She was a wonderful woman. All his love, all his reverence, had returned; and she knew it.

"It is a French receipe of my grandmother's," said Mrs. Ramsay, speaking with a ring of great pleasure in her voice. Of course it was French. What passes for cookery in England is an abomination (they agreed). It is putting cabbages in water. It is roasting meat till it is like leather. It is cutting off the delicious skins of vegetables. "In which," said Mr. Bankes, "all the virtue of the vegetable is contained." And the waste, said Mrs. Ramsay. A whole French family could live on what an English cook throws away. Spurred on by her sense that William's affection had come back to her, and that everything was all right again, and that her suspense was over, and that now she was free both to triumph and to mock, she laughed, she gesticulated, till

Lily thought, How childlike, how absurd she was, sitting up there with all her beauty opened again in her, talking about the skins of vegetables. There was something frightening about her. She was irresistible. . . .

"Then," said Mr. Bankes, "there is that liquid the English call coffee."

"Oh, coffee!" said Mrs. Ramsay. But it was much rather a question (she was thoroughly roused, Lily could see, and talked very emphatically) of real butter and clean milk. Speaking with warmth and eloquence, she described the iniquity of the English dairy system, and in what state milk was delivered at the door, and was about to prove her charges, for she had gone into the matter, when all round the table, beginning with Andrew in the middle, like a fire leaping from tuft to tuft of furze, her children laughed; her husband laughed; she was laughed at, fire-encircled, and forced to veil her crest, dismount her batteries, and only retaliate by displaying the raillery and ridicule of the table to Mr. Bankes as an example of what one suffered if one attacked the prejudices of the British Public.

No, she said, she did not want a pear. Indeed she had been keeping guard over the dish of fruit (without realising it) jealously, hoping that nobody would touch it. Her eyes had been going in and out among the curves and shadows of the fruit, among the rich purples of the lowland grapes, then over the horny ridge of the shell, putting a yellow against a purple, a curved shape against a round shape, without knowing why she did it, or why, every time she did it, she felt more and more serene; until, oh, what a pity that they should do it—a hand reached out, took a pear, and spoilt the whole thing. In sympathy she looked at Rose. She looked at Rose sitting between Jasper and Prue. How odd that one's child should do that!

How odd to see them sitting there, in a row, her children, Jasper, Rose, Prue, Andrew, almost silent, but with some joke of their own going on, she guessed, from the twitching at their lips. It was something quite apart from everything else, something they were hoarding up to laugh over in their own room. It was not about their father, she hoped. No, she thought not. What was it, she wondered, sadly rather, for it seemed to her that they would laugh when she was not there. There was all that hoarded behind those rather set, still, mask-like faces, for they did not join in easily; they were like watchers, surveyors, a little raised or set apart from the grown-up people. . . .

. . . But dinner was over. It was time to go. They were only playing with things on their plates. She would wait until they had done laughing at some story her husband was telling. . . . Then she would get up. . . .

She tucked her napkin under the edge of her plate. Well, were they done now? No. That story had led to another story. Her husband was in great spirits tonight, and wishing, she supposed, to make it all right with old Augustus after that scene about the soup, had drawn him in—they were telling stories about some one they had both known at college. She looked at the window in which the candle flames burnt brighter now that the panes were black, and looking at the outside the voices came to her very strangely, as if they were voices at a service in a cathedral, for she did not listen to the words. The sudden bursts of laughter and then one voice (Minta's) speaking alone, reminded her of men and boys crying out the Latin words of a service in some Roman Catholic cathedral. She waited. Her husband spoke. He was repeating something, and she knew it was poetry from the rhythm and the ring of exultation, and melancholy in his voice:

> Come out and climb the garden path,
>   Luriana, Lurilee.
> The China rose is all abloom and buzzing with the yellow bee.

The words (she was looking at the window) sounded as if they were floating like flowers on water out there, cut off from them all, as if no one had said them, but they had come into existence of themselves.

"And all the lives we ever lived and all the lives to be are full of trees and changing leaves." She did not know what they meant, but, like music, the words seemed to be spoken by her own voice, outside her self, saying quite easily and naturally what had been in her mind the whole evening while she said different things. She knew, without looking round, that every one at the table was listening to the voice saying:

> I wonder if it seems to you,
>   Luriana, Lurilee

with the same sort of relief and pleasure that she had, as if this were, at last, the natural thing to say, this were their own voice speaking.

But the voice stopped. She looked round. She made herself get up. Augustus Carmichael had risen and, holding his table napkin so that it looked like a long white robe, he stood chanting:

> To see the Kings go riding by
> Over lawn and daisy lea
> With their palm leaves and cedar sheaves,
>   Luriana, Lurilee

and as she passed him, he turned slightly towards her repeating the last words:

> Luriana, Lurilee

and bowed to her as if he did her homage. Without knowing why, she felt that he liked her better than he had ever done before; and with a feeling of relief and gratitude she returned his bow and passed through the door which he held open for her.

X

THIS NOBLE FLUMMERY

Fantasy

Fantasy, according to the *Oxford Dictionary*, is a noun meaning "Faculty of imagination, esp. when extravagant; mental image; fanciful design, speculation, etc.," all of which leads me to think that lexicographers are as much baffled by a definition for the thing as are its amateurs. I, for instance, can give examples of what it is, but I cannot tell why they are fantastic to me and something else is not, even when it is equally imaginative and "impossible."

The excerpts I have chosen are, to me, fantasy, but I know that to many other readers they may seem merely nonsense or whimsy. They are irreconcilable with logical and normal human behavior; they are monstrously exaggerated or deeply understated, but all with such a complete assumption of truth that their readers are almost too easily persuaded to wonder at their seeming actualities.

"That which is unreal, never was; that which is real, never was not." It took thought to make such a statement, and such a statement takes much thought to think about at all. How better can one say what is so obvious about Alice's tea-party, for instance?

If it was unreal, then it never did happen. But if it was real, then it happened as surely as ever any woman struggled to be polite and bright-faced at a confusing social flibflab. . . .

From *Alice's Adventures in Wonderland* by Lewis Carroll, 1832–1898

There was a table set out under a tree in front of the house, and the March Hare and the Hatter were having tea at it: a Dormouse was sitting between them, fast asleep, and the other two were resting their elbows on it, and talking over its head. "Very uncomfortable for the Dormouse," thought Alice; "only, as it's asleep, I suppose it doesn't mind."

The table was a large one, but the three were all crowded together at one corner of it. "No room! No room!" they cried out when they saw Alice coming. "There's *plenty* of room!" said Alice indignantly, and she sat down in a large arm-chair at one end of the table.

"Have some wine," the March Hare said in an encouraging tone.

Alice looked all round the table, but there was nothing on it but tea. "I don't see any wine," she remarked.

"There isn't any," said the March Hare.

"Then it wasn't very civil of you to offer it," said Alice angrily.

"It wasn't very civil of you to sit down without being invited," said the March Hare.

"I didn't know it was *your* table," said Alice; "it's laid for a great many more than three."

"Your hair wants cutting," said the Hatter. He had been looking at Alice for some time with great curiosity, and this was his first speech.

"You shouldn't make personal remarks," Alice said with some severity; "it's very rude."

The Hatter opened his eyes very wide on hearing this; but all he *said* was, "Why is a raven like a writing-desk?"

"Come, we shall have some fun now!" thought Alice. "I'm glad they've begun asking riddles.—I believe I can guess that," she added aloud.

"Do you mean that you think you can find out the answer to it?" said the March Hare.

"Exactly so," said Alice.

"Then you should say what you mean," the March Hare went on.

"I do," Alice hastily replied; "at least—at least I mean what I say— that's the same thing, you know."

"Not the same thing a bit!" said the Hatter. "You might just as well say that 'I see what I eat' is the same thing as 'I eat what I see'!"

"You might just as well say," added the March Hare, "that 'I like what I get' is the same thing as 'I get what I like'!"

"You might just as well say," added the Dormouse, who seemed to be talking in his sleep, "that 'I breathe when I sleep' is the same thing as 'I sleep when I breathe'!"

"It *is* the same thing with you," said the Hatter, and here the conversation dropped, and the party sat silent for a minute, while Alice thought over all she could remember about ravens and writing-desks, which wasn't much.

The Hatter was the first to break the silence. "What day of the month is it?" he said, turning to Alice: he had taken his watch out of his pocket, and was looking at it uneasily, shaking it every now and then, and holding it to his ear.

Alice considered a little, and then said, "The fourth."

"Two days wrong!" sighed the Hatter. "I told you butter wouldn't suit the works!" he added, looking angrily at the March Hare.

"It was the *best* butter," the March Hare meekly replied.

"Yes, but some crumbs must have got in as well," the Hatter grumbled: "you shouldn't have put it in with the bread-knife."

The March Hare took the watch and looked at it gloomily: then he dipped it into his cup of tea, and looked at it again: but he could think of nothing better to say than his first remark, "It was the *best* butter, you know."

Alice had been looking over his shoulder with some curiosity. "What a funny watch!" she remarked. "It tells the day of the month, and doesn't tell what o'clock it is!"

"Why should it?" muttered the Hatter. "Does *your* watch tell you what year it is?"

"Of course not," Alice replied very readily: "but that's because it stays the same year for such a long time together."

"Which is just the case with *mine*," said the Hatter.

Alice felt dreadfully puzzled. The Hatter's remark seemed to have no meaning in it, and yet it was certainly English. "I don't quite understand," she said, as politely as she could.

"The Dormouse is asleep again," said the Hatter, and he poured a little hot tea upon its nose.

The Dormouse shook its head impatiently, and said, without opening its eyes, "Of course, of course; just what I was going to remark myself."

"Have you guessed the riddle yet?" the Hatter said, turning to Alice again.

"No, I give it up," Alice replied: "what's the answer?"

"I haven't the slightest idea," said the Hatter.

"Nor I," said the March Hare.

Alice sighed wearily. "I think you might do something better with the time," she said, "than waste it asking riddles with no answers."

"If you knew Time as well as I do," said the Hatter, "you wouldn't talk about wasting *it*. It's *him*."

"I don't know what you mean," said Alice.

"Of course you don't!" the Hatter said, tossing his head contemptuously. "I dare say you never even spoke to Time!"

"Perhaps not," Alice cautiously replied: "but I know I have to beat time when I learn music."

"Ah! that accounts for it," said the Hatter. "He won't stand beating. Now, if you only kept on good terms with him, he'd do almost anything you liked with the clock. For instance, suppose it were nine o'clock in the morning, just time to begin lessons: you'd only have to whisper a hint to Time, and round goes the clock in a twinkling! Half-past one, time for dinner!"

("I only wish it was," the March Hare said to itself in a whisper.)

"That would be grand, certainly," said Alice thoughtfully: "but then— I shouldn't be hungry for it, you know."

"Not at first, perhaps," said the Hatter: "but you could keep it to half-past one as long as you liked."

"Is that the way *you* manage?" Alice asked.

The Hatter shook his head mournfully. "Not I!" he replied. "We quarrelled last March—just before *he* went mad, you know—" (pointing with his teaspoon at the March Hare) "—it was at the great concert given by the Queen of Hearts, and I had to sing

Twinkle, twinkle, little bat!
How I wonder what you're at!

"You know the song, perhaps?"

"I've heard something like it," said Alice.

"It goes on, you know," the Hatter continued, "in this way:

Up above the world you fly,
Like a tea-tray in the sky.
        Twinkle, twinkle—"

Here the Dormouse shook itself, and began singing in its sleep, "Twinkle, twinkle, twinkle, twinkle—" and went on so long that they had to pinch it to make it stop.

"Well, I'd hardly finished the first verse," said the Hatter, "when the Queen jumped up and bawled out, 'He's murdering the time! Off with his head!'"

"How dreadfully savage!" exclaimed Alice.

"And ever since that," the Hatter went on in a mournful tone, "he won't do a thing I ask! It's always six o'clock now."

A bright idea came into Alice's head. "Is that the reason so many tea-things are put out here?" she asked.

"Yes, that's it," said the Hatter with a sigh: "it's always tea-time, and we've no time to wash the things between whiles."

"Then you keep moving round, I suppose?" said Alice.

"Exactly so," said the Hatter: "as the things get used up."

"But what happens when you come to the beginning again?" Alice ventured to ask.

"Suppose we change the subject," the March Hare interrupted, yawning. "I'm getting tired of this. I vote the young lady tells us a story."

"I'm afraid I don't know one," said Alice, rather alarmed at the proposal.

"Then the Dormouse shall!" they both cried. "Wake up, Dormouse!" And they pinched it on both sides at once.

The Dormouse slowly opened his eyes. "I wasn't asleep," he said in a hoarse, feeble voice: "I heard every word you fellows were saying."

"Tell us a story!" said the March Hare.

"Yes, please do!" pleaded Alice.

"And be quick about it," added the Hatter, "or you'll be asleep again before it's done."

"Once upon a time there were three little sisters," the Dormouse began in a great hurry; "and their names were Elsie, Lacie, and Tillie; and they lived at the bottom of a well—"

"What did they live on?" said Alice, who always took a great interest in questions of eating and drinking.

"They lived on treacle," said the Dormouse, after thinking a minute or two.

"They couldn't have done that, you know," Alice gently remarked; "they'd have been ill."

"So they were," said the Dormouse; "*very* ill."

Alice tried to fancy to herself what such an extraordinary way of living would be like, but it puzzled her too much, so she went on: "But why did they live at the bottom of a well?"

"Take some more tea," the March Hare said to Alice, very earnestly.

"I've had nothing yet," Alice replied in an offended tone, "so I can't take more."

"You mean you can't take *less*," said the Hatter: "it's very easy to take *more* than nothing."

"Nobody asked *your* opinion," said Alice.

"Who's making personal remarks now?" the Hatter asked triumphantly.

Alice did not quite know what to say to this: so she helped herself to some tea and bread-and-butter, and then turned to the Dormouse, and repeated her question: "Why did they live at the bottom of a well?"

The Dormouse again took a minute or two to think about it, and then said, "It was a treacle-well."

"There's no such thing!" Alice was beginning very angrily, but the Hatter and the March Hare went "Sh! sh!" and the Dormouse sulkily remarked, "If you can't be civil, you'd better finish the story for yourself."

"No, please go on!" Alice said. "I won't interrupt again. I dare say there may be *one*."

"One, indeed!" said the Dormouse indignantly. However, he consented to go on: "And so these three little sisters—they were learning to draw, you know—"

"What did they draw?" said Alice, quite forgetting her promise.

"Treacle," said the Dormouse, without considering at all this time.

"I want a clean cup," interrupted the Hatter: "let's all move one place on."

He moved on as he spoke, and the Dormouse followed him: the March Hare moved into the Dormouse's place, and Alice rather unwillingly took the place of the March Hare. The Hatter was the only one who got any advantage from the change: and Alice was a good deal worse off, as the March Hare had just upset the milk-jug into his plate.

Alice did not wish to offend the Dormouse again, so she began very cautiously: "But I don't understand. Where did they draw the treacle from?"

"You can draw water out of a water-well," said the Hatter; "so I should think you could draw treacle out of a treacle-well—eh, stupid?"

"But they were *in* the well," Alice said to the Dormouse, not choosing to notice this last remark.

"Of course they were," said the Dormouse; "—well in."

This answer so confused poor Alice, that she let the Dormouse go on for some time without interrupting it.

"They were learning to draw," the Dormouse went on, yawning and rubbing its eyes, for it was getting very sleepy; "and they drew all manner of things—everything that begins with an M—"

"Why with an M?" said Alice.

"Why not?" said the March Hare.

Alice was silent.

The Dormouse had closed its eyes by this time, and was going off into a doze; but, on being pinched by the Hatter, it woke up again with a little shriek, and went on: "—that begins with an M, such as mouse-traps, and the moon, and memory, and muchness—you know you say things are 'much of a muchness'—did you ever see such a thing as a drawing of a muchness?"

"Really, now you ask me," said Alice, very much confused, "I don't think—"

"Then you shouldn't talk," said the Hatter.

This piece of rudeness was more than Alice could bear: she got up in great disgust, and walked off; the Dormouse fell asleep instantly, and neither of the others took the least notice of her going, though she looked back once or twice, half hoping that they would call after her: the last time she saw them, they were trying to put the Dormouse into the teapot.

"At any rate I'll never go *there* again!" said Alice as she picked her way through the wood. "It's the stupidest tea-party I ever was at in all my life!"

As Sir Thomas More said in the last sentence of his *Utopia*, "There are many things in the Commonwealth that I rather wish, than hope, to see followed."

And the description of the dining habits of his Syphogrants will prove, if that be needed, that any Utopia must be based on an idealization of the human animal rather than on his reality!

From *Utopia* by Sir Thomas More, 1478–1535

... At the hours of dinner and supper, the whole Syphogranty being called together by sound of trumpet, they meet and eat together except only such as are in the hospitals, or lie sick at home. Yet after the halls are served, no man is hindered to carry provisions home from the market-place; for they know that none does that but for some good reason; for though any that will may eat at home, yet none does it willingly, since it is both ridiculous and foolish for any to give themselves the trouble to make ready an ill dinner at home, when there is a much more plentiful one made ready for him so near at hand. All the uneasy and sordid services about these halls are performed by the slaves; but the dressing and cooking their meat and the ordering their tables belong only to the women, all those of every family taking it by turns. They sit at three or more tables, according to their number; the men sit toward the wall, and the women sit on the other side, that if any of them should be taken suddenly ill, which is no uncommon case among women with child, she may, without disturbing the rest, rise and go to the nurse's room, who are there with the sucking children; where there is always clean water at hand, and cradles in which they may lay the young children, if there is occasion for it, and a fire that they may shift and dress them before it. Every child is nursed by its own mother, if death or sickness does not intervene, and in that case the Syphogrants' wives find out a nurse quickly, which is no hard matter; for any one that can do it, offers herself cheerfully; for as they are much inclined to that piece of mercy, so the child whom they nurse considers the nurse as its mother. All the children under five years old sit among the nurses, the rest of the younger sort of both sexes, till they are fit for marriage, either serve those that sit at table, or if they are not strong enough for that, stand by them in great silence, and eat what is given them; nor have they any other formality of dining. In the middle of the first table, which stands across the upper end of the hall, sit the Syphogrant and his wife; for that is the chief and most conspicuous place; next to him sit two of the most ancient, for there go always four to a mess. If there is a temple within that Syphogranty, the priest and his wife sit with the Syphogrant above all the rest: next them there is a mixture of old and young, who are so placed, that as the young are set near others, so they are mixed with the more ancient; which they say was appointed on this account, that the gravity of the old people, and the reverence that is due to them, might restrain the younger from all indecent words and gestures. Dishes are not served up to the whole table at first, but the best are first set before the old, whose seats are distinguished from the young, and after them all the rest are served alike. The old men distribute to the younger any curious meats that happen to be set before them, if there is not such an abundance of them that the whole company may be served alike.

Thus old men are honored with a particular respect; yet all the rest fare as well as they. Both dinner and supper are begun with some lecture of morality that is read to them; but it is so short, that it is not tedious nor uneasy to them to hear it: from hence the old men take occasion to entertain those about them with some useful and pleasant enlargements; but they do not engross the whole discourse so to themselves during their meals that the younger may not put in for a share: on the contrary, they engage them to talk, that so they may in that free way of conversation find out the force of every one's spirit, and observe his temper. They dispatch their dinners quickly, but sit long at supper; because they go to work after the one, and are to sleep after the other, during which they think the stomach carries on the concoction more vigorously. They never sup without music; and there is always fruit served up after meat; while they are at table, some burn perfumes, and sprinkle about fragrant ointments and sweet waters: in short, they want nothing that may cheer up their spirits: they give themselves a large allowance that way, and indulge themselves in all such pleasures as are attended with no inconvenience. Thus do those that are in the towns live together; but in the country, where they live at great distance, every one eats at home, and no family wants any necessary sort of provision, for it is from them that provisions are sent unto those that live in the towns.

The step from a philosophical to a satirical attitude is a short one, with men who observe as well as think. That is why Jonathan Swift's bitter lashing of his fellows in *Gulliver's Travels* is, in spite of the difference in feeling between

it and *Utopia*, simply the second side of a mirror which is as clear gastronomically as otherwise. . . .

Here, then, are a few pages from *Travels Into Several Remote Nations of the
World, in Four Parts, by Lemuel Gulliver, First a Surgeon and Then a Captain
of Several Ships*. First, in these excerpts, Gulliver is in Lilliput, where the people are tiny; then he is in Brobdingnag, where he seems Lilliputian himself in
contrast to the great inhabitants; finally he is among the Houyhnhnms, noble
horses (and faring none too well, either, on their oats):

From A Voyage to *Lilliput* by Jonathan Swift, 1667–1745

Being almost famished with hunger, having not eaten a morsel for some
hours before I left the ship, I found the demands of nature so strong upon
me, that I could not forbear shewing my impatience (perhaps against the
strict rules of decency) by putting my finger frequently to my mouth, to
signify that I wanted food. The Hurgo (for so they call a great lord, as I
afterwards learnt) understood me very well. He descended from the stage,
and commanded that several ladders should be applied to my sides, on
which above an hundred of the inhabitants mounted, and walked towards
my mouth, laden with baskets full of meat, which had been provided and
sent thither by the king's orders, upon the first intelligence he received of
me. I observed there was the flesh of several animals, but could not distinguish them by the taste. There were shoulders, legs, and loins, shaped
like those of mutton, and very well dressed, but smaller than the wings of
a lark. I eat them by two or three at a mouthful, and took three loaves at a
time, about the bigness of musket bullets. They supplied me as they could,
shewing a thousand marks of wonder and astonishment at my bulk and
appetite. I then made another sign that I wanted drink. They found by
my eating, that a small quantity would not suffice me, and being a most
ingenious people, they flung up with great dexterity one of their largest
hogsheads, then rolled it towards my hand, and beat out the top; I drank
it off at a draught, which I might well do, for it did not hold half a pint,
and tasted like a small wine of Burgundy, but much more delicious. They
brought me a second hogshead, which I drank in the same manner, and
made signs for more; but they had none to give me. When I had performed
these wonders, they shouted for joy, and danced upon my breast, repeating
several times as they did at first, *Hekinah degul*. . . .

I had three hundred cooks to dress my victuals, in little convenient huts built about my house, where they and their families lived, and prepared me two dishes apiece. I took up twenty waiters in my hand, and placed them on the table, an hundred more attended below on the ground, some with dishes of meat, and some with barrels of wine and other liquors, slung on their shoulders, all of which the waiters above drew up as I wanted, in a very ingenious manner, by certain cords, as we draw the bucket up a well in Europe. A dish of their meat was a good mouthful, and a barrel of their liquor a reasonable draught. Their mutton yields to ours, but their beef is excellent. I have had a surloin so large, that I have been forced to make three bites of it; but this is rare. My servants were astonished to see me eat it bones and all, as in our country we do the leg of a lark. Their geese and turkeys I usually eat at a mouthful; and, I must confess, they far exceed ours. Of their smaller fowl, I could take up twenty or thirty at the end of my knife.

One day His Imperial Majesty, being informed of my way of living, desired that himself and his royal consort, with the young princes of the blood of both sexes, might have the happiness (as he was pleased to call it) of dining with me. They came accordingly, and I placed them upon chairs of state on my table, just over against me, with their guards about them. Flimnap, the lord high treasurer, attended there likewise, with his white staff; and I observed he often looked on me with a sour countenance, which I would not seem to regard, but eat more than usual, in honour to my dear country, as well as to fill the court with admiration.

From A Voyage to Brobdingnag by Jonathan Swift, 1667–1745

It was about twelve at noon, and a servant brought in dinner. It was only one substantial dish of meat (fit for the plain condition of an husband-man), in a dish of about four and twenty feet diameter. The company were the farmer and his wife, three children, and an old grandmother. When they were set down, the farmer placed me at some distance from him on the table, which was thirty feet high from the floor. I was in a terrible fright, and kept as far as I could from the edge, for fear of falling. The wife minced a bit of meat, then crumbled some bread on a trencher, and placed it before me. I made her a low bow, took out my knife and fork, and fell to eat, which gave them exceeding delight. The

mistress sent her maid for a small dram cup, which held about two gallons, and filled it with drink; I took up the vessel with much difficulty
in both hands, and, in a most respectful manner, drank to her ladyship's
health, expressing the words as loud as I could in English, which made
the company laugh so heartily that I was almost deafened with the noise.
This liquor tasted like a small cyder, and was not unpleasant. Then the
master made me a sign to come to his trencher-side; but as I walked on
the table, being in great surprise all the time, as the indulgent reader
will easily conceive and excuse, I happened to stumble against a crust,
and fell flat on my face, but received no hurt. I got up immediately, and
observing the good people to be in much concern, I took my hat (which
I held under my arm out of good manners) and, waving it over my head,
made three huzzas, to show I had got no mischief by my fall. . . .

The queen became so fond of my company that she could not dine
without me. I had a table placed upon the same at which Her Majesty ate,
just at her left elbow, and a chair to sit on. Glumdalclitch stood on a stool
on the floor, near my table, to assist and take care of me. I had an entire
set of silver dishes and plates, and other necessaries which, in proportion
to those of the queen's, were not much bigger than what I have seen of the
same kind in a London toy-shop for the furniture of a baby-house. These
my little nurse kept in her pocket in a silver box, and gave me at meals as
I wanted them, always cleaning them herself. No person dined with the
queen but the two princesses royal, the elder sixteen years old, and the
younger at that time thirteen and a month. Her Majesty used to put a bit
of meat upon one of my dishes out of which I carved for myself; and her
diversion was to see me eat in miniature. For the queen (who had, indeed,
but a weak stomach) took up at one mouthful as much as a dozen English
farmers could eat at a meal, which, to me, was for some time a very nauseous sight. She would crunch the wing of a lark, bones and all, between
her teeth, although it were nine times as large as that of a full-grown turkey;
and put a bit of bread into her mouth as big as two twelve-penny loaves.
She drank out of a golden cup, above a hogshead at a draught. Her knives
were twice as long as a scythe, set straight upon the handle. The spoons,
forks, and other instruments were all in the same proportion. I remember,
when Glumdalclitch carried me out of curiosity to see some of the tables at

court, where ten or a dozen of these enormous knives and forks were lifted up together, I thought I had never, till then, beheld so terrible a sight.

It is the custom that every Wednesday (which, as I have before observed, was their Sabbath) the king and queen, with the royal issue of both sexes, dine together in the apartment of His Majesty, to whom I was now become a great favourite; and at these times my little chair and table were placed at his left hand, before one of the salt-cellars. This prince took a pleasure in conversing with me, enquiring into the manners, religion, laws, government, and learning of Europe; wherein I gave him the best account I was able. His apprehension was so clear, and his judgment so exact, that he made very wise reflections and observations upon all I said. But I confess, that after I had been a little too copious in talking of my own beloved country, of our trade, and wars by sea and land, of our schisms in religion, and parties in the State; the prejudices of his education prevailed so far, that he could not forbear taking me up in his right hand, and, stroking me gently with the other, after an hearty fit of laughing, asked me whether I was a Whig or Tory. Then turning to his first minister, who waited behind him with a white staff, near as tall as the mainmast of the *Royal Sovereign,* he observed how contemptible a thing was human grandeur, which could be mimicked by such diminutive insects as I: "And yet," says he, "I dare engage, these creatures have their titles and distinctions of honour, they contrive little nests and burrows that they call houses and cities; they make a figure in dress and equipage; they love, they fight, they dispute, they cheat, they betray." And thus he continued on, while my colour came and went several times, with indignation, to hear our noble country, the mistress of arts and arms, the scourge of France, the arbitress of Europe, the seat of virtue, piety, honour, and truth, the pride and envy of the world, so contemptuously treated.

From A Voyage to the Land of the Houyhnhnms by Jonathan Swift, 1667–1745

The sorrel nag offered me a root, which he held (after their manner, as we shall describe in its proper place) between his hoof and pastern; I took it in my hand, and, having smelt it, returned it to him again as civilly as I could. He brought out of the Yahoo's kennel a piece of ass's flesh, but it smelt so offensively that I turned from it with loathing; he then threw it to the Yahoo, by whom it was greedily devoured. He afterwards shewed me a wisp of hay, a fetlock full of oats; but I shook my head, to signify that neither of these were food for me. And, indeed, I now apprehended that I must absolutely starve, if I did not get to some of my own species: for as to those filthy Yahoos, although there were few greater lovers of mankind, at that time, than myself, yet, I confess I never saw any sensitive being so detestable on all accounts, and the more I came near them, the more hateful they grew, while I stayed in that country. This the master horse observed by my behaviour, and therefore sent the Yahoo back to his kennel. He then put his fore-hoof to his mouth, at which I was much surprised, although he did it with ease, and with a motion that appeared perfectly natural; and made other signs to know what I would eat; but I could not return him such an answer as he was able to apprehend; and, if he had understood me, I did not see how it was possible to contrive any way for finding myself nourishment. While we were thus engaged, I observed a cow passing by, whereupon I pointed to her, and expressed a desire to let me go and milk her. This had its effect; for he led me back into the house, and ordered a mare servant to open a room, where a good store of milk lay in earthen and wooden vessels, after a very orderly and cleanly manner. She gave me a large bowl full, of which I drank very heartily, and found myself well refreshed.

About noon, I saw coming towards the house a kind of vehicle, drawn, like a sledge, by four Yahoos. There was in it an old steed, who seemed to be of quality; he alighted with his hind feet forward, having, by accident, got a hurt in his fore-foot. He came to dine with our horse, who received him with great civility. They dined in the best room and had oats boiled in milk for the second course, which the old horse eat warm, but the rest cold. Their mangers were placed circular in the middle of the room, and divided into several partitions, round which they sat on their haunches upon bosses of straw. In the middle was a large rack, with angles answering to every partition of the manger; so that each horse and mare ate their own hay, and their own mash of oats and milk, with much decency and regularity. The behaviour of the young colt and foal appeared very modest; and that of the master and mistress extremely cheerful and complaisant to their guest. The grey ordered me to stand by him; and much discourse passed between him and his friend concerning me, as I found by the stranger's often looking on me, and the frequent repetition of the word Yahoo.

I happened to wear my gloves, which the master grey observing, seemed perplexed, discovering signs of wonder what I had done to my fore-feet; he put his hoof three or four times to them, as if he would signify, that I should reduce them to their former shape, which I presently did, pulling off both my gloves, and putting them into my pocket. This occasioned far-ther talk, and I saw the company was pleased with my behaviour, whereof I soon found the good effects. I was ordered to speak the few words I under-stood; and while they were at dinner, the master taught me the names for oats, milk, fire, water, and some others; which I could readily pronounce after him, having from my youth a great facility in learning languages.

When dinner was done, the master horse took me aside, and by signs and words, made me understand the concern that he was in, that I had nothing to eat. Oats, in their tongue, are called *hluunh.* This word I pro-nounced two or three times; for although I had refused them at first, yet, upon second thoughts, I considered that I could contrive to make of them a kind of bread, which might be sufficient, with milk, to keep me alive, till I could make my escape to some other country, and to creatures of my own species. The horse immediately ordered a white mare servant, of his family, to bring me a good quantity of oats on a sort of wooden tray. These I heated before the fire, as well as I could, and rubbed them till the husks came off, which I made a shift to winnow from the grain; I ground and beat them between two stones, then took water, and made them into a paste or cake, which I toasted at the fire, and ate warm with milk. It was at first a very insipid diet, though common enough in many parts of Europe, but grew tolerable by time; and, having been often reduced to hard fare in my life, this was not the first experiment I had made, how easily nature is satisfied. And I cannot but observe, that I never had one hour's sickness while I stayed in this island. It is true, I sometimes made a shift to catch a rabbit, or bird, by springs made of Yahoo's hairs; and I often gathered wholesome herbs, which I boiled, or eat as salads with my bread; and now and then for a rarity I made a little butter and drank the whey. I was first at a great loss for salt; but custom soon reconciled the want of it; and I am confident that the frequent use of salt among us is an effect of luxury, and was first introduced only as a provocative to drink; except where it is necessary for preserving of flesh in long voyages, or in places remote from great markets. For we observe no animal to be fond of it but man: and as to myself, when

I left this country, it was a great while before I could endure the taste of it in anything that I ate.

It takes a long time to grow up to *Gargantua and Pantagruel*.

Almost every person who is beginning to feel educated goes through a period or, unfortunately, remains in it, when he reads skippingly some parts of these five great books, and refers to any remark that is even faintly gastronomical, pornographic, or scatological as "Rabelaisian," with the appropriate winks, nudges, and leers. This period is either boring or actively nauseating in retrospect, of course, and happy is the man who can count it well behind him.

Even happier is he who finally reaches the stage where Rabelais is a depthless source of social philosophy, human observation, merriment.

The great doctor said to his readers, ". . . take in perfect part all I write or do; revere the cheese-shaped brain which feeds you this noble flummery; strive diligently to keep me ever jocund . . . be gay, and gayly read the rest, with ease of body and in the best of kidney! . . . remember to drink to me gallantly, and I will counter with a toast at once."

Ronsard wrote of him something that referred to more than his great physical thirst, probably:

> If, from a rotted corpse at rest,
> Nature can breed and manifest
> New life; if generations can
> Rise from corrupted things or man,
> Surely, some vine will grow from out
> The paunch and belly of our stout
> Friend Rabelais, who never tried
> To curb his drinking ere he died.

In the pages I have chosen to put here, the first tell of how Ponocrates instructed the unruly young Gargantua to spend his time and his energies so that nothing was wasted.

Then come a description of a feast of welcome Pantagruel gave for his son, and the ridiculous story, which Swift might have written later, of the sadly sanctimonious adventure of six pilgrims who got swallowed by Gargantua in a salad.

Finally there is the account, scornful and mocking, of the behavior of the Gastrolaters, the swinish gluttons, the belly-worshipers who live always, everywhere. "Some," Rabelais says, "were gay, wanton, downy milksops. Others were solemn, stern, grim, dour; utterly idle, working at nothing, they formed a useless weight and burden on earth. In so far as we could judge, what they most feared was to offend or reduce their bellies."

In their futile viciousness they were then, as they are now, extravagantly, enormously superhuman, just as the thirsts and appetites of all Rabelais's creatures were impossibly larger than life. That was his weapon, and that is why it takes a few years of ripening perspective for us to know what he was really saying. . . .

From *Gargantua and Pantagruel* by François Rabelais, 1483–1553

Meanwhile My Lord Appetite put in an appearance and they sat down most opportunely to table.

At the beginning of the meal, they listened to the reading of some agreeable chronicle of chivalry in ancient times, until Gargantua gave the signal for wine to be served. Then, if they wished, the reading went on or they could talk merrily together. Often they discussed the virtues, property, efficacy, and nature of what was served at table: bread, wine, water, salt, meat, fish, fruit, herbs, roots, and their preparation. Thus Gargantua soon knew all the relevant passages in Pliny's *Natural History* . . . in the grammarian Anthenæus' *Deipnosophistes* or *The Banquet of the Sages,* which treats of flowers, fruits, and their various uses . . . in Dioscorides' famous medical treatise, the bible of apothecaries . . . in the *Vocabularium* by Julius Pollux, a grammarian and sophist of Marcus Aurelius' day, who wrote of hunting and fishing . . . in Galen's numerous dissertations upon alimentation . . . in the works of Porphyrius, the third-century Greek author of a *Treatise upon Abstinence from Meat*. . . in Oppian's two poems, *Cynegetica* which deals with venery and *Halieutica* with angling . . . in *Of Healthy Diet* by Polybius of Cos, disciple and son-in-law of Hippocrates . . . in Heliodorus of Emesa, Syrian Bishop of Tricca and a celebrated novelist of the fourth century . . . in Aristotle's essays on natural history . . . in the Greek works upon animals by Claudius Ælianus, a Roman contemporary of Heliogabalus . . . and in various other tomes. . . . Often for surer authority as they argued, they would have the book in question brought to the table. Gargantua so thoroughly and cogently learned and assimilated all he heard that no physician of his times knew one-half so much as he.

They discussed the lessons they had learned that morning and topped their meal off with quiddany, a sort of quince marmalade and an excellent digestive. After which Gargantua picked his teeth with a fragment of mastic, washed his hands and daubed his eyes with cool clear water, and, instead of saying grace, sang the glory of God in noble hymns, composed in praise of divine bounty and munificence.

Presently cards were brought them and they played, not for the sake of the pastime itself but to learn a thousand new tricks and inventions all based on arithmetic.

Thus Gargantua developed a keen enthusiasm for mathematics, spending his leisure after dinner and supper every evening as pleasantly as once he had, dicing and gaming. As a result, he knew so much about its theory and practice that Cuthbert Tunstal, Bishop of Durham and secretary to King Henry VIII, a voluminous writer on the subject, confessed that, beside Gargantua, he knew no more about arithmetic than he did about Old High Gothic. Nor was it arithmetic alone our hero learned, but also such sister sciences as geometry, astronomy, and music.

Now the digestion of foods is a most important matter. There is the first stage, which occurs in the stomach, where the viands are changed into chyle; the second, in the liver, where the chyle is transformed into blood; the third, in the habit of the body, where the blood is finally converted into the substance of each part. So, whilst Gargantua awaited the first stage of digestion, they made a thousand delightful instruments, drew geometrical figures, and even applied the principles of astronomy.

After, they amused themselves singing a five-part score or improvising on a theme chosen at random. As for musical instruments, Gargantua learned to play the lute, the spinet, the harp, the nine-holed transverse or German flute, the viol, and the sackbut or trombone.

Having spent an hour thus and completed his digestion, he discharged his natural excrements and then settled down again to work three hours or more at his principal study. Either he revised the morning reading, or proceeded in the text at hand or practised penmanship in the most carefully formed characters of modern Roman and ancient Gothic script.

Thereupon supper was prepared, and in honor of the special occasion they added to the regular menu sixteen oxen, three heifers, thirty-two calves, sixty-three young kids, ninety-five wethers, three hundred milch-sows soaked in sweet wine, eleven-score partridges, seven hundred wood-cocks, four hundred capons from Loudun and Cornouailles in Brittany, six thousand pullets and as many pigeons again, six hundred crammed hens, fourteen hundred young hares, three hundred and three bustards, and one thousand and seven fat capons. As for venison, all they could obtain was eleven wild boars sent by the Abbot of Turpenay, eighteen fallow deer presented by My Lord of Grandmont, and sevenscore pheasants from My Lord of Les Essards. In addition, there were dozens of ringdoves and riverfowl, ducks, drakes, bitterns, curlews, plovers, francolins, sheldrakes, Poitou woodcocks, lapwings, shovellers, herons, moorhens, storks, orange flamingos, cranes, geese, ptarmigans, turkey hens, prepared with quantities of soups, broths, sauces and stew.

Beyond all doubt, here were victuals aplenty, cooked to a turn by Grangousier's cooks Wolfsauce, Hotchpot, and Lickjuice. The stewards, Jock-bottle, Guzzletun, and Clearglass, kept their beakers brimful with wine.

We must now relate what happened to six pilgrims who were returning from St. Sebastien-d'Aigne, near Nantes. Afraid of the enemy, they sought shelter that night in the garden, crouched among the cabbage, lettuce, and peas.

Gargantua, being somewhat thirsty, asked for some lettuce salad. When they told him the lettuce in that garden was the greatest and finest in the land (some heads were tall as plum trees or walnut trees) he determined to pick it himself. Plucking what he thought good, he also carried off in the hollow of his hand the six pilgrims, who were too terrified to cough, let alone to speak.

While Gargantua was washing the heads of lettuce in the fountain, the pilgrims plucked up their courage and held a whispered consultation.

"What can we do?"

"We're drowning in all this lettuce!"

"Dare we speak?"

"If we speak, he'll kill us for spies."

Amid their deliberations, Gargantua put them with the lettuce in a bowl of Grangousier's large as the tun at the Abbey of Cîteaux, in Burgundy, a fine huge cask reputed to hold three hundred hogsheads. Then he doused the leaves (and pilgrims) with salt, vinegar, and oil, and, for refreshment before supper, began to eat. He had already swallowed five pilgrims and the sixth lay under a leaf, completely invisible save for his staff, when Grangousier pointed to the latter.

"Look, Gargantua, that's a snail's horn. Don't eat it!"

"Why not? Snails are good this month."

Picking up staff and pilgrim, he swallowed them neat, then drank a terrific draught of red Burgundy while awaiting his supper.

The pilgrims thus devoured crept out of his gullet as best they could, avoiding the millstones of his teeth. They believed they had been cast into the pit of the lowest dungeon in a prison. When Gargantua downed his wine, they all but drowned; the crimson torrent almost swept them down again into the abyss of his belly. However, leaping on their staffs as the Mont St. Michel pilgrims do, they found shelter in the chinks between his teeth. Unhappily one of them, sounding the lay of the land with his staff to ascertain its safety, struck hard into the cavity of a sore tooth and hit the mandibulary nerve. Gargantua screamed with pain, then, for relief, reached for his toothpick. Strolling out towards the great walnut tree in the garden, he proceeded to dislodge our six gentlemen pilgrims. He jerked one out by the legs, another by the shoulders, a third by his scrip, a fourth by his pouch, a fifth by his neckerchief and the last, the poor devil who had hurt him, he pulled out by the codpiece. . . .

The pilgrims, thus dislodged, scurried away at top speed. Gargantua's toothache subsided, just as Eudemon announced dinner.

"Very well," said Gargantua. "I shall piss away my misfortune."

Which he proceeded to do so copiously that the pilgrims' road was washed away and they were forced to wade through this vast, foamy salt lake. Skirting a small wood, all but Fournillier were swept off their feet into a trap set for wolves. But they finally escaped, thanks to the industry of

Fournillier, who broke all the snares and ropes. Free once again, they spent the rest of the night in a hut near Le Coudray, where they drew comfort in their misfortune from the words of one of their number, Lasdaller or Dogweary, who reminded them that this adventure had been foretold by the prophet David in his *Psalms*.

We were observing the faces and gestures of those craven, great-gullied Gastrolaters when, to our amazement, we heard a carillon. At once, they drew up in rank and file, each according to his office, degree and seniority. In this formation, they advanced towards Master Gaster. Their leader was a fat, potbellied youth; he bore a long, richly gilt staff, with, at its end, an ill-carved, roughly bedaubed statue. Plautus, Juvenal, and Pompeius Festus have described it; at Lyons, in Carnival time, it is called Gnawcrust. The Gastrolaters called it Manducus.

A monstrous, hideous, ridiculous figure it was, too, calculated to terrify children, equipped with eyes larger than its belly, topped by a head larger than the rest of its body. Its jaws, wide, broad, and alarming, were lined with teeth which, by means of a small wire within the hollow gold staff, were made to rattle together as dreadfully as those of St. Clement's dragon in the processions at Metz on Rogation Days.

Drawing close to the Gastrolaters, I noticed that they were followed by cohorts of fat varlets, bearing baskets, hampers, dishes, bags, pots, and kettles. Manducus in the lead, they advanced, singing God knows what *dithyrambics* (wild songs) *cræpalcomes* (chants of drunken revelry) and *epænons* (canticles of praise). Opening their baskets and pots, they offered up to their god all manner of gifts, as listed below.

White hippocras or spiced wine, with toasts and sippets... plain white bread and bread of the snowiest dough ... *carbonados* or grilled meats of six different varieties ... *Couscous*, an Arabian stew ... haslets, pluck and fry ... fricassées of nine sorts ... bread and dripping, bread and cheese ... gravy soup, hotchpotch, and potroast ... shortbread and household loaf... *cabirotado* or grilled viands ... cold loins of veal, spiced with ginger, meat pies and broths flavored with bay leaves ... marrow-bones of beef with cabbage ... salmagundi, which is a mixed dish of chopped meat and pickled herring, with oil, vinegar, pepper, and onions.

(Drink after drink, eternally, it seemed, provided the transition from course to course. First came a brisk, tartish white wine; next claret; then a dry red wine, iced to polar temperature and served in great silver cups.)

Next came sausages, caparisoned with choice mustard, chitterlings, smoked oxtongue, salted meats of various sorts, pork's back with peas, pig's haslets, blood sausages, brain sausages, Bolognas, hams, boars' heads, dried venison with turnips, chicken livers on the spit, olives-in-oil.

(These dishes were accompanied by sempiternal bibbage.)

Next, they poured into his maw the following fare: shoulder of mutton with garlic, meat pies with hot sauce, pork chops with onion sauce, roast capons basted in their own dripping, spring capons . . . goose, kid, fawn and deer, hare and leveret, partridge and choice young partridges, pheasant and delicate young pheasants, peacock and toothsome young peacocks . . . stork and storklet, woodcock, snipe, ortolan, turkey; gobbler, hen and pullet. . . ringdove, wood pigeon, pork with wine sauce, duck with onion sauce, blackbird, rail, heron and excellent young herons, bustard and wild turkey, figpecker or *beccafico*, and Italian warbler fed on sweet fruits . . . young guinea hen, plover, goose and gosling, rockdove, wild duck, mavis, and flamingo. . . .

(To these dishes were added vast quantities of vinegar.)

Then, they fed Gaster pies and pasties of venison, lark, dormouse, roebuck, pigeon, chamois, capon, and bacon . . . hogs feet in lard, fried piecrust, stuffed capons, cheese, and juicy peaches. . . artichoke, sea grouse, crier, crane, egret, teal, diver and loon, bittern and stake driver, curlew, wood duck, water hen with leeks, hedgehog, kid, shoulder of mutton with caper sauce. . . beef royal, breast of veal, boiled chicken and stuffed capon with blancmange, pullet and pullen, rabbit and cony, waterfowl, cormorant, francolin, ringdove, cottontail, porcupine, rail. . . .

Next, they filled him with pastries, including cream tarts, fruit squares, sweet biscuits, sugar plums, fritters, tarts of sixteen varieties, waffles, pancakes, quince rolls, curds and cream, whipped cream, preserved myrobalans or prunes, and jellies.

(With, of course, red and pale hippocras to wash them down.)

And, finally, seventy-eight species of dry and liquid preserves and jams, sweetmeats of one hundred different colors, cream cakes, and light confections.

(Vinegar followed, for fear of quinsy, and toasts, to scour the teeth.)

Where the bee sucks, there suck I;

In a cowslip's bell I lie;

There I couch when owls do cry.

On the bat's back I do fly

After summer merrily.

Merrily, merrily shall I live now

Under the blossom that hangs on the bough.*

It is not a prank I play, to place after the final garglings of the Gastrolaters this fairy-song of nourishment. Nor is it a piece of personal whimsy to copy a few paragraphs from that subtle, haunting story, *The Memoirs of a Midget*, by Walter de la Mare.

Such changes, even if shocking and violent, are as restful to the soul's palate as a leaf of crisp cool lettuce after a rich sauce, as a draught of beer after a plate of *chilis rellenos*.

The Memoirs, "sealed up with Miss M.'s usual scrupulous neatness in numerous small, square brown-paper packages, and laid carefully away in her old nursery," were left to her friend Sir Walter, and he in turn had the minute handwriting deciphered and typed and then saw to it that they should not appear until after his own death.

"It is possible," Miss M. said in her letter to him left with the manuscript, "that after reading my small, endless story you may be very thankful that you are not a Midget too." But that is never the case with those who like this provocative, tantalizing piece of fantasy.

Here is the story of Miss M.'s first dinner with her new friend Mrs. Bowater:

From *The Memoirs of a Midget* by Walter de la Mare, 1873–1956

To my ear, Mrs. Bowater's was what I should describe as a low, roaring voice, like falling water out of a black cloven rock in a hill-side; but what a balm was its sound in my ear, and how solacing this dignified address to jaded nerves still smarting a little after my victory on the London, Chatham, and Dover Railway. Making my way around a grandfather's clock that ticked hollowly beside the door, I followed her into a room on the left

---

* From *The Tempest*, by William Shakespeare.

of the passage, from either wall of which a pair of enormous antlers threat-ened each other under the discoloured ceiling. For a moment the glare within and the vista of furniture legs confused my eyes. But Mrs. Bowater came to my rescue.

"Food was never mentioned," she remarked reflectively, "being as I see nothing to be considered except as food so-called. But you will find everything clean and comfortable; and I am sure, miss, what with your sad bereavements and all, as I have heard from Mr. Pellew, I hope it will be a home to you. There being nothing else as I suppose that we may expect."

My mind ran about in a hasty attempt to explore these sentiments. They soothed away many misgivings, though it was clear that Mrs. Bowa-ter's lodger was even less in dimensions than Mrs. Bowater had supposed. *Clean:* after so many months of Mrs. Sheppey's habits, it was this word that sang in my head. Wood, glass, metal flattered the light of gas and coal, and for the first time I heard my own voice float up into my new "apartment": "It looks *very* comfortable, thank you, Mrs. Bowater; and I am quite sure I shall be happy in my new abode." There was nothing intentionally affected in this formal little speech.

"Which being so," replied Mrs. Bowater, "there seems to be trouble with the cabman, and the day's drawing in, perhaps you will take a seat by the fire."

A stool nicely to my height stood by the steel fender, the flames played in the chimney; and for a moment I was left alone. "Thank God," said I, and took off my hat, and pushed back my hair. . . . Alone. Only for a moment, though. Its mistress gone, as fine a black cat as ever I have seen appeared in the doorway and stood, green-eyed, regarding me. To judge from its countenance, this must have been a remarkable experience.

I cried seductively, "Puss."

But with a blink of one eye and a shake of its forepaw, as if inadver-tently it had trodden in water, it turned itself about again and disappeared. In spite of all my cajoleries, Henry and I were never to be friends.

Whatever Pollie's trouble with the cabman may have been, Mrs. Bowa-ter made short work of it. Pollie was shown to the room in which she was to sleep that night. I took off my bodice and bathed face, hands, and arms to the elbow in the shallow bowl Mrs. Bowater had provided for me. And soon, wonderfully refreshed and talkative, Pollie and I were seated over the last meal we were to share together for many a long day.

There were snippets of bread and butter for me, a little omelette, two sizes too large, a sugared cherry or two sprinkled with "hundreds and thousands," and a gay little bumper of milk gilded with the enwreathed letters, "A Present from Dover." Alack-a-day for that omelette! I must have kept a whole family of bantams steadily engaged for weeks together. But I was often at my wits' end to dispose of their produce. Fortunately Mrs. Bowater kept merry fires burning in the evening—"Ladies of some sizes can't warm the air as much as most," as she put it. So at some little risk to myself among the steel fire-irons, the boiled became the roast. At last I made a clean breast of my horror of eggs, and since by that time my landlady and I were the best of friends, no harm came of it. She merely bestowed on me a grim smile of unadulterated amusement, and the bantams patronised some less fastidious stomach.

The things Paul Bunyan the Mightiest Logger did and said, even when they are told in the most pedestrian or pedagogic prose, or in the most obnoxious "Wal naow" ballad-style, are too important a part of the literature of fantasy to ignore.

They are completely American: tall tales, perhaps the tallest in the world, of a giant of power and benevolence and humor. It is surprising that they have not been better sung, but nevertheless they are absorbing, and a lot of fun to read and to think about in the dark.

They always manage to recall a few other private but equally Bunyan-esque (or Gargantuan) happenings . . . such as, for me, visits to the Raleigh Inn. It is gone now, burned to the ground with a fire started in its clean but well-buttered kitchen.

It was a long-galleried wooden building, two stories tall, about as old as California itself since it became one of "us," and there were forty-eight bedrooms, each named for a state in the union, and one cold-water bathroom. Downstairs were a big brown entrance hall with a fireplace and a ceaseless game of chess, and some postcards; rooms (I suppose) for the owners and the servants, and the offices for feeding all the miners and hunters and sybarites who came there.

The dining room was high and bleak, with strips of flypaper in the air and a few ancient spotted pictures of Cunard liners on the walls. Most of the tables seated eight or more people, and they were always covered with good clean linen, under the thick plates and tumblers. It was, that is to say, much like a pension in a small French town, even to the local "girls" who waited on table, and called the proprietors "Mama" and "Papa."

I doubt if much was ever bought from stores . . . the waitresses and their families managed to supply everything, even to the rather watery and salty butter and the tough bread, which in contrast to the standardized California commercial "bread" and butter tasted like gods' food. As for the vegetables and fruits, they were the same: tough but fresh carrots and peas and beets; twisted little apples like the ones from Normandy, with an unforgettable nip to them; lettuces nibbled by caterpillars and snails but infinitely tasteful after the hard pure heads sold in super-markets.

The specialty of the Raleigh Inn was "The Chicken Dinner," which seemed to be ready any day at noontime (only city slickers ate dinner there at night) for twenty-five cents extra . . . and when you said weakly, under the eager insistent gaze of your "girl," that you would take it, you did not mean you would take fried chicken, or broiled or roasted or fricasseed chicken, nor yet chicken pie, nor yet boiled chicken with dumplings. You meant all those kinds of chicken served at once in their respective gold or crisp or pale or soft disguises, each in its basin or platter, spread before you on the generous white table with accompanying bowls of sauces and gravies and spiced relishes and pickles, and surrounded by perhaps three different kinds of potatoes, say French-fried and plain boiled and baked, and then several bowls of vegetables like corn on the cob and carrots in butter with parsley and hot little beets cooked with their tops, and then another bowl, of lettuce with tomatoes sliced thick on a plate with scallions and slivers of green pepper.

There would be three kinds of hot bread, besides the dumplings and the baking-powder biscuits served as companions to the stewed chicken and the fried chicken: corn bread, pocketbook rolls, and salt-rising bread, with a bowl of dark pungent mountain honey to spread over the butter on them.

But the desserts at the Raleigh, for some reason, were nothing much . . . just a big bowl of sun-warm berries with thick cream and a slab of pound cake, or in the winter hot apple pie.

There was lots of coffee, good coffee . . . "Mama" thought drinkin-likka was nonsense, and if you wanted a snort before dinner, to give you an appetite, you had to take it in your dim, sparse bedroom, with its lumpy iron bed and its naked light bulb swinging, fly-hung, from the high ceiling.

The Raleigh Inn was a rare spot, not so much because of its insanely laden tables as its feeling of the old America, the free extravagant lusty America of Paul Bunyan's days. It was a fairy tale, as he is, and yet completely real: that is to say, it was of the stuff of fantasy.

Here, then, is the story of the mighty Black Duck Dinner, as told by James Stevens:

From *Paul Bunyan* by James Stevens, 1892–1950

. . . Paul Bunyan . . . worked his men twelve hours a day, and, had they thought about it, they would have been astounded by any idea of working less. And they would have been perplexed by any other scheme to ease their lot. If there were not to be great exertions, they would have asked, why their sturdy frames, their eager muscular force? If they were not meant to face hazards, why was daring in their hearts? A noble breed, those loggers of Paul Bunyan's, greatly worthy of their captain! He himself told them in a speech he made at the finishing of the Onion River Drive that they were "a good band of bullies, a fine bunch of savages." I should like to quote this speech in its entirety, for it celebrated the accomplishment of a historical logging enterprise, and it was a master oration which showed the full range and force of Paul Bunyan's oratorical powers. But as nine days and eight nights were required for its delivery, it is obvious that no publication save the *Congressional Record* could give all of it. It was at this time that Paul Bunyan served his great black duck dinner. . . .

All night fires roared in the ranges as preparations went on for the great dinner. The elevators brought a load of vegetables every minute from the deep bins, potatoes were pared and washed, kettles and roasting pans were made ready, and sauces and dressings were devised. The black ducks were scalded, plucked, and cleaned by the Preparations Department, and by morning the cranemen were bringing them by the hundreds to the Finishing Department, where the kettles and pans were waiting for them.

Most of the loggers stayed in their bunks this morning, and those who did come to breakfast ate sparingly, saving their appetites. Time passed quietly in the camp. The loggers washed and mended their clothes and greased their boots, but they did not worry themselves with bed-making. The other Sunday morning chores finished, they stretched out on their unmade bunks and smoked. They were silent and preoccupied, but now and again a breeze blowing from the direction of the cookhouse would cause them to sigh. What enchantment was in the air, so redolent with the aroma of roasting duck and stewing cabbages, so sharply sweet with the fragrance of hot ginger and cinnamon from the bakery where Cream Puff Fatty fashioned his creations! A logger who was shaving would take a deep breath of this incense, and the blood would trickle unnoticed from a slash in his cheek; another, in his bunk, would let his pipe slip from his hand and enjoy ardent inhalations, blissfully unaware of his burning shirt; yet another, engaged in greasing his boots, would halt his task and sit in motionless beatitude, his head thrown back, his eyes closed, quite unconscious of the grease that poured from a tilted can into a prized boot.

At half past eleven the hungriest of the loggers began to mass before the cookhouse door, and as the minutes passed the throng swiftly increased. At five minutes to noon all the bunkhouses were empty and the furthest fringe of the crowd was far up Onion River valley. The ground shook under a restless trampling, and the faces of the loggers were glowing and eager as they hearkened to the clatter and rumble inside the cookhouse, as four-horse teams hauled in loads of salt, pepper and sugar for the shakers and bowls. Then the loggers began to stamp and shout as they heard the flunkies, led by the Galloping Kid on his white horse, rushing the platters and bowls of food to the tables. Tantalizing smells wafted forth from the steaming dishes. The loggers grew more restless and eager; they surged to and fro in a tidal movement; jests and glad oaths made a joyous clamor over the throng. This was softened into a universal sigh as the doors swung open and Hot Biscuit Slim, in spotless cap and apron, appeared wearing the impressive mien of a conquering general. He lifted an iron bar with a majestic gesture, paused for dramatic effect amid a breathless hush, and then struck a resounding note from the steel triangle that hung from the wall. At the sound a heaving torrent of men began to pour through the doors in a rush that was like the roaring plunge of water when the gate of a dam is lifted. The chief cook continued to pound out clanging rhythms until the last impatient logger was inside.

Then Hot Biscuit Slim re-entered the cookhouse. He was reminded of a forested plain veiled in thin fog as he surveyed the assemblage of darkly clad figures, wreathed with white and fragrant blooms of steam. His impression was made the more vivid when the loggers plunged their spoons into the deep bowls of oyster soup, for the ensuing sounds seemed like the soughing of wind in the woods. The chief cook marched to the kitchen with dignity and pride, glancing to right and left at the tables that held his masterwork. He asked for no praise or acclaim; the ecstasy that now transfigured the plainest face was a sufficient light of glory for him.

The soup bowls pushed aside, the loggers began to fill their plates, which were of such circumference that even a long-armed man could hardly reach across one. The black ducks, of course, received first attention. And great as the plates were, by the time one was heaped with a brown fried drumstick, a ladle of duck dumplings, several large fragments of duck fricassee, a slab of duck baked gumbo style, a rich portion of stewed duck, and a mound of crisp brown dressing, all immersed in golden duck gravy, a formidable space was covered. Yet there was room for tender leaves of odorous cabbage beaded and streaked with creamy sauce; for mashed potatoes which seemed like fluffs of snow beside the darkness of duck and gravy; for brittle and savory potato cakes, marvelously right as to texture and thickness; for stewed tomatoes of a sultry ruddiness, pungent and ticklish with mysterious spices; for a hot cob of corn as long as a man's forearm, golden with sirupy kernels as big as buns; for fat and juicy baked beans, plump peas, sunny applesauce, and buttered lettuce, not to mention various condiments. Squares of cornbread and hot biscuits were buttered and leaned against the plate; a pot-bellied coffee-pot was tilted over a gaping cup, into which it gushed an aromatic beverage of drowsy charm; a kingly pleasure was prepared. More than one logger swooned with delight this day when his plate was filled and, red-faced, hot-eyed, wet-lipped, he bent over it for the first mouthful with the joy of a lover claiming a first embrace.

In the kitchen the chief cook, the baker, and their helpers watched and listened. At first the volume of sounds that filled the vast room was like the roar and crash of an avalanche, as dishes were rattled and banged about. Then the duck bones crackled like the limbs of falling trees. At last came a steady sound of eating, a sound of seventy threshing machines devouring bundles of wheat. It persisted far beyond the usual length of time, and Hot Biscuit Slim brought out his field glasses and surveyed the tables. The

loggers were still bent tensely over their plates, and their elbows rose and
fell with an energetic movement as they scooped up the food with undi-
minished vigor.

"Still eatin' duck," marveled Hot Biscuit Slim.

"They won't be more'n able to *smell* my cream puffs," said the baker
enviously.

The loggers ate on. They had now spent twice their usual length of
time at the table. Each plate was in a dark shadow from tall rows of slick
black duck bones and heaps of corn cobs. But—

"Still eatin' duck," reported Hot Biscuit Slim.

That no one might see his grief, Cream Puff Fatty moved to a dark
corner. He was now certain that none of the loggers could have room for
his pastries. They ate on. They had now spent three times their usual length
of time at the table. The baker was sweating and weeping; he was soaked
with despair. Then, suddenly:

"They're eatin' cream puffs!" cried Hot Biscuit Slim.

Cream Puff Fatty could not believe it, but a thrill of hope urged him to
see for himself. True enough, the loggers were tackling the pastries at last.
On each plate cream puffs the size of squashes lay in golden mounds. As
the spoons struck them their creamy contents oozed forth from breaks and
crevices. Stimulated by their rich flavor, the loggers ate on with renewed
gusto. They had now stayed four times as long as usual at the table. Other
enchantments still kept them in their seats: lemon pies with airy frostings,
yellow pumpkin pies strewn with brown spice specks, cherry pies with
cracks in their flaky crusts through which the red fruit winked, custard
pies with russet freckles on their golden faces, fat apple pies odorous with
cinnamon, cool, snowy cream pies, peach cobblers, chocolate puddings,
glittering cakes of many colors, slabs of gingerbread, sugar-powdered jelly
rolls, doughnuts as large around as saucers and as thick through as cups,
and so soft and toothsome that a morsel from one melted on the tongue
like cream. So endearing were the flavors of these pastries that the loggers
consumed them all.

Cream Puff Fatty and Hot Biscuit Slim solemnly shook hands. There
was glory enough for both of them.

At last there were no sounds at the tables save those of heavy breathing.
The loggers arose in a body and moved sluggishly and wordlessly from the

cookhouse. They labored over the ground towards the bunkhouses as wearily as though they had just finished a day of deadening toil. Soon Onion River valley resounded with their snores and groans....

At supper time, when Hot Biscuit Slim rang the gong, Cream Puff Fatty stood by his side. This was to be the supreme test of their achievement. For five minutes the chief cook beat the triangle, and then a solitary logger appeared in the door of a bunkhouse. He stared at them dully for a moment and then staggered back into the darkness. This was indeed a triumph! Great as other feasts in the cookhouse had been, never before had all the loggers been unable to appear for supper. This was a historic day. Cream Puff Fatty and Hot Biscuit Slim embraced and mingled rapturous tears. It was their high moment. They would not have traded it for all the glory that was Greece and the grandeur that was Rome. . . .They had intimations of immortality....

XI

O PIONEERS!

America

It is a good thing that we have in this country a day set aside for the special thanksgiving to our gods for what mercies they have let fall upon us during the past year. It is good, too, that we choose to show our gratitude by the age-old gesture of eating and drinking in their names.

Of course it can be said with some rightness that occasionally we dwell more on the gastronomical delights of Thanksgiving Day than we should upon the mystical significance of our well-filled bellies. That has doubtless been so since the first of such holidays was celebrated by the Pilgrims with a three-day orgy of venison and wine . . . and prayers in their proper places. Certainly it was so when I was a child and the Day became, for one reason and another, a routine observance of my grandparents' wishes, complete with bilious attacks and over-stuffed emotions which, on the part of the children, at least, had nothing to do with giving thanks.

We were unconscious of any reason for doing so. We had been raised to think that good and plenteous food, and warmth and protection as well, were the prerogatives of little middle-class Americans. We had no conception of hunger as such, in practice or even in theory.

Things have changed, perhaps for the better. At any rate we are wise enough now to acknowledge the existence of other kinds of starvation than that of the human body, and to give thanks humbly for whatever we can cultivate to feed our souls.

The legend of the first Thanksgiving, in 1621, has become more and more apocryphal, naturally, as it has been retold by men of varying creeds and political bents. I like it best, because it seems least varnished with religious hero-worship and patriotism, as it is reported by George F. Willison:

From *Saints and Strangers* by George F. Willison, 1896–

Indian summer soon came in a blaze of glory, and it was time to bring in the crops. All in all, their first harvest was a disappointment. Their twenty acres of corn, thanks to Squanto, had done well enough. But the Pilgrims failed miserably with more familiar crops. Their six or seven acres of English wheat, barley, and peas came to nothing, and Bradford was certainly on safe ground in attributing this either to "ye badnes of ye seed, or latenes of ye season, or both, or some other defecte." Still, it was possible to make a substantial increase in the individual weekly food ration which for months had consisted merely of a peck of meal from the stores brought on the Mayflower. This was now doubled by adding a peck of maize a week, and the company decreed a holiday so that all might, "after a more special manner, rejoyce together."

The Pilgrims had other things to be thankful for. They had made peace with the Indians and walked "as peaceably and safely in the woods as in the highways in England." A start had been made in the beaver trade. There had been no sickness for months. Eleven houses now lined the street—seven private dwellings and four buildings for common use. There had been no recurrence of mutiny and dissension. Faced with common dangers, Saints and Strangers had drawn closer together, sinking doctrinal differences for a time. Nothing had disturbed the peace but a duel, the first and last fought in the colony, with Stephen Hopkins' spirited young servants, Edward Dotey and Edward Leister, as principals.

As the day of the harvest festival approached, four men were sent out to shoot waterfowl, returning with enough to supply the company for a week. Massasoit was invited to attend and shortly arrived—with ninety ravenous braves! The strain on the larder was somewhat eased when some of these went out and bagged five deer. Captain Standish staged a military review, there were games of skill and chance, and for three days the

Pilgrims and their guests gorged themselves on venison, roast duck, roast goose, clams and other shellfish, succulent eels, white bread, corn bread, leeks and watercress and other "sallet herbes," with wild plums and dried berries as dessert—all washed down with wine, made of the wild grape, both white and red, which the Pilgrims praised as "very sweete & strong." At this first Thanksgiving feast in New England the company may have enjoyed, though there is no mention of it in the record, some of the long-legged "Turkies" whose speed of foot in the woods constantly amazed the Pilgrims. And there were cranberries by the bushel in neighboring bogs. It is very doubtful, however, if the Pilgrims had yet contrived a happy use for them. Nor was the table graced with a later and even more felicitous invention—pumpkin pie.

The celebration was a great success, warmly satisfying to body and soul alike, and the Pilgrims held another the next year, repeating it more or less regularly for generations. In time it became traditional throughout New England to enjoy the harvest feast with Pilgrim trimmings, a tradition carried to other parts of the country as restless Yankees moved westward. But it remained a regional or local holiday until 1863 when President Lincoln, in the midst of the Civil War, proclaimed the first national Thanksgiving, setting aside the last Thursday in November for the purpose, disregarding the centuries-old Pilgrim custom of holding it somewhat earlier, usually in October as on this first occasion.

There are two other bits from books I like that are a part of the picture of Thanksgiving Day as a completely and wholeheartedly American festival. Although there can be no comparison between them as literature, they are alike in their sensuous preoccupation with what is almost an idealization, a dream-telling, of plenty . . . plenty to eat, plenty to see and smell and then feast upon.

The first is about a family Thanksgiving in Michigan toward the end of the last century. It is, in its own kindly nostalgic way, almost a caricature of such traditional "harvest-homes," like a magazine cover by Norman Rockwell.

It is taken, more or less piecemeal (if such a banquet could be referred to even indirectly by so stark a word as meal!), from *The Country Kitchen*, by

Della T. Lutes, and is, by courtesy, the story of Little Runt, the predestined baked-meat for the feast:

From *The Country Kitchen*, 1936, by Della T. Lutes

Thanksgiving was the day of days, after my father's birthday, for intimate family gathering and unstinted feasting. There were times when my mother resented the invasions of my father's numerous relatives, but on this day she welcomed numbers. Only numbers could provide suitable scope for her prowess as a cook. A meagre family of three, even though augmented by a hired man, was no excuse for the array of meats, vegetables, cakes, cookies, pies and puddings and bread, and the orgy of preparation which, on this day, were her great delight.

Such preparations were sometimes in progress far ahead of the eventful date, as in one particular instance when Aunts Hanner and Sophrony, Uncle Frank and Aunt Catherine, with Amelia and Saryette, their daughters, and Uncle Matt and Aunt Martha, who were all within reasonable visiting distance, were invited to partake of the Thanksgiving dinner.

That year a young sow mistook, in the exuberance of her youth, the proper season for mating and, in early fall, presented herself with a lively litter of thirteen husky pigs. All but the thirteenth. The thirteenth was one too many for the calculations of nature and he, being shriveled and feeble, was rooted out of place by the others and repudiated by his mother. My father brought him into the house, scrawny, unable to stand on his little spindling legs, blear-eyed and livid, and laid him on my mother's lap. . . .

"Fat him up," said my father . . . , "and we'll have him for Thanksgiving dinner. I've always wanted roast pig for Thanksgiving."

My mother reminded him that he had had roast pig once some years before at Uncle Frank's house and that he had not liked it. In fact he had pronounced the whole dinner an utter failure because he had not liked the Pig.

"Fed on sour milk," retorted my father tersely. "Flabby and tough. Frank's too tarnation stingy to feed a pig fit for roasting. Feed the critter up," he advised, "on sweet milk and corn-meal mush, get him nice and fat, and we'll ask the ole curmudgeon over here Thanksgiving and show him what a roast pig's like."

So Little Runt was fed on sweet milk, fresh corn meal and vegetables, and he throve to a state of porcine beauty beyond all rightful expectation, considering his early state. . . .

He tagged at my mother's skirts when she looked for eggs and when she fed the hens, always sniffing at everything in his path, continuously expressing his affection, gratitude, and general satisfaction in life, with cheerful little ungh-ungh-unghs or a high-pitched protesting squeal.

He allowed me to wash and scrub him until his skin was pink and smooth and firm as that of any buxom farmer's child, and made no serious objection to the still pinker ribbon sometimes tied about his neck. With his little round quirking nose, his small bright watchful eyes, and his up-curled wiry tail, Little Runt was a pig to be proud of . . .

"Going to look pretty good spread out on a dripping pan 'long about the twenty-ninth," observed my father early in November, sitting on the back stoop and watching Little Runt nuzzle the cats away from their rightful pan of milk.

Mother made no reply, and as for myself I looked at my father with positive distaste. . . .

"Just how," queried my father at another time, as Little Runt grew in stature and rotundity, "do you make the stuffing for roast pig?"

For quite a few moments my mother did not reply. Her face reflected none of the gustatory fervor that lightened my father's, and she even turned her head away from where he was scratching Little Runt's back with a stick. . . .

Surprised at her silence, he set his penetrating eyes upon her and said, "Huh?"

"Stuffing?" she repeated with apparent reluctance. "Oh, I make it 'bout the same as for turkey. Little more sage, maybe."

"Umm-m!" My father made plesant reminiscent sounds in his throat. "Sage! You picked the sage yet?"

"Yes," she replied, "long ago. Savory, too, and all the herbs."

"Put any onion in it?" With the pertinacity of the obstinate mind, he seemed intent upon teasing his always latent appetite.

"Yes," said my mother, shortly, "plenty of it."

After an interval of silence in which Little Runt kept up a running commentary on the salubrious effect of back-scratching, he asked solicitously, "You begun to save up dried bread yet?"

My mother lifted her hands impatiently. "Good gracious!" she exclaimed irritably. "What do you think that pig's goin' to be—an elephant?" With which crushing remark she left the room.

And then, all of a sudden, Little Runt took to following my father about, his nose close to the heel of the man whose favor he seemed to think it vital that he should gain. . . .

And into my father's voice crept an extra note of bravado when he referred to the succulent dish so soon to be served upon his plate.

"You goin' to have anything besides roast pig?" he asked of my mother in what was intended for a casual tone, but which certainly bordered upon the anxious.

"Potatoes," replied my mother promptly, "and squash, and boiled onions—"

"I mean any—any other—*meat?*" he persisted in a manner strangely hesitating for one of his forthright spirit. "I didn't know as just the—the— pig'd be enough."

"Well," said my mother judicially, "I didn't know as 'twould be, myself, seein' how your mouth's waterin' for it. So I thought I'd roast a turkey. Old Tom's good and fat."

My father's face lightened unwarrantably.

"May be's well," he replied carelessly. "When you want him killed?"

"Any way, not yet," replied my mother shortly. "You can kill him when you butcher the pig "

My father rose and went outside, where we heard him vociferously greeted by Little Runt, with his own response made in loud and threatening tones. My mother smiled with her eyes, but her lips were tightly shut as she went about her work of clearing away supper. After that he talked loud and often of the Thanksgiving feast so rapidly approaching. He asked my mother if she was going to put a raw apple or a cooked one in Little Runt's mouth. He enlarged the daily rations of meal and milk and even gave him a few small ears of corn. He cut up pumpkins and fed him bit by bit. He stood by the pen (Little Runt now had a shelter all his own, so, as my father said, he "wouldn't run the fat off") and scratched his back and talked to him, always loudly and truculently of his approaching fate when anyone was within hearing. . . .

With the imminent approach of the festal day, my father haunted the kitchen. He watched the filling of the cookie jars—gray stone for sugar cookies and a brown glazed one for molasses. He sampled each batch of doughnuts as it came from the kettle and said they were not quite up to my mother's usual standard. He took, at my mother's invitation, repeated tastes of the mincemeat under preparation and with the air of a connoisseur suggested the addition of a *lee-tle* more boiled cider, just a *speck* more of allspice, and, finally, with a tentative glance at my mother's face, just a *touch* of brandy. Adding and mixing and stirring and tasting, together they brought the concoction to what both were satisfied was a state of perfection. . . .

Two days before Thanksgiving my father beheaded Old Tom, filled the big brass kettle with boiling water, scalded and plucked him. The wing tips were cut off whole for brushing the hearth and the tail feathers were finally gathered up and tied together in the form of a duster. He was then handed over to my mother with the somewhat ostentatious remark, "There's your turkey. I'll fetch the pig in tonight. Stib Obart's goin' to butcher him for me." . . .

. . . My mother lifted a corner of her apron to wipe her eyes. As for me, I was openly bawling. No miracle had happened, no ram in the bushes to save Little Runt. Stib Obart and his hideous knife stood, a menacing shadow, in the too near future. . . .

After supper that night [my father] set off with Little Runt, squealing, kicking, protesting, in a box in the back of the pung, it having snowed enough during the day to warrant the use of that vehicle. . . .

Along about nine o'clock [he] returned. He put the horse in the barn and then came stomping up to the door—the back kitchen door where a light had been left burning.

"Where you want him?" he called lustily.

"Put him down cellar," my mother replied. "On the table."

She did not rise, she made no inquiries. She took me off to bed and sat with me until I slept.

My mother always stuffed her meats at least twenty-four hours before roasting, so for one day Old Tom hung head down in an outer room to cool, while the little pig lay supinely upon the mahogany table in the cellar.

I crept down once for a peep at him, but the sight of the now too-white form sticking stiff, inglorious feet in the air was too much for me. I ran whimpering upstairs to the comfort of my mother's arms.

Early in the morning of the day before the feast a big bowl of stuffing was prepared—sage, savory, marjoram, and thyme crumbled between the fingers into well-moistened bread; onion chopped and added; salt and pepper, and lastly the generous half cup of melted butter, with frequent tastings as the rite proceeded.

When it was finally enriched to my mother's satisfaction, the turkey's ample cavities were filled and sewed. The wings were trussed, the neck bent back; and then, dipping her hand in the moist stuffing, my mother rubbed the entire exterior of the bird with the savory dressing. Over this paper-thin slices of fat salt pork were laid, and the bird, now in the roaster, was again consigned to the cold room to await his final call to glory.

On Thanksgiving morning the family were early astir. There was much to be done. The company would begin to arrive before eleven and my mother wanted to make progress before they came.

"Once your Aunt Catherine gets here, and your Aunt Hanner, there'll be so much talk I shan't be able to think."

The little pink carcass was brought up as soon as breakfast was over, and at sight of it I burst into tears and fled the kitchen, but could not remain long away. And neither could my father....

Particularly he was interested in the preparation of the pig for roasting. "You *do* rub it with butter, don't you?" he demanded with eager interest.

"Who said I didn't?" countered my mother a shade tartly, as well she might with a small girl following her about, tiptoe with excitement, and a restless, curious man under her feet when she had a thousand things to do....

"I wish you'd get out of the kitchen, 'Lije Thompson," she told him..., "and go and *do* something. Fill up the wood box and the water pail, and *stay* out."

He went, and so did I, for I could bear neither the sight of Little Runt in his defenseless state of abrogation, nor my mother's face as she bent over him....

Holidays and company-coming were usually the occasion for exuberant spirits on all our parts, for excited anticipation, chatter, and comment, but today my mother's grim face cast a shadow upon the day and there was small pleasure in the prospect of a bountiful table, the *pièce de résistance* of which was to be our so recent companion.

Time, however, is no respecter of emotion, and as the hours wore on the tempo of activity increased. Potatoes were pared and left in a kettle of cold water that they might not discolor. My father brought a huge Hubbard squash up from the sand pit in the cellar, . . . broke it into small pieces with the axe . . . scraped out the seeds and loose pulp, emptied the waste, and stacked the green and golden sections neatly on the kitchen table.

"Anything more I can do, 'Miry?" he inquired solicitously, only to meet with a suspicious glance from my mother.

"Yes," she said shortly, "you can peel the onions." This was more than he had bargained for, but his quick, rather shocked look into her face brought him no quarter.

"They're in the butt'ry," she said tersely, "and you better peel 'em all."

To my certain knowledge, my father had never up to this time peeled an onion or any other vegetable in his whole life. Nor had he ever washed a dish or in any other way shown any inclination toward self-preservation so far as the preparation of food was concerned. My mother often said that if he were left alone he would probably starve to death before he would cook himself a meal. And now there he was standing at a kitchen table peeling onions and surreptitiously wiping his weeping eyes, while my mother stepped briskly from room to room, her hands filled with one delectable dish after another, her lips grimly set, her eyes unsmiling and hard.

The onions peeled and standing in a pan of water, my father scrubbed his hands in the tin basin, wiped them on the roller towel hanging on the back of a door, and then, without a word or a glance in my mother's direction, put on his hat and escaped.

To a little girl accustomed to basking in the warmth, the approval, the impregnable security of a united family life, there was something oppressive and sinister in the atmosphere of this morning. Still, there was assurance in the wealth of delicacies stored against the day.

In the buttery were the pumpkin pies that had been baked earlier in the morning, the ruffled edges of their biscuit-brown crusts encircling smooth plaques of yellow custard coated with a thin, almost transparent veil of dappled russet and bronze.

From these were exhaled a most flavorsome odor reminiscent of autumn days when the lusty vine strewed its golden fruit wantonly amongst the corn, mingled with the spicy fragrance of cinnamon, nutmeg, ginger, and allspice.

Alongside these were the mince pies baked a week earlier, stored in cold and now brought out to be warmed at the last moment on the oven top. Marked with an "M" they were, and through the delicate tracery of the letter one caught tantalizing whiffs of meat preserved in heavenly juices, apple, currant, and raisin all melded into one sweetly tart aroma, itself bathed in the effluvious bouquet of rich old brandy, such aroma as the Olympian gods may have dreamed of but never met.

Here, too, arranged in glass sauce dishes, pickle dishes, preserve dishes that were the possessions of but ordinary women, but which are now elevated to the high estate of the rare, were pickled peaches with the pointed ears of cloves dotting their amber sides; mustard pickles to neutralize the too-rich content of the young pork; bowls of crimson cranberry sauce; globules of currant jelly for those who did not favor the fruit of the bog; long, green sections of cucumber pickle standing upright in the crystal dish swinging censer-like in its silver frame with hanging fork beside.

And then, here was the comp'ny! Uncle Frank and Aunt Catherine with the two third cousins, Saryette and Amelia.... The horses having been attended to, and greetings exchanged, Uncle Frank and my father betook themselves to the front room, where the round chunk stove sent vibrations of heat quivering upon the air. Aunt Catherine unfolded a voluminous apron from her sewing bag, tied it around her ample waist, and laid capable hands to the setting of the table. By the time Aunt Hanner and Aunt 'Phrony had arrived with the remainder of the guests, the table was dressed in its long white linen cloth, the tall silver caster and its five crystal bottles as a centrepiece, and the various relishes, jellies, and preserves clustered about it.

At two o'clock the family was seated around the board, the turkey, his crisp juicy skin bursting here and there in the plenitude of his stuffed insides, before my mother at one end of the table, and the rosy-brown, crackling-coated, well-rounded porcine frame before my father. The little

pig's legs, now untied, squatted wantonly beneath his well-padded hams
and shoulders, his golden belly crouched upon the plate.

… My mother had left the head intact, with upstanding ears and truculently extended snout. In his mouth was a beautiful red apple, polished
(for I saw him do it) on the sleeve of my father's wamus, and inserted by
him, at my mother's request, into the open mouth after the pig was placed
on the table. Over his haunches a small crisp tail upcurled with a realism
seldom equaled in culinary lore.

A beautiful creature he certainly was, smoking, steaming, reeking of
succulent juices, and rich with fragrance of herbs sun-ripened in our own
garden.

"How do I carve him?" inquired my father with suspicious alacrity,
poising his instruments above the plate before him, and ignoring the expectant silence with which my mother always recognized religious ten-
dencies accorded to Uncle Frank. Dismissing the too-previous question
as unheard, my mother turned in the direction of her guest and politely
inquired if he would like to ask a blessing.

Uncle Frank, knowing my father's contempt for an attitude that he
considered lacking in sincerity, waved dismissal of the courtesy.

"Best way to thank the Lord," observed my father benignly, slipping
the razor-edged knife well under the skin of the succulent pig and watching with round eyes the free rich juices run, "is to fall to and eat. Pass up
your plate, Cathy, for some of the best roast pig you ever tasted in your life.
'Miry'll tend to the turkey."

One by one he filled the huge plates—a slice of well-done pinkish-
white young pork, a bit of crackling brown skin, a spoonful of mashed
potatoes whipped with cream and butter to a very froth of delectable flavor,
a spoonful of the stuffing. My mother, brooding eyes intent upon the work
before her, was carving the turkey—a thin piece of white meat rimmed
with chestnut-brown, a bit of the dark, laying the pieces on the side of the
platter and transferring them to the plates as they reached her.

Finally all were taken care of except Mother, and Father, holding his
knife above the riddled carcass, said with odd gusto, "Now, 'Miry, I'm
goin' to cut *you* a nice juicy slice."

My mother, struggling to control herself, said, "I don't care for any,
thank you," and burst into tears.

We all with one accord turned to look at her, the guests in astonish-ment, I with streaming eyes and sobbing breath, and my father in conster-nation and apparent anger.

"Well!" he said with what would seem to be a righteous indignation. "I been wonderin' if you was goin' to show some signs of feelin', 'Miry. Wait a minute."

He threw down his napkin, shoved back his chair, dashed through the kitchen, snatched his hat from a nail as he went—all, it seemed, in one whirlwind of motion, his guests staring after him in rooted amazement.

My mother wiped her eyes, and in a shamed and shaken voice said, "It was Little Runt. I fed him by hand—he t-tagged us around—I didn't see—h-how he *could*—I d-don't know what he's up to—"

But her tearful, broken apology was interrupted by a confusion of the strangest sounds—a mingling of the sharp, staccato squeals of a struggling pig, snuffles and grunts, my father's voice raised in affectionate abuse, the back door opening.

"Hol' your tongue, you tarnation fool-cuss"—and there he was, white hair flying, hat awry, and in his arms, legs kicking, snout wrinkling, small pink body squirming, was—sure as you live—Little Runt!

"There!" said my father, wheezing a bit from exertion. "*Now* what you think?"

Every chair had been pushed back. Food was cooling on the plates. I had flown from my chair to greet Little Runt and pull him into my lap.

"Why!" cried my mother, gasping. "What—where—"

"Well," said my father, flinging off his hat and smoothing hair and beard, and beaming with satisfaction in his own exploit, "when I see you [address-ing my mother] was really *bent* on roast pig for dinner [my mother lifted her hands, opened her mouth, and remained silent], I thought I'd have to fix it some way to save Little Runt's hide. You see," he now turned eagerly to the dumbfounded guests, "this was a runt we raised by hand and he took to fol-lowing me round, so when it came time I didn't have the heart to—so I took one of the others over to Stib Obart's instead." Then, with a swift turn from the still silent table, he addressed the contented, adventuring pig.

"Come along now," he said, and, executing a flank movement, caught Little Runt by his hind leg and hoisted him to his arms, admonishing him sonorously.

"Thanksgiving for *you*, all right, you fool runt, you, but hogs don't celebrate it in the house," and in an uproar of squeals and protesting kicks Little Runt was borne away.

"'Lije," said Uncle Frank sententiously in his absence, "always was a sentimental old fool."

"Let me," urged my mother politely, ignoring the remark, "give you some of the turkey."

Almost immediately my father was at his place washed and brushed, passing the squash, asking for the cranberries, urging second helpings where the first were hardly touched. He made complimentary and utterly absurd remarks about Aunt Catherine's fine looks, joshed Uncle Frank about a horse trade he had recently made, and otherwise disported himself as the benignant and genial host. To my mother he was especially considerate, but could not at the last deny himself the pleasure of a subtle thrust which would reflect upon his own clever scheming.

"Well, 'Miry," he said handsomely as the guests, replete with food and hospitable content, drove away in the dusk of blue-white snow and creeping night, "ain't you glad *now* that I done something about Little Runt?"

"You better go feed him," said my mother dryly, which he did. . . .

The other thing I have chosen to put in this packaging of Thanksgiving excerpts is from *Look Homeward, Angel*, by Thomas Wolfe. It is about his very young days, as Eugene Gant.

It tells of Christmas and Thanksgiving, true, but it is really a hymn to the yearlong feasting in the Gant household, when the mother Eliza with her smoking cookstove alchemy would create a kind of antidote to all the ragings and bickerings and silent hatreds of the family.

They were big people, and they ate like big people.

From *Look Homeward, Angel* by Thomas Wolfe, 1900–1938

They fed stupendously. Eugene began to observe the food and the seasons. In the autumn, they barrelled huge frosty apples in the cellar. Gant bought whole hogs from the butcher, returning home early to salt them, wearing a long work-apron, and rolling his sleeves half up his lean hairy arms. Smoked bacons hung in the pantry, the great bins were full of flour, the dark recessed shelves groaned with preserved cherries, peaches, plums, quinces, apples, pears. All that he touched waxed in rich pungent life: his Spring gardens, wrought in the black wet earth below the fruit trees, flourished in huge crinkled lettuces that wrenched cleanly from the loamy soil with small black clots stuck to their crisp stocks; fat red radishes; heavy tomatoes. The rich plums lay bursted on the grass; his huge cherry trees oozed with heavy gum jewels; his apple trees bent with thick green clusters. The earth was spermy for him like a big woman.

Spring was full of cool dewy mornings, spurting winds, and storms of intoxicating blossoms, and in this enchantment Eugene first felt the mixed lonely ache and promise of the seasons.

In the morning they rose in a house pungent with breakfast cookery, and they sat at a smoking table loaded with brains and eggs, ham, hot biscuit, fried apples seething in their gummed syrups, honey, golden butter, fried steak, scalding coffee. Or there were stacked batter-cakes, rum-colored molasses, fragrant brown sausages, a bowl of wet cherries, plums, fat juicy bacon, jam. At the mid-day meal, they ate heavily: a huge hot roast of beef, fat buttered lima-beans, tender corn smoking on the cob, thick red slabs of sliced tomatoes, rough savory spinach, hot yellow cornbread, flaky biscuits, a deep-dish peach and apple cobbler spiced with cinnamon, tender cabbage, deep glass dishes piled with preserved fruits—cherries, pears, peaches. At night they might eat fried steak, hot squares of grits fried in egg and butter, pork-chops, fish, young fried chicken.

For the Thanksgiving and Christmas feasts four heavy turkeys were bought and fattened for weeks: Eugene fed them with cans of shelled corn several times a day, but he could not bear to be present at their executions, because by that time their cheerful excited gobbles made echoes in his heart. Eliza baked for weeks in advance: the whole energy of the family focussed upon the great ritual of the feast. A day or two before, the auxiliary dainties arrived in piled grocer's boxes—the magic of strange foods and fruits was added to familiar fare: there were glossed sticky dates, cold rich figs, cramped belly to belly in small boxes, dusty raisins, mixed nuts—the almond, pecan, the meaty Brazil nut, the walnut, sacks of assorted candies, piles of yellow Florida oranges, tangerines, sharp, acrid, nostalgic odors.

Seated before a roast or a fowl, Gant began a heavy clangor on his steel and carving knife, distributing thereafter Gargantuan portions to each plate. Eugene feasted from a high chair by his father's side, filled his distending belly until it was drum-tight, and was permitted to stop eating by his watchful sire only when his stomach was impregnable to the heavy prod of Gant's big finger.

"There's a soft place there," he would roar, and he would cover the scoured plate of his infant son with another heavy slab of beef. That their machinery withstood this hammer-handed treatment was a tribute to their vitality and Eliza's cookery.

America in the Colonial period was a strange mixture of European sophistication and primitive backwoods simplicity, gastronomically as well as in other social ways.

Gentlemen lived perhaps more graciously than they ever have since, on such breathtakingly beautiful estates as Monticello and Mount Vernon, with most of the amenities and few of the inconveniences (political, at least) of a comparable existence in England or France. There were slaves, black mostly, not really thought of as human beings, and the townspeople lived much as they would in the older countries, in fatness or filth according to their incomes and their natural proclivities.

A decent existence was much easier even for the very poor "whites" than it had ever been in Europe, mainly because the new country was so generous. Game roamed within gunshot in the fields and forests, and flew overhead in great convenient flocks. Wild fruits and vegetables lay everywhere for the picking, and almost all the cultivated seeds flourished with a new enthusiasm in the fresh soil. The sea was full of fish, sporting everywhere along the boundless Atlantic coast. And ships sailed in and out of the fine harbors, laden with delicacies from abroad, and rum and wine and spices.

Parties in Boston and in Williamsburg and everywhere between were very gay; and although some of the "Rules for Behavior" set down by young gentlemen like George Washington indicate a certain crudity of table manners in such things as belching, spitting, and picking of the teeth, there was a real graciousness of living then, for almost everyone.

It shows in the architecture, and in the portraits and furnishings that have lasted; in the recipes written by great hostesses; in unimportant jingles like the following one, composed sometime late in the eighteenth century to amuse and instruct the future matrons of New England:

Anonymous, 18th Century

A Recipe for all Young Ladies that are going to be Married.
To Make a Sack-Posset

From famed Barbadoes on the Western Main
    Fetch sugar half a pound; fetch Sack from Spain
A pint; and from the Eastern Indian Coast
    Nutmeg, the glory of our Northern toast;
O'er flaming coals together let them heat
    Till the all-conquering Sack dissolves the sweet,
O'er such another fire set eggs, twice ten
    Newborn from crowing cock and speckled hen;
Stir them with steady hand, and conscience pricking
    To see the untimely fate of twenty chicken.
From shining shelf take down your brazen skillet,
    A quart of milk from gentle cow will fill it;
When boiled and cooked put milk and Sack to egg,
    Unite them firmly like the triple league.
Then, covered close, together let them dwell
    Till Miss sings twice, "You must not kiss and tell!"
Each lad and lass snatch up their murdering spoon,
    And fall on fiercely like a starved dragoon.

One of the accidents of fate that made life much more exciting than it might have been for the Colonial Americans was the presence of hundreds of refugees from restless Europe. Some of them became stylish dancing-masters and wig-curlers and even cooks and colonels. Others taught French or Italian or German. Most of them, naturally, were courageous men, and many of them were charming, to boot.

One of the most delightful, to my way of thinking, must have been Anthelme Brillat-Savarin, temporarily "studying" in America until his political reputation cooled off in France and he could go back to live quietly and work on his great *Physiology of Taste*.

Much of the best of that inimitable book concerns his days in this country: he seemed to look back on them with an especial delicacy and pleasure, which I always share with him in the rereading.

This anecdote is called "An Exploit of the Professor":

From *The Physiology of Taste* by Anthelme Brillat-Savarin, 1755–1826
While I was in Hartford, in Connecticut, I had the good luck to kill a wild turkey. This deed deserves to go down in history, and I shall recount it all the more eagerly since I myself am its hero.

A worthy old landowner (AMERICAN FARMER) had invited me to come hunt on his property; he lived in the backwoods of the State (BACK GROUNDS), promised me partridges, grey squirrels, and wild turkeys (WILD COCKS), and gave me the privilege of bringing with me one or two of my chosen friends.

As a result, one fine day of October 1794 we set out, Monsieur King and I, mounted on two hired nags, with the hope of arriving by nightfall at Monsieur Bulow's farm, situated five whole ungodly leagues from Hartford.

M. King was a hunter of an extraordinary kind: he loved the sport passionately, but when he had killed any game he looked on himself as a murderer, and delivered himself of sensitive moral speculations and elegies on the final passing of his victims, which of course did not in the least keep him from starting the hunt all over again.

Although our road was hardly more than a track, we arrived without accident, and were received with that kind of cordial and wordless hospitality which expresses itself by its actions, which is to say that in a very few minutes all of us had been looked after, refreshed, and lodged—men, horses, and dogs according to their particular needs.

We spent some two hours in looking over the farm and its dependencies. I could describe all of that if I wished to, but I much prefer picturing to the reader M. Bulow's four fine daughters (BUXUM LASSES), for whom our visit was a great event.

Their ages ranged from sixteen to twenty; they were radiant with freshness and good health, and there was about all of them such simplicity, such graceful naturalness, that their most ordinary actions endowed them with a thousand charms.

Shortly after we returned from our walk we sat down around a plenti-fully laden table: a handsome piece of CORN'D BEEF, A STEW'D goose, and a magnificent leg of mutton, then root-vegetables of all kinds (PLENTY), and at the two ends of the table two enormous jugs of an excellent cider, of which I could not drink enough.

When we had proved to our host that we were genuine hunters, at least in our appetite, he began to talk of the real purpose of our visit: he de-scribed to the best of his ability the places where we would find our game, the landmarks which we must watch for to guide us safely back again, and above all the farms where we could find refreshment.

During this conversation the ladies had prepared some excellent tea, of which we drank several cups; then they showed us to a room with two beds in it, where the day's exercise and the good food soon sent us off into a delicious sleep.

The next morning we set out for the hunt a little late, and soon coming to the edge of the clearings made by M. Bulow's workmen, I found myself for the first time in my life in virgin forest, where the sound of the axe had never been heard.

I wandered through it with delight, observing the benefits and the ravages of time, which both creates and destroys, and I amused myself by following every period in the life of an oak tree, from the moment it emerges two-leaved from the earth until that one when nothing is left of it but a long black smudge which is its heart's dust.

M. King chided me for my wandering attention, and we took up the hunt more seriously. First of all we killed some of those pretty little grey partridges which are so plump and so tender. Then we knocked down six or seven grey squirrels, highly thought of in that country; and finally our lucky start led us into the midst of a flock of wild turkeys.

They arose, one after another, in quick noisy flight, screaming loudly. M. King fired first, and ran ahead: the others were by now out of range; then the laziest of them rose from the earth not ten paces from me; I fired at it through a break in the woods, and it fell, stone dead.

Only a hunter will understand the bliss such a lucky shot gave me. I picked up the superb winged creature, and stood admiring it from every angle for a good quarter-hour, when I heard M. King cry out for help; I ran to him, and found that he was only calling me to aid him in the search for a turkey which he declared he had killed, but which had nonetheless completely disappeared.

I put my dog on the scent, but he led us into thickets so dense and thorny that a serpent could not have gone through them, and we were forced to give up, which threw my companion into a temper which lasted until we returned to the farm.

The rest of our hunt is hardly worth describing. On the way back, we lost ourselves in the boundless woods, and were in great danger of having to spend the night in them, had it not been for the silvery voices of the young Bulows and the deep bass of their father, who had been kind enough to come in search of us, and who helped lead us out of the forest.

The four sisters had put on their full battle dress; freshly laundered frocks, new sashes, pretty hats and neatly shining shoes told that they had gone to some expense for our benefits; and as for me, I was willing enough to be my most agreeable to the one of these young ladies who took my arm with as much a proprietary air as any wife.

When we got back to the farm we found supper ready for us; but, before starting to eat, we sat down for a few minutes before a lively blazing fire which had been lighted, even though the weather would not have seemed to call for it. We found it very comforting indeed, and were refreshed by it almost magically.

This custom doubtless came from the Indians, who always have a fire burning in their wigwams. Perhaps it is also a custom given to us by Saint Francis of Sales, who once said that a fire is good twelve months of the year. (*Non liquet.*)

We ate as if we were starved; a generous bowl of punch helped us to finish off the evening, and a discussion in which our host talked much more freely than the day before held us late into the night.

We talked of the War of Independence, in which M. Bulow had served as a ranking officer; of M. de La Fayette, steadily greater in the minds of the Americans, who always spoke of him familiarly by his title (THE MAR-QUIS); of agriculture, which during that period was enriching the United States, and finally of my own dear France, which I loved much more since I had been forced to leave it.

From time to time, as an interlude in our conversation, M. Bulow would say to his oldest daughter: "Mariah! Give us a song." And she sang to us without more urging, and with a charming shyness, the national air YANKEE DUDDE, and the lament of Queen Mary and the one of Major Andrew, both of them very popular in this country. Mariah had taken a few lessons, and there in the backwoods was thought to be something of an artist; but her singing was praiseworthy mainly because of the quality of her voice, which was at once sweet, fresh, and unaffected.

The next day we left, in spite of the friendliest protests, for even in America I had certain duties to perform. While the horses were being saddled, M. Bulow, having drawn me to one side, spoke in the following profoundly interesting way:

"You see in me, my dear sir, a happy man, if such there be on earth: everything around you and all that you have so far observed is a product of what I own. These stockings I wear were knitted by my daughters; my shoes and my clothes come from my own sheep; they help also, with my gardens and barnyards, to furnish me with simple nourishing food; and what makes our government so admirable is that here in Connecticut there are thousands of farmers just as happy as I am, and whose doors, like mine, are never bolted.

"Taxes here are almost nothing; and as long as they are paid we can sleep in peace. Congress does everything in its power to help our newborn industry; agents come from every direction to buy up whatever we have to sell; and I have cash on hand for a long time, for I have just sold for twenty-four dollars a barrel the wheat I usually get eight for.

"All this is the result of the liberty which we have fought for and founded on good laws. I am master in my own house, and you will not be astonished to know that we never hear the sound of the drum here, nor, except for the fourth of July, the glorious anniversary of our independence, do we ever see soldiers, or uniforms, or bayonets."

During the whole of our trip homeward I was plunged in profound thought. It may be believed that I was pondering the parting speech of M. Bulow, but I had something quite different on my mind: I was considering how best I should cook my turkey, and I was not without some worries, for I feared that in Hartford I might not find all the ingredients I would need—and I was determined to raise a worthy monument to the spoils of my skill.

I inflict on myself a painful sacrifice in leaving out the details of the elaborate preparations I made for the fitting and distinguished way I planned to entertain my American dinner guests. It is enough to say that the partridge wings were served *en papillote*, and the grey squirrels simmered in Madeira.

As for the turkey, which was our only roast, it was charming to look at, flattering to the sense of smell, and delicious to the taste. And as the last morsel of it disappeared, there arose from the whole table the words: "VERY GOOD! EXCEEDINGLY GOOD! OH! DEAR SIR, WHAT A GLORIOUS BIT!"

Hungry men think of everything in their lives, from their sweethearts to their religious principles, in terms of food. One of the most amusing proofs of this fact in American literature is Washington Irving's description of the lanky scarecrow Ichabod Crane and how he felt about Katrina Van Tassel and her succulent possessions. She would have appealed to any man, of course, but to one as chronically lean and starved as the schoolteacher she was irresistible:

From *The Legend of Sleepy Hollow* by Washington Irving, 1783–1859

Among the musical disciples who assembled one evening in each week to receive ... instructions in psalmody, was Katrina Van Tassel, the daughter and only child of a substantial Dutch farmer. She was a blooming lass of fresh eighteen; plump as a partridge; ripe and melting and rosy-cheeked as one of her father's peaches, and universally famed, not merely for her beauty, but her vast expectations. She was, withal, a little of a coquette, as might be perceived even in her dress, which was a mixture of ancient and modern fashions, as most suited to set off her charms. She wore the ornaments of pure yellow gold, which her great-great-grandmother had brought over from Saardam; the tempting stomacher of the olden time; and withal a provokingly short petticoat, to display the prettiest foot and ankle in the country round.

Ichabod Crane had a soft and foolish heart towards the sex, and it is not to be wondered at that so tempting a morsel soon found favour in his eyes, more especially after he had visited her in her paternal mansion. Old Baltus Van Tassel was a perfect picture of a thriving, contented, liberal-hearted farmer. He seldom, it is true, sent either his eyes or his thoughts beyond the boundaries of his own farm; but within those, everything was snug, happy, and well-conditioned. He was satisfied with his wealth, but not proud of it; and piqued himself upon the hearty abundance, rather than the style in which he lived. His stronghold was situated on the banks of the Hudson, in one of those green, sheltered, fertile nooks, in which the Dutch farmers are so fond of nestling. A great elm-tree spread its broad branches over it, at the foot of which bubbled up a spring of the softest and sweetest water, in a little well formed of a barrel, and then stole sparkling away through the grass to a neighbouring brook that bubbled along among alders and dwarf willows. Hard by the farm-house was a vast barn that might have served for a church, every window and crevice of which seemed bursting forth with the treasures of the farm; the flail was busily resounding within it from morning to night; swallows and martins skimmed twittering about the eaves; and rows of pigeons, some with one eye turned up, as if watching the weather, some with their heads under their wings, or buried in their bosoms, and others swelling, and cooing, and bowing about their dames, were enjoying the sunshine on the roof. Sleek unwieldy porkers were grunting in the repose and abundance of their pens, whence sallied forth now and then troops of suckling pigs, as if to snuff the air. A stately squadron of snowy geese were riding in an adjoining pond, convoying whole fleets of ducks; regiments of turkeys were gobbling through the farm-yard, and guinea-fowls fretting about it, like ill-tempered housewives, with their peevish, discontented cry. Before the barn door strutted the gallant cock, that pattern of a husband, a warrior, and a fine gentleman, clapping his burnished wings, and crowing in the pride and gladness of his heart—sometimes tearing up the earth with his feet, and then generously calling his ever-hungry family of wives and children to enjoy the rich morsel which he had discovered.

The pedagogue's mouth watered as he looked upon this sumptuous promise of luxurious winter fare. In his devouring mind's eye he pictured to himself every roasting-pig running about with a pudding in his belly, and an apple in his mouth; the pigeons were snugly put to bed in a comfortable pie, and tucked in with a coverlet of crust; the geese were swimming in their own gravy; and the ducks pairing cosily in dishes, like snug married couples, with a decent competency of onion sauce. In the porkers he saw carved out the future sleek side of bacon and juicy relishing ham; not a turkey but he beheld daintily trussed-up, with its gizzard under its wing, and, peradventure, a necklace of savoury sausages; and even bright chanticleer himself lay sprawling on his back in a side-dish, with uplifted claws, as if craving that quarter which his chivalrous spirit disdained to ask while living.

As the enraptured Ichabod fancied all this, and as he rolled his great green eyes over the fat meadow-lands, the rich fields of wheat, of rye, of buckwheat, and Indian corn, and the orchards burthened with ruddy fruit, which surrounded the warm tenement of Van Tassel, his heart yearned after the damsel who was to inherit these domains, and his imagination expanded with the idea, how they might be readily turned into cash, and the money invested in immense tracts of wild land, and shingle palaces in the wilderness. Nay, his busy fancy already realized his hopes, and presented to him the blooming Katrina, with a whole family of children, mounted on the top of a waggon loaded with household trumpery, with pots and kettles dangling beneath; and he beheld himself bestriding a pacing mare, with a colt at her heels, setting out for Kentucky, Tennessee, or the Lord knows where.

When he entered the house, the conquest of his heart was complete. It was one of those spacious farmhouses, with high-ridged, but lowly-sloping roofs, built in the style handed down from the first Dutch settlers; the low projecting eaves forming a piazza along the front, capable of being closed up in bad weather. Under this were hung flails, harness, various utensils of husbandry, and nets for fishing in the neighbouring river. Benches were built along the sides for summer use; and a great spinning-wheel at one end, and a churn at the other, showed the various uses to which this important porch might be devoted. From this piazza the wondering Ichabod entered the hall, which formed the centre of the mansion and the place of usual residence. Here rows of resplendent pewter, ranged on a long dresser, dazzled his eyes. In one corner stood a huge bag of wool ready to be spun; in another, a quantity of linsey-woolsey just from the loom; ears of Indian corn, and strings of dried apples and peaches, hung in gay festoons along the wall, mingled with the gaud of red peppers; and a door left ajar gave him a peep into the best parlour, where the claw-footed chairs and dark mahogany tables shone like mirrors; andirons, with their accompanying shovel and tongs, glistened from their covert of asparagus tops; mock oranges and conch-shells decorated the mantel-piece; strings of various coloured birds' eggs were suspended above it; a great ostrich egg was hung from the centre of the room, and a corner-cupboard, knowingly left open, displayed immense treasures of old silver and well-mended china.

As Ichabod jogged slowly on his way, his eye, ever open to every symptom of culinary abundance, ranged with delight over the treasures of jolly autumn. On all sides he beheld vast stores of apples; some hanging in oppressive opulence on the trees; some gathered into baskets and barrels for the market; others heaped up in rich piles for the cider-press. Further on he beheld great fields of Indian corn, with its golden ears peeping from their leafy coverts, and holding out the promise of cakes and hasty-pudding; and the yellow pumpkins lying beneath them, turning up their fair round bellies to the sun, and giving ample prospects of the most luxurious of pies; and anon he passed the fragrant buckwheat fields, breathing the odour of the bee-hive, and as he beheld them, soft anticipations stole over his mind of dainty slapjacks, well buttered, and garnished with honey or treacle, by the delicate little dimpled hand of Katrina Van Tassel. . . .

Fain would I pause to dwell upon the world of charms that burst upon the enraptured gaze of my hero, as he entered the state parlour of Van Tassel's mansion. Not those of the bevy of buxom lasses, with their luxurious display of red and white; but the ample charms of a genuine Dutch country tea-table in the sumptuous time of autumn. Such heaped-up platters of cakes of various and almost indescribable kinds, known only to experienced Dutch housewives! There was the doughty dough-nut, the tenderer oly koek, and the crisp and crumbling kruller; sweet-cakes and shortcakes, ginger-cakes and honey-cakes, and the whole family of cakes. And then there were apple-pies and peach-pies and pumpkin-pies; besides slices of ham and smoked beef; and, moreover, delectable dishes of preserved plums, and peaches, and pears, and quinces; not to mention broiled shad and roasted chickens; together with bowls of milk and cream, all mingled higgledy-piggledy, pretty much as I have enumerated them, with the motherly teapot sending up its clouds of vapour from the midst—Heaven bless the mark! I want breath and time to discuss this banquet as it deserves, and am too eager to get on with my story. Happily, Ichabod Crane was not in so great a hurry as his historian, but did ample justice to every dainty.

He was a kind and thankful creature, whose heart dilated in proportion as his skin was filled with good cheer; and whose spirits rose with eating as some men's do with drink. He could not help, too, rolling his large eyes round him as he ate, and chuckling with the possibility that he might one day be lord of all this scene of almost unimaginable luxury and splendour. Then he thought, how soon he'd turn his back upon the old school-house, snap his fingers in the face of Hans Van Ripper, and every other niggardly patron, and kick any itinerant pedagogue out of doors that should dare to call him comrade!

The first half of the nineteenth century found a new type of visitor in America: the observer of our table-manners and church-morals rather than the grateful partaker of our political and religious freedoms. European refugees gave way to a flood of writers, some of them very good ones, and most of them from England.

Mrs. Trollope really blazed the path, in 1832, and set our society buzzing with rage at her candid picture of it in *Domestic Manners of the Americans*. She wrote well, as the mother of Anthony would be expected to do, and her book is amusing to read now, but it is easy to see why its bluntly critical attitude enraged the people who had been hospitable and kind to her on her energetic tour.

Another writer, and this time one more widely known and much beloved, hurt the proud feelings of the Americans with his book of *Notes*; Charles Dickens, who came to this country in 1842, and set down with a regrettably supercilious tone what he saw and thought of our obvious crudities as well as our irrefutable graces.

The *Notes* are still by Dickens, however, and thus are good reading in spite of their sour overtones. (And when you consider the difficulties of travel then, you cannot see how even the strongest and most insensitive of men could survive a trip unruffled, if at all.)

This cutting is typical, about a steamboat ride on the *Messenger* from Pittsburgh to Cincinnati.

From *American Notes* by Charles Dickens, 1812–1870

. . . There is one long narrow cabin, the whole length of the boat; from which the state-rooms open, on both sides. A small portion of it at the stern is partitioned off for the ladies: and the bar is at the opposite extreme. There is a long table down the centre, and at either end a stove. The washing apparatus is forward, on the deck. It is a little better than on board the canal boat, but not much. In all modes of travelling, the American customs, with reference to the means of personal cleanliness and wholesome ablution, are extremely negligent and filthy; and I strongly incline to the belief that a considerable amount of illness is referable to this cause.

We are to be on board the Messenger three days; arriving at Cincinnati (barring accidents) on Monday morning. There are three meals a day. Breakfast at seven, dinner at half-past twelve, supper about six. At each, there are a great many small dishes and plates upon the table, with very little in them; so that although there is every appearance of a mighty "spread," there is seldom really more than a joint: except for those who fancy slices of beet-root, shreds of dried beef, complicated entanglements of yellow pickle; maize, Indian corn, apple-sauce, and pumpkin.

Some people fancy all these little dainties together (and sweet preserves beside), by way of relish to their roast pig. They are generally those dyspeptic ladies and gentlemen who eat unheard-of quantities of hot corn bread (almost as good for the digestion as a kneaded pin-cushion), for breakfast, and for supper. Those who do not observe this custom, and who help themselves several times instead, usually suck their knives and forks meditatively, until they have decided what to take next: then pull them out of their mouths: put them in the dish; help themselves; and fall to work again. At dinner, there is nothing to drink upon the table, but great jugs full of cold water. Nobody says anything, at any meal, to anybody. All the passengers are very dismal, and seem to have tremendous secrets weighing on their minds. There is no conversation, no laughter, no cheerfulness, no sociality, except in spitting; and that is done in silent fellowship round the stove, when the meal is over. Every man sits down, dull and languid; swallows his fare as if breakfasts, dinners, and suppers, were necessities of nature never to be coupled with recreation or enjoyment; and having bolted his food in a gloomy silence, bolts himself, in the same state. But for these animal observances, you might suppose the whole male portion of the company to be the melancholy ghosts of departed bookkeepers, who had fallen dead at the desk: such is their weary air of business and calculation. Undertakers on duty would be sprightly beside them; and a collation of funeral-baked meats, in comparison with these meals, would be a sparkling festivity.

The Peterkin Papers are as American as apple pie ... *or baked beans and brown bread* ... or whatever it is that to each of us means something that can be savored in no other country than this one.

As a book they are even funnier to grown-up people than to the children who first giggled helplessly at the incredible blunders of Elizabeth Eliza Peterkin and her family, and shrieked with a familiar but unchanging relief when the Lady from Philadelphia settled one affair after another with her obnoxiously right suggestions. They are fantasy, really, but the naive language of their telling, and the forthrightness of their nonsense, make them Alice in Wonderland, the universal child-person.

Here, then, is one of the *Papers*, about "The Lady Who Put Salt in Her Coffee":

From *The Peterkin Papers* by Lucretia P. Hale, 1820–1900

This was Mrs. Peterkin. It was a mistake. She had poured out a delicious cup of coffee, and, just as she was helping herself to cream, she found she had put in salt instead of sugar! It tasted bad. What should she do? Of course she couldn't drink the coffee; so she called in the family, for she was sitting at a late breakfast all alone. The family came in; they all tasted, and looked, and wondered what should be done, and all sat down to think.

At last Agamemnon, who had been to college, said, "Why don't we go over and ask the advice of the chemist?" (For the chemist lived over the way, and was a very wise man.)

Mrs. Peterkin said, "Yes," and Mr. Peterkin said, "Very well," and all the children said they would go too. So the little boys put on their india-rubber boots, and over they went.

Now the chemist was just trying to find out something which should turn everything it touched into gold; and he had a large glass bottle into which he put all kinds of gold and silver, and many other valuable things, and melted them all up over the fire, till he had almost found what he wanted. He could turn things into almost gold. But just now he had used up all the gold that he had round the house, and gold was high. He had used up his wife's gold thimble and his great-grandfather's gold-bowed spectacles; and he had melted up the gold head of his great-great-grandfather's cane; and, just as the Peterkin family came in, he was down on his knees before his wife, asking her to let him have her wedding ring to melt up with all the rest, because this time he knew he should succeed, and should be able to turn everything into gold; and then she could have a new wedding ring of diamonds, all set in emeralds and rubies and topazes, and all the furniture could be turned into the finest of gold.

Now his wife was just consenting when the Peterkin family burst in. You can imagine how mad the chemist was! He came near throwing his crucible—that was the name of his melting-pot—at their heads. But he didn't. He listened as calmly as he could to the story of how Mrs. Peterkin had put salt in her coffee.

At first he said he couldn't do anything about it; but when Agamemnon said they would pay in gold if he would only go, he packed up his bottles in a leather case, and went back with them all.

First he looked at the coffee, and then stirred it. Then he put in a little chlorate of potassium, and the family tried it all round; but it tasted no better. Then he stirred in a little bichlorate of magnesia. But Mrs. Peterkin didn't like that. Then he added some tartaric acid and some hypersulphate of lime. But no; it was no better. "I have it!" exclaimed the chemist—"a little ammonia is just the thing!" No, it wasn't the thing at all.

Then he tried, each in turn, some oxalic, cyanic, acetic, phosphoric, chloric, hyperchloric, sulphuric, boracic, silicic, nitric, formic, nitrous nitric, and carbonic acids. Mrs. Peterkin tasted each, and said the flavor was pleasant, but not precisely that of coffee. So then he tried a little calcium, aluminum, barium, and strontium, a little clear bitumen, and a half of a third of a sixteenth of a grain of arsenic. This gave rather a pretty color; but still Mrs. Peterkin ungratefully said it tasted of anything but coffee. The chemist was not discouraged. He put in a little belladonna and atropine, some granulated hydrogen, some potash, and a very little antimony, finishing off with a little pure carbon. But still Mrs. Peterkin was not satisfied.

The chemist said that all he had done ought to have taken out the salt. The theory remained the same, although the experiment had failed. Perhaps a little starch would have some effect. If not, that was all the time he could give. He should like to be paid, and go. They were all much obliged to him, and willing to give him $1.37½ in gold. Gold was now 2.693 3/4, so Mr. Peterkin found in the newspaper. This gave Agamemnon a pretty little sum. He sat himself down to do it. But there was the coffee! All sat and thought awhile, till Elizabeth Eliza said, "Why don't we go to the herb-woman?" Elizabeth Eliza was the only daughter. She was named after her two aunts—Elizabeth, from the sister of her father; Eliza, from her mother's sister. Now, the herb-woman was an old woman who came round to sell herbs, and knew a great deal. They all shouted with joy at the idea of asking her, and Solomon John and the younger children agreed to go and find her too. The herb-woman lived down at the very end of the street; so the boys put on their india-rubber boots again, and they set off. It was a long walk through the village, but they came at last to the herb-woman's house, at the foot of a high hill. They went through her little garden. Here she had marigolds and hollyhocks, and old maids and tall sunflowers, and all kinds of sweet-smelling herbs, so that the air was full of tansy-tea and elder-blow. Over the porch grew a hop-vine, and a brandy-cherry tree shaded the door, and a luxuriant cranberry-vine flung its delicious fruit across the window. They went into a small parlor, which smelt very spicy. All around hung little bags full of catnip, and peppermint, and all kinds of herbs; and dried stalks hung from the ceiling; and on the shelves were jars of rhubarb, senna, manna, and the like.

But there was no little old woman. She had gone up into the woods to get some more wild herbs, so they all thought they would follow her— Elizabeth Eliza, Solomon John, and the little boys. They had to climb up over high rocks, and in among huckleberry-bushes and blackberry-vines. But the little boys had their india-rubber boots. At last they discovered the little old woman. They knew her by her hat. It was steeple-crowned, without any vane. They saw her digging with her trowel round a sassafras bush. They told her their story—how their mother had put salt in her coffee, and how the chemist had made it worse instead of better, and how their mother couldn't drink it, and wouldn't she come and see what she could do? And she said she would, and took up her little old apron, with pockets all round, all filled with everlasting and pennyroyal, and went back to her house.

There she stopped, and stuffed her huge pockets with some of all the kinds of herbs. She took some tansy and peppermint, and caraway-seed and dill, spearmint and cloves, pennyroyal and sweet marjoram, basil and rosemary, wild thyme and some of the other time—such as you have in clocks—sappermint and oppermint, catnip, valerian, and hop; indeed, there isn't a kind of herb you can think of that the little old woman didn't have done up in her little paper bags, that had all been dried in her little Dutch oven. She packed these all up, and then went back with the children, taking her stick.

Meanwhile Mrs. Peterkin was getting quite impatient for her coffee.

As soon as the little old woman came she had it set over the fire, and began to stir in the different herbs. First she put in a little hop for the bitter. Mrs. Peterkin said it tasted like hop-tea, and not at all like coffee. Then she tried a little flagroot and snakeroot, then some spruce gum, and some caraway and some dill, some rue and rosemary, some sweet marjoram and sour, some oppermint and sappermint, a little spearmint and peppermint, some wild thyme, and some of the other tame time, some tansy and basil, and catnip and valerian, and sassafras, ginger, and pennyroyal. The children tasted after each mixture, but made up dreadful faces. Mrs. Peterkin tasted, and did the same. The more the old woman stirred, and the more she put in, the worse it all seemed to taste.

So the old woman shook her head, and muttered a few words, and said she must go. She believed the coffee was bewitched. She bundled up her packets of herbs, and took her trowel, and her basket, and her stick, and went back to her root of sassafras, that she had left half in the air and half out. And all she would take for pay was five cents in currency.

Then the family were in despair, and all sat and thought a great while. It was growing late in the day, and Mrs. Peterkin hadn't had her cup of coffee. At last Elizabeth Eliza said, "They say that the Lady from Philadelphia, who is staying in town, is very wise. Suppose I go and ask her what is best to be done." To this they all agreed, it was a great thought, and off Elizabeth Eliza went.

She told the Lady from Philadelphia the whole story—how her mother had put salt in the coffee; how the chemist had been called in; how he tried everything but could make it no better; and how they went for the little old herb-woman, and how she had tried in vain, for her mother couldn't drink the coffee. The Lady from Philadelphia listened very attentively, and then said, "Why doesn't your mother make a fresh cup of coffee?" Elizabeth Eliza started with surprise. Solomon John shouted with joy; so did Agamemnon, who had just finished his sum; so did the little boys, who had followed on. "Why didn't we think of that?" said Elizabeth Eliza; and they all went back to their mother, and she had her cup of coffee.

It is hard for people who have passed the age of, say, fifty to remember with any charity the hunger of their own puberty and adolescence, the days when they winced and whitened at the prospect of waiting politely a few more hours for food, when their guts howled for meat-bread-candy-fruit-cheese-milkmilkmilk-old wilted toast-ANYTHING IN THE WORLD TO EAT. . . .

The anger and exasperation that older people feel, when they discover soon after the advent of two or three youths, or even one, that the cupboards are bare, stripped, devastated, is not based on stinginess or stupidity. It is, very simply, that they have forgotten how to eat much at a time. Their own needs for nourishment have dwindled. They have with the years acquired a discretion, a cautious distaste for surfeit, painful as well as unintelligible to young and healthy humans. They are out of the habit of stuffing.

It might perhaps be a good thing, at least for social relations between uncles and nephews, parents and their prep-school hostages, if older people deliberately cultivated an unshared but planned generosity at table. They need eat no more themselves, but they should not gauge others' hunger by their lack of it.

And perhaps, now and then, they should read some such story as "The Great Pancake Record.". . .

From *The Prodigious Hickey* by Owen Johnson, 1878–1952
With each succeeding week Hungry Smeed comprehended more fully the enormity of his offense in doing nothing and weighing one hundred and six pounds. He saw the new boys arrive, pass through the fire of chastening, give respectable weights and go forth to the gridiron to be whipped into shape by Turkey and the Butcher, who played on the school eleven. Smeed humbly and thankfully went down each afternoon to the practice, carrying the sweaters and shin-guards, like the grateful little beast of burden that he was. He watched his juniors, Spider and Red Dog, rolling in the mud or flung gloriously under an avalanche of bodies; but then, they weighed over one hundred and thirty, while he was still at one hundred and six—a dead loss! The fever of the house loyalty invaded him; he even came to look with resentment on the Faculty and to repeat secretly to himself that they never would have unloaded him on the Dickinson if they hadn't been willing to stoop to any methods to prevent the House again securing the championship.

The fact that the Dickinson, in an extraordinary manner, finally won by the closest of margins, consoled Smeed but a little while. There were no more sweaters to carry, or pails of barley water to fetch, or guard to be mounted on the old rail fence, to make certain that the spies from the Davis and Kennedy did not surprise the secret plays which Hickey and Slugger Jones had craftily evolved.

With the long winter months he felt more keenly his obscurity and the hopelessness of ever leaving a mark on the great desert of school life that would bring honor to the Dickinson. He resented even the lack of the mild hazing the other boys received—he was too insignificant to be so honored. He was only a dead loss, good for nothing but to squeeze through his recitations, to sleep enormously, and to eat like a glutton with a hunger that could never be satisfied, little suspecting the future that lay in this famine of his stomach.

For it was written in the inscrutable fates that Hungry Smeed should leave a name that would go down imperishably to decades of schoolboys, when Dibbles' touchdown against Princeton and Kafer's home run should be only tinkling sounds. So it happened, and the agent of this divine destiny was Hickey.

It so happened that examinations being still in the threatening distance, Hickey's fertile brain was unoccupied with methods of facilitating his scholarly progress by homely inventions that allowed formulas and dates to be concealed in the palm and disappear obligingly up the sleeve on the approach of the Natural Enemy. Moreover, Hickey and Hickey's friends were in straitened circumstances, with all credit gone at the jigger-shop, and the appetite for jiggers in an acute stage of deprivation.

In this keenly sensitive, famished state of his imagination, Hickey suddenly became aware of a fact fraught with possibilities. Hungry Smeed had an appetite distinguished and remarkable even in that company of aching voids.

No sooner had this pregnant idea become his property than Hickey confided his hopes to Doc Macnooder, his chum and partner in plans that were dark and mysterious. Macnooder saw in a flash the glorious and lucrative possibilities. A very short series of tests sufficed to convince the twain that in little Smeed they had a phenomenon who needed only to be properly developed to pass into history.

Accordingly, on a certain muddy morning in March, Hickey and Doc Macnooder, with Smeed in tow, stole into the jigger-shop at an hour in defiance of regulations and fraught with delightful risks of detection.

Al, the watch-dog of the jigger, was tilted back, near a farther window, the parted tow hair falling doglike over his eyes, absorbed in the reading of Spenser's *Faerie Queen,* an abnormal taste which made him absolutely incomprehensible to the boyish mind. At the sound of the stolen entrance, Al put down the volume and started mechanically to rise. Then, recognizing his visitors, he returned to his chair, saying wearily:

"Nothing doing, Hickey."

"Guess again," said Hickey, cheerily. "We're not asking you to hang us up this time, Al."

"You haven't got any money," said Al, the recorder of allowances; "not unless you stole it."

"Al, we don't come to take your hard-earned money, but to do you good," put in Macnooder impudently. "We're bringing you a little sporting proposition."

"Have you come to pay up that account of yours?" said Al. "If not, run along, you Macnooder; don't waste my time, with your wildcat schemes."

"Al, this is a sporting proposition," took up Hickey.

"Has *he* any money?" said Al, who suddenly remembered that Smeed was not yet under suspicion.

"See here, Al," said Macnooder, "we'll back Smeed to eat the jiggers against you—for the crowd!"

"Where's your money?"

"Here," said Hickey; "this goes up if we lose." He produced a gold watch of Smeed's, and was about to tender it when he withdrew it with a sudden caution. "On the condition, if we win I get it back and you won't hold it up against my account."

"All right. Let's see it."

The watch was given to Al, who looked it over, grunted in approval, and then looked at little Smeed.

"Now, Al," said Macnooder softly, "give us a gambling chance; he's only a runt."

Al considered, and Al was wise. The proposition came often and he never lost. A jigger is unlike any other ice cream; it is dipped from the creamy tin by a cone-shaped scoop called a jigger, which gives it an unusual and peculiar flavor. Since those days the original jigger has been contaminated and made ridiculous by offensive alliances with upstart syrups, meringues and macaroons with absurd titles; but then the boy went to the simple jigger as the sturdy Roman went to the cold waters of the Tiber. A double jigger fills a large soda glass when ten cents has been laid on the counter, and two such glasses quench all desire in the normal appetite.

"If he can eat twelve double jiggers," Al said slowly, "I'll set them up and the jiggers for youse. Otherwise, I'll hold the watch."

At this there was a protest from the backers of the champion, with the result that the limit was reduced to ten.

"Is it a go?" Al said, turning to Smeed, who had waited modestly in the background.

"Sure," he answered, with calm certainty.

"You've got nerve, you have," said Al, with a scornful smile, scooping up the first jiggers and shoving the glass to him. "Ten doubles is the record in these parts, young fellow!"

Then little Smeed, methodically, and without apparent pain, ate the ten doubles.

Conover's was not in the catalogue that anxious parents study, but then catalogues are like epitaphs in a cemetery. Next to the jiggershop, Conover's was quite the most important institution in the school. In a little white Colonial Cottage, Conover, veteran of the late war, and Mrs. Conover, still in active service, supplied pancakes and maple syrup on a cash basis, two dollars credit to second-year boys in good repute. Conover's, too, had its traditions. Twenty-six pancakes, large and thick, in one continuous sitting, was the record, five years old, standing to the credit of Guzzler Wilkins, which succeeding classes had attacked in vain. Wily Conover, to stimulate such profitable tests, had solemnly pledged himself to the delivery of free pancakes to all comers during that day on which any boy, at one continuous sitting, unaided, should succeed in swallowing the awful number of thirty-two. Conover was not considered a prodigal.

This deed of heroic accomplishment and public benefaction was the true goal of Hickey's planning. The test of the jigger-shop was but a preliminary trying out. With medical caution, Doc Macnooder refused to permit

Smeed to go beyond the ten doubles, holding very wisely that the jigger record could wait for a further day. The amazed Al was sworn to secrecy.

It was Wednesday, and the following Saturday was decided upon for the supreme test at Conover's. Smeed at once was subjected to a graduated system of starvation. Thursday he was hungry, but Friday he was so ravenous that a watch was instituted on all his movements.

The next morning the Dickinson House, let into the secret, accompanied Smeed to Conover's. If there was even a possibility of free pancakes, the House intended to be satisfied before the deluge broke.

Great was the astonishment at Conover's at the arrival of the procession.

"Mr. Conover," said Hickey, in the quality of manager, "we're going after that pancake record."

"Mr. Wilkins' record?" said Conover, seeking vainly the champion in the crowd.

"No—after that record of *yours*," answered Hickey. "Thirty-two pancakes—we're here to get free pancakes today—that's what we're here for."

"So, boys, so," said Conover, smiling pleasantly; "and you want to begin now?"

"Right off the bat."

"Well, where is he?"

Little Smeed, famished to the point of tears, was thrust forward. Conover, who was expecting something on the lines of a buffalo, smiled confidently.

"So, boys, so," he said, leading the way with alacrity. "I guess we're ready, too."

"Thirty-two pancakes, Conover—and we get 'em free!"

"That's right," answered Conover, secure in his know ledge of boyish capacity. "If that little boy there can eat thirty-two I'll make them all day free to the school. That's what I said, and what I say goes—and that's what I say now."

Hickey and Doc Macnooder whispered the last instructions in Smeed's ear.

"Cut out the syrup."

"Loosen your belt."

"Eat slowly."

In a low room, with the white rafters impending over his head, beside a basement window flanked with geraniums, little Smeed sat down to battle for the honor of the Dickinson and the record of the school. Directly under his eyes, carved on the wooden table, a name challenged him, standing out of the numerous initials—Guzzler Wilkins.

"I'll keep count," said Hickey. "Macnooder and Turkey, watch the pancakes."

"Regulation size, Conover," cried that cautious Red Dog; "no doubling now. All fair and above board."

"All right, Hickey, all right," said Conover, leering wickedly from the door; "if that little grasshopper can do it, you get the cakes."

"Now, Hungry," said Turkey, clapping Smeed on the shoulder. "Here is where you get your chance. Remember, Kid, old sport, it's for the Dickinson."

Smeed heard in ecstasy; it was just the way Turkey talked to the eleven on the eve of a match. He nodded his head with a grim little shake and smiled nervously at the thirty-odd Dickinsonians who formed around him a pit of expectant and hungry boyhood from the floor to the ceiling.

"All ready!" sang out Turkey, from the doorway.

"Six pancakes!"

"Six it is," replied Hickey, chalking up a monster 6 on the slate that swung from the rafters. The pancakes placed before the ravenous Smeed vanished like snow-flakes on a July lawn.

A cheer went up, mingled with cries of caution.

"Not so fast."

"Take your time."

"Don't let them be too hot."

"Not too hot, Hickey!"

Macnooder was instructed to watch carefully over the temperature as well as the dimensions.

"Ready again," came the cry.

"Ready—how many?"

"Six more."

"Six it is," said Mickey, adding a second figure to the score. "Six and six are twelve."

The second batch went the way of the first.

"Why, that boy is starving," said Conover, opening his eyes.

"Sure he is," said Hickey. "He's eating 'way back in last week—he hasn't had a thing for ten days."

"Six more," cried Macnooder.

"Six it is," answered Hickey. "Six and twelve is eighteen."

"Eat them one at a time, Hungry."

"No, let him alone."

"He knows best."

"Not too fast, Hungry, not too fast."

"Eighteen for Hungry, eighteen. Hurrah!"

"Thirty-two is a long ways to go," said Conover, gazing apprehensively at the little David who had come so impudently into his domain; "fourteen pancakes is an awful lot."

"Shut up, Conover."

"No trying to influence him there."

"Don't listen to him, Hungry."

"He's only trying to get you nervous."

"Fourteen more, Hungry—fourteen more."

"Ready again," sang out Macnooder.

"Ready here."

"Three pancakes."

"Three it is," responded Hickey. "Eighteen and three is twenty-one."

But a storm of protest arose.

"Here, that's not fair!"

"I say, Hickey, don't let them do that."

"I say, Hickey, it's twice as hard that way."

"Oh, goon."

"Sure it is."

"Of course it is."

"Don't you know that you can't drink a glass of beer if you take it with a teaspoon?"

"That's right, Red Dog's right! Six at a time."

"Six at a time!"

A hurried consultation was now held and the reasoning approved. Macnooder was charged with the responsibility of seeing to the number as well as the temperature and dimensions.

Meanwhile Smeed had eaten the pancakes.

"Coming again!"

"All ready here."

"Six pancakes!"

"Six," said Hickey; "twenty-one and six is twenty-seven."

"That'll beat Guzzler Wilkins."

"So it will."

"Five more makes thirty-two."

"Easy, Hungry, easy."

"Hungry's done it; he's done it."

"Twenty-seven and the record!"

"Hurrah!"

At this point Smeed looked about anxiously.

"It's pretty dry," he said, speaking for the first time.

Instantly there was a panic. Smeed was reaching his limit—a groan went up.

"Oh, Hungry."

"Only five more."

"Give him some water."

"Water, you loon; do you want to end him?"

"Why?"

"Water'll swell up the pancakes, crazy."

"No water, no water."

Hickey approached his man with anxiety.

"What is it, Hungry? Anything wrong?" he said tenderly.

"No, only it's a little dry," said Smeed, unmoved. "I'm all right, but I'd like just a drop of syrup now."

The syrup was discussed, approved and voted.

"You're sure you're all right," said Hickey.

"Oh, yes."

Conover, in the last ditch, said carefully:

"I don't want no fits around here."

A cry of protest greeted him.

"Well, son, that boy can't stand much more. That's just like the Guzzler. He was taken short and we had to work over him for an hour."

"Conover, shut up!"

"Conover, you're beaten."

"Conover, that's an old game."

"Get out."

"Shut up."

"Fair play."

"Fair play! Fair play!"

A new interruption came from the kitchen. Macnooder claimed that Mrs. Conover was doubling the size of the cakes. The dish was brought. There was no doubt about it. The cakes were swollen. Pandemonium broke loose. Conover capitulated, the cakes were rejected.

"Don't be feazed by that," said Hickey, warningly to Smeed.

"I'm not," said Smeed.

"All ready," came Macnooder's cry.

"Ready here."

"Six pancakes!"

"Regulation size?"

"Regulation."

"Six it is," said Hickey, at the slate. "Six and twenty-seven is thirty-three."

"Wait a moment," sang out the Butcher. "He has only to eat thirty-two."

"That's so—take one off."

"Give him five—five only."

"If Hungry says he can eat six," said Hickey, firmly, glancing at his protégé, "he can. We're out for big things. Can you do it, Hungry?"

And Smeed, fired with the heroism of the moment, answered in disdainful simplicity:

"Sure!"

A cheer that brought two Davis House boys running in greeted the disappearance of the thirty-third. Then everything was forgotten in the amazement of the deed.

"Please, I'd like to go on," said Smeed.

"Oh, Hungry, can you do it?"

"Really?"

"You're goin' on?"

"Holy cats!"

"How'll you take them?" said Hickey, anxiously.

"I'll try another six," said Smeed, thoughtfully, "and then we'll see."

Conover, vanquished and convinced, no longer sought to intimidate him with horrid suggestions.

"Mr. Smeed," he said, giving him his hand in admiration, "you go ahead; you make a great record."

"Six more," cried Macnooder.

"Six it is," said Hickey, in an awed voice; "six and thirty-three makes thirty-nine!"

Mrs. Conover and Macnooder, no longer antagonists, came in from the kitchen to watch the great spectacle. Little Smeed alone, calm and unconscious, with the light of a great ambition on his forehead, ate steadily, without vacillation.

"Gee, what a stride!"

"By Jiminy, where does he put it?" said Conover, staring helplessly.

"Holy cats!"

"Thirty-nine—thirty-nine pancakes—gee!!!"

"Hungry," said Hickey, entreatingly, "do you think you could eat another—make it an even forty?"

"Three more," said Smeed, pounding the table with a new authority. This time no voice rose in remonstrance. The clouds had rolled away. They were in the presence of a master.

"Pancakes coming."

"Bring them in!"

"Three more."

"Three it is," said Hickey, faintly. "Thirty-nine and three makes forty-two—forty-two. Gee!"

In profound silence the three pancakes passed regularly from the plate down the throat of little Smeed. Forty-two pancakes!

"Three more," said Smeed.

Doc Macnooder rushed in hysterically.

"Hungry, go the limit—the limit! If anything happens I'll bleed you."

"Shut up, Doc!"

"Get out, you wild man."

Macnooder was sent ignominiously back into the kitchen, with the curses of the Dickinson, and Smeed assured of their unfaltering protection.

"Three more," came the cry from the chastened Macnooder.

"Three it is," said Hickey. "Forty-two and three makes—forty-five."

"Holy cats!"

Still little Smeed, without appreciable abatement of hunger, continued to eat. A sense of impending calamity and alarm began to spread. Forty-five pancakes, and still eating! It might turn into a tragedy.

"Say, bub—say, now," said Hickey, gazing anxiously down into the pointed face, "you've done enough—don't get rash."

"I'll stop when it's time," said Smeed; "bring 'em on now, one at a time."

"Forty-six, forty-seven, forty-eight, forty-nine!"

Suddenly, at the moment when they expected him to go on forever, little Smeed stopped, gazed at his plate, then at the fiftieth pancake, and said:

"That's all."

Forty-nine pancakes! Then, and only then, did they return to a realization of what had happened. They cheered Smeed, they sang his praises, they cheered again, and then, pounding the table, they cried, in a mighty chorus:

"We want pancakes!"

"Bring us pancakes!"

"Pancakes, pancakes, we want pancakes!"

Twenty minutes later, Red Dog and the Egghead, fed to bursting, rolled out of Conover's, spreading the uproarious news.

"Free pancakes! Free pancakes!"

The nearest houses, the Davis and the Rouse, heard and came with a rush.

Red Dog and the Egghead staggered down into the village and over to the circle of houses, throwing out their arms like returning bacchanalians.

"Free pancakes!"

"Hungry Smeed's broken the record!"

"Pancakes at Conover's—free pancakes!"

The word jumped from house to house, the campus was emptied in a trice. The road became choked with the hungry stream that struggled, fought, laughed and shouted as it stormed to Conover's.

"Free pancakes! Free pancakes!"

"Hurrah for Smeed!"

"Hurrah for Hungry Smeed!!"

There have always been more miracles about hunger and its solace than any other of the human needs. Jesus of Nazareth knew that good wine from water and a plenitude of fishes and fine bread could succor the starved soul as well as any promise of immortality ... and older gods, too, made pitchers give endlessly of their sweet liquor and cakes never shrink upon their plates.

Tortilla Flat, by John Steinbeck, and then "No Trouble at All," from *Hotel Bemelmans*, by Ludwig himself, are proofs that the gods are still on hand, no matter how minor.

From *Tortilla Flat* by John Steinbeck, 1902–1968

Señora Teresina Cortez and her eight children and her ancient mother lived in a pleasant cottage on the edge of the deep gulch that defines the southern frontier of Tortilla Flat. Teresina was a good figure of a mature woman, nearing thirty. Her mother, that ancient, dried, toothless one, relict of a past generation, was nearly fifty. It was long since any one had remembered that her name was Angelica.

During the week work was ready to this vieja's hand, for it was her duty to feed, punish, cajole, dress and bed down seven of the eight children. Teresina was busy with the eighth, and with making certain preparations for the ninth.

On Sunday, however, the vieja, clad in black satin more ancient even than she, hatted in a grim and durable affair of black straw, on which were fastened two true cherries of enameled plaster, threw duty to the wind and went firmly to church, where she sat as motionless as the saints in their niches. Once a month, in the afternoon, she went to confession. It would be interesting to know what sins she confessed, and where she found the time to commit them, for in Teresina's house there were creepers, crawlers, stumblers, shriekers, cat-killers, fallers-out-of-trees; and each one of these charges could be trusted to be ravenous every two hours.

Is it any wonder that the vieja had a remote soul and nerves of steel? Any other kind would have gone screaming out of her body like little skyrockets.

Teresina was a mildly puzzled woman, as far as her mind was concerned. Her body was one of those perfect retorts for the distillation of children. The first baby, conceived when she was fourteen, had been a shock to her; such a shock, that she delivered it in the ball park at night, wrapped it in newspaper and left it for the night watchman to find. This is a secret. Even now Teresina might get into trouble if it were known.

When she was sixteen, Mr. Alfred Cortez married her and gave her his name and the two foundations of her family, Alfredo and Ernie. Mr. Cortez gave her that name gladly. He was only using it temporarily anyway. His name, before he came to Monterey and after he left, was Guggliemo. He went away after Ernie was born. Perhaps he foresaw that being married to Teresina was not going to be a quiet life.

The regularity with which she became a mother always astonished Teresina. It occurred sometimes that she could not remember who the father of the impending baby was; and occasionally she almost grew convinced that no lover was necessary. In the time when she had been under quarantine as a diphtheria carrier she conceived just the same. However, when a question became too complicated for her mind to unravel, she usually laid that problem in the arms of the Mother of Jesus who, she knew, had more knowledge of, interest in and time for such things than she.

Teresina went often to confession. She was the despair of Father Ramon. Indeed he had seen that while her knees, her hands and her lips did penance for an old sin, her modest and provocative eyes, flashing under drawn lashes, laid the foundations for a new one.

During the time I have been telling this, Teresina's ninth child was born, and for the moment she was unengaged. The vieja received another charge; Alfredo entered his third year in the first grade, Ernie his second, and Panchito went to school for the first time.

At about this time in California it became the stylish thing for school nurses to visit the classes and to catechize the children on intimate details of their home life. In the first grade, Alfredo was called to the principal's office, for it was thought that he looked thin.

The visiting nurse, trained in child psychology, said kindly, "Freddie, do you get enough to eat?"

"Sure," said Alfredo.

"Well, now. Tell me what you have for breakfast."

"Tortillas and beans," said Alfredo.

The nurse nodded her head dismally to the principal. "What do you have when you go home for lunch?"

"I don't go home."

"Don't you eat at noon?"

"Sure. I bring some beans wrapped up in a tortilla."

Actual alarm showed in the nurse's eyes, but she controlled herself. "At night what do you have to eat?"

"Tortillas and beans."

Her psychology deserted her. "Do you mean to stand there and tell me you eat nothing but tortillas and beans?"

Alfredo was astonished. "Jesus Christ," he said, "what more do you want?"

In due course the school doctor listened to the nurse's horrified report. One day he drove up to Teresina's house to look into the matter. As he walked through the yard the creepers, the crawlers and the stumblers were shrieking one terrible symphony. The doctor stood in the open kitchen door. With his own eyes he saw the vieja go to the stove, dip a great spoon into a kettle and sow the floor with boiled beans. Instantly the noise ceased. Creepers, crawlers and stumblers went to work with silent industry, moving from bean to bean, pausing only to eat them. The vieja went back to her chair for a few moments of peace. Under the bed, under the chairs, under the stove the children crawled with the intentness of little bugs. The doctor stayed two hours, for his scientific interest was piqued. He went away shaking his head.

He shook his head incredulously while he made his report. "I gave them every test I know of," he said, "teeth, skin, blood, skeleton, eyes, co-ordination. Gentlemen, they are living on what constitutes a slow poison, and they have from birth. Gentlemen, I tell you I have never seen healthier children in my life!" His emotion overcame him. "The little beasts," he cried. "I never saw such teeth in my life. I *never* saw such teeth!"

You will wonder how Teresina procured food for her family. When the bean threshers have passed, you will see, where they have stopped, big piles of bean chaff. If you will spread a blanket on the ground, and, on a windy afternoon, toss the chaff in the air over the blanket, you will understand that the threshers are not infallible. For an afternoon of work you may collect twenty or more pounds of beans.

In the autumn the vieja and those children who could walk went into the fields and winnowed the chaff. The landowners did not mind, for she did no harm. It was a bad year when the vieja did not collect three or four hundred pounds of beans.

When you have four hundred pounds of beans in the house, you need have no fear of starvation. Other things, delicacies such as sugar, tomatoes, peppers, coffee, fish or meat may come sometimes miraculously, through the intercession of the Virgin, sometimes through industry or cleverness; but your beans are there, and you are safe. Beans are a roof over your stomach. Beans are a warm cloak against economic cold.

Only one thing could threaten the lives and happiness of the family of the Señora Teresina Cortez; that was a failure of the bean crop.

When the beans are ripe, the little bushes are pulled and gathered into piles, to dry crisp for the threshers. Then is the time to pray that the rain may hold off. When the little piles of beans lie in lines, yellow against the dark fields, you will see the farmers watching the sky, scowling with dread at every cloud that sails over; for if a rain comes, the bean piles must be turned over to dry again. And if more rain falls before they are dry, they must be turned again. If a third shower falls, mildew and rot set in, and the crop is lost.

When the beans were drying, it was the vieja's custom to burn a candle to the Virgin.

In the year of which I speak, the beans were piled and the candle had been burned. At Teresina's house, the gunny sacks were laid out in readiness.

The threshing machines were oiled and cleaned.

A shower fell.

Extra hands rushed to the fields and turned the sodden hummocks of beans. The vieja burned another candle.

More rain fell.

Then the vieja bought two candles with a little gold piece she had kept for many years. The field hands turned over the beans to the sun again; and then came a downpour of cold streaking rain. Not a bean was harvested in all Monterey County. The soggy lumps were turned under by the plows.

Oh, then distress entered the house of Señora Teresina Cortez. The staff of life was broken; the little roof destroyed. Gone was that eternal verity, beans. At night the children cried with terror at the approaching starvation. They were not told, but they knew. The vieja sat in church, as always, but her lips drew back in a sneer when she looked at the Virgin. "You took my candles," she thought. "Ohee, yes. Greedy you are for candles. Oh, thoughtless one." And sullenly she transferred her allegiance to Santa Clara. She told Santa Clara of the injustice that had been done. She permitted herself a little malicious thought at the Virgin birth. "You know, sometimes Teresina can't remember either," she told Santa Clara viciously.

It has been said that Jesus Maria Corcoran was a great-hearted man. He had also that gift some humanitarians possess of being inevitably drawn toward those spheres where his instinct was needed. How many times had he not come upon young ladies when they needed comforting. Toward any pain or sorrow he was irresistibly drawn. He had not been to Teresina's house for many months. If there is no mystical attraction between pain and humanitarianism, how did it happen that he went there to call on the very day when the last of the old year's beans were put in the pot?

He sat in Teresina's kitchen, gently brushing children off his legs. And he looked at Teresina with polite and pained eyes while she told of the calamity. He watched, fascinated, when she turned the last bean sack inside out to show that not one single bean was left. He nodded sympathetically when she pointed out the children, so soon to be skeletons, so soon to die of starvation.

Then the vieja told bitterly how she had been tricked by the Virgin. But upon this point, Jesus Maria was not sympathetic.

"What do you know, old one?" he said sternly. "Maybe the Blessed Virgin had business some place else."

"But four candles I burned," the vieja insisted shrilly.

Jesus Maria regarded her coldly. "What are four candles to Her?" he said. "I have seen one church where She had hundreds. She is no miser of candles."

But his mind burned with Teresina's trouble. That evening he talked mightily and piteously to the friends at Danny's house. Out of his great heart he drew a compelling oratory, a passionate plea for those little children who had no beans. And so telling was his speech that the fire in his heart ignited the hearts of his friends. They leaped up. Their eyes glowed.

"The children shall not starve," they cried. "It shall be our trust!"

"We live in luxury," Pilon said.

"We shall give of our substance," Danny agreed. "And if they needed a house, they could live here."

"Tomorrow we shall start," Pablo exclaimed. "No more laziness! To work! There are things to be done!"

Jesus Maria felt the gratification of a leader with followers.

Theirs was no idle boast. Fish they collected. The vegetable patch of the Hotel Del Monte they raided. It was a glorious game. Theft robbed of the stigma of theft, crime altruistically committed—What is more gratifying?

The Pirate raised the price of kindlings to thirty cents and went to three new restaurants every morning. Big Joe stole Mrs. Palochico's goat over and over again, and each time it went home.

Now food began to accumulate in the house of Teresina. Boxes of lettuce lay on her porch, spoiled mackerel filled the neighborhood with a strong odor. And still the flame of charity burned in the friends.

If you could see the complaint book at the Monterey Police Department, you would notice that during this time there was a minor crime wave in Monterey. The police car hurried from place to place. Here a chicken was taken, there a whole patch of pumpkins. Paladini Company reported the loss of two one-hundred-pound cases of abalone steaks.

Teresina's house was growing crowded. The kitchen was stacked high with food. The back porch overflowed with vegetables. Odors like those of a packing house permeated Tortilla Flat. Breathlessly the friends dashed about at their larcenies, and long they talked and planned with Teresina.

At first Teresina was maddened with joy at so much food, and her head was turned by the compliment. After a week of it, she was not so sure. The baby was down with colic, Ernie had some kind of bowel trouble, Alfredo's face was flushed. The creepers and crawlers cried all the time. Teresina was ashamed to tell the friends what she must tell them. It took her several days to get her courage up; and during that time there arrived fifty pounds of celery and a crate of cantaloupes. At last she had to tell them. The neighbors were beginning to look at her with lifted brows.

She asked all of Danny's friends into her kitchen, and then she informed them of the trouble, modestly and carefully, that their feelings might not be hurt.

"Green things and fruit are not good for children," she explained. "Milk is constipating to a baby after it is weaned." She pointed to the flushed and irritable children. See, they were all sick. They were not getting the proper food.

"What is the proper food?" Pilon demanded.

"Beans," she said. "There you have something to trust, something that will not go right through you."

The friends went silently away. They pretended to themselves to be disheartened, but they knew that the first fire of their enthusiasm had been lacking for several days.

At Danny's house they held a conference.

This must not be told in some circles, for the charge might be serious.

Long after midnight, four dark forms who shall be nameless, moved like shadows through the town. Four indistinct shapes crept up on the Western Warehouse Company platform. The watchman said, afterward, that he heard sounds, investigated and saw nothing. He could not say how the thing was done, how a lock was broken and the door forced. Only four men know that the watchman was sound asleep, and they will never tell on him.

A little later the four shadows left the warehouse, and now they were bent under tremendous loads. Pantings and snortings came from the shadows.

At three o'clock in the morning Teresina was awakened by hearing her back door open. "Who is there?" she cried.

There was no answer, but she heard four great thumps that shook the house. She lighted a candle and went to the kitchen in her bare feet. There, against the wall, stood four one-hundred-pound sacks of pink beans.

Teresina rushed in and awakened the vieja. "A miracle!" she cried. "Come look in the kitchen."

The vieja regarded with shame the plump full sacks. "Oh, miserable dirty sinner am I," she moaned. "Oh, Holy Mother, look with pity on an old fool. Every month thou shalt have a candle, as long as I live."

At Danny's house, four friends were lying happily in their blankets. What pillow can one have like a good conscience? They slept well into the afternoon, for their work was done.

And Teresina discovered, by a method she had found to be infallible, that she was going to have a baby. As she poured a quart of the new beans into the kettle, she wondered idly which one of Danny's friends was responsible.

No Trouble at All by Ludwig Bemelmans, 1898–1962

The world is full of maîtres d'hôtel, many of whom are able, well-informed men. But only one in a hundred thousand is blessed with that rarest, most priceless of qualities so generously evident in Gabriel, the Maître of the Cocofinger Palace Hotel in New York.

We see this peculiar talent in the profile below, behind the ear, under "Detail and Executive Ability." It is the faculty of "Anticipation," an astral clairvoyance with which to sense catastrophe anywhere in the wide realm of his authority. Not only to feel it ahead, but to prepare for it, and minimize the effect thereof.

One more look at the graph and it is evident to anyone why, with such talents, Gabriel has come up, up, up, from the position of third piccolo at the humble Red Ox Tavern in Obergurgl, through the pantries and over the red carpets of Madame Sacher's, the Negresco, Shepheard's, the Meurice, Claridge's, up to the golden doors of the restaurant of the hotel of hotels—the Cocofinger Palace in New York.

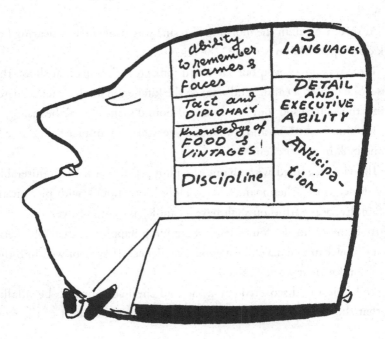

Gabriel smokes Dimitrinos, he has twenty dozen shirts, he thinks in French, his hats come from London, and both Noel Coward and Cole Porter have asked him who builds his faultless tail coats.

To his many subordinates, he speaks through his assistant, one Hector de Malherbes. Between the Maître and Malherbes is perfect, wordless understanding. Never were Gabriel's great talents and the mute felicity of Malherbes more clearly demonstrated than on the night and day of February the twenty-fifth, 1937.

On that Thursday at three-fifteen in the afternoon, when the last luncheon guests had left, Gabriel leaned on his desk with its seven drawers, one for each day of the week, and nodded gently to Malherbes. Malherbes bent down to the drawer Jeudi—because it was Thursday—and took from it a salmon-colored folder with a sulphur label on which was written: "Birthday Party, February 25, 1937, Mrs. George Washington Kelly."

Gabriel carried the folder up to his room. Malherbes bowed and left. In his room Gabriel took off the faultless tail coat which was rounded from much bowing, hung it up, sat on his bed, and carefully unfolded the bills that five-, ten-, and one-dollar patrons had pressed into his hand. He added them up and entered into a little crimson book: "February 25, Déjeuner, $56." Then he took off his boots, leaned back into the pillows, stretched his toes in the sheer black Sulka silk socks, and opened the salmon-colored folder.

Madame George Washington Kelly was a very difficult and exacting client. The Italian waiters called her "bestia," the French "canaille," and the Germans "die alte Sau." She had a desperate countenance, partly concealed by a veil; behind this her face shone the color of indigo. Her skin had the texture of volcanic rock seen from the air with dirty snow swept into the crevices.

She dressed with complete immunity to fashion, except for the Beaux Arts Ball. On the night of that elaborate affaire she had come with her friend, the "Spirit of the Midnight Sun," and together they had engaged the rooms and made the preliminary plans for this birthday party, of which Malherbes had said to Monsieur Gabriel in sotto voce French, "It is not a birthday party—it is a centennial celebration." Gabriel had stared him into silence.

After many more visits and consultations with architects, stage de-signers, and florists, Madame had decided to build at the end of the ball-room a replica of her Miami retreat, "O Sole Mio," in its original noble dimensions. This was to be set among hibiscus, poinciana, and orange trees in bloom, surrounded by forty-three-foot royal palm trees and fronted by wide terraces. Cutting through the center of the room, from the terrace on the north to a magnificent flight of stairs on the south, ran the lagoon, filled with real water, and in this water was to float the genuine gondola which Mr. George Washington Kelly had brought as a souvenir from Ven-ice and taken all the way to Miami. The stairs on the north end rose to a balcony; from there, a birthday cake was to be carried down, placed on the gondola, and rowed across to Sole Mio, where Mrs. Kelly's own servants would bring it to her table to be cut.

The gondola was in Miami, also the royal palms, also the four white-haired servants, brothers named Morandus. The Fire Department had sent a captain to study the position of the hydrants and windows, to connect a pumping truck, and to fill the lagoon, which it was estimated would take fourteen hours.

To do all this properly, the complete entertaining facilities of the Co-cofinger Palace Hotel had been rented for a week ahead of the party and a week following it, to clear away the debris. Mr. George Washington Kelly was many times a millionaire.

Since Monday of the first week, the Cocofinger Palace had been filled with drafts from open doors and windows, with tall ladders and empty smilax crates. Careless carpenters, careless stagehands, and careless plumb-ers and florists ruined the peace and the carpets of the hotel with ham-mering, riveting, and soldering together the two-hundred-foot tank that was to serve as the lagoon. Following on the heels of the plumbers came the painters, who painted the sides of the lagoon emerald green and put a pattern of underwater scenery on its bottom. An eminent artist from Coral Gables supervised this.

The menu for this party was dictated by Madame herself, without ben-efit of Gabriel's advice. It was in the tradition of her entertainments and composed itself—at twenty dollars a cover for four hundred guests—of the following: Caviar aux blinis, borscht, homard Sole Mio, faisan Miami, puree de marrons, pommes soufflées, salade Georges et Marthe, bombe Washington, café.

For the one thousand five hundred additional guests for supper, she had chosen an equally unfortunate repast. This, at ten dollars a cover, consisted of velouté Marthe aux croûtons, poussin en cocotte Washington, nouilles polonaise, petits pois parisiennes, bombe Sole Mio aux fraises cardinal, gâteaux Georges, café.

Breakfast was to be served from four o'clock on, at two dollars and fifty cents a person. Provision was also made for eighty musicians' suppers, suppers for chauffeurs, maids, the secretaries at the door, and the announcer and the detectives, at one dollar a person.

Cocktails were to be served during the reception: a fantastic violent drink of Madame's own invention, named "High Diddle," the most secret formula for which Madame fortunately gave to no one. Closely guarded, her trusty servants—the Morandi—were to mix this, bringing most of the ingredients themselves from Florida.

After Gabriel had read the papers thoroughly and made several notes, he rose, looked into the mirror, and took a loose smoking jacket from his closet. He slipped on a pair of white gloves and walked below. Malherbes was waiting for him. It was six o'clock.

Gabriel nodded, and his assistant followed him with a silver pencil and a morocco portfolio.

They walked through the kitchen, where the cooks fished red lobster out of steaming casseroles and chopped them in half. From there they went to the cellar; here, men broke open cases of Cordon Rouge 1921 and put them away in tubs. From here, they walked up to the ballroom proper. The tables, seating eight guests each, were set to the left and right of the lagoon. Sole Mio was finished, and on the lower terraces in front of it—as indicated on the plan—was the crescent-shaped table, facing the room. Here, Monsieur and Madame George Washington Kelly and their son George Washington Kelly, Jr., as well as their most intimate friends, would sit.

Two painters were busy pouring and stirring fifty gallons of turquoise ink into the lagoon, to give it the precise color of the waters around Miami. The Coral Gables artist had left with them a sample of that shade on a piece of water-color paper, and from time to time they compared this and then added more ink. Up on the balcony of Sole Mio, two electricians were focusing spotlights across the room, up to a magenta curtain on the other side.

From the street could be heard the "poooommmph, puuuuumph, poomph" of the Fire Department pumping-truck which filled the lagoon with water.

Gabriel, walking into the hall, saw the last of twenty royal palms—in tubs, with their leaves carefully bandaged—being carried upstairs, and below from the street appeared the neck of the Venetian gondola.

The great Maître nodded to Malherbes. Malherbes ran down to the door and told the men: "Watch out for the paint, you." Later on, in the office, he made certain that a gondolier had been engaged. Yes, he had. He was to report at the ballroom in costume, with a knowledge of how to row the gondola and the ability to sing "O Sole Mio."

Gabriel went to his room, lit a cigarette, and rested in his bath for half an hour. Then he dressed.

As on every evening, so now, he received the dinner guests of the hotel at the door of the restaurant.

Madame George Washington Kelly's party over in the ballroom was in the able hands of his third assistant, Monsieur Rudi, a withered onetime stableboy of Prince Esterházy's.

At regular intervals a courier crossed from the ballroom and whispered to Malherbes, "The guests are arriving." Then again, "The cocktails are being passed." After this, "The guests are entering the ballroom." Then, "Madame George Washington Kelly is very pleased," and on to "The guests are sitting down," and "The soup is being served." These bulletins were translated into French by Malherbes and whispered on to Gabriel, who nodded.

Dinner was almost over in the restaurant when Gabriel went into a little side room where, on a table behind a screen, a plain meal was prepared for him. It consisted of some cold pheasant cut from the bones, field salad with lemon dressing, and a plain compote of black cherries cooked without sugar. In ice under the table was his favorite wine, an elegant, slim bottle of Steinberger Kabinett, Preussische Staatsdomäne, 1921.

In the middle of the meal, before he had touched the great wine, Gabriel rose abruptly and quickly walked across the restaurant. Malherbes, who had eaten out in the second little room off the restaurant, swallowed quickly and followed him. Almost running, they crossed the entrance hall of the ballroom and went up the staircase, to the third palm.

Gabriel suddenly stopped there, and beside him, as always, stopped Hector de Malherbes. The dessert had just been served, the remnants of the bombe Washington were being carried from the room by the waiters, and, as set forth in the sheet of instructions, the lights were lowered.

Two heralds sounded the *Aïda* theme as a command to silence and attention.

The heavy magenta curtains sailed back, and high above the audience appeared the birthday cake. It was magnificent, of generous proportions and truly beautiful, the masterpiece of Brillat Bonafou, chef pâtissier of the Cocofinger Palace Hotel, twice the winner of the Médaille d'Or de la Société Culinaire de Paris, Founder and President of the Institut des Chefs Pâtissiers de France. In weeks of patient, sensitive, loving labor he had built a monument of sugar, tier upon tier, ten feet high, of raisin and almond cake. It was of classic simplicity, yet covered with innumerable ornaments that depicted scenes from a happy sporting life. Up and down the cake dozens of cherubim were busy carrying ribbons; these—Bordeaux and emerald—represented the racing colors of the G. W. K. stables.

But the most wonderful part of the wonderful cake was its top. There, complete in all details, stood a miniature replica of O Sole Mio, correct as to palms, orange trees, the lagoon, the gondola. Under the portico, an inch high, smiling, hand in hand, stood Monsieur and Madame George Washington Kelly: Madame with a bouquet of roses, Monsieur with his ever-present cigar, an Hoyo de Monterrey, at the end of which was a microscopic tuft of cotton. That was, however, not all. Over the miniature Sole Mio hovered a brace of doves. In their beaks, most artfully held, were electric wires, so arranged that flashing on and off they spelled first "George" and then "Martha," "George" in Bordeaux, and "Martha" in emerald green. Five lady midgets, dressed as the Quintuplets, carried the cake downstairs in the light of the amber spotlights.

An Hawaiian orchestra played "Happy Birthday to You, Happy Birthday to You." Everyone sang, and all eyes were moist.

The gondolier started to punt down the lagoon to receive the cake.

At that moment, with all eyes upon them, one of the Quintuplets, Yvonne, stepped on an olive pit, and turned her ankle. The cake trembled,

swayed, and fell into the lagoon, taking the midgets with it. "Ffssss-hsss,"
went the electric wires.

But where is Gabriel?

He stood under the royal palm and nodded quietly to Malherbes.
Malherbes lifted one finger and looked up at the man with the spotlight.

The amber light left the lagoon and raced up the stairs. Out came the
trumpeters again and sounded the *Aïda* theme, the curtain swung open
once more, again the Hawaiians played "Happy Birthday to You, Happy
Birthday to You."

As if the last dreadful minutes had never been on the watches of this
world, there appeared to the unbelieving eyes of Monsieur and Madame
George Washington Kelly and their guests and friends—THE CAKE again,
unharmed, made with equal devotion, again the work of Brillat Bonafou,
identically perfect and complete, with the scenes of the happy life, the
cherubim, cigar and smoke, lagoon and gondola, and the lights in the
dove-beaks flashing on and off, "George" in Bordeaux and "Martha" in
emerald green; the new cake was carried on the shoulders of a new set of
Quintuplets.

The miserable first set of midgets swam to the shore of the lagoon,
scrambled out, and tried to leave the ballroom in the shade of the tables.

Gabriel hissed "Imbéciles!" to Malherbes. Malherbes hissed "Imbéciles!" down to the wet midgets.

The new cake was rowed across, besung, carried to the table, cut, and
served. Not until then did the great maître d'hôtel leave the protecting
shadow of the royal palm. Now he walked quietly, unseen, to his room; for,
in spite of possessing every talent, and, besides, the gift of "Anticipation,"
Monsieur Gabriel was a very modest man.

There are several things from what Ernest Hemingway has written that I
would like to put here, to end this section about America and this whole book
about feasting with a writer who is American and who is good.

From all that he has said, though, about how human beings eat and
drink and exist, I have chosen to print one morsel from *For Whom the Bell
Tolls*. What the people in Spain ate and drank in their doomed vitality upon
a hillside is a part of their being real.

From *For Whom the Bell Tolls* by Ernest Hemingway, 1899–1961

Now the morning was late May, the sky was high and clear and the wind blew warm on Robert Jordan's shoulders. The snow was going fast and they were eating breakfast. There were two big sandwiches of meat and the goaty cheese apiece, and Robert Jordan had cut thick slices of onion with his clasp knife and put them on each side of the meat and cheese between the chunks of bread.

"You will have a breath that will carry through the forest to the fascists," Agustín said, his own mouth full.

"Give me the wineskin and I will rinse the mouth," Robert Jordan said, his mouth full of meat, cheese, onion and chewed bread.

He had never been hungrier and he filled his mouth with wine, faintly tarry-tasting from the leather bag, and swallowed. Then he took another big mouthful of wine, lifting the bag up to let the jet of wine spurt into the back of his mouth, the wineskin touching the needles of the blind of pine branches that covered the automatic rifle as he lifted his hand, his head leaning against the pine branches as he bent it back to let the wine run down.

"Dost thou want this other sandwich?" Agustín asked him, handing it toward him across the gun.

"No. Thank you. Eat it."

"I cannot. I am not accustomed to eat in the morning."

"You do not want it, truly?"

"Nay. Take it."

Robert Jordan took it and laid it on his lap while he got the onion out of his side jacket pocket where the grenades were and opened his knife to slice it. He cut off a thin sliver of the surface that had dirtied in his pocket, then cut a thick slice. An outer segment fell and he picked it up and bent the circle together and put it into the sandwich.

"Eatest thou always onions for breakfast?" Agustín asked.

"When there are any."

"Do all in thy country do this?"

"Nay," Robert Jordan said. "It is looked on badly there."

"I am glad," Agustín said. "I had always considered America a civilized country."

"What hast thou against the onion?"

"The odor. Nothing more. Otherwise it is like the rose."

Robert Jordan grinned at him with his mouth full.

"Like the rose," he said. "Mighty like the rose. A rose is a rose is an onion."

"Thy onions are affecting thy brain," Agustín said. "Take care."

"An onion is an onion is an onion," Robert Jordan said cheerily and, he thought, a stone is a stein is a rock is a boulder is a pebble.

"Rinse thy mouth with wine," Augustín said. "Thou art very rare, *Inglés*. There is a great difference between thee and the last dynamiter who worked with us."

"There is one great difference."

"Tell it to me."

"I am alive and he is dead," Robert Jordan said.

THE END

We are alive indeed, fed by the countless feasts of other men, other times. As long as we breathe we can thus nourish ourselves, valiant fleas upon the lion's lip, sucking richness and strength from what has always been written, and always will be, about the manners and the meanings of broken bread, poured wine, and the communion of two or three of us gathered together . . .

ACKNOWLEDGMENTS

Every effort has been made to trace the ownership of copyrighted material and to make full acknowledgment of its use. If errors or omissions have occurred, they will be corrected in subsequent editions upon notification in writing to the publisher. The author wishes to thank the following for their kind permission to reprint in this volume excerpts from the following sources:

Rinehart & Company, N.Y.: *The Green Pastures* by Marc Connelly. Copyright 1929 by Marc Connelly.

The John Day Company, N.Y.: *My Country and My People* by Lin Yutang. Copyright 1935 by The John Day Company.

Little, Brown & Company, Boston: *Father and Glorious Descendant* by Pardee Lowe. Copyright 1937, 1943 by Pardee Lowe.

David Lloyd, N. Y.: *The Good Earth* by Pearl S. Buck. Copyright 1931 by Pearl S. Buck. The John Day Company.

Liveright Publishing Corporation, N.Y.: *The Travels of Marco Polo*, edited by Manuel Komroff. Copyright 1926, 1930 by Horace Liveright, Inc.

Doubleday and Company, N.Y., and Jonathan Cape, London, on behalf of Lawrence executors: *Seven Pillars of Wisdom* by T. E. Lawrence. Copyright 1926 by Doubleday, Doran and Company, Inc.

The George Macy Companies, N.Y.: *Gargantua and Pantagruel* by François Rabelais, translated by Jacques LeClercq. Copyright 1936 by The Limited Editions Club.

Henry Holt and Company, N.Y.: *A Shropshire Lad* by A. E. Housman; the Society of Authors, London, representing the trustees of the author's estate, and Jonathan Cape, London: *Collected Poems of A. E. Housman.*

Alfred A. Knopf, N.Y.: *The Bridal Wreath* by Sigrid Undset. Copyright 1925 by Alfred A. Knopf, Inc.

Harper & Brothers, N.Y.: Description of Mr. Hastings by Anthony Cooper, First Earl of Shaftesbury, quoted in *Texts and Pretexts* by Aldous Huxley. Copyright 1933 by Aldous Huxley.

Chatto & Windus, London: *Dead Souls* by Nikolai Gogol, translated by Constance Garnett. Copyright 1923 by Mrs. Edward Garnett. Alfred A. Knopf.

Oxford University Press and representatives of the late Aylmer Maude, London: *War and Peace* by Leo Tolstoy, translated by Louise and Aylmer Maude.

Maxim Lieber, N.Y.: *Against the Grain* by J. K. Huysmans, translated by John Howard. Copyright 1922 by Lieber & Lewis.

André Simon and The Wine and Food Society, London: "Esau to Escoffier" from *The Wine and Food Quarterly*, Winter 1940 issue.

Mrs. W. A. Bradley, Paris: *César Ritz: Host to the World* by Madame Marie Ritz. Copyright 1938 by J. B. Lippincott Company.

Alfred A. Knopf, N.Y.: *Buddenbrooks* by Thomas Mann, translated by H. T. Lowe-Porter. Copyright 1923 by Alfred A. Knopf, Inc.

Macmillan Publishing Company: Reprinted by permission from *Notes on a Cellar-Book* by George Saintsbury. Copyright 1933 by Macmillan Publishing Company.

Doubleday and Company, N.Y.: *Of Human Bondage* by W. Somerset Maugham. Copyright 1915 by Doubleday, Doran and Company, Inc., 1943 by W. Somerset Maugham.

André Simon and The Wine and Food Society, London: "Memorable Meals, No. 1" from *The Wine and Food Quarterly*, Spring 1942 issue.

The Society of Authors as the literary representatives of the estate of G. B. Stern: *Bouquet* by G. B. Stern. Copyright 1927 by G. B. Stern. Alfred A. Knopf.

Harcourt, Brace and Company, N.Y.: *To the Lighthouse* by Virginia Woolf. Copyright 1927 by Harcourt, Brace and Company, Inc.

The Literary Trustees of Walter de la Mare and The Society of Authors as their representative: *The Memoirs of a Midget* by Walter de la Mare. Copyright 1922 by Walter de la Mare. Alfred A. Knopf.

Alfred A. Knopf, N.Y.: *Paul Bunyan* by James Stevens. Copyright 1924 by Alfred A. Knopf, Inc.

Reynal & Hitchcock, N.Y.: *Saints and Strangers* by George F. Willison. Copyright 1945 by George F. Willison.

Little, Brown & Company and Atlantic Monthly Press, Boston: *The Country Kitchen* by Della T. Lutes. Copyright 1935, 1936 by Della T. Lutes.

Charles Scribner's Sons, N.Y.: *Look Homeward, Angel* by Thomas Wolfe. Copyright 1929 by Charles Scribner's Sons.

INDEX

MARY FRANCES KENNEDY FISHER was the preeminent American food writer. She wrote thirty-three books, including a translation of *The Physiology of Taste* by Jean Anthelme Brillat-Savarin. Her first book, *Serve It Forth*, was published in 1937. Fisher's books are an amalgam of food literature, travel, and memoir.

BETTY FUSSELL was born in Southern California in 1927. Her most recent book is *Eat, Live, Love, Die*. She was recently celebrated, along with other winners of the Silver Spoon Award, by *Food Arts* magazine.

Printed in the United States
by Baker & Taylor Publisher Services